THE CHANGING
AMERICAN
NEIGHBORHOOD

THE CHANGING AMERICAN NEIGHBORHOOD

The Meaning of Place in
the Twenty-First Century

Alan Mallach and Todd Swanstrom

CORNELL UNIVERSITY PRESS ITHACA AND LONDON

First published 2023 by Cornell University Press

Library of Congress Cataloging-in-Publication Data

Names: Mallach, Alan, author. | Swanstrom, Todd, author.
Title: The changing American neighborhood : the meaning of place
   in the twenty-first century / Alan Mallach and Todd Swanstrom.
Description: Ithaca [New York] : Cornell University Press, 2023. |
   Includes bibliographical references and index.
Identifiers: LCCN 2023003097 (print) | LCCN 2023003098 (ebook) |
   ISBN 9781501770890 (hardcover) | ISBN 9781501771132 (paperback) |
   ISBN 9781501770906 (pdf) | ISBN 9781501770913 (epub)
Subjects: LCSH: Neighborhoods—Social aspects—United States. |
   Neighborhoods—Economic aspects—United States. | City and
   town life—United States. | Urban economics.
Classification: LCC HT123 .M18 2023 (print) | LCC HT123 (ebook) |
   DDC 307.3/362—dc23/eng/20230303
LC record available at https://lccn.loc.gov/2023003097
LC ebook record available at https://lccn.loc.gov/2023003098

In memory of my beloved life partner Robin Gould

—Alan Mallach

To my dear sister Mary Claire Schultz

—Todd Swanstrom

Neighbor is not a geographic term. It is a moral concept.
—Rabbi Joachim Prinz, from his remarks at the
March on Washington, 1963

Contents

Preface

The idea for this book did not suddenly spring full-blown into our minds. It was preceded by years of personal and professional evolution based on our experiences, our observations, and innumerable conversations over the years with scholars and practitioners. We recently calculated, with equal parts pride and embarrassment, that together we have been engaged in neighborhood work and scholarship for over ninety years, the greater part of it in struggling, often shrinking cities in America's Northeast and Midwest. These experiences have colored our perspective on life and human behavior and left an indelible imprint on our thinking. This book also went through an extended, although not ninety-year-long, evolution before taking its final form.

As an undergraduate in the early 1960s, Alan joined the New Haven chapter of the Congress of Racial Equality, spending many hours in African American neighborhoods that were about to be demolished to make way for urban renewal and talking to people living in homes already owned by the city and soon to disappear. Years later, while working in Atlantic City in the 1980s and in Trenton during the 1990s, he became deeply engaged with the struggles of America's older cities and the challenges of their neighborhoods, which has been the principal focus of his subsequent life's work. Since then, first with the Brookings Institution and for the last ten years with the Center for Community Progress, Alan has led efforts to address the challenge of housing vacancy and abandonment and, more broadly, the strangely contradictory crisis and revival of America's legacy cities, the once-industrial cities such as Detroit and Pittsburgh that have lost much of their population and still more of their economic base. In his book *The Divided City*, Alan brought both the crisis and the revival to wider attention, grappling with how urban decline continues in the midst of surging, if selective, urban revival.

In 1979, Todd moved to Cleveland to pursue his PhD and go to work for the urban populist administration of Mayor Dennis Kucinich. It was an exciting time for Todd, at the height of the era of what we call in this book "neighborhoodism," the idea that many, if not most, of society's problems can be addressed by empowering neighborhoods. Todd's PhD dissertation and subsequent book, *The Crisis of Growth Politics*, profiled urban populism as confrontational organizing moved from the neighborhoods into city politics, mobilizing people around pithy slogans such as "invest in neighborhoods not downtown." It was a

hard time for older central cities, which were being devastated by deindustrialization and white flight, and as we describe, urban populism proved unsustainable, although it has many echoes in today's battles over gentrification and racial
justice.

After nineteen years in Albany at the State University of New York, where he
worked with community development corporations and the local tenants' union,
Todd moved to St. Louis, Missouri, one of America's fastest-shrinking cities.
Blessed with a pool of resources that came with his endowed professorship at the
University of Missouri–St. Louis, he first used those funds to help form the Community Builders Network, a coalition of about eighty organizations working to
build better neighborhoods in St. Louis. Recognizing, though, that there were not
nearly enough resources in the community development system to address
neighborhood decline, he later directed his endowment's funds to support the
St. Louis Anchor Action Network, a coalition made up of the major institutions
of higher education and medical services in St. Louis. What these anchor institutions can do to turn around the many declining neighborhoods in the city of
St. Louis and in St. Louis County of course remains an open question.

The story of how our thinking about neighborhoods evolved into this book
began in 2015 when, together with our colleague Brett Theodos of the Urban Institute, we organized a panel on neighborhood change in older industrial cities
at an International Sociological Association gathering in Chicago. Reflecting the
work that each of us had done separately, a central theme of the panel was our
growing conviction that the hot-button issue of gentrification was distracting
scholarly attention away from the more serious problem of neighborhood decline. Although we half-expected to be assailed by progressives for our seeming
indifference to the threat posed by gentrification, the response to the panel was
strongly positive and led us to start thinking about how we could build on the
work we had already done.

One thing the three of us began talking about was how we could encourage
scholarly research to more productively inform the work of people in community development, addressing neighborhood change on the ground. The next year
we helped pull together a workshop in Washington, D.C., where about twenty
scholars and practitioners came together to talk about how they could work together more effectively. Cosponsored by the Center for Community Progress,
the Urban Institute, and the Lincoln Institute of Land Policy, the workshop
brought home the fact that while social scientists were producing a large corpus
of research on neighborhood change, this research appeared to have little or no
impact on community development practice. It may not surprise the reader that
part of the problem was the dense, barely comprehensible academic prose and
the inaccessibility of the journals in which it was published. That was not the

only problem, however. As we reviewed the research, we came to realize that with rare exceptions, it was all of a piece. Quantitative research using sophisticated econometric techniques to isolate the effect of individual variables—such as housing demolition and the greening of vacant lots—seemed oblivious to the complex interactions of economic, social, and political forces shaping neighborhood trajectories and the importance of local context, factors seen as essential by practitioners in both understanding neighborhoods and guiding action to change them.

Despite our frustration with much of what we read, we continued to feel that there were ways scholarly research could be used to more effectively guide local action. For the most part we did not believe that the findings and conclusions of the research were wrong, although sometimes we believe that to be the case and point that out in the pages that follow. The reader will notice, in fact, that we repeatedly draw on the large body of quantitative neighborhood research. That research offers many valuable, even striking insights. The problem is not so much that the research is wrong but that it is fragmentary, lacking in a broader context or framework to ground it in the complex reality of neighborhoods, with their many interactions and feedback loops. It is almost as if the sheer amount of data available, along with the stunning increase in the power of computers and geographic information systems to store and analyze that data, has caused researchers to progressively narrow their field of vision. We were struck that neighborhood research from earlier eras often examined neighborhoods through a wider, more panoramic lens, drawing insights from different disciplines and integrating quantitative research with qualitative analyses and case studies that were more sensitive to neighborhood context and history.

The United States has a long and proud tradition, which can be traced back to the settlement house movement of the late nineteenth century, of using data and scientific methods, both qualitative and quantitative, to better understand neighborhood conditions and neighborhood change. For all its flaws, the Chicago School of Human Ecology at its heyday in the 1920s placed urban neighborhoods within the context of local, national, and even global trends. While the Chicago School is widely seen as discredited today, reflecting the ways in which much of its research was used to justify the racial discrimination of the following decades, its effort to grasp neighborhoods as a whole is still worthy of emulation.

A second burst of neighborhood research emerged in the 1970s that in many respects was a reaction to the failures and excesses of postwar urban renewal. This research stressed the importance of local knowledge, seeking to integrate resident perceptions and behavior into the analysis of the dynamics of neighborhood change. In contrast to the deterministic, even fatalistic, stance toward neighborhood change of the Chicago School, scholar-practitioners, such as Rolf Goetze and Paul Brophy, stressed the possibility of intervention and in many respects provided the intellectual basis for the community development movement in the United States that was emerging at the time.

Our initial idea was to focus on lifting up this rich body of neighborhood thinking, which led us to believe that an edited book that both highlighted and contextualized the best neighborhood research over the past century would be valuable. To that end, we began to talk with Michael McGandy at Cornell University Press about what form such an edited volume could take. As Michael kept pushing us on what we wanted to say with an edited book, our thinking gradually shifted and became more focused. When we realized that what we wanted to say could not be conveyed in an edited volume, we moved from that format to an original book that we would coauthor. As we did that, we came to feel that what we wanted to do went well beyond synthesizing existing research on neighborhoods or even putting that research within a broader framework and that the book should reflect our own thinking about neighborhoods and their place and prospects in American cities today. Fortunately, our thinking had evolved along largely parallel tracks, and despite the need to iron out many small differences, we shared a common perspective on the big questions we were trying to answer.

As the project took on increasingly ambitious dimensions, Brett, blessed with an overabundance of work and family obligations, wisely bowed out. The two of us soldiered on, unaware that we were about to embark on a four-year journey that would be interrupted by a global pandemic, medical challenges, and the loss of loved ones. This book is the product of that journey. It is a work of scholarship, but it is also one that is grounded in what neighborhoods have meant and continue to mean to those who live in them and, to the best of our ability, in their full complexity and variety.

Finally, a major challenge of writing a book about neighborhoods in twenty-first-century America is that it is easy to think of the subject as obsolete or even trivial. After all, with the technological changes of the last few decades and the enhanced transportation and communications networks that are part of our everyday life, most notably the handheld devices we all carry that enable us to connect to our social networks or play Final Fantasy XV, neighborhood social relations grounded in physical proximity are not nearly as central to our lives as they once were. While the two us of enjoy the neighborhoods we live in, we had to admit that we do not sit on the front stoop for hours each day schmoozing with our neighbors. Indeed, we have little more than a passing acquaintance with most of our neighbors. Our close networks of family and friends are widely dispersed.

Our acknowledgment that many, perhaps most, people today perceive neighborhood ties as marginal to their lives clashed with our conviction that neighborhoods were still important. Gradually, after many emails and conversations, we came to the realization that, ironically, it is precisely the coolness of neighborhood ties that makes them so important in modern society. We are not the first to observe that neighborhood social relations are distinctive. Sixty years ago, Jane Jacobs wrote about how urban neighborhoods can nurture social capital while still preserving individuality and privacy. Even as neighborhoods have become less central to our lives, the importance of neighborhood relations has grown. As our nation becomes increasingly divided by almost every social, economic, demographic, and cultural fault line imaginable, we believe that the weak ties nurtured in neighborhoods can help us bridge the intense polarization that bedevils our society and risks tearing it apart. We offer this book in that spirit in the hope that it will contribute to the important work of building or rebuilding better neighborhoods and in homage to those who have dedicated their lives to that work.

Acknowledgments

We both want to thank our three readers, Karen Black, Charles Duff, and John Shapiro, who offered sometimes critical but always thoughtful and constructive comments and suggestions; Jim Lance, our editor at Cornell University Press, for his consistent support and encouragement; and Brett Theodos, who was part of the initial conversations that ultimately led to this book.

Over many years Alan has had the opportunity to learn about cities and neighborhoods from numerous people, perhaps beginning with George Sternlieb at Rutgers, whose clear-headed view of the urban condition in the 1970s and 1980s was an invaluable experience. The late David Lewis, founder of Urban Design Associates, and the late Colin Ward, the one Welsh and the other English, were two people who were early inspirations as Alan began his career in this field. During Alan's long involvement with the Housing and Community Development Network from its founding in 1988, he learned from a host of New Jersey's community development leaders, including Sean Closkey, Pilar Hogan Closkey, Ray Ocasio, Joe Della Fave, Patrick Morrisy, and above all the network's founding executive director, Diane Sterner, who has been my valued friend, critic, and sounding board for many years. Working for the City of Trenton during the 1990s opened Alan's eyes to the many complexities of urban and neighborhood change and enabled him to learn from an amazing cast of characters, including among many others Marty and Liz Johnson, Gwendolyn Long Harris, Blanca Valentin, the late Ken Russo, Father Brian McCormick, the late Albert "Bo" Robinson, Bill Watson, and the people of Trenton themselves. More recently as Alan has worked in cities around the country, he has been fortunate to meet wonderful and dedicated practitioners who have shared their challenges and insights, including Rick Sauer in Philadelphia; Frank Ford, Linda Warren, and Tony Brancatelli in Cleveland; Annika Goss, Steve Tobocman, and Maggie DeSantis in Detroit; Ian Beniston in Youngstown; Presley Gillespie, first in Youngstown and now in Pittsburgh; Chris Ryer and Gerard Joab in Baltimore; and many more whom he hopes will forgive him for not mentioning them by name.

One of Alan's great rewards of working on cities and neighborhoods has been the ability to work with a remarkable collection of colleagues, both practitioners and scholars, including Paul Brophy, the late Michael Schubert, David Boehlke, Sabina Deitrick, George Galster, Margie Dewar, Dennis Keating, Jennifer Leonard, Robert Beauregard, Robert Weissbourd, Karen Beck Pooley, Dan

Immergluck, Ira Goldstein and many others. Alan particularly wants to thank Michael Braverman, Karen Black, Lavea Brachman, Charles Buki, Bill Gilchrist, John Shapiro and Marcia Nedland, who have become friends of long standing and to whom Alan looks regularly to obtain good advice, valuable insights, and wise counsel.

Alan is grateful to CEO Akilah Watkins and her colleagues Tarik Abdelazim, Rob Finn, Kim Graziani, Courtney Knox, Danielle Lewinski, and former CEO Tamar Shapiro at the Center for Community Progress and to CEO Mac McCarthy and in particular Jessie Grogan at the Lincoln Institute of Land Policy for their constant support and encouragement and the many opportunities both organizations gave Alan to engage with the past, present and future of America's neighborhoods.

Finally, Alan wants, one more time, to thank Robin, his lifelong partner, who passed away in the summer of 2020, as this book was being written. For many decades, her love, moral support, and encouragement were his mainstay, and this book is dedicated to her.

Over the years Todd has had the privilege of learning from community development practitioners working on the ground in St. Louis. Under the leadership of Jenny Connelly-Bowen, the Community Builders Network has been a constant source of inspiration and insight. There are too many people to acknowledge here, but Tom Pickel has been a special source of sage advice. Participating in the civic experiment called the St. Louis Anchor Action Network has also been eye-opening. Karl Guenther, Stefani Weeden-Smith, Prima Wagan, Hank Webber, Jason Purnell, Nishesh Chalise, Ifeanyi Ukpabi, and Rachel Lewis have been stimulating collaborators as we have tried to figure out how anchor institutions can revitalize disinvested neighborhoods. Led by Dana Malkus, the Vacancy Collaborative Reading Group critically examined several chapters from the book. Among many other members of the group, Peter Hoffman, Zach Kassman, Laura Ginn, Ian Trivers, Bob Lewis, Kathryn Shackelford, and Brian Adler deserve a special shout-out for stimulating conversations about the challenges of disinvested neighborhoods. Austin Harrison has also helped both Todd and Alan think critically about the literature on neighborhood change.

Todd would like to thank Allie Huddleston and Zack Schwartz for research assistance. Madeleine Swanstrom also conducted valuable research for the book as well as endless hours of stimulating conversation about things urban. Todd benefited greatly from Napoleon Williams's work on the struggles of older suburbs in St. Louis. Bob Kerstein, Ben Looker, and Margaret Weir provided helpful commentary on parts of the manuscript. The St. Louis–Dortmund exchange provoked new thinking about gentrification from a cross-national point of view. We want to especially thank Jörg Plöger, Susanne Frank, Sabine Weck, Heike

Hanhörster, Florian Sichling, and Adriano Udani for their many insights. The students from St. Louis who, together with their collaborators from TU Dortmund University, won "The Future of My City" competition also deserve recognition for generating insights on gentrification: Mark Kasen, Liz Gerard, Adam Brown, Nathan Theus, Jodie Lloyd, Sydney Gosik, and Julia Spoerry. Todd's collaborators on the Home Repair Grant funded by the RRF Foundation for Aging, including Kiley Bednar, Adam Brown, John Robinson, Cynthia Palazzolo, Terry Jones, and Rachel Goldmeier, helped him to understand the huge need for more investment in older homes. Norm Krumholz passed away while this book was being written, but his dedication to equity planning continues be a source of inspiration.

Finally, Todd wants to thank his wife Catherine for being so patient and supportive as he drifted off to his study, physically and mentally, to write the book. He wants to especially acknowledge the incredibly generous and intelligent support she provided during his recent medical challenges. In this case, it is not a cliché: He could not have done it without her.

THE CHANGING
AMERICAN
NEIGHBORHOOD

INTRODUCTION

Everyone who has lived in a place more than briefly has been shaped, knowingly or otherwise, by the experience. We are no exception. Todd grew up in a community that could reasonably be described as a good neighborhood. Sandwiched between the Mississippi River and I-94, the Desnoyer Park neighborhood is located on the west side of St. Paul, Minnesota, not far from the University of Minnesota. When Todd was growing up there in the 1950s and 1960s, it had everything from millionaires' mansions on the River Boulevard to working- and middle-class single-family homes to modest apartment buildings. It was far from perfect—Todd does not remember a single person of color living in the neighborhood, for example—but it was a secure and stimulating place to grow up.

The three-room K–4 Desnoyer Park School was the center of the community. It had a large playground with a jungle gym and a baseball field, and every winter the fire hydrant was tapped to flood two ice rinks, one recreational and one for hockey. Every year the PTA held a winter carnival with games of chance in the school and Strauss waltzes played over loudspeakers for the skaters. Todd's immediate neighborhood on Otis Avenue was especially close. On summer evenings kids would gather for games of tag and Simon Says, and every Fourth of July Mrs. Stoddard held a community picnic. To this day, Todd remembers the names of dozens of families who lived on his street.

Since 1984 Alan has lived in Roosevelt, a small village in what was once rural but is now exurban New Jersey. Built in the 1930s as a New Deal agricultural-industrial cooperative community and with barely nine hundred residents, it can be seen as a single neighborhood.[1] Although neighborliness today is less intense than it was in the 1930s and 1940s, when old-timers years later described it as "one big family where doors were always open and neighbors could drop in on each other pretty much any time," it remains an intimate, involved, and engaged community, the sort of place where people greet each other and often stop for a chat when they pass each other in the street.[2]

Over a hundred residents, with or without children in the village K–5 school, show up each year for the school graduation ceremony in the village, while local artists, poets, and musicians have been putting on regular events in town every year since 1987. But some of the connections are fraying. The volunteer fire department was disbanded for lack of members a few years ago, and ever since Herb Johnson and Les Weiner died, there are no more annual Hiroshima Day memorial events in the village amphitheater.

These places matter, but how? Our book is focused on that central question: What is the significance of neighborhoods in twenty-first-century America when, as so many observers have noted, we seem more absorbed in our digital devices than in the social environment immediately around us? As physical containers of social relations, we argue, neighborhoods still matter deeply, and yet their role is different than for earlier generations.

In the most fundamental sense, a neighborhood is a place, a geographic entity. The word "neighbor" itself comes from Old English, meaning "people living near to a certain place."[3] Therefore, from an etymological standpoint, a neighborhood is a group of people living close to each other, or a "body of neighbors." From the earliest cities large enough to be considered cities in the modern sense, the creation of intermediate spaces, bigger than one's dwelling or family compound but smaller than the city as a whole, has paralleled the creation of cities. "Despite profound differences in urbanization processes," Emily Talen writes, neighborhoods, or localized spaces that people identify with and that facilitate human relationships, "emerged as a regular feature of urban experience all over the globe."[4] The Roman emperor Augustus gave official recognition to Rome's neighborhoods, known as *vici*, each of which had its own religious shrines and civic administration.[5] Over the millennia neighborhoods have varied in their physical form, official status, and governance, but every major city has had "little worlds" inside it that people cared about and related to. It is a constantly changing yet remarkably persistent motif of human society.

People understand a neighborhood as a physical space, but it is not just any physical space. It is an intermediate space. It is a recognized space. Its boundaries may be fuzzy, and people may well disagree about the borders of their own neighborhood or about what their neighborhood should be called, but neighborhoods are places that are clearly understood to exist and are recognized by the people who live there. The principal reason people all but universally identify with a place is, of course, that neighborhoods are far more than physical spaces and geographic entities. At its core, a neighborhood is about proximity, about people living close to one another and therefore developing distinctive social relations.

As befits such a significant, resilient feature of society, a neighborhood is complex. It is simultaneously a geographic entity, an economic unit, and a social organism. Thus, to understand a neighborhood, one must look at it through a multidisciplinary lens, recognizing its diversity and complexity. While we respect what many scholars have written about neighborhoods, we find that much of it is narrow and confined by disciplinary boundaries, projecting an image that recalls the parable of the blind men and the elephant.[6] Similarly, neighborhoods need to be understood holistically. Our understanding of neighborhoods needs to be both contextual and dynamic. Neighborhoods are dynamic organisms, constantly changing, embodying a complex system of interactions and feedback loops, much like echo chambers where every action reverberates back and forth in a circular process of causation. With the possible exception of the very wealthiest and very poorest, neighborhoods are in constant flux, moving upward, downward, or sideways but always changing. Trying to stop neighborhoods from changing is no more practical than the apocryphal story of King Canute, who ordered the tides to stop without success.

Not only are neighborhoods internally complex, but they are also situated within larger contexts of both time and space. Neighborhoods are a product of both their histories and the larger forces operating around them, beginning with the city of which they are a part and extending to the global economy. They are *affected* by all of these forces but not *determined* by them. Far too much of today's discourse about neighborhoods sees them purely as the passive products of larger forces, whether racial discrimination, public policies, institutional frameworks, or global capital flows. All such forces are important, but such thinking leaves room for agency, for the effects of the actions and choices of the millions of people who live in America's neighborhoods and the organizations they have created to act on their behalf. People mold their neighborhoods just as their neighborhoods mold them.

The Idea of the Good Neighborhood

At the center of our argument is the idea of the "good neighborhood." One could also call them healthy, vital, or decent neighborhoods or, in Emily Talen's expression, "everyday" neighborhoods.[7] When we talk about "good neighborhoods," however, we do so with care. It is a term fraught with potential misunderstandings

and stereotypes, smacking of popular but trivial stories about "the ten best neighborhoods in Houston" or "finding the best place to raise your family." It is also
tinged with nostalgia for the good old days when, in the refrain of the theme song
for the sitcom *Cheers*, "Everybody knew your name." This sort of nostalgia seems
harmless but can easily shade into a yearning for bygone social hierarchies of racial and gender power and subordination.

The good neighborhood can also conjure up racist stereotypes. Real estate
agents have often used "good neighborhoods" as code words for white middle-
class neighborhoods.[8] The reader may reasonably ask, how can we call the neighborhood in St. Paul, Minnesota, where one of us grew up, a "good neighborhood"
when it was completely segregated? We are using the term "good," however, not in
the sense of a moral concept or Platonic ideal but in a narrower pragmatic sense:
whether a neighborhood is good or not depends on how well it functions for the
people who live there at that time. It is possible to acknowledge that a place
worked for the people who lived there and try to understand why it worked for
them so we can learn from that experience while at the same time condemning
the racism that unjustly blocked people from living there because of the color of
their skin.

Race is an inescapable presence in any discussion of American neighborhoods, linked as neighborhoods are to historic systems of oppression and discrimination that are far from merely a bad memory. When it comes to the
dynamics of the American neighborhood, however, it is always about race but is
never *only* about race. The white flight from the cities after World War II was
about race, but it was also about desperate housing shortages and the sheer shab-
biness of the postwar American city after fifteen years of neglect. However, it
was racial discrimination, private and public, that made it *white* flight. In the
course of this book, we will try to disentangle the many strands connecting race
and neighborhoods.

Good neighborhoods must be understood through an interdisciplinary lens,
not reduced to one dimension. Just as neighborhoods should not be reduced to
their racial dimension, neither should they be reduced to economics. Some might
argue that a neighborhood with a strong housing market—one with high and
rising property values where buyers are clamoring to get in—is ipso facto a good
neighborhood. We disagree. The market is a blunt instrument. In global cities
such as New York and London, many homes in expensive neighborhoods are
owned by speculators who may occupy them for only a few weeks of the year,
while other units have become Airbnb rentals, turning the neighborhood into
an endless stream of transients. A neighborhood may be a market success, yet it
is not a good neighborhood if it fails to nurture social connections or sunders
those that previously existed. Still, a strong housing market is an important

element in most good neighborhoods if not a threshold condition of a good neighborhood.

If we know what good neighborhoods are not, then what are they? How are they defined? A good neighborhood, we readily admit, is not a concept capable of precise definition or quantitative measurement. Intuitively, most people know or think they know a good neighborhood when they see one. They might say that someone "bought a house in a good neighborhood" or "don't go there at night, that's a bad neighborhood." These judgments, of course, can be and often are infected with misinformation and subjective bias. As we use the term "good neighborhood," it has two necessary elements that, while they may be difficult to apply in any specific neighborhood, are analytically distinct and observable: access to things that are necessary for a good life and the nurturance of distinctive social relations.

First, a good neighborhood gives its residents connections to the things that are necessary for a decent life while not inflicting on them those things that prevent them from living such a life. This includes decent schools, well-functioning civic institutions and public services, access to jobs, and a healthy environment, including clean air, healthy food, and safe open spaces. A good neighborhood is reasonably safe and supports stable or rising property values so that residents can accumulate a modicum of wealth. Good neighborhoods are places where, in the words of one pioneering community development figure, "families can raise their children with the hope that their children's lives will be better than their own."[9]

Few neighborhoods can meet every aspiration. When choosing a neighborhood, all but the wealthiest people need to evaluate and make trade-offs. They may choose a neighborhood because it has excellent schools and pleasant parks even though the nearest grocery store is miles away. Good neighborhoods do not need to be perfect; they just need to work well enough for the people who live there. Indeed, we toyed with the idea of substituting the term "good enough neighborhood." That modest term reflects the reality that while neighborhoods matter, the lives and identities of most twenty-first-century Americans are far less interwoven with neighborhood connections than was true of past generations.

Neighborhoods, though, need to be good enough to meet those needs that still must be met by neighborhoods. And this will vary across different groups in society. With their far-flung social networks, affluent people depend less on neighborhood connections to meet their needs. They may, for example, send their children not to the local public school but instead to a distant private school or even a boarding school. Lower-income households are far more reliant on the neighborhood's amenities and social support networks.

The second necessary characteristic of a good neighborhood is that it nurtures distinctive social relations, the social connections epitomized by Mark

Granovetter's concept of "weak ties."[10] Unlike "strong ties" of kinship and friendship, weak ties do not involve substantial intimacy or powerful reciprocal obligations. They are crucial, however, for information sharing, trust building, and mobilizing diverse groups to defend the neighborhood. In chapter 1 we develop the idea of weak ties further. Suffice it to say at this point that weak ties perform crucial functions in good neighborhoods.

Weak ties are crucial for addressing two growing problems in American society: excessive individualism at the cost of community and social/political polarization. In their recent book *The Upswing*, Robert Putnam and Shaylyn Garrett present an impressive array of surveys and other measures to show how, after steady growth in the United States of economic equality, political comity, and communitarian values from the end of the nineteenth century to the 1950s or 1960s, that trend abruptly reversed itself as the country turned away from communitarian to individualistic values. As Putnam and Garrett put it, from having been very much a "we" society in the 1950s and 1960s, the United States "has become demonstrably—indeed measurably—a more 'I' society."[11] At the same time, the country has engaged in what journalist Bill Bishop calls "the big sort," separating ourselves geographically into separate enclaves of political, economic, and social tribes and thus eroding trust and undermining our ability to achieve political consensus.[12]

While hardly a solution in themselves, weak ties nurtured in good neighborhoods can help address these divisions. Precisely because of their informality and lack of intimacy, weak ties enable people to develop connections across economic, social, and even political divides. Weak ties do not require conformity to a single body of values or perspectives but instead nurture looser connections of tolerance and respect. By helping people to get along at the same time that they get ahead, weak ties work to reconcile the life between individualism and community in American life.

We do not look at every permutation of the American neighborhood in our book. Both the shortness of life and the strictures of our publisher constrain us. Our focus is principally on what might be called "traditional" neighborhoods, where the proximity inherent in the meaning of the word "neighbor" encourages face-to-face encounters in public spaces that nurture weak ties. Such neighborhoods include those of America's older cities as well as for the most part those in the inner-ring suburbs and newer cities built during the first few decades after World War II. For this reason, we have little to say about the newer very low-density exurban neighborhoods, where virtually every form of human activity or contact requires an automobile. While those communities undoubtedly meet many people's needs, we wonder whether the term "neighborhood" is even applicable. With distance and the absence of face-to-face contact forcing residents to be very intentional about whom they interact with, in some respects they are more communities of interest than neighborhoods. Perhaps they are the birthplace of new forms of neighboring and social connection, but if so that is a topic for a different book by someone else.

While our concept of neighborhood includes the neighborhoods of the rich and the poor, much of our focus is on those urban and suburban neighborhoods that are coming to be known as "middle neighborhoods," the neighborhoods that have historically housed America's vast middle class.[13] As Henry Webber writes, they "have traditionally been the heart of American cities. They are the neighborhoods where working- and middle-class citizens live; raise families; pay taxes; send their children to school; go to church, synagogue or mosque; and shop at the local grocer."[14] Despite their erosion in recent decades, these neighborhoods, which still make up a large part of the universe of neighborhoods, are not only at risk of further decline but also have been far less studied than they deserve.

We do not, however, ignore the neighborhoods of the poor or the rich, particularly the former. The future of the nation's low-income neighborhoods, particularly those low-income communities of color where disinvestment and discrimination have played such a destructive role, is a critical part of the neighborhood conversation. We address those neighborhoods directly in chapter 12.

Why Are Good Neighborhoods Threatened?

Our work is motivated by the conviction that everyone, whatever their economic condition, should be able to live in a good neighborhood and that however difficult it may be, this is an achievable aspiration. Yet, the challenge is that by any reasonable standard, far too few neighborhoods today, particularly those occupied by the less prosperous members of American society and by people of color, meet even a modest definition of what a good enough neighborhood should be. For all the disproportionate attention given to gentrification, outside a handful of hot markets it is the exception rather than the rule. The dominant trend of neighborhood change in recent decades has been decline, while access to good neighborhoods has increasingly become an elite good.

There are many possible explanations for the decline of good neighborhoods. Technological changes have played a part. Things as mundane as the rise of television and air conditioning during the second half of the twentieth century meant that fewer people sit on front stoops or porches or take strolls around the block on summer evenings, all activities conducive to neighborliness. More recent developments, such as the internet and social media, have further attenuated place-based social ties. The rise of shopping malls and big box stores undid count-less neighborhood shopping streets, once critical stitches in the neighborhood fabric, and more recently those neighborhood shopping venues are being undone by the rise of ecommerce.

Another fundamental force is the change in the American family since the 1960s. The number of husband-and-wife couples raising children together, the backbone of earlier tightly knit neighborhoods, has dropped from nearly half of all American households to fewer than 20 percent. Stay-at-home mothers have all but disappeared from the scene. With people marrying later and living lon-ger, far more of us live alone. While the young people who have flocked to the vibrant urban scenes of New York City, Chicago, Philadelphia, and many other cities may want some kind of neighborhood connection, they look for it in high-density, mixed-use enclaves, not the blocks of one- and two-family houses that make up the traditional neighborhoods of our cities and postwar suburbs. While their dramatic rise as a share of the American urban population since 2000 has undermined some traditional neighborhoods, it has also led to the growth of a new type of good neighborhood dominated by educated, affluent, and above all young residents.

Our economy has also changed fundamentally. The shift from an industrial to a so-called knowledge economy has led to the hollowing out of the American middle class, the heart of the traditional neighborhood. We have more rich and poor families—and fewer middle-class families—than we did a couple of gen-erations ago. That reflects in turn many changes, including the shift from well-paying industrial jobs to lower-wage service jobs, the collapse of the unions that played such an important role in working-class life, and the growing earnings gap between those with and those without a college degree, all of which has made America's haves and have-nots into two almost separate societies.

Economic polarization has been paralleled by spatial polarization. Not only do we have fewer middle-income families, but we also have even fewer middle neigh-borhoods, as households have increasingly sorted themselves by income. Although racial segregation has slowly declined in American neighborhoods since the 1960s, in its place we have far more economic, social, and even partisan political segrega-tion. As a recent study concluded, "high partisan segregation [exists] across the country, with most voters of both political parties living in partisan bubbles with little exposure to the other party."[15] Not only have neighborhoods pulled apart economically, but neighborly relations more broadly have also deteriorated. In-volvement in local organizations has dropped, voting in local elections has de-clined, and Americans report spending less time with their neighbors.[16]

Does this mean that neighborhoods no longer exist or are in danger of dis-appearing? Hardly. Human beings are social animals, and neighborhoods provide for human interaction that is fundamental to our being. But they have become weaker, both as frames for human connection and places that offer people, particularly people of color and those not affluent enough to have many choices about where to live, a decent quality of life and opportunities for them and their children. Too often, neighborhoods are places where families have little hope for their children's futures.

Plan of the Book

This book examines how American neighborhoods have changed, what factors have driven those changes, and what challenges our neighborhoods face today in the early twenty-first century. Our approach is deliberately concrete and grounded in the lived reality of neighborhoods. While we are both scholars, we have also been practitioners, and that experience animates this book. We are interested in knowledge for its own sake but even more in knowledge that can guide action to support good neighborhoods and rebuild struggling ones. We are interested in *neighborhoods*, not an abstraction called "The Neighborhood."

Chapters 1 and 2 frame the argument of the book. Chapter 1 elaborates on the idea of the good neighborhood that we have sketched out above, making the case for why good neighborhoods are important and why they are threatened. Chapter 2 develops our approach to studying neighborhood change. Placing our work in the context of prior thinking about neighborhoods, we argue that thinking about neighborhood change must be interdisciplinary, applying insights from fields such as sociology, economics, political science; contextual, taking into account the effects of different geographical scales on neighborhoods; and historical, recognizing the overlapping and multidimensional effects of time. To reflect all of these realities, neighborhoods cannot be grasped with linear reasoning; instead, they must be understood as dynamic systems with powerful feedback effects and tipping points.

Reflecting the importance of history to today's reality, chapters 3 through 5 explore the constantly changing dynamics of American neighborhoods from the colonial era to the present. Neighborhood change has reflected shifts in the role of the American city as it has moved from being a mercantile to an industrial center and today a center of education and health care or, to some, a "creative" city. Neighborhoods have also mirrored changes in American attitudes and values, the shifting meanings of race and ethnicity and, particularly since World War II, the shifting public policies and institutional frameworks that have emerged as neighborhoods came to be perceived as a problem to be solved rather than simply part of the reality of people's lives.

At the same time, we try to show how the people who live in cities have fought to create vital neighborhoods, from the immigrant enclaves of the early twentieth century and the segregated Black ghettos of the 1920s to today's community development movement. A key to our approach is that historical periods do not end; they continue on as new historical forces are layered on top of old ones. The contemporary city, for example, is primarily a product of the forces of two historical periods: the forces of urban revival that began gathering steam in the 1990s are overlaid on the forces of urban decline that, while they may have peaked in the 1960s and 1970s, are still very much alive in American cities.

The next four chapters explore key forces and agents of neighborhood change. Chapter 6 addresses the pervasive role of the housing market in neighborhood change and shows how market factors operate within and are central to the larger neighborhood feedback system. Chapter 7 looks at the larger demographic, economic, and social changes that have affected neighborhoods since the end of World War II, while chapter 8 grapples with the pervasive but changing role of race. We stress the ways in which people, both Black and white, have used their agency to create successful Black and integrated neighborhoods while recognizing the pressures and threats to these neighborhoods posed by the continued presence of structural racism in American society. Chapter 9 then looks at the agents of neighborhood change and the ways in which neighborhoods and their residents are affected by institutional and organizational actors, beginning with city governments but including institutions such as universities and medical centers, which have come to play an outsize and sometimes positive but often problematic role in neighborhood change.

Reflecting our critique of theories of neighborhood change that overgeneralize across different neighborhood contexts, chapters 10 to 13 are organized around three different types of neighborhoods that have different yet related dynamics and challenges. Chapter 10 examines gentrification, arguably the most widely discussed and probably the most widely misunderstood form of neighborhood change in American cities today. We drill down into the dynamics of gentrification—who gentrifies, what neighborhoods gentrify, and why—but also into the relationship of gentrification and power and the significance of gentrification as one link in the larger context of the ongoing dynamic of neighborhood change.

If gentrification can be seen as a form of neighborhood revival, however problematic, the next three chapters look at different variations on the theme of neighborhood decline. Chapter 11 explores the decline of the traditional middle neighborhood, particularly the Black middle neighborhoods that largely emerged in the 1960s and 1970s. Chapter 12 turns to the persistent challenge of neighborhoods of concentrated poverty, tracing their origins and current conditions and posing the question of whether and how such neighborhoods can become good neighborhoods, a question we answer cautiously in the affirmative. Finally, chapter 13 addresses the increasing challenges faced by many suburban neighborhoods, particularly in the inner-ring suburbs built in the postwar suburban boom.

In the final chapter we tie together the themes that animate our thinking and ask the central question: How should scholars and practitioners be rethinking the theory and practice of neighborhood change to make them more intellectually compelling and practically useful in the twenty-first century? Ultimately, we need a robust multidimensional understanding of how and why neighborhoods change to be a framework for not only more productive research but also to support creative, effective policies and practices by neighborhood change agents that can move us toward a reality where the ability to live in a good neighborhood is available to all, not just a fortunate few.

Postscript: A Note on the Pandemic

Beginning in early 2020, COVID-19 changed everything. It caused us to appreciate neighborly connections more than ever but also to recognize their fragility

FIGURE 0.1. A community refrigerator in Colton, California

(Photo by Annakai Geschlider/IECN)

and contingency. Neighborhoods are all about face-to-face encounters. With so-cial distancing, we suddenly found that we could not even share a cup of coffee with a friend at a local café. Initially, even sidewalk encounters seemed hazard-ous. We missed these human connections. At the same time, we discovered that neighborhoods have qualities that can compensate, at least up to a point, for the risks created by propinquity, fostering social connection even while physically distancing. Forced to stay home, people found that they had more opportunities to nurture neighborhood connections and to appreciate how valuable those con-nections could be.

People formed neighborhood pods, hyperlocal text message groups, and phone trees. Neighbors joined together to share childcare, a pressing need for working parents after many childcare centers closed. Mutual aid societies fos-tered reciprocal helping relationships outside of government or market exchanges, an idea rooted in the anarchist tradition. Innumerable acts of neighboring, care-fully organized or spontaneous, took place in cities and towns across the country, such as community refrigerators that popped up in front yards and on sidewalks (figure 0.1).

It would be heartwarming to report that neighborhood connections wove a tight safety net around those vulnerable to COVID-19, but that would be far from the truth. The safety net may be tightly woven in some neighborhoods but so loosely woven in others as to be all but meaningless. Even at best, it cannot sub-stitute for the loss of income or jobs and can provide only limited comfort for the loss of a loved one. At the same time that COVID-19 prompted so many ex-amples of neighborhood vitality, it also exposed the deep inequality across neighborhoods. Rates of COVID-19 infection and death were highest in low-income, immigrant, and African American neighborhoods. The pandemic brought out the continuing resilience of neighborhoods but also exposed their stunning inequality and the deep racial roots of that inequality, themes we re-turn to often in this book.

WHY GOOD NEIGHBORHOODS?

As we wrote in the introduction, we focus on what we refer to as the "good neighborhood." What that means is not a simple matter. While the idea of a neighborhood is straightforward, determining what constitutes a good neighborhood is complicated because it implies a value judgment about which people can legitimately disagree. In this chapter, we explore the idea of the good neighborhood and examine why it is threatened. In the next chapter we develop an approach for understanding neighborhood change that can help us both better understand how and why neighborhoods change as well as help guide action to sustain good neighborhoods.

The Idea of the Good Neighborhood

The good neighborhood is not a monolithic, one-size-fits-all concept. Whether a neighborhood is good is determined not by any objective standard but instead by the people who live there. Different people need and want different things from their neighborhood, which vary with the social and economic condition of the neighborhood and the individuals who make it up. To the extent that neighborhood support systems are an important part of the good neighborhood, those systems may be seen as relatively unimportant by many affluent people whose personal support networks, such as they may be, are more widely dispersed geographically. For many others, though, neighbors are an essential part of a web of mutual support that sustains them in their lives. As sociologist

Suzanne Keller has written, "the neighbor is the helper in times of need who is expected to step in when other resources fail."[1] Lower-income people generally have more geographically confined social networks and are more likely to live in proximity to their family members. Their economic and even physical survival may depend on a network of reciprocal neighboring or neighborhood-based kinship relationships. Ironically, the affluent few, who rely on neighborly relations the least in their daily lives, are the ones increasingly reaping the benefits of strong neighborhoods with rising home prices.

The roles that neighborhoods play also vary from one historical period to the next. Neighborhoods in American cities have lost much of the central role they played in people's lives a hundred years ago, when many neighborhoods were virtually self-sufficient units. A great deal of mischief indeed has been made by people pining for the days of the urban ethnic neighborhood or the close-knit suburbs of the 1950s. We need to avoid that form of nostalgia and acknowledge the ambiguity and complexity of America's neighborhood heritage. Those tightly knit neighborhoods were highly gendered and racialized. Much has changed since then. Women are far more likely to work than stay home raising children, and racial boundaries, although still present, are far more porous than they once were. These are all positive changes.

The social relations nurtured by twenty-first-century neighborhoods are far less all-encompassing than in previous generations. People's social networks as well as their work, shopping, and entertainment destinations are dispersed over a wider landscape; in recent years, they have increasingly become virtual through the internet and social media platforms such as Facebook and Instagram. But this does not mean that neighborhoods are unimportant. Indeed, in the age of digital connections and social fragmentation, the bridging social ties nurtured in good neighborhoods are more important than ever. If we needed reminding, the COVID-19 pandemic served that purpose.

Good neighborhoods promote diversity and tolerance without undermining group cohesion or solidarity. To be sure, many neighborhoods today are highly segregated and exclusionary. While most Americans would not want to live in a neighborhood where everybody is alike, few would want to live in a neighborhood where residents have almost nothing in common and where life in the neighborhood is a constant clash of conflicting values and lifestyles. Finding the balance between diversity and cohesion in a neighborhood is difficult. While condemning racism and exclusion, we should be careful not to elevate an abstract ideal of diversity to an ultimate value at the price of other neighborhood values.[2] While research has shown that greater diversity can make building community cohesion more difficult, the research is also clear that racially diverse neighborhoods can reduce racial conflict and tension, especially when people of different races and ethnicities but similar socioeconomic status work toward shared goals.[3]

How are good neighborhoods able to reconcile the competing values of diversity and solidarity? A key to the answer lies in recognizing that neighborhoods do not have to be all things to all people, intense hubs of social interaction or, as William Holly Whyte put it in *The Organization Man*, "hotbeds of Participation."[4] Neighborhoods don't have to be Good in some abstract, Platonic sense; they just have to be good enough. Neighborhood ties do not need to be all-encompassing; they just need to work for the people who live there. The informal limited ties that good neighborhoods nurture are part of the formula for successful diverse neighborhoods.

Much frustration has been created by expecting too much of neighborly relations. Although good when it happens, it is unrealistic as a general proposition to expect people from widely varying racial, social, and economic backgrounds to become close friends, invite each other over for dinner, and share the intimate details of their lives. And indeed, none of that is necessary for a neighborhood to be a good neighborhood. It is both desirable and realistic, however, for diverse groups of people to mingle in neighborhoods, share public spaces, appreciate each other's cultures, and learn to get along with one another.

Although neighborhoods no longer play as prominent a role in people's lives as they did in earlier times, they still perform crucial functions. Perhaps counterintuitively, we argue, in an age of digital connections, social fragmentation, and increasing diversity and partisan polarization, the weak ties nurtured in neighborhoods are more important than ever. Neighborhoods can help people get ahead in life and get along with others. Good neighborhoods both build community and foster better individual life outcomes.

Good Neighborhoods Nurture Community

Human beings are social animals. We may grudgingly admire people who choose to live off the grid or survive by foraging in the wilds of Alaska, but few of us will ever choose to emulate them. Our human relationships are part and parcel of our being and run the gamut from the friendly but casual nod we give the barista at our regular café when she says "the usual?" to the most intense bonds of friendship, kinship, and love. We are individuals, but rarely by choice are we isolated individuals. We want both privacy and community. As Jane Jacobs wrote, "a good city street neighborhood achieves a marvel of balance between its people's determination to have essential privacy and their simultaneous wishes for differing degrees of contact, enjoyment or help from the people around."[5]

Good neighborhoods help to reconcile the tension between individualism and community. Good neighborhoods generate norms of "generalized reciprocity," as anthropologists say. Those norms prompt me to watch my neighbors' homes when they are out of town on the expectation that they will do the same for me in the future or reciprocate with some other favor, such as helping push my car out of a snowdrift. Those connections enhance my individual well-being, acting like social savings accounts. As Robert Putnam puts it, "An effective norm of generalized reciprocity enables the reconciliation of self-interest and good neighborliness."[6] It is not that people who live in good neighborhoods have put aside self-interest in the name of community. Rather, they have embraced what Alexis de Tocqueville memorably called "self-interest rightly understood."[7]

Philosopher Nancy Rosenblum posits an ethic of neighborliness grounded in sharing a common space and recognizing the value of reciprocity between neighbors.[8] In a good neighborhood, residents act out of a sense of community connection, not just individual well-being. Communities vary in the degree to which residents are willing to engage in altruistic actions and pursue what is right or good for the community. Sociologist Robert Sampson found, for example, that the willingness to conduct cardiopulmonary resuscitation on a stranger or intervene in public to address threats to civic order or even conduct such mundane tasks as picking up a letter from the ground and putting it in a mailbox varied significantly across Chicago neighborhoods.[9]

Neighborly relations form a crucial middle ground in our network of social ties, less intense than the bonds that link us to friends and family but often more significant than the casual connections we make between ourselves and casual acquaintances, including most coworkers. They are a middle ground not only geographically but also in the web of human relationships that tie us together. They are rarely people's most important relationships. Neighbors are not friends as such, although some may become friends. Nevertheless, they are important; as Rosenblum writes, "neighbors are not just people living nearby. Neighbors are our environment."[10]

In many ways, the low intensity and informality of neighborly relations is what makes them function as neighborhood glue. Neighborhood relationships are part of what sociologist Mark Granovetter called "weak ties," as distinct from the "strong ties" of close friendship and kinship networks.[11] Weak ties do not involve substantial obligations or intimacy. But neighborly relations play a crucial role in our array of human connections. It is through those weak ties that neighborhoods become repositories of social capital. Robert Putnam, who did not invent the term but has popularized it through his writings, describes social capital as "the collective value of all 'social networks' [who people know] and the inclinations that arise from these networks to do things for each other ['norms of reciprocity']. . . . When a group of neighbors informally keep an eye on one another's homes, that's social capital in action."[12]

A related concept, developed by Robert Sampson and his colleagues, is collective efficacy, which can be defined as the ability of people in a neighborhood to establish norms and enforce them through informal social controls.[13] Collective efficacy goes beyond social capital in the important sense that while starting with the existence of a social network and a body of neighbors motivated to support one another, it adds two critical dimensions: those neighbors share a body of norms about what constitutes proper neighboring behavior and are willing to enforce them through informal means. In many respects, this is what the overused phrase "it takes a village" is about. Sampson and others have found that crime rates and other levels of disorder are lower in neighborhoods with high levels of collective efficacy.[14]

Social capital and collective efficacy combine two basic concepts: the existence of a social network connecting people and the ways in which that network motivates people to behave in mutually supportive ways. As a distinct form of social capital, neighborly relations are primarily what Putnam calls bridging social capital as opposed to bonding social capital.[15] Bonding social capital is demanding and inward-looking; it is often found among homogeneous groups sharing a kinship, ethnicity, or religious affiliation. Bridging social capital cuts across these identities. People can bridge social divides when they live in the same neighborhood and develop a sense of reciprocal responsibility for a shared space. It is partly because of the casual, even weak nature of neighborly relations that it is possible for people of different religions, economic backgrounds, and ethnicities or races to mingle and get along.

Paradoxically, it may seem that strong ties, such as intimate friendship and kinship relations, can hinder the effective workings of neighborhood social capital, undermining the weaker connections that are needed to bind the neighborhood together across social groups. Tight neighborhood subunits, whether one calls them cliques, clans, families, or gangs organized along the lines of kinship, race, religion, or other strong ties, can fragment the community and weaken neighborhood-level social capital. In his study of Boston's West End, Herbert Gans found that the community was unable to form an organization to fight against urban renewal, which ultimately destroyed the community even though it boasted tight social and extended family connections.[16] To Granovetter, this can be explained by the fact that the West End was organized into tight "cliques" and lacked the weak ties that could form bridges across the entire community to organize community-wide action.[17] Similarly, it explains how some low-income neighborhoods, which many struggling families value because they offer a strong familial support network, can also be areas of sustained crime and drug activity, taking place in the gaps between those networks created by the absence of weak ties.

How people perceive themselves and are perceived by others is interwoven with their and others' perception of their neighborhoods. Neighborhoods have identities based on fact, rumor, reputation, or all of the above that affect how residents of the city perceive them and the associations they have with them. If you move to a different neighborhood that has a different image, while you may think of yourself as unchanged, other people's perceptions of you may change. Moving may also challenge or even change your own self-image. For many people who have moved into changing urban neighborhoods in recent years, whether to see oneself as a gentrifier and if so how one should behave as a result have become highly charged questions involving not only behavioral but also ethical choices. At the other end of the economic spectrum, both comparative poverty and levels of neighborhood disorder have been found to have a negative effect on individuals' self-esteem.[18]

Neighborhood characteristics affect not only the quantity but the quality of civic participation. Alexis de Tocqueville famously observed that "town-meetings are to liberty what primary schools are to science; they bring it within people's reach; they teach people how to use and enjoy it."[19] By "liberty" Tocqueville meant the ability of citizens to govern their public and private lives. Many Americans experience politics first in their neighborhood, where they attend meetings and acquire the skills necessary for effective political engagement. Participation in neighborhood organizations is especially valuable because at that level one can more readily see the connection between individual and community well-being, Tocqueville's self-interest "rightly understood."

Neighborhoods that may appear to lack connections may actually have powerful latent organizational strength. We say "latent" because many healthy neighborhoods, particularly middle-class and affluent ones, may have no visible, ongoing neighborhood organizations to speak of. Yet, when something arises such as a proposal for a noxious land use or a change in local land use regulations that appears to threaten the neighborhood's character, organizations form within what seems like milliseconds, petitions are circulated, meetings are held, and local officials are bombarded with opposition to the proposal. Weak ties form the building blocks of latent as well as visible neighborhood civic capacity. Informal interactions and relationships, more than close friendships or family ties, are the means by which neighbors organize to fight for and fend off threats to their community.

Good Neighborhoods Improve Life Outcomes

At the same time that good neighborhoods promote social ties, they also promote individual success, often in ways their inhabitants may be unaware of. A growing and compelling body of research has demonstrated that the features of a person's neighborhood, after controlling for individual characteristics, exert a profound influence over their physical and mental health, economic success, and quality of life. It may even affect their identity and self-image in ways that individuals may not consciously realize.

While it has long been believed that that the neighborhood one grows up in affects one's future success, until recently the data was not available to measure the magnitude of this effect. In recent years, Harvard economist Raj Chetty and his colleagues have developed data sets that make it possible to measure the impact that growing up in different neighborhoods has on economic mobility.[20] By linking tax returns with individual-level data from the US Census Bureau, they mapped children born between 1978 and 1983 by census tract and then followed them into adulthood to see how they fared economically. After controlling for the race and income of parents, they found that the neighborhood children grow up in has a huge impact on their future economic mobility. For example, a Black man growing up in the 1980s and 1990s in a poor family in Atlanta might on average be earning today anything from $5,000 or less to over $40,000, depending on which census tract he grew up in. Low-income Black men who grew up in one neighborhood in the city of Compton, just outside Los Angeles, made three times as much as comparable Black men growing up in different circumstances in the Watts neighborhood of Los Angeles. Where we grow up and where we live powerfully affect our life trajectories.[21]

Equally powerful have been the findings about the relationship between neighborhoods and health. In Mercer County, a small New Jersey county bookended by struggling Trenton and wealthy Princeton, average life expectancy is over ninety years in Princeton but only seventy-two years in an impoverished neighborhood of Trenton, only ten miles away.[22] Researchers studying the vast socioeconomic disparities in life expectancy in the United States have concluded that only 10 percent of the variation is attributable to differences in access to medical care, with another 20 percent attributable to genetic factors.[23] The balance is a function of environmental factors, that is, lifestyle and behavioral factors, all of which are powerfully influenced by neighborhood conditions. Among the most powerful behavioral factors is chronic stress; an Atlanta-based study found that the incidence of post-traumatic stress disorder (PTSD) among low-income Black residents was closely associated with higher levels of neighborhood disorder. High levels of community cohesion, however, reduced this association.[24] Neighborhoods can be either beneficial or hazardous to your health.

Living in a disadvantaged neighborhood can be especially detrimental to children. Researchers in Chicago found out that simply living in proximity to a violent crime can affect brain functioning. Research by Patrick Sharkey found that "children do substantially worse on standard tests of cognitive skills . . . when there has been a homicide near their home." "Local violence does not make children less intelligent. . . . Rather, it occupies their minds."[25] These effects can be cumulative and difficult to reverse.

As the above examples suggest, most of the research in this area has been done in low-income neighborhoods. Yet, whether with respect to economic mobility, life expectancy, or childhood development, it is not about the neighborhood being low-income as such but instead about how well the neighborhood functions. Chetty and his colleagues found many low-income neighborhoods where children were growing up successfully and who as adults were earning substantially more than their cohorts from relatively more affluent neighborhoods. In his book *Heat Wave*, Eric Klinenberg tells the story of how Chicago's neighborhoods coped with the scorching heat wave of 1995. As temperatures and humidity reached unprecedented levels, deaths soared; in one week in July, 739 more people than expected died in the city of Chicago. Klinenberg found that eight of the ten community areas with the highest death rates were predominantly African American, with high levels of poverty and violent crime. At the same time, three of the ten neighborhoods with the lowest heat deaths were also predominantly African American, poor, and crime-ridden.[26] Those neighborhoods had social ties that protected the elderly from social isolation and death. What all this tells us is that a neighborhood's social and interpersonal dynamics can make a vast difference in the lives of the people who live there.

None of this should be taken to mean that external factors, such as concentrated poverty, racial segregation and discrimination, physical isolation, environmental contamination, and vacant dilapidated houses do not matter. They matter deeply, and the more pervasive they are, the more obstacles they put in the path of a neighborhood's chances of being or becoming a good neighborhood. Many people assume, however, that they are the only things that matter. The less tangible social dynamics of the neighborhood also matter and in the best cases can undo much of the damage done by negative external factors affecting the neighborhood. Neighboring, in all its manifold meanings, is an essential part of what makes a neighborhood a good neighborhood.

It is crucial to understand that the ability of families to access good neighborhoods is powerfully impacted by racial discrimination. African American children are seven times more likely than non-Hispanic white children to grow up in concentrated poverty neighborhoods.[27] Even when middle-class Black families are able to move into better low-poverty neighborhoods, those neighborhoods are often located in a broader geography of disadvantage that negatively impacts them.[28]

Neighborhoods also affect residents' ability to build wealth. For most American families, particularly those who are not in the top 10 or 20 percent by wealth and income, equity in their home is far and away their largest financial asset. Not quite two-thirds of American families are homeowners, and a still larger percentage have been homeowners at one point or another in their lives. Arguably, the most important economic decision, which is also a personal and emotional decision, that most families make during their lifetime is where to buy a home.[29] Where they buy that home, in turn, affects whether or not it appreciates after they purchase it. While the features of the house itself obviously matter, they matter less than the location or neighborhood; as the popular real estate saw goes, the three most important rules of real estate are "location, location, location."

Homeownership is far from a guaranteed path to wealth building, as millions of families learned during the mortgage crisis and the Great Recession, but for most American families it is the only option, as few families without significant capital to invest have realistic alternative paths to gain wealth. Moreover, homeownership usually works. Although families who bought at the height of the bubble often saw their equity disappear, homeowner equity has grown steadily over most time periods during the past half century or more.[30]

Black families have accumulated less household wealth through homeownership than white families, primarily because of the neighborhoods they have been historically relegated to by racial discrimination. In 2019, white median income was 1.65 times Black median income, but median white household wealth was over 7.8 times that of Black households ($188,200 vs. $24,100).[31] More than anything else, this disparity is the result of different rates of homeownership and home appreciation of Blacks compared to whites, reflecting in turn the long history of neighborhood segregation. Prior to the passage of civil rights laws in the 1960s, African Americans were routinely barred from most neighborhoods by private practices reinforced by public policies, a subject we discuss in chapter 8. Discrimination by real estate agents and mortgage lenders was all but universal. While that has largely changed, the effects of that racist history of exclusion perpetuate and exacerbate racial inequities to this day. Without accumulated wealth, African Americans are less able to afford college, start a business, or help their children buy a home in a good neighborhood to build their own wealth. At the same time, while it is generally known that Black homeowners were hit hardest by the mortgage crisis, it is less well known that Black home buyers who have bought homes after the crisis have widely seen significant appreciation in their value.[32]

One further neighborhood effect may seem counterintuitive, yet it is significant and another example of the strength of weak ties. More than half of all job opportunities come through word of mouth.[33] Most people who find jobs this way do so not through their strong ties, such as friends and relatives, but instead through their weak ties, casual acquaintances, and neighbors. The reasons for this have been widely explored since Granovetter first pointed this out, but the implications for neighborhoods are profound.[34] If you move to a neighborhood where people are well connected to the local labor market, your job and career options are likely to be greater than if you move into a neighborhood where fewer people have jobs or where they mostly work in fields remote from your skills and interests.

The Decline of Good Neighborhoods

Many Americans miss the close-knit neighborhoods that flourished in the early twentieth century, although some of them might find them less appealing in reality than in hazy retrospect. In 1999, National Public Radio host Ray Suarez wrote a book titled *The Old Neighborhood*, which laments the great white suburban flight that "left the very idea of 'neighborhoods' behind."[35] According to Suarez, people "yearn for the closeness, the coherence, that an old urban neighborhood gave their lives," for a time when "we *never* had to lock our doors." Interest has recently revived in Fred Rogers, the creator and star of *Mr. Rogers' Neighborhood*, which aired nationally on public television from 1968 to 2001. Creating a simulacrum of the community in which he grew up in 1930s Latrobe, Pennsylvania, his show was for decades a comforting presence for millions of children. Rogers's biographer suggests that at a time when "the geographical concept of the neighborhood in the United States is vastly diminished," Mr. Rogers "pointed to the way back to the neighborhood."[36] We would suggest, rather, that he offered a beguiling nostalgic perspective on a version of neighborhood that few of us experience today.

Putting nostalgia aside, however, there is compelling evidence that the supply of good neighborhoods in American towns and cities is shrinking. Compelling research shows that neighborhoods no longer perform as well as they once did with respect to two of their key historical roles: promoting social mobility and fostering social cohesion and trust.

The geographical sorting of the American population is a major contributor to the decline of good neighborhoods. While racial segregation in American cities has steadily, if slowly, declined since the 1960s, economic segregation has increased significantly. Increasingly, rich and poor live in different neighborhoods, and the number of middle-income and economically mixed neighborhoods has fallen. As researchers Sean Reardon and Kendra Bischoff sum up their findings for the period 1970–2009, "high- and low-income families have become increasingly less likely to live near one another. Mixed-income neighborhoods have grown rarer, while affluent and poor neighborhoods have grown much more common."[37] Joe Cortright and Dillon Mahmoudi found that the number of high-poverty neighborhoods in the United States tripled between 1970 and 2010.[38] With some exceptions, neighborhoods with high rates of poverty or housing abandonment reduce the likelihood of individual success whether in school or the job market and, as we noted, undermine physical and mental health. Few such neighborhoods are good enough for the people who live in them.

The shift away from mixed-income neighborhoods has been even more pronounced among African Americans. As Reardon and Bischoff document, predominantly Black neighborhoods were more economically mixed than white neighborhoods in 1970, but by 2010 predominantly Black neighborhoods had become less economically diverse than their white counterparts. Increasingly, middle-class and low-income Blacks live in separate neighborhoods. Millions of low-income families, disproportionately African American, are, in Patrick Sharkey's words, "stuck in place," trapped in neighborhoods that reinforce multigenerational poverty. "A mountain of research," Sharkey asserts, "has demonstrated the ways in which neighborhood structural disadvantage and social organization affect individual and collective social outcomes."[39]

Besides the loss of individual mobility and interaction across economic lines, considerable evidence supports the conclusion that many neighborhoods are doing a poorer job of promoting social cohesion and community. As we discussed earlier, social cohesion and individual success can be mutually reinforcing. Through the cluster of neighborly behaviors and relationships, good neighborhoods provide children with role models and mentors, connect them to job opportunities, and support success in school. The evidence, however, points strongly toward a decline of neighboring. In *The Upswing*, Putnam and Garrett update the analysis that Putnam began in *Bowling Alone* of the decline of community in the United States. Mining many different data sources, they conclude that "active involvement in local organizations fell by more than half in the last several decades of the twentieth century."[40]

Drawing from the General Social Survey, Joe Cortright reports that since the 1970s the percentage of Americans who report spending time with a neighbor at least twice weekly fell from 30 percent to about 20 percent.[41] Turnout in local elections is also down. According to one study, local voting turnout in thirty-eight cities declined 20 percent between 1978 and 2003. Only about one in four eligible voters turns out in local elections.[42] In ten of America's thirty largest cities, voter turnout for mayoral elections was less than 15 percent.[43] As Putnam puts it, "Declining electoral participation is merely the most visible symptom of a broader disengagement from community life."[44] Despite increasing affluence and steady improvement in housing quality, there is considerable evidence that the supply of good neighborhoods has fallen.

What Has Caused the Decline of Good Neighborhoods?

Many factors have caused the decline of good neighborhoods. Economic, technological, and demographic trends that threaten good neighborhoods have become entrenched and will be difficult if not impossible to alter. The hollowing out of the middle class, continued job and housing sprawl, and the rise first of television and then the internet, along with striking changes to the American family, all present challenges for traditional neighborhoods. This does not mean that good neighborhoods will disappear. Many people continue to seek out good neighborhoods in one fashion or another, while the nation's growing immigrant population and the movement of young people to the cities have created new pathways for creating good neighborhoods, both reviving older forms of neighborhood and building new kinds of good neighborhoods. Still, the forces and trends working against them are powerful. While we discuss many of them in detail in later chapters, it is useful to provide an overview here.

Technology has played an important role. Even if nothing else had changed, the technologies that have emerged since World War II would have undermined face-to-face neighborly relations. With the spread of air conditioning, fewer people sat on front porches on sultry nights greeting their neighbors as they walked by. In 2000, Putnam estimated that about 25 percent of the decline of social capital in the United States could be accounted for by the spread of electronic entertainment, largely television.[45] The internet has further disconnected people from their physical surroundings. No longer do people have to live close to one another to stay connected, which they can now do on Facebook, Twitter, and other social media. Ecommerce means that people can shop almost effortlessly online, usually at Amazon, rather than patronize local stores. These trends accelerated during the COVID-19 pandemic and the spread of remote working and Zoom-based social interactions. Some of this is likely to persist beyond the pandemic even after it is totally safe to engage in face-to-face relations.

Technology can support place-based communities as well but only up to a point. Some scholars argue that the internet can be used as a tool to further face-to-face connections and facilitate neighborhood connections.[46] Nextdoor.com is a social networking service where information is posted that is distributed only within the neighborhood. Residents use it to keep up with neighborhood news, exchange recommendations for service providers, and sell or exchange goods. That and similar services may be valuable tools, but the experience of millions during the pandemic has made it abundantly clear that a Zoom call is not the same as sitting next to someone and that online connections can never fully replace face-to-face relationships.

So-called third places, such as coffee shops, farmers markets, and even, despite Amazon, independent bookstores, have proliferated.[47] While these all testify to the importance of direct experience in the internet age, in many cases their connection to the idea of neighborhood is tenuous, and where they are part of a neighborhood fabric, the economics of such places dictates that they tend to be disproportionately clustered in neighborhoods largely populated by high-earning college graduates. This suggests a further point to which we will often return: the extent to which access to good neighborhoods has increasingly become associated with affluence rather than being a common good available to all segments of society.

While technology can undermine neighborhood connections, it is not as serious a threat to good neighborhoods as the hollowing out of the middle class. As we noted earlier, the number of middle-income neighborhoods with middle-class residents or a mix of people of different incomes has declined steadily for decades. If we define the middle class as families earning between 75 percent and 150 percent of the national median family income, then 43 percent of all families fell into that class in 1960. Today it is 34 percent.[48] We have many more rich and poor families and fewer middle-class families than in the past. This reflects many changes, including the shift from well-paying industrial jobs to lower-wage service jobs, the decline of unions, and the growing earnings disparity between college graduates and those without a college degree. Increasingly the top 10 or 20 percent, and even more the top 1 percent (or 0.1 percent), have pulled away from the rest of society. Rising income inequality is a major reason why we are losing so many of the neighborhoods in the middle, neighborhoods that have historically been the backbone of America's cities.

Economic changes have been paralleled by demographic changes. In the 1950 and 1960s we were a nation of families, more specifically, a nation of married-couple families with children. In 1960, 75 percent of American households were married couples, with almost 60 percent of them raising children under age eighteen.[49] Most of the rest were probably planning to have children or had finally pushed the last one out of the family home. It is not necessary to glorify the traditional American family to recognize that married couples raising children were the fundamental building block of both the postwar suburbs and earlier urban neighborhoods. Between 1960 and 2020, the percentage of US households composed of a married couple with children fell from 44 percent to 19 percent.[50] Cities in particular have fewer families with children and have become populated by young people, singles, and nontraditional households. While the number of child-rearing married couples has declined across the United States, it has plummeted further in central cities. Such families make up 19 percent of all households in the United States today but only 11 percent of households in Washington, D.C., and 9 percent in Pittsburgh. Nearly half of the households in both cities are single individuals living alone. As the number of single individuals and others in informal relationships grows, however, they may be inventing their own versions of good neighborhoods, often in areas such as downtowns and former industrial areas that had never before been residential neighborhoods.

Along with the preponderance of married couples in the 1950s and 1960s, stay-at-home wives and mothers were the backbone of that era's good neighborhoods. In 1955, only one out of six women in married couples with children under age six was in the labor force, rising to only one out of three for women with children ages six to seventeen. Mothers watched the children play, nurtured local connections, and took action to repel neighborhood threats. As Alan Ehrenhalt writes about a neighborhood in southwest Chicago, its "streets were being monitored during all the waking hours of the day by the informal law enforcement system of the neighborhood, the at-home mothers who devoted much of their time to keeping it glued together."[51]

This is no longer the case. Whether single or married and with or without children, women are now overwhelmingly part of the labor force. In 2019 the labor force participation rate, the share of the adult population working or looking for work, for women with children under age eighteen was 72.3 percent.[52] There was little difference between mothers in married couples and single mothers. We would not want to go back to the days when women were discriminated against and systematically excluded from many jobs. The entry of women into the workforce, however, has not been completely voluntary. A solid middle-class way of life today is increasingly difficult for all but a few families without two wage earners. Single mothers, of course, usually lack even the illusion of choice.

As we stress throughout the book, neighborhoods do not just reflect societal trends; they are active players in those trends. The decline of good neighborhoods is both a product of the pressures on the middle class and a contributor to those pressures. Causation runs in both directions. Neighborhood change is part of the story of the plight of the middle class. Elizabeth Warren (now Senator Warren) and Amelia Tyagi argued that many women have felt compelled to work to supplement the family's income so they could afford a house in a better

neighborhood, usually defined as a place with low crime and good schools. Warren and Tyagi wrote, "But as families saw urban centers as increasingly unat-
tractive places to live, the range of desirable housing options began to shrink and
parents' desires to escape from failing schools began to take on a sense of ur-
gency."[53] As the supply of good neighborhoods has shrunk, the competition for
them has intensified, driving up prices. This drives more women into the workforce and also requires both men and women to undertake longer commutes to
be able to afford a home in what they consider a good neighborhood.

Older urban neighborhoods were especially hard hit by demographic and economic trends, including changes in family structure, the suburbanization of
much of the white middle class, and the loss of well-paying industrial jobs. While
some urban middle neighborhoods became home to the Black middle class and
remained strong neighborhoods, many did not, triggering the growth of the concentrated poverty neighborhoods that persist to this day in America's cities.
While under the right circumstances a high-poverty neighborhood can be a good
neighborhood, providing support and a decent quality of life for its residents, it
is a difficult proposition, as we discuss in chapter 12. Moreover, as we noted
earlier, even after controlling for individual characteristics, including poverty
itself, people who live in high-poverty neighborhoods have worse outcomes than
those who live elsewhere.

Economic classes have increasingly sorted into different neighborhoods,
something Robert Reich called the "secession of the successful."[54] The fragmented
nature of American land-use powers enabled suburban governments to pass exclusionary zoning laws that facilitated them to become enclaves of affluence
and whiteness. When resource-rich households fled to the suburbs, the neighborhoods they left behind faced stagnating property values, falling retail opportunities, and rising crime. Notwithstanding the much-heralded urban revival,
the effects of the urban crisis that began in the 1960s, with its white flight, disinvestment, and housing abandonment, persist in large swaths of American cities
today, destroying good neighborhoods.

For many neighborhoods already struggling with the manifold challenges of
demographic change, economic decline, and an aging housing stock, the crush-
ing blow was the decade that began with the onset of subprime or predatory lending in the late 1990s, reaching its climax a decade later with the foreclosure
crisis and the Great Recession. Predatory lending did not markedly affect the
areas that were already disinvested and abandoned, but it did great damage
to areas that still retained much of the physical and social fabric of the good neighborhood, including large parts of cities such as Detroit and Cleveland that had
been sustained by middle-class Black families after the white flight of the 1960s
and 1970s.

Subprime lending was particularly devastating for African American neighborhoods, both in the central cities and in the inner-ring suburbs around them. These neighborhoods, as has become widely known, were targeted by lenders for high-cost, so-called exotic loans, often with the knowing or unwitting collaboration of prominent neighborhood figures.[55] In Cleveland, three out of every five home purchase loans in neighborhoods that were more than 80 percent Black in 2005 were subprime or high-cost mortgages, compared to one out of three in neighborhoods that were less than 20 percent Black.[56] With thousands of borrowers receiving mortgage loans that they had no realistic prospect of paying back, the outcome was predictable.

By 2007, waves of mortgage foreclosures were sweeping through these neighborhoods at the same time that the Great Recession was triggering massive job losses. Home prices plummeted, while vacant and abandoned houses began to appear on once-pristine blocks. Homeownership rates collapsed as lenders sold thousands of foreclosed properties to investors, triggering new waves of instability. As neighborhoods destabilized, many of the remaining homeowners decamped to the suburbs. A decade after the Great Recession, many of these neighborhoods have not recovered. They are still neighborhoods at least in the physical sense, but they provide less of the social fabric of neighboring and the springboard to opportunity that makes a geographic space a good neighborhood.

At the same time, the media increasingly presented our times as an age of urban revival, promoting a narrative in which the central urban problem today is not the flight of the middle class or the decline of urban neighborhoods but rather the invasion by the affluent of the neighborhoods of the poor, forcing them out of their homes. While gentrification as a phenomenon of neighborhood change is real, it is also a hot-button issue not only in neighborhood change but also as a shorthand for a variety of social, cultural, ideological, and political battles. As we discuss in detail in chapter 10 it is not the whole story, though.

The reality is that our age of urban revival is simultaneously an age of urban crisis in what we call the "layering" of different historical periods and forces. Modern American urban history can be seen as a shifting balance between forces of reurbanization and de-urbanization, something that varies over time as well as within and between cities. Over the past roughly forty years, the United States has diverged spatially. The predominantly coastal winner-take-all and strong market metros such as Boston and San Francisco have drawn the great majority of the jobs and investment in the new technology economy, while many other metros, especially smaller metros in the middle of the country, have fallen further and further behind.

Affluent in-migrants bid prices up in hot markets, while thousands of homes sit vacant and abandoned in weak markets. This disparity can be seen even within the overlapping metropolitan areas of Baltimore and Washington, D.C., where bricks from demolished row houses in Baltimore are trucked forty miles down the road to give a faux-historic aura to million-dollar condos in gentrifying Washington, D.C., neighborhoods.[57] Both extremes undermine neighborhood stability, whether by creating too much demand that overheats prices or too little demand that leaves abandoned houses behind.

Spatial inequality is also widening across neighborhoods within metropolitan areas. Since the 1990s, young well-educated single individuals and nontraditional households have sought out urban neighborhoods for their density, diversity, and lively youth-oriented social scene. Those people, sometimes referred to as the millennial generation, are the driving force of what is often referred to as gentrification. That phenomenon plays out differently, however, in different settings. Cities with rapidly growing technology-based economies, high levels of both immigration and in-migration, and severe constraints on new housing construction, such as restrictive zoning laws and physical barriers imposed by oceans and mountains, have few neighborhoods with weak housing markets. In distressed neighborhoods in Washington, D.C., where household incomes are barely $30,000, developers are buying and rehabilitating houses that go on the market for nearly $600,000.[58] In these cities, the primary threat to good neighborhoods comes not from blight but instead from hyperprosperity. Good neighborhoods for working- and middle-class households are disappearing.

Gentrification has become a dirty word in many circles—something that needs to be stopped in its tracks. This is unrealistic. Gentrification is not an isolated phenomenon but is part of the broader dynamic of neighborhood change that has operated ever since neighborhoods have existed, and it is not going to disappear. Moreover, while gentrification brings both harms and benefits, neighborhood decline brings little but harm. Neighborhoods are going to change; the question is whether the benefits of that change can be spread more broadly benefit only a few. How gentrification plays out depends on the context, on whether local policy decisions exacerbate its potentially destructive tendencies or manage them for the benefit of the entire community.

In all likelihood, more metros in the United States have weak housing markets than strong ones. Even with the real estate price rises triggered by the pandemic, as of June 30, 2021, two-thirds of the two hundred largest regions in the country had median house values under $300,000.[59] In many weak market metro areas such as Cleveland and St. Louis, gentrification is creating pockets of reinvestment in older industrial cities that have suffered from decades of disinvestment. In many ways that is a welcome trend in those cities, replenishing the tax base and in some respects building good neighborhoods that are often much more diverse racially and economically than is widely believed. These neighborhoods are emerging in and near the downtowns of older cities, from eastern Nashville to Cincinnati's Over-the-Rhine neighborhood and in neighborhoods adjacent to major universities or medical centers, such as Hampden in Baltimore and St. Louis's Central West End. But the number of in-migrants and would-be gentrifiers in these cities is relatively small, and as a group they are too few to sustain more than a handful of healthy neighborhoods. The greater problem in most older cities is not gentrification but rather its opposite, the continued flight of middle- and working-class families, who today are as or more likely to be Black or Latinx than non-Latinx white, from older urban neighborhoods.

Context Matters

Good urban and suburban neighborhoods still perform an important function in American society by providing settings within which it is possible to reconcile or balance individualism and community, a central challenge of our times. Good neighborhoods are not *the* solution to the problems of unbridled individualism and declining community, but they can be *part* of the solution. The weak ties and informal relations in good neighborhoods form bridging social capital that is especially important in an increasingly diverse and divided nation. Yet, with the decline of good neighborhoods, fewer and fewer are performing those functions.

Neighborhood change is closely tied to the national crisis of widening economic inequality and the shrinking middle class. Trends in the broader political economy that are driving increased polarization of both income and wealth put stress on good neighborhoods, while at the same time neighborhood change is itself part of the story of rising inequality. Concentrated poverty neighborhoods create poverty traps especially for African Americans, whose long exclusion from opportunity still resonates in the racial and economic distribution of American neighborhoods today. Affluent neighborhoods hoard opportunities and the social ties that help people access opportunity. The good neighborhoods in the middle that provided generations of average Americans with a shot at the American dream are shrinking. Good neighborhoods are in danger of becoming a luxury good.

There is no simple solution to the decline of good neighborhoods. Broad social and economic forces are buffeting neighborhoods, but they play out in varied ways on the ground. Context is powerful, as economic, social, and political forces interact to produce neighborhood change. As powerful a force as race is, for example, it cannot be understood apart from economic class. How race and class affect neighborhood change will be different in strong housing markets compared to weak ones and in metropolitan areas with high immigration and multiple or overlapping racial and ethnic identities compared to areas with a binary opposition of Black and white racial identities.

Not only does the larger context in which neighborhoods exist matter, but each neighborhood also creates its own context based on its unique history, identity, and the constellation of people, organizations, and networks that animate it. Local knowledge is not just important; it is essential. Every neighborhood is constantly changing but in a direction defined by its distinct context and character. And any efforts to intervene in that process of change need to be adapted to that context and character. In the next chapter, we explore how to think about and understand the process of neighborhood change.

A DYNAMIC SYSTEMS APPROACH TO UNDERSTANDING NEIGHBORHOOD CHANGE

Discussions of the prospects of cities and their neighborhoods tend to lurch between paralyzing pessimism and gushing optimism. From the 1960s through the 1990s, the words "urban crisis" seemed part of every conversation about cities. Many commentators declared that older central cities were dying if not already dead. As late as 1991, *Newsweek* posed the question "Are Cities Obsolete?" in a bold headline. In response, prominent legal scholar Daniel Mandelker was quoted as saying that "the basic problem is that big cities are no longer functional. A handful of cities—New York, San Francisco, maybe Boston—are redefining their roles. But the rest are losing their place in society. We don't need them anymore."[1] Such sentiments were widespread.

In recent years the media have been much more likely to take the opposite view, with one writer proclaiming that we are now in "the golden age of American cities."[2] Alan Ehrenhalt calls our era "the great inversion." "The truth is," he writes, "we are living in a moment in which the massive outward migration of the affluent that characterized the second half of the twentieth century is coming to an end."[3] Another commentator, with considerable exaggeration, claimed that "once, Americans fled inner cities for a suburban paradise. Now an urban revival is making the suburbs the home of the poor."[4] The preference of the millennial generation for urban living is heralded, while gentrification has become a touchstone for city planners, community advocates, and others across the United States.

There is some limited but important truth to that picture. Urban revival, which started in coastal cities such as Boston and San Francisco, has spread to the older industrial cities in the American interior such as Cleveland and Pittsburgh. However, sweeping proclamations of a new age of urban revival and suburban decline, let alone a golden age for the cities, are almost risible overstatements. While some neighborhoods may be colonized by millennials, larger numbers of neighborhoods are losing ground and becoming areas of concentrated poverty. Middle-class and affluent Americans are still moving to the suburbs in droves, and the McMansions of exurbia have yet to become squatter colonies, as some pundits predicted during the foreclosure crisis.[5]

We are living not in an age of urban revival but instead in a complex age of simultaneous urban revival and decline. The same is true of the suburbs. Many are booming and others are stable, while an increasing number are declining. The neighborhood landscape in our cities and metropolitan areas is now far more complex and varied than it has been for many decades or perhaps ever. The one constant is change. Neighborhoods are continually in flux, moving upward or downward, changing economically, socially, and demographically, sometimes gradually over decades and sometimes seemingly overnight.

In this book, we add our voice to the many scholars who have tried to understand neighborhood change in its multidimensional complexity over the past hundred years.[6] We will review their efforts and present our perspective. We begin with the fundamental premise that to capture the complexities of neighborhood change, our thinking must be grounded in four basic principles:

1. It must be **contextual**. Neighborhood change is not just a product of the forces internal to each neighborhood, nor is it solely determined by overwhelming global forces. Explanations of neighborhood change must take into account both factors inside the neighborhood and factors operating at ever broader geographies—citywide, regional, national, and even global—and the interactions between them, integrating them into a coherent framework.

2. It must take **history** into account. As William Faulkner famously wrote, "The past is not dead, it is not even past."[7] What happened in the past, even many decades ago, continues to influence neighborhoods in the present. We never start with a blank slate, yet we must avoid the trap of seeing neighborhood change as no more than the playing out of historical forces. However powerfully history shapes the future, it does not determine it.

3. It must be **interdisciplinary**. Neighborhood change as a subject for inquiry does not fit into a single academic discipline. Research that is grounded in a single discipline—economics, sociology, or political science, for example—or relies on a single causal theory is bound to be

inadequate. While each field along with its particular body of theory has something important to say about neighborhood change, neighborhoods are where all of the various human processes that different disciplines study come together in complex ways.

4. It must treat neighborhoods as **dynamic systems**. Neighborhood change is not a linear process in which A leads to B, which leads to C. We need to understand neighborhood change as a dynamic process with powerful feedback effects. Neighborhoods are like echo chambers where every action reverberates back and forth in circular causal relationships; what was a cause at one time becomes an effect at another time. We question the conventional narratives of neighborhood decline or gentrification that view them as linear processes with predictable results. Neighborhood change is more complex and unpredictable.

In this chapter, we offer a framework for such a dynamic systems approach to neighborhood change. Before that point, however, it will be useful to present an overview of prior thinking about neighborhood change not only because of its inherent interest but also because in many respects prior theories continue to mold our thinking, often unconsciously, about neighborhoods and their processes of transformation even when they can be shown to be empirically flawed. This overview begins with the work of the Chicago School of Human Ecology.

Learning from the Chicago School

The Chicago School of Human Ecology (or Sociology) was formed by a body of scholars working in Chicago in the 1920s and 1930s who sought to create a comprehensive and systematic theory of neighborhood change and whose work dominated most twentieth-century thinking on the subject. In retrospect, their theories were limited by their origins in Chicago's particular conditions during the first decades of the twentieth century, a period of frenzied urbanization, immigration, and industrialization. Nevertheless, both their strengths and weaknesses remain instructive.

Chicago School thinking was grounded in modernization theory. Influenced by Max Weber, Georg Simmel, and Ferdinand Tönnies, the great German theorists of modernization, Chicago School thinkers addressed the problem of creating and maintaining a stable social order as people moved from traditional rural societies to modern cities. They viewed the need to reconstitute social order in the wake of the disruption of social ties caused by urbanization and modernization as the central issue in neighborhood change. Louis Wirth's classic essay "Urbanism as a Way of Life" highlighted the disruptive effects of urbanization. "For sociological purposes a city is a relatively large, dense, and permanent settlement of heterogeneous individuals. Large numbers account for individual variability, the relative absence of intimate personal acquaintanceship, the segmentalization of human relations which are largely anonymous, superficial, and transitory. . . . Density involves diversification and specialization, the coincidence of social relations, glaring contrasts, a complex pattern of segregation, the predominance of formal social control, and accentuated friction."[8]

To human ecologists, modernization can be seen as the process of successful adaptation to urbanization. As people move from traditional rural societies to big cities, the informal social bonds that create order in pre-modern societies are severed, but over time urban migrants habituate themselves to urban life and re-create social order by embracing new forms of solidarity rooted in secondary, instrumental relations and the rule of law. As urban dwellers, they become rational actors, engaging with their social and economic surroundings in order to advance their interests and becoming aware of their interdependence with one another through their complementary functions in the increasingly complex division of labor in modern urban societies.

The social attachments that arise from urbanization may lack the warmth and intimacy of traditional social relations, but to the Chicago School they can be equally powerful. The challenge presented by urbanization, however, is that in the course of moving from tradition to modernity many people get stuck in between, where they have lost their traditional primary ties but have failed to develop new instrumental ties in the modern city. The Chicago School saw this problem of transition at the heart of urban crime, vice, and antisocial behavior.

On its face, this theory would appear to have little relationship to neighborhood change. To the Chicago School thinkers, however, the process of modernization expressed itself spatially in distinctive and dynamic neighborhood settlement patterns. To explain this process, they developed the idea of neighborhood invasion and succession, a model of neighborhood change that still underlies much contemporary thinking. One such pattern is laid out in Ernest Burgess's concentric zone model of neighborhood succession (figure 2.1). The center is the downtown or central business district where jobs and businesses are concentrated. The next ring is the "zone of transition," which is characterized by business and light manufacturing mixed with the housing of immigrants and other low-income city dwellers who can only afford to live in this transient area of the city. Over time, upward economic mobility enables some newcomers to escape into the next ring of working-class homes. Farther out are more desirable residential zones, and

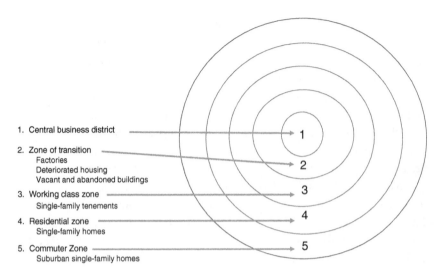

1. Central business district

2. Zone of transition
   Factories
   Deteriorated housing
   Vacant and abandoned buildings

3. Working class zone
   Single-family tenements

4. Residential zone
   Single-family homes

5. Commuter Zone
   Suburban single-family homes

FIGURE 2.1. The Burgess concentric zone model of metropolitan development

(Authors' work based on Ernest Burgess)

beyond them are the suburbs that form the commuter zone. Starting from the center, each zone expands outward in an ongoing process of neighborhood succession in which populations move, along with social disorganization and decay, outward from the center. As urban newcomers gradually work their way up and into modern society, more affluent families move to more desirable environments in an ever-expanding suburban periphery.

The highly influential theory of housing filtering grows directly from the neighborhood succession model.[9] Filtering is the proposition that older homes move—or filter—down a price and quality chain as their more affluent occupants move outward, leaving the homes behind for those just below them on the socioeconomic ladder. The succession of moves assumed by the model ultimately gives lower-income households the opportunity to move into at least marginally better housing. As it suggests, both economists and human ecologists view urban growth as a largely utilitarian process that tends toward equilibrium, in which urban residents are seen as individual strivers rationally pursuing their material interests.

The concepts of invasion and succession were derived from plant ecology, the branch of biology that studies the succession of plant species as they compete for dominance in natural habitats. Like plants, ecologists suggested, residents and businesses compete for space in urban environments, ultimately settling in the areas that give them the best chance of succeeding. One of the most influential human ecologists, Robert Park, described a metropolis as "a great sifting and sorting mechanism, which, in ways that are not yet fully understood, infallibly selects out of the population as a whole individuals best suited to live in a particular region and a particular milieu."[10] Ultimately, the process should lead to an equilibrium state whereby every urban species occupies its optimal niche in the ecological system. Chicago ecologists were not naive optimists, however. They observed that the constant arrival of new populations, immigrants with little experience in city living as was happening in 1920s Chicago, led to a rapid invasion and succession of inner-city neighborhoods, causing social problems that prevented the system from reaching equilibrium.

From the ecological perspective, the segregation of economic functions as well as of ethnic and racial groups was seen as both natural and desirable. Urbanization was viewed as a process of rationalization and modernization that divided cities into "natural areas," enabling them to achieve higher levels of rationality and efficiency. "As the community grows," sociologist Roderick McKenzie wrote, "there is not just a multiplication of houses and roads but a process of differentiation and segregation takes place as well."[11] Diverse economic functions—industrial, wholesale, retail, office, entertainment, and so on—sort across the landscape in ways that maximize their efficiency.

Ethnic and racial sorting in neighborhoods mimics the sorting of economic functions. Racial and ethnic segregation is natural and even beneficial, Chicago School human ecologists argued, because homogeneous communities, other things being equal, are more socially cohesive. Chicago School researchers sought to understand the dynamics of these communities by conducting detailed ethnographic studies of Polish immigrants, the Jewish ghetto, Little Italy, Greektown, Chinatown, and the Black Belt with its "free and disorderly life."[12] As Park observed about this "constellation of natural areas," they "touch but never completely penetrate."[13] Human ecologists saw disordered urban ghettos as a transition stage to modernity from which urban newcomers would move upward and outward into American society. In contrast to efforts by settlement houses to acculturate ghetto residents and assist in their upward mobility, Chicago School thinkers viewed efforts to upgrade or revive their neighborhoods as not only futile but even potentially harmful.

Both housing filtering and neighborhood succession theory implicitly viewed neighborhoods as having a natural life cycle, leading subsequent theorists to propose life cycles as a fundamental law of neighborhood change. As we will see, such theories have had a long and problematic history in guiding thinking and practice about urban neighborhoods, including at times demolishing them in the name of progress.

Neighborhood Change Theory after the Chicago School

The Chicago School thinkers got many things right. They recognized that neighborhood change must be understood in the context of broader forces of economic restructuring and population flows that operate at regional, national, and even international scales. They identified the crucial role that social organization plays in stabilizing neighborhoods and protecting them from threats. Troubled neighborhoods, they argued, were a product not of individual failures but rather of the forces driving social disorganization in the areas they dubbed zones of transition. Above all, they argued, neighborhoods are powerful shapers of identities, values, and social relations. As Robert Park wrote, "there is not now, if there ever was, any question that the individual's conception of himself, the role which he plays in any society, and the character which eventually he acquires are very largely determined by the associations which he makes and, in general, by the world in which he lives."[14] Neighborhoods shape people as much as people shape neighborhoods.

At the same time, the Chicago School thinkers got many things wrong. Their theory is egregiously deterministic, suggesting that neighborhoods inevitably follow a single script. While subsequent scholars modified Burgess's concentric zone theory to reflect the variety of urban physical forms and the significance of transportation arteries, these writers did not challenge its deterministic logic, leaving little role room for human agency whether through public policies or neighborhood initiatives. Indeed, the ecological model that underlies their thinking is grounded in the idea of change as the impersonal, mindless working of forces beyond the control of any individual, group, or organization.

Many of the weaknesses of the Chicago School thinkers can be traced to their tendency to overgeneralize from a particular place and time. Their intellectual neighborhood, one might say, was the city of Chicago at its peak of industrial might and population growth, a city with teeming immigrant ghettos and noxious industries surrounding its central commercial core. Economist Homer Hoyt, a disciple of the Chicago School who exerted a powerful influence on housing policy into the 1950s, saw outward migration from central cities as all but a law of nature, writing that "high rent or high-grade neighborhoods must almost necessarily move outward toward the periphery of the city. The wealthy seldom reverse their steps and move backward into the obsolete houses which they are giving up."[15] The most cursory view of the contemporary postindustrial city, with its gentrification pressures and knowledge economy, renders this proposition deeply flawed if not simply wrong.

The flaws in human ecology are also rooted in its uncritical acceptance of modernization theory, which depicts cities as moving inexorably through a mechanistic process of rationalization to a brighter future. That perspective was not unique to the Chicago School, however, and one should not blame its thinkers for the urban devastation committed in the name of modernization. They were part of a larger zeitgeist. The goals of rationalization, efficiency, and modernism later reflected in urban renewal and its promotion of an automobile-dominated metropolis were the common language of the time, beginning with the eccentric Italian Futurists of the 1910s and including architects such as Le Corbusier, with his 1926 Plan Voisin, and the Bauhaus school, not to mention Soviet ideologues with their visions of a New Socialist Man.

Nonetheless, the ideas of the Chicago School dominated thinking about neighborhood change for many years. In 1934, Hoyt became principal housing economist at the newly created Federal Housing Administration and, as we discuss in chapter 4, played a critical role in designing the policies that subsequently contributed to both the devaluation of urban neighborhoods and the enforcement of racial segregation in the postwar Levittowns and their many suburban counterparts. The idea of neighborhood life cycles had an even longer life. The concept of neighborhood life cycles, implicit in the work of the Chicago School, was explicitly articulated in the formative text of real estate appraisal in the 1930s, Frederic Babcock's *The Valuation of Real Estate*: "A residential district seems to go through a very definite and *inevitable* course of development when not affected by forces which can entirely change its use. This cycle is characterized by the gradual decline in quality of people through the years accompanied by population increases and the more intensive residential use of ground."[16]

In the postwar era, neighborhood life cycle theory was articulated by economists Edgar Hoover and Raymond Vernon in 1959[17] and by the Real Estate Research Corporation (RERC) in *The Dynamics of Neighborhood Change*, a report commissioned and disseminated in 1975 by the US Department of Housing and Urban Development.[18] The RERC report identified five stages in the neighborhood life cycle:

Stage 1: *Healthy.* Homogeneous housing and moderate to upper income, insurance, and conventional financing available.

Stage 2: *Incipient decline.* Aging housing, decline in income and education level, influx of middle-income minorities, and fear of racial transition.

Stage 3: *Clearly declining.* Higher density, visible deterioration, decrease in white in-movers, more minority children in schools, mostly rental housing, and problems in securing insurance and financing.

Stage 4: *Accelerating decline.* Increasing vacancies, predominantly low income and minority tenants or elderly ethnics, high unemployment, fear of crime, no insurance or institutional financing available, declining public services, and absentee-owned properties.

Stage 5: *Abandoned.* Severe dilapidation, poverty and squatters, high crime and arson, and negative cash flow from buildings.

While a later widely cited but tendentious article argued that the RERC, along with its use of life cycle theory, was largely responsible for the urban decline of the 1960s and 1970s, the reality was more nearly the opposite; that is, urban decline reinforced the theory.[19] RERC, the Department of Housing and Urban Development, and a host of other researchers and policymakers were frantically trying to grasp the underlying forces driving what they perceived at the time as the inevitable decline of the American city and its neighborhoods. Life cycle theory was a way urban policymakers thought they could make sense of the unprecedented decline of the South Bronx and a host of other urban neighborhoods taking place at the time.

By the 1960s, however, a critique of this way of thinking was beginning to emerge. In her 1961 classic *The Death and Life of Great American Cities*, Jane Jacobs challenged the modernist vision that sought to "sort and sift out of the whole certain simple uses, and to arrange each of these in relative self-containment," suggesting instead that cities were problems of "organized complexity, in which a half dozen or several dozen quantities are all varying simultaneously *and in subtly interconnected ways.*"[20]

Although Jacobs did not develop a full-fledged theory of neighborhood change, her discussion of "unslumming and slumming" stressed that "slums operate as vicious circles," recognizing the power of human agency to break the cycle in contrast to the deterministic predictions of the life cycle theorists.[21] Scholars such as William F. Whyte and Herbert Gans documented the extent of social order in seemingly disorganized "slum" neighborhoods, suggesting the presence of far more complexity than reflected in Chicago School models.[22]

Growing recognition of the destructive nature of racial segregation undercut the perspective that segregation was a fundamentally benign transitional process, while research on housing filtering showed that it was a more complex and damaging process than had been assumed, shaped by both regional market and neighborhood conditions rather than simply by housing aging and obsolescence. In strong markets, particularly where production of new housing is constrained, older properties filter upward rather than downward, while in weaker markets housing filtering can be rapid and chaotic, with many older properties ending up vacant and abandoned, burdening remaining residents with crime and social decay.[23]

Meanwhile, in the 1970s a new generation of thoughtful community development practitioners began to develop new models of neighborhood change that took account of the multifaceted nature of neighborhood improvement and decline, recognizing that neighborhood change was contingent, not determined. Rolf Goetze, reflecting on his experience in Boston, showed how neighborhood change is molded by perceptions and expectations and the ways policies and interventions could change expectations.[24] Roger Ahlbrandt and Paul Brophy, both engaged in neighborhood revitalization in Pittsburgh, built a model centering on housing demand and highlighting the critical role of public- and private-sector interventions in shaping demand.[25] Subsequently, Kenneth Temkin and William Rohe built a model that synthesized the relationships between perceptions, external forces, and interventions.[26] Our thinking builds on their work.

Do these new and improved theories mean that the Chicago School is irrelevant? Are we now in an age of urban revival, as some assert, in which the course of metropolitan development has pushed the poor to the periphery and the rich to the center? The answer is an emphatic *no*. The forces of decentralization identified by the Chicago School and that dominated the last half of the twentieth century are still present today. Cities today are shaped simultaneously by forces of de-urbanization and reurbanization. The Chicago School model of outward movement from the urban core is not wrong, just radically incomplete.

Many patterns of neighborhood development that the Chicago School identified are still present today. Central cities across the United States are still centers of economic activity, although today they produce more services than manufactured goods. The outward movement of affluent households continues. A recent study of neighborhood change from 1970 to 2010 in the one hundred largest metros found that "high-status neighborhoods were and continue to be disproportionately located in suburban communities."[27]

At the same time, countertendencies are also powerful. The idea of the "crisis of function" of the older cities, which was widespread during the urban crisis era, has been put to rest. Driven by growing economies grounded in vast higher education and health care complexes, many older cities are regaining thousands of new residents and billions of dollars in new investment. Large numbers of young college graduates, along with smaller numbers of empty nesters, are gravitating to dense, mixed-use, urban downtowns and nearby neighborhoods. Home prices and rents are soaring in hot market cities such as New York, San Francisco, and Seattle, where both incomes and house prices are higher in the central city than in the suburbs. For many of these cities, household incomes are now highest in the heart of the urban core.[28] And although poverty rates continue to be higher in central cities, more poor people now live in suburbs.[29]

The different eras of the American cities—from the market cities of colonial times to the manufacturing cities of the late nineteenth and early twentieth centuries and from the cities of the postwar urban crisis to today's unevenly and partially reviving cities grounded in the knowledge economy—are layered on top of one another, each forming a part of the matrix that drives the trajectories of today's urban neighborhoods. Neighborhood change, as we noted earlier, is contextual; that context is constantly changing and neighborhoods with it. But it is also multidimensional and above all interactive. Neighborhoods resemble large echo chambers in which multiple causes and effects interact in complex causal loops.

Neighborhoods as Dynamic Feedback Systems

Over a century of social science research on neighborhood change has generated important insights into what drives such change. In some ways, though, we have moved backwards. The Chicago School, for all the flaws in its analysis, aimed for a holistic understanding of neighborhood change. Similarly, the scholars and practitioner-scholars, beginning with Jane Jacobs, who reframed neighborhood change during the 1960s and 1970s, were also looking to understand change as a gestalt phenomenon, particularly in Temkin and Rohe's proposed synthesis. The vast majority of current research on neighborhood change, however, focuses on isolating single variables and attributing significance to them in a linear process of causation. While experienced community development practitioners intuitively know that one cannot understand a neighborhood by focusing on the effect of an isolated variable, that is the thrust of most research on neighborhoods today.

Social scientists studying neighborhood change have tried to emulate the hard sciences, whose gold standard is the experimental method in which a single variable is isolated and studied to determine if it has a causal effect on the dependent variable, or the outcome in question. The ideal method is to conduct a controlled experiment in which researchers randomly assign some subjects to an experimental group and others to a control group. Under properly controlled conditions, if researchers find that outcomes on the dependent variable are different between the two groups, they can confidently conclude that the independent variable must have caused the difference.

Fortunately, researchers cannot conduct controlled random experiments on neighborhoods.[30] Researchers can, however, imitate the experimental method by using statistical techniques, most often multiple regression analysis, to hold a wide range of variables constant in order to isolate the effect of an independent variable on a dependent variable to, for example, measure the effect of vacant properties on the prices of homes in the vicinity while controlling for race, income, and other neighborhood features. Such techniques yield probabilistic outcomes, measuring whether there is an association between the two variables and the strength of the association.[31] In theory, this method should permit researchers to gradually accumulate knowledge of all the individual factors that influence neighborhood decline or renewal and then add them up to develop a comprehensive causal explanation of neighborhood change.

Angus Deaton has dubbed the adherents of this philosophy "randomistas."[32] The problem with the randomista approach, as Robert Sampson has persuasively argued, is not only that it is almost impossible to isolate the impact of a single variable on neighborhood change, but more importantly, the effort to isolate variables fundamentally distorts our understanding of how neighborhood change happens.[33] Endogeneity, the statistical process that takes place when interaction effects among variables confound the relationship between the independent and dependent variables, is seen by researchers as a problem that needs to be solved by statistical techniques. For neighborhood processes, however, endogeneity is inherent in their very nature. As Sampson writes, "unlike medical treatments that approximate a closed system, human behavior in social settings is interdependent—*nothing is ever 'held constant.'*"[34]

Much of the research on property effects suffers from these distorting effects. A number of studies in the wake of the foreclosure crisis, for example, argued that foreclosures led to increased crime in the surrounding area. This is patently illogical; foreclosure is no more or less than a legal procedure. The effects they were finding were not effects of foreclosure as such but instead effects triggered by complex interactions between foreclosure and other factors operating within neighborhoods. Indeed, subsequent research by Cui Lin and Randall Walsh found that the foreclosure effects disappeared except when conditions associated with the foreclosure led to the property becoming vacant, with the most significant effects only appearing after prolonged vacancy.[35]

Even then, that begs the real question. It is not the vacant house as a physical object that causes crime to increase, except in the narrow sense that some criminals may use vacant houses for nefarious purposes or causes properties in the vicinity to lose value, but rather how its neighbors perceive the vacant house, or how its presence affects others' perception of the block, and how people then behave on the basis of those perceptions. Either way, something needs to be done about the vacant house. However, understanding the pathways leading from a home foreclosure to people's perceptions and behavior and from there to its measurable effects can have a significant bearing on how one goes about intervening and prioritizing limited resources.

Neighborhoods are neither closed systems nor mechanical systems that allow one to predict their trajectory by aggregating isolated factors into a comprehensive explanation. In neighborhood change, variables interact with one another through circular paths of causation. In the dynamic system that is a neighborhood, a variable can be simultaneously both a cause and an effect. Neighborhoods cannot be understood as the sum of relationships between individual, isolated variables acting in a linear fashion. Neighborhoods are dynamic feedback systems and must be understood that way.

Systems dynamics modeling provides a way to understand how different forces influencing neighborhood change interact with each other in a system of circular causation.[36] Systems dynamics recognizes two basic kinds of causal loops: balancing loops and reinforcing loops. Reinforcing loops are like a runaway train or an arms race in which every feedback loop reinforces the process and magnifies the effects. Balancing loops are like a thermostat, constantly establishing and reestablishing equilibrium or homeostasis. Classical economic land market models, for example, are based on balancing loops. They assume that declining land values will eventually draw new buyers back into the neighborhood, bringing supply and demand back to equilibrium. From the viewpoint of classical market economics, efforts to intervene in weak markets are unnecessary or even counterproductive.[37]

The flaw in that thinking is that behavior is viewed as the sum of individual decisions made by autonomous rational actors, overlooking the fundamentally social dimension of market interactions. Neighborhood market actors are social creatures. They are influenced by the actions of other actors and are heavily dependent on the many actors' varying perceptions of the underlying reality. In this environment, the number and variety of actors whose perceptions and behavior are salient to neighborhood market outcomes, as we describe in chapter 6, is almost inconceivably large, and the interactions among them are exceedingly complex. Equilibrium cannot be assumed and in the real world is the exception rather than the norm. Often declining neighborhoods end up with a collapsed market where supply greatly exceeds demand and many properties are abandoned.

One important feature of these interactions, something intuitively understood by anyone who has worked extensively with or closely observed neighborhood dynamics, is the extreme variability of neighborhood change processes, including wide variation in the rate of change over time and the presence of threshold effects, or tipping points. George Galster and his colleagues have shown how changes in both the poverty rate and the rental rate in neighborhoods begin to have powerful effects only beyond a certain threshold.[38] In chapter 11, we discuss how inadequate home buyer demand can trigger a vicious cycle of neighborhood decline, a process that is painfully apparent in many Black middle neighborhoods. While the relationship between each step in the process is well documented, the outcome is the product of interaction among many the different factors, operating, once again, through both perceptions and overt behavior.

Other threshold effects can include the pace of upward market change when a neighborhood is "discovered" or, conversely, the accelerated process of housing abandonment that takes place when some tipping point associated with loss of confidence in the neighborhood is reached and the neighborhood enters a vicious cycle of decline.

Economists working out of the tradition of welfare economics recognize social interdependencies and spillovers and their ability to generate reinforcing cycles of decline, as exemplified in Galster's work.[39] According to welfare economics, however, the way to address these market failures is to internalize the externalities associated with them, that is, to require those actors who generate the negative externalities to compensate those on whom they have imposed the costs. That in turn produces outcomes that are designed to create an ersatz housing and land market operating as if the market participants were acting independently, motivated solely by individual utility maximization. We find this proposition (perhaps) plausible in some contexts but ultimately problematic from the perspective of the inherently interactive nature of neighborhood dynamics or from a values perspective. Good neighborhoods are not produced by actors motivated solely by the desire to maximize individual utility but instead by residents who balance individual aspiration and social commitments. As we argued in chapter 1, the value of good neighborhoods lies in their ability to balance, or reconcile, individualism (market behavior) and community (social behavior).

While neighborhoods can be subject to vicious cycles of decline, they can also benefit from virtuous circles rooted in prosocial behavior. Studies have found that decisions by homeowners to maintain or improve their properties are influenced by the level of social cohesion and interaction in a neighborhood; put differently, decisions are influenced by what one sees one's neighbors doing. A few such decisions can create a virtuous cycle.[40] Even homeowners with modest incomes will invest in improving their property if they perceive the neighborhood as improving. As we describe in chapter 8, successful collective action has maintained stable racially integrated communities in challenging environments.

Ultimately, what matters in neighborhood change is less the measurable objective factors, such as homeownership rates, median incomes, and racial change as such, but how people, both inside and outside the neighborhood, perceive those factors and act on them. Neighborhoods are containers of social relations.

The feedback effects generated in the neighborhood echo chamber may lead to cumulative causation that can result in neighborhood improvement or decline. Design, physical conditions, and economic trends all contribute to shaping a neighborhood's dynamics and creating a frame for its social relations, but ultimately the neighborhood's fate will be determined by how residents as well as outsiders perceive those conditions and trends and whether their perceptions foster the supportive, prosocial relations that sustain good neighborhoods or trigger behaviors that lead to decline. Neither is inevitable.

While neighborhood residents have agency and are not merely passive spectators to their neighborhood's revival or decline, their powers are limited. The surroundings of the neighborhood matter, as does its larger citywide and regional setting. Within that setting are many actors whose perceptions and behavior directly or indirectly affect neighborhoods, even when they may be barely familiar with the neighborhood and are unaware of the effect of their behavior. Multiple geographical scales must be integrated into a comprehensive model of neighborhood change.

Modeling Neighborhood Change

It is impossible to understand neighborhood change by focusing on isolated variables, however many are investigated. Instead, the focus should shift from *variables to pathways*. Neighborhoods are always changing, but they can change in many ways and move in many different directions rather than through any predictable linear life cycle. An approach to neighborhood change that synthesizes the different forces operating on neighborhoods at different geographical scales to produce distinctive neighborhood pathways is called for.

Neighborhoods are affected by economic, social, and political or institutional forces. Each represents a distinct way that humans have evolved for relating to each other and building complex societies. Each also embodies a distinct way of thinking by those—economists, sociologists, political scientists, and others—engaged in practicing their particular discipline.

Economic forces. In an idealized market economy, individuals seek to maximize utility, and corporations seek to maximize profits. Price is determined by supply and demand, while price mechanisms ration goods according to consumers' ability to pay. Larger economic forces, including overall economic growth, mortgage interest rates, and wage levels, shape the supply of and demand for housing. In a well-functioning neighborhood housing market, supply and demand are in reasonable balance, and housing price changes are consistent with larger economic trends.

Social forces. Unlike economics, which views human behavior as fundamentally individualistic and goal-oriented, sociologists view behavior as socially interdependent and expressive. Humans desire to be part of a society that has developed a body of cultural values and status hierarchies transmitted from one generation to the next. Social behavior at the neighborhood level, reflected in social capital, cohesion, and collective efficacy, powerfully affects the quality of life and stability of neighborhoods.

Political/institutional forces. Human behavior is organized and social order is maintained through the exercise of legal and political authority and ultimately by the power of the state, which provides public goods and services that neither markets nor social networks can supply. The effects of political systems and governmental power, from resource allocation to the delivery of services such as policing and public education, pervade every aspect of neighborhood life. The role of institutions, ranging from neighborhood-level organizations to global universities and medical centers, is hardly less significant.

Although these three types of forces are conceptually distinct, they are actually closely interwoven with one another. Public resources, such as safety and the quality of public schools, affect house prices, while a neighborhood's level of social cohesion in turn affects its ability to fend off political actions it perceives as negative or destabilizing. All these forces and their interactions with one another are mediated by perceptions. Neighborhoods are socially constructed, and in the final analysis the key to change is less the objective conditions in a neighborhood than how they are perceived. The physical condition of a neighborhood shapes perceptions, to be sure, but does not determine them. As the late neighborhood planner Michael Schubert wrote, "the work of neighborhood revitalization is as much about managing meaning as it is about managing projects and producing a narrative rather than producing housing units."[41]

The forces that drive neighborhoods operate at different scales. Broader economic, social, and political/institutional forces provide the context that defines the "opportunity space" for good neighborhoods to flourish or that raises barriers to others flourishing. For example, access to loan capital is widely recognized as one factor that drives neighborhood change. Capital access, however, is subject to a wide range of external influences, including the strength of the economy, Federal Reserve policies affecting interest rates, Fannie Mae and Freddie Mac underwriting standards, appraisal rules adopted by federal agencies, and the presence and practices of both bank and nonbank lenders in the local area, among others. All these factors are mediated by the social, cultural, and racial attitudes and perceptions of the actors. The effects of a breakdown in that system were brought home by the subprime lending wave early in the millennium and the subsequent foreclosure crisis and more than a decade later are still

affecting the vitality of hundreds of American neighborhoods. Neighborhood
activists see the city's mayor as a key protagonist in their neighborhood's future,
yet few are aware of the often far more powerful role of state officials in a faraway state capital.[42]

A unified theory of neighborhood change that would be capable of explain-
ing such change and predicting neighborhood outcomes across different times
and places does not exist and is unlikely ever to exist. Instead of such a theory,
our goal is an integrated *model* of neighborhood change. Such a model cannot
fully explain or predict neighborhood change. It can, however, help us think
clearly about the process and better understand the most important forces that
impact neighborhoods and the critical relationships between them. Figure 2.2
depicts our model of neighborhood change.

In the model, forces that originate outside the neighborhood, or exogenous
forces in larger economic, social, and political systems, are the starting point of
change. These forces can range from massive forces such as economic recessions
or large-scale migratory movements to changes in mortgage lending practices
or laws regulating racial and ethnic discrimination. External forces, however,
do not lead to sustained neighborhood change; their effect is always mediated
by the perceptions and behavior of local and neighborhood actors. Neighbor-

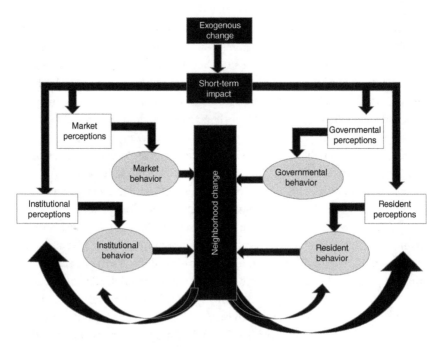

FIGURE 2.2.   A model of neighborhood change

hood house prices are directly driven not by changes in the national economy but instead by the ways in which local actors—builders, home buyers, realtors, bankers and others—perceive the relationship between those changes and specific neighborhood conditions and then act on those perceptions.

The model suggests that there are four distinct clusters of actors whose perceptions and behavior, taken as a whole, lead to change: market or economic, political, institutional, and social actors. While market actors are both local and regional, political and institutional actors are principally local but can be regional or even national, while social actors, including informal community ties and social capital, operate mostly at the neighborhood level.

Feedback effects (causal arrows that form loops) are a critical part of the model. They are concentrated at the local level both within and between neighborhoods. Local actors have little effect on national polices or economic conditions, but within the neighborhood echo chamber they are constantly influencing one another's perceptions and behavior in a perpetual feedback system. As a result, all the causal arrows within the neighborhood system run both ways. Local market choices, institutional actions, political decisions, and community social and organizational behavior all influence neighborhood change; the course of neighborhood change then shapes economic, institutional, political, and social behavior.

A further implication of our model is that neighborhood change, not neighborhood conditions, is the central focus of analysis. Neighborhoods are constantly in flux, continually absorbing, reflecting, and sometimes deflecting the effects of larger citywide, regional, and national forces. Decades of observation of neighborhoods by the authors suggests that the only neighborhoods that do not change significantly and often unpredictably over time are the few at the extreme ends of the social and economic spectrum: the handful of very strong neighborhoods that are so solidly established as to seem impervious to decline and the handful of neighborhoods that are so extensively disinvested that they are equally impervious to revitalization efforts.

We do not make extravagant claims for this model. It is not a unified theory of neighborhood change applicable to all times and types of neighborhoods. It does not specify how economic, political, institutional, and social forces interact to produce neighborhood change, although we suggest that investigation of those interactive dynamics would be a more fruitful pursuit by future scholars than randomista searches for statistical relationships between individual neighborhood variables across many different contexts. The model is situated within what Robert Merton called "middle-range theory," which eschews grand theoretical generalizations along with narrow empiricism. As Merton wrote, middle-range theory "is intermediate to general theories of social systems which are too remote from particular classes of social behavior, organization, and change to account for what is observed and to those detailed orderly descriptions of particulars that are not generalized at all."[43] It is impossible to generalize across all neighborhoods at all times. We believe it is possible, however, to theorize about pathways of neighborhood change for *specific* types of neighborhoods in *specific* historical periods—as we do in the chapters that follow. Middle-range theory empowers practitioners to think systematically about the nature of the forces driving change in their neighborhood and place those forces in a framework that will make it possible to understand them better and take effective action to influence neighborhood actors' perceptions and behavior.

Closing Note

The purpose of this chapter has been to describe the ways in which scholars and practitioners have sought to understand and explain neighborhood change, to elucidate the fundamental dynamics of change as we have come to understand them, and to offer a framework that we believe can help others understand the complex cluster of perceptions and behaviors summed up in the term "neighborhood change." Although the sheer number of external actors and forces with the power to shape neighborhoods may appear daunting, we believe that the more neighborhood-level actors understand those forces, the more they will begin to see the possibilities for effective intervention. To quote the physicist Albert Einstein, "Once we accept our limits, we go beyond them."

THE RISE OF THE AMERICAN URBAN NEIGHBORHOOD, 1860–1950

The idea and reality of the distinctive, identifiable urban neighborhood emerged slowly in American history. Early American cities, whose primary economic function was trade, huddled along harbors. Residences, workshops, and merchants' offices were jumbled together in a city that could be traversed on foot in less than half an hour, and separate neighborhoods were rare. Industrialization shattered this intimate world, creating large anonymous cities increasingly differentiated by function, status, and ethnic origin as the rich moved farther out and the millions of immigrants who flocked to the cities sorted themselves into neighborhood enclaves. Those neighborhoods became their home, refuges where they could find support from people like themselves and shelter from the anonymity and relentless demands of the capitalist world as well as the indifference and frequent hostility of the larger society. From the late nineteenth century to the middle of the twentieth century, the neighborhood played a central role in the daily lives of most Americans. Neighborhoods also played an important part in America's self-identification as a pluralist society, grounded in the idea that neighborhoods were a microcosm of the nation and seedbeds of democracy. We had become, in Benjamin Looker's evocative phrase, "a nation of neighborhoods."[1]

The neighborhoods that had emerged in American cities during the first half of the twentieth century, we argue, were mostly good neighborhoods for the people who lived in them. They should not be romanticized, however. Many were overcrowded, and much of their housing, particularly in older neighborhoods that predated the building boom of the 1920s, was substandard. They were also segregated not just racially but also ethnically and religiously, as Black people were relegated to the worst areas with few opportunities for good jobs in the mainstream economy. At the same time, traditional neighborhoods offered their residents access to most of what they needed for a good life. Their physical form, with its interplay of homes, shops, and schools, promoted neighborly connections. This was true to a large extent also of segregated Black neighborhoods, which in many respects provided their residents with a haven from a racist society.[2]

In the second half of the twentieth century, however, urban neighborhoods were challenged by threats to their vitality and in many cases their very existence. Since then, the centrality of neighborhoods and their role in American society have become increasingly contested as the conditions that led to the emergence of America's urban neighborhoods have changed beyond recognition. Yet these neighborhoods still matter. This chapter chronicles the rise of neighborhoods up to midcentury, while in the subsequent chapters we examine the vicissitudes of the American urban neighborhood since that time and how they have been affected by the economic, social, and physical transformation of American life.

Cities before Neighborhoods: The Early Market City

Neighborhoods did not play a large role in colonial and early post-Revolutionary American cities. Colonial cities, like most of their European counterparts, resembled more the cities of the Middle Ages or antiquity than what they would become over the next two centuries. Although some neighborhoods undoubtedly existed in colonial cities, those cities were compact places in which land uses and building types were far more mixed together than was true later. They were also small. As late as 1820, among all American cities only New York City had a population over one hundred thousand, although Philadelphia, together with the adjacent smaller cities of Southwark and Northern Liberties, both of which it absorbed some years later, came close.

Preindustrial cities in the United States were largely ports and trading centers dotted with small workshops; a directory of 1819 Cincinnati, a city of fewer than ten thousand at the time, listed two foundries, six tinsmiths, four coppersmiths, and nine silversmiths along with sixteen coopers (barrel makers) and fifteen cabinetmakers. These workshops were run by their owners, master craftsmen, with rarely more than one or two apprentices or journeyman helpers. The cities' populations were concentrated in tightly clustered blocks around their harbors, with residences, workshops, stores, warehouses, taverns, and coffeehouses mixed together in a jumble of land uses and building types. In Philadelphia, the largest American city in 1776, barely twelve of the nearly two hundred city blocks laid out in William Penn's plan for the city were largely developed. Those blocks formed a triangle, with its base defined by the bustling wharves and piers along the Delaware River (figure 3.1). The State House, now known as Independence Hall, where the signers of the Declaration of Independence gathered, was near the edge of the city, with open fields only a block away.

To be sure, the colonial city was spatially differentiated by economic class. The most prosperous families typically lived nearest the center and those with less farther away, while the poorest families often lived in shanty settlements outside the urban core. Distinct neighborhoods, though, were atypical. As urban historian Patricia Mooney-Melvin writes, "neighborhoods, as identifiable units in the American cityscape, emerged as major urban centers underwent the transition from the pedestrian city of the eighteenth and early nineteenth centuries to the expanded and differentiated urban structure of the early twentieth century."[3]

Colonial cities were haphazard affairs where builders for the most part, in architectural historian Charlie Duff's words, "viewed their buildings and streets as tools, made for use rather than for elegance, and they were quite ready to discard them when better came along."[4] A handful of remnants of the colonial city, modeled after the row houses of London and other British cities, still stand today, such as Elfreth's Alley in Philadelphia, with houses dating back to the 1720s, but most of what we think of as colonial dates from the early nineteenth century, such as Mount Vernon Square in Baltimore and Acorn Street in Boston's Beacon Hill neighborhood (figure 3.2). Acorn Street was initially built for artisans, not poor but not gentry, many of whom conducted their businesses from the premises. Houses on Acorn Street that come on the market today sell for upwards of $3 million.

The Rise of the Industrial City and the Immigrant Neighborhood

The urban neighborhood as a pervasive presence and defining feature of the American urban fabric was the product of post–Civil War urban expansion. That expansion was unique in world history up to that point, making the earlier growth of European industrial cities such as Manchester pale by comparison. Chicago added nearly 20,000 people per year to its population between 1860 and 1880 and 60,000 per year from 1880 to 1900, a growth rate that continued until World War 1.[5] From a village of fewer than 5,000 people in 1840, it had become a metropolis of 2.7 million in 1920. Chicago was far from alone. In 1820, places such as Buffalo, Cleveland, Detroit, and Pittsburgh were modest settlements, barely even villages. One hundred years later each was a major city of over half

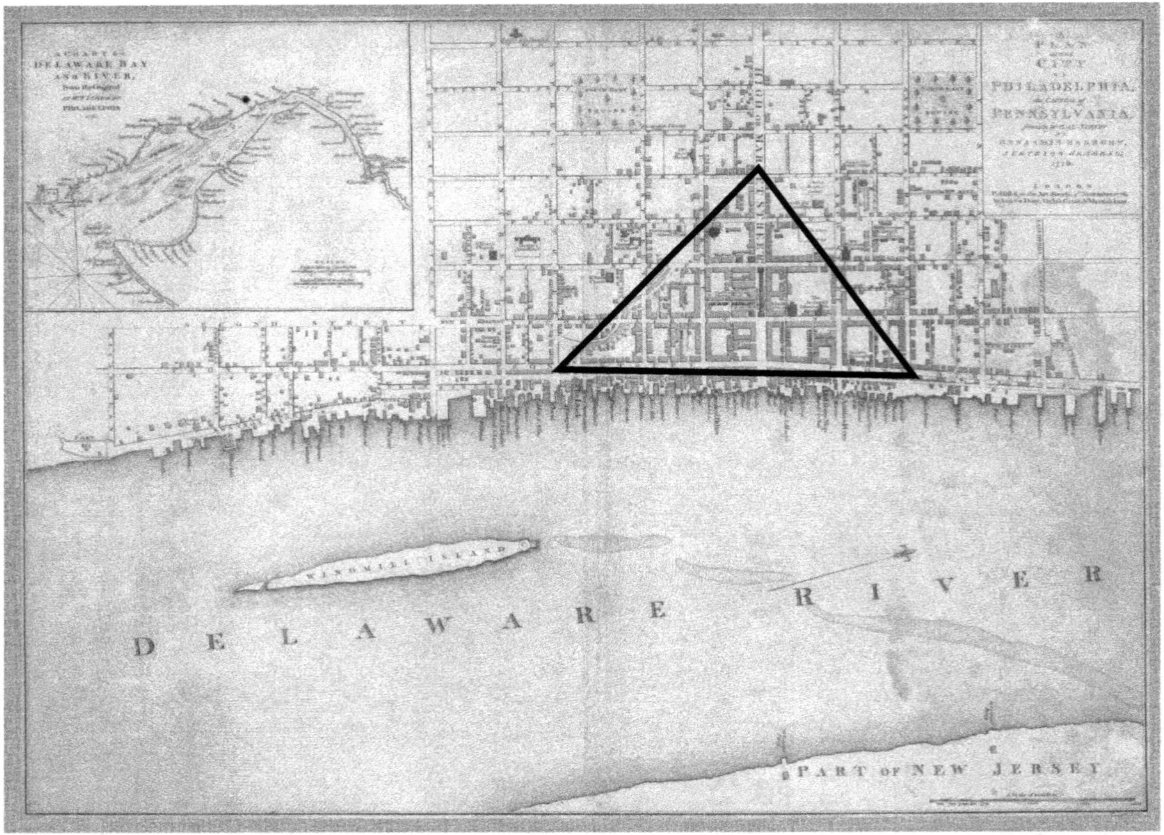

FIGURE 3.1. Philadelphia in 1776

(Source: Library of Congress, Geography and Map Division. Overlay by Bill Nelson)

FIGURE 3.2.   Acorn Street, a typical early nineteenth-century street in Boston

(Photograph by Michael Browning)

a million people, with Detroit close to a million. The Philadelphia of 1776 had become little more than a tiny corner of little importance in the vastly larger 1876 city, while the centers of commerce and government had moved westward away from the increasingly industrial Delaware River waterfront (figure 3.3). At the same time, along with the handful of behemoths such as Chicago and Detroit, urban expansion turned hundreds of other towns—such as Trenton, New Jersey; Lima, Ohio; and Reading, Pennsylvania—into smaller cities, each replicating the features of the larger industrial cities in miniature. All of this was part and parcel of the process by which the United States became the world's dominant industrial nation.

Historians and economists have identified so many different reasons for the simultaneous explosion of industrialization and urbanism in late nineteenth-century America that the outcome seems to have been all but inevitable. America had everything needed for industrial supremacy: vast natural resources of coal and iron, ample and inexpensive sources of energy, an extensive and efficient transportation infrastructure built first around navigable rivers and then around the spread of the railroads, a growing and increasingly affluent domestic market, technological innovations such as the Kelly-Bessemer steelmaking process, a flourishing entrepreneurial culture subject to few legal or customary restraints, seemingly inexhaustible sources of inexpensive immigrant labor, and

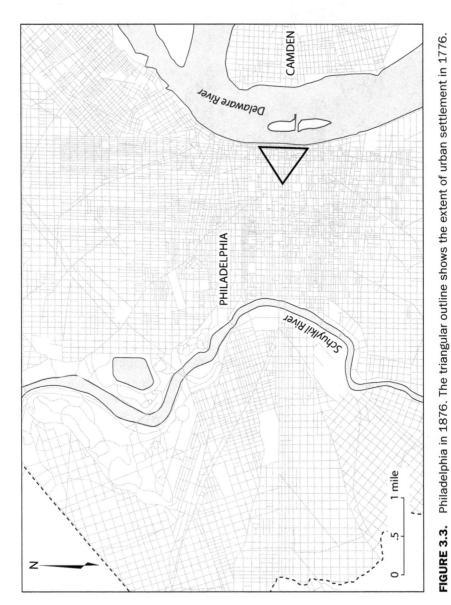

FIGURE 3.3. Philadelphia in 1876. The triangular outline shows the extent of urban settlement in 1776.

(Wikimedia Commons, overlay by Bill Nelson)

finally, the creative energy of the both acclaimed and reviled band of inventors, financiers, and industrial barons, among them Andrew Carnegie, Thomas Edison, John Pierpont Morgan Sr., John D. Rockefeller, and Cornelius Vanderbilt.

Unlike earlier workshops, the new factories were vast establishments, running on the labor of hundreds and often thousands of workers. While the workforce for America's first factories, New England's early nineteenth-century textile mills, was drawn from the region's rural population surplus, that surplus had disappeared by midcentury as Americans headed to western lands that were opened up for settlement early in the nineteenth century after the Native Americans who had inhabited them had been brutally dispossessed.[6] The post–Civil War industrial explosion was fueled by millions of men and women from almost every European nation fleeing poverty, hunger, exploitation, political unrest, and oppression or simply looking for a better life.

From a trickle in the 1820s and 1830s, immigration increased steadily through the nineteenth century and up to World War I, exceeding 1.2 million in 1907 and again in 1914 (figure 3.4). The initial waves were from Ireland, Scandinavia, and

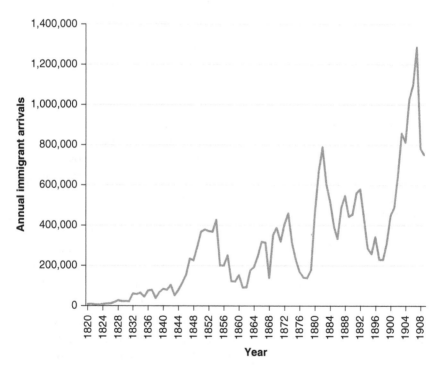

FIGURE 3.4. Legal permanent residents admitted to the United States by decade, 1820–1909

(Authors' work based on public data compiled by the Migration Policy Institute)

Germany, triggered by hunger, poverty, and the failed German revolutions of 1848. Eastern and Southern Europe contributed ever-larger shares of immigrants in later decades, most prominently Italians largely from southern Italy and Sicily; Poles, Czechs, Slovaks, and other Slavic peoples; and the persecuted, impoverished Jewish residents of the Russian and Austro-Hungarian Empires. The color bar in effect throughout this period meant that the great majority of immigrants were European, and if not fully accepted as "white," they were neither Asian nor Black. Few Asian, African, or Afro-Caribbean immigrants made it to the United States; although Chicago sociologist Harvey Zorbaugh refers to a "Persian" community in that city early in the twentieth century, it was probably either an Arab or Armenian rather than Iranian community.[7] Despite the porous Mexican border of the time, few Latinx immigrants arrived in northern cities.

As the cities grew, their character changed. While the eighteenth- and early nineteenth-century city was one in which different land uses and building types were mingled widely with few distinct residential neighborhoods as such, land uses and activities gradually became more sharply defined and separated. Downtowns became districts for the conduct of commerce, with large office buildings and stores including the grand department stores that emerged late in the century. Except for the occasional Skid Row, downtowns had largely lost what residential populations they once had by the end of the nineteenth century.[8] Surrounding residential quarters grew, increasingly differentiated by income, social status, and place of origin. The elites built neighborhoods of fine houses sometimes close to downtown, such as Philadelphia's Rittenhouse Square, but sometimes in landscaped settings such as Llewellyn Park in West Orange, New Jersey, laid out in 1853 as "a suburban community of country estates ... [with] finely crafted homes stand[ing] amid majestic trees and running streams."[9]

In-town elite neighborhoods increasingly became islands in a working-class sea. By the end of the nineteenth century, immigrants and their native-born children vastly outnumbered the population of "native" stock in America's cities. When Jacob Riis asked an old-timer in New York City in the 1880s where the "Americans" lived, he answered "I don't know. . . . I wish I did. Some went to California in '49, some to the war and never came back. The rest, I expect, have gone to heaven, or somewhere. I don't see them 'round here."[10] In 1910, over three-quarters of the populations in Chicago, 74 percent in Detroit, and fully 85 percent in the small New Jersey industrial city of Passaic were made up of immigrants and their native-born children. What Oliver Zunz has written about Detroit can stand for almost any American city: "a description of the ethnic neighborhoods in this large industrial city in the late nineteenth century is in many respects a description of the entire population."[11]

The greater part of each city was taken up by factories and housing for immigrant workers. While immigrant quarters contained stores to serve their residents' needs along with small workshops or sweatshops, their principal function was to house the families of the workers in nearby factories. The factories themselves, often vast complexes covering hundreds of acres, were part of the urban fabric, not set apart in industrial parks. Tenements and row houses often faced hulking factory buildings across a city street, an alley, or a postage stamp backyard.

The process by which distinctive immigrant neighborhoods emerged paralleled the growth and industrialization of cities. It was not an orderly process, nor was there a single model of an "immigrant neighborhood." A neighborhood might be settled by one immigrant group, only to give way to another and then another over time. As Zorbaugh describes one Chicago neighborhood, "wave after wave of immigrants has swept over the area—Irish, Swedish, German, Italian, Greek, Persian and Negro—forming colonies, staying a while, then giving way to others."[12] Alternatively, an immigrant group might settle in one area, as in Trenton's Chambersburg, which became a distinct Italian neighborhood late in the nineteenth century and stayed that way until the 1990s, when a shrinking Italian community gradually gave way to today's mixed Latinx population. St. Louis's Hill neighborhood, childhood home of baseball Hall of Famer Yogi Berra, was settled by Italian immigrants in the late nineteenth century and remains an Italian neighborhood to this day.

While some neighborhoods were dominated by a single immigrant community, others were a jumble of different nationalities and religions, sometimes coexisting peacefully but often living in a state of conflict that could range from occasional slurs and gestures to outright warfare. As Zorbaugh writes about the same neighborhood, "while the Irish and Swedish had gotten on well as neighbors, neither could or would live peaceably with the Sicilian[s]."[13] In an 1895 survey of its environs, Chicago's Hull House found eighteen different distinct nationalities living in an area of less than a third of a square mile within which were smaller and more homogenous pockets with clusters of Italian, Czech, Jewish, and Irish immigrants.

Living conditions in these neighborhoods were often crowded, unsafe, and unhealthy. Riis describes one tenement apartment he visited in lower Manhattan:

> Look into any of these houses, everywhere the same piles of rags, of malodorous bones and musty paper, all of which the sanitary police flatter themselves they have banished to the dumps and the warehouses. Here is a "flat" of "parlor" and two pitch-dark coops called bedrooms. Truly, the bed is all there is room for. The family teakettle is on the stove, doing

duty for the time being as a wash-boiler. . . . One, two, three beds are there, if the old boxes and heaps of foul straw can be called by that name; a broken stove with crazy pipe from which the smoke leaks at every joint, a table of rough boards propped up on boxes, piles of rubbish in the corner. The closeness and smell are appalling.[14]

The sheer density of New York may have made it extreme but not unique. A Chicago social worker described her city's immigrant quarters in similar language. "Little idea can be given of the filthy and rotten tenements, the dingy courts and tumble-down sheds, the foul stables and dilapidated outhouses, the broken sewer-pipes, the piles of garbage fairly alive with diseased odors, and of the numbers of children filling every nook, working and playing in every room, eating and sleeping in every window-sill, pouring in and out of every door, and seeming literally to pave every scrap of 'yard.'"[15]

The 1910 census laconically reports that the city of Boston contained 74,000 dwellings but 140,000 families. Riis describes one dwelling in New York's Lower East Side, where "two small rooms in a six-story tenement were made to hold a 'family' of father and mother, twelve children, and six boarders."[16] Conditions were typically somewhat better in the newer, less densely built cities of the Midwest such as Detroit and Cleveland, where an immigrant family had a better chance of having a house or apartment to themselves.

Exploitation and poverty were the rule. Factory jobs were long and dangerous and paid little. In Andrew Carnegie's mills in Pittsburgh, workers worked twelve-hour days, seven days a week with only the Fourth of July off, while fatal accidents in the city's mills accounted for 20 percent of the city's male deaths in the 1880s.[17] Yet, contemporary writers often compare the factories favorably to what was known as the "sweating system" under which "sweaters," or middlemen, bought fabric or unfinished clothes from manufacturers and in turn farmed the work out to men, women, and children working long hours for pennies in their apartments or rooms, using their feet to power their machines, among damp, fumes, and sick or screaming children. Riis describes such a scene:

> Up two flights of dark stairs, three, four, . . . on every landing, whirring sewing machines behind closed doors betraying what goes on within, to the door that opens to admit the bundle and the man. . . . Five men and a woman, two young girls, not fifteen, and a boy who says unasked that he is fifteen, and lies in saying it, are at the machines sewing knickerbockers, "knee-pants" in the Ludlow Street dialect. The floor is littered ankle-deep with half-sewn garments. In the alcove, on a couch of many dozens of "pants" ready for the finisher, a bare-legged baby with pinched face is asleep.[18]

Reformer Florence Kelley estimated that twenty-five thousand to thirty thousand Chicagoans, almost all Jewish and Italian immigrants, were employed in similar conditions.[19] In the 1890s, the sweating system was a pervasive reality wherever garments were manufactured in American cities.

Reformers such as Kelley, Riis, and their counterparts provided a valuable service in bringing the exploitation of immigrants to wider attention, yet they often failed to see beyond the poverty and disease that initially overwhelmed them. Their writings often betray a sense that these immigrants and their families were inferior to people of solid "American" stock, something that also reverberated in much of the writings of the Chicago School as well as in popular discourse until the end of World War II.

However deplorable the housing conditions of the late nineteenth-century immigrant neighborhoods were, middle-class reformers such as Riis and Kelley erred badly in assuming that their physical conditions were signs of pervasive social depravity and economic despair. On the contrary, as Hymowitz writes, "some of the enclaves became reeking, overcrowded slums that would catalyze progressive reformers. . . . But they also hummed with Tocquevillian energy. Immigrant civic groups sprang up to meet every sort of need from the medical to the recreational to the spiritual. The social benefits of the immigrant enclave were immense."[20] Immigrants did not let the squalor of the moment dim their aspirations for the future. They were adapting to a new country, building institutions, and in large numbers slowly but steadily moving up economically. Ironically, for all its abuses, the sweating system was a vehicle for upward mobility. A pieceworker might more easily make the transition to becoming a sweater than find comparable opportunities elsewhere, earn a little more, and eventually perhaps move into a better neighborhood and into the middle class.

As immigrants from different nations, speaking little or no English and adrift in the new country, each reached critical mass, and the institutions they created both sustained their ties to now faraway Europe and helped support their adjustment to a new life in the United States. The process of immigrant neighborhood formation was very much an informal and iterative one in which the first group of immigrants would arrive in a city and found a church, synagogue, or other center that would become a focal point around which more people of their nationality or religion congregated. The first wave of settlers did not typically form themselves into a cohesive ethnic neighborhood. It was the process of institution building over time that led to the formation of cohesive ethnic neighborhoods.

By the eve of World War I, American cities were almost all "cities of neighborhoods," mostly distinguished by ethnic or religious identities. While small cities might have a single distinct "Italian neighborhood" or "Polish neighborhood," larger cities tended to have something more like an archipelago of ethnic neighborhoods with multiple ethnic clusters, some large distinct neighborhoods with others no more than a block or two. Few ethnic neighborhoods, though, were ever entirely the terrain of a single group. Except for the Black ghettos that emerged in the 1920s, which formed a special case and which we discuss below, neighborhoods were mixed to varying degrees, but usually one national, ethnic, or religious group dominated the mix. Immigrants created institutions such as the Dom Polski (Polish House), built in 1889 in the Buffalo neighborhood known as Out Broadway, or Polonia. The Dom Polski was the home of Polish cultural and fraternal groups and became the de facto clubhouse for thousands of neighborhood residents. Shown in figure 3.5, it stood at the intersection of Broadway and Fillmore, known as "the Polish Main Street." That business district was

FIGURE 3.5. Buffalo's Dom Polski

(Photograph by Andre Carrotflower)

equivalent to the main street of a midsize Northeast city, reputedly boasting 2,930 Polish-owned businesses and 14 community banks.[21]

Early twentieth-century neighborhoods such as Polonia were all but self-contained, self-sufficient entities. Residents could spend their entire lives there without ever stepping outside its boundaries. Many of the men worked in nearby factories, while the neighborhood shopping street provided everything people needed for their day-to-day lives, from the taverns where the men went to unwind after their shifts to the grocery stores and bakeries from which their wives and children brought food home for dinner. The children went to the neighborhood public or parochial school, the family went to the picture show in the neighborhood movie theater on Saturday, and on Sunday they worshipped in a neighborhood church. Excursions to downtown department stores or to the country were special events, for which one dressed as if for church or a family wedding. For some, their first trip outside the neighborhood may have been the ride in the hearse—owned by a neighborhood funeral parlor—that took them to the cemetery.

Not all neighborhoods in 1900 cities were ethnic, immigrant neighborhoods. Cities had elite neighborhoods as well as a few other neighborhoods where most of the residents were what the makers of an 1895 nationalities map of New York City referred to as "natives," meaning white households of "native" as distinct from immigrant stock. Most cities also had small African American pockets, and some had so-called Chinatowns. But the European ethnic immigrant neighborhood was the dominant neighborhood type that gave early twentieth-century American cities their distinctive character.

The Rise of African American Neighborhoods

Although some southern cities such as Atlanta and New Orleans had substantial Black populations since the nineteenth century, most northern cities of that era had far fewer Black residents than would be the case in later years. In 1900, there were thirty thousand African Americans living in Chicago, thirty-six thousand in St. Louis, and sixty-three thousand in Philadelphia. With seventy-nine thousand Black residents, Baltimore was the nation's largest urban Black community, reflecting that city's mixture of southern and northern roots.

While distinct Black neighborhoods such as Sweet Auburn in Atlanta and Tremé in New Orleans go back to the late nineteenth century, northern cities, while far from integrated, had few distinct Black neighborhoods. Typically, Black families lived in small clusters or pockets—all-Black buildings or largely Black blocks or block faces—inside larger neighborhoods they shared with poor white families. Few Blacks owned their homes, and the buildings they lived in were often the most dilapidated ones in the vicinity, although their rents were no lower than in nearby buildings occupied by white families that were often in better condition.

While members of white ethnic communities who succeeded economically and assimilated culturally could—and often did—move into mixed or predominantly "native" neighborhoods, middle-class African Americans were no more welcome than poor ones in white neighborhoods even then. As an early sociologist noted in 1912, "the strong prejudice among the white people against having colored people living on white residence streets, colored children attending schools with white children, or entering into other semi-social relations with them, confines the opportunities for residence open to colored people *of all positions in life* to relatively small and well-defined areas."[22] When a respectable Black lawyer and his wife moved onto a white block in Baltimore in 1910, the uproar ultimately led to the city enacting the first racial zoning ordinance, barring Black families from moving onto any city block "wherein more than half the residents are white."[23]

That changed with the First Great Migration, as it is known, which took place from 1910 to 1940 and brought some 1.6 million southern Blacks to northern cities, many of whom filled labor gaps left by the drop in immigration following the immigrant exclusion acts of the 1920s.[24] Cleveland's Black population went from 8,000 in 1910 to 72,000 by 1930; over the same period, Detroit's Black population grew from 6,000 to over 120,000. The thousands of newly arrived African American migrants put severe pressures on existing Black enclaves, foreshadowing the far better-known story of racial pressures and white flight of the 1960s and 1970s, described in Horace Cayton's and St. Clair Drake's classic study of Chicago's Black community, *Black Metropolis*. The "tremendous demand for houses resulted in an immediate skyrocketing of rents for all available accommodations and in the opening of new residential areas to Negroes. There were tremendous profits to be made by both colored and white realtors who could provide houses. . . . Artificial panics were sometimes created in white areas by enterprising realtors who raised the cry 'the Negroes are coming' and then proceeded to double the rents after the whites had fled."[25]

It was during the 1920s that Black neighborhoods, in both their scale and their largely self-contained network of social institutions and economic activity, took on a character similar to that of the immigrant neighborhoods but with one important difference, as Drake and Cayton point out. "Negroes are not finally absorbed in the general population. Black Metropolis remains athwart the least desirable residential zones. Its population grows larger and larger, unable either to expand freely or to scatter."[26] It was thus that they came to be referred to as ghettos, reflecting the painful truth—as was true of the original Jewish ghettos of early modern Europe, from which the term came—that Black residency of those areas was imposed by legal and extralegal pressure from outside. Although in 1917 the US Supreme Court struck down the explicitly racial zoning that Baltimore had pioneered and other cities had copied—albeit on property rights rather than civil rights grounds—restrictive covenants, social pressures, and often outright violence kept most Black families pent up in racially defined ghettos until after World War II.[27]

Despite being penned in and partly for that same reason, Black neighborhoods were vital communities. Black-owned businesses lined the streets of Bronzeville, including Black-owned banks and insurance companies, while hundreds of social clubs, churches, nightclubs, and theaters provided solace, sociability, and entertainment. As Drake and Cayton note, "on eight square miles of land a Black Metropolis was growing in the womb of the white," visible in a 1934 map of Chicago (figure 3.6).[28]

Bronzeville had counterparts in almost every major American city from Harlem in New York to Black Bottom in Detroit, which had been the heart of Detroit's Jewish community at the end of the nineteenth century and got its name from its rich alluvial soils long before it became an African American community. These neighborhoods shared rich community networks along with appalling housing conditions, which got worse as more and more people moved north and crowded into already-teeming areas. Between 1920 and 1950 Chicago's Black population grew from one hundred thousand to nearly half a million and that of Detroit from forty thousand to three hundred thousand, while few opportunities existed to move beyond the borders of the ghetto.

Homeownership opportunities in neighborhoods such as Black Bottom and Bronzeville were few and far between, and living conditions for all but the well-to-do were often inadequate or worse. Conditions in Black Bottom, in a 1917 account, were "unspeakably vile," as a reporter wrote, with "tumbledown shacks . . . [that] fairly bulge with their human population, herded into stuffy quarters without proper light or ventilation, eating, living and sleeping in a single room."[29]

The Beginnings of the Urban Neighborhood Transformation

The 1920s saw significant changes come to American cities. After the Immigration Act of 1924, mass immigration came to an end. From over eight million

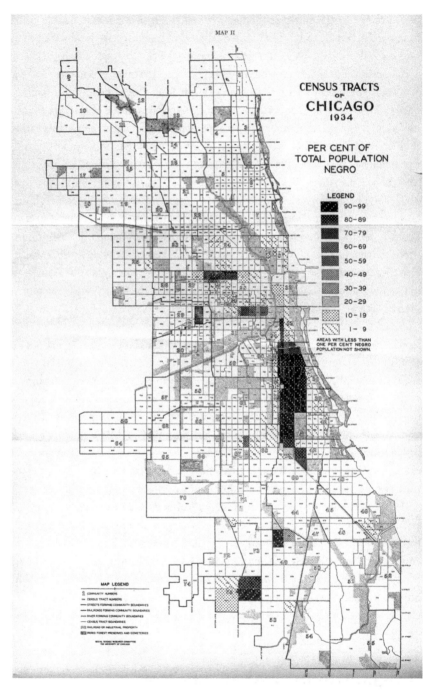

FIGURE 3.6. Bronzeville stands out vividly in this 1930s map of Chicago's Black population

(Map courtesy of the Newberry Library, Chicago)

immigrants in the first decade of the twentieth century and over six million—despite World War I—in the 1910s, immigration to the United States dropped to four million in the 1920s (mostly arriving before 1925) and to fewer than seven hundred thousand in the 1930s. At the same time urban Black populations grew rapidly, and the first distinct Black neighborhoods emerged in most American cities.

The 1920s were also the years when the spatial transformation of American life that was to become a reality after World War II first became clearly visible. It was when the automobile became a product for the masses rather than a toy for the elite. By 1925, over seventeen million private cars were on the road, more than ten times the number in 1914, roughly one for every two American households. Almost every feature of America's car-oriented society can be traced back to the 1920s, from the first motels and drive-in restaurants to the growth of the suburbs. Freed from their dependence on streetcar and commuter rail lines, suburbs could now be built anywhere that a car could reasonably reach. Although cities continued to grow during the 1920s and added more people than their suburbs, the 1920s was the first decade when suburbs grew at a faster percentage rate than central cities.

The 1920s also saw an unprecedented volume of homebuilding in urban America. With large tracts of vacant land remaining inside most central cities, much "suburban" construction took place within the cities as their boundaries were filled in with bungalows, row houses, and other housing types meeting the demands of a growing middle class. Relative to the size of the existing housing stock, that decade—particularly the years from 1923 to 1927—still stands as the greatest housing boom era in American history.[30] More 1920s buildings still stand in Chicago today than from any other decade before or since.[31]

Neighborhoods changed but less than might have been expected considering these dramatic social and economic changes. Scholars of the Chicago School argued that as immigrants moved upward socioeconomically they would slough off their parochial commitments, embrace a modern identity characterized by rational and instrumental relations, and move steadily into the so-called melting pot, but they were at least partly wrong. While immigrants shared the American aspiration for a house and yard of their own, as they began to prosper and realize that aspiration, their tendency was less to assimilate into ethnically neutral environments than to remain in familiar ethnic settings by either upgrading sections of existing neighborhoods into areas that often came to be known as "doctors' row" or "lawyers' row", or forming new more comfortable but still largely ethnically defined neighborhoods within newly built parts of the same cities.[32] Upwardly mobile New York Jewish families moved from the Lower East Side to the Bronx's Grand Concourse, while their Pittsburgh counterparts moved from Lower Hill to Squirrel Hill. The old ethnic neighborhoods, though, often remained the centers of ethnic social life and commercial activity. Residents of the newer ethnic neighborhoods continued for years to return to the old neighborhood to shop, worship, and participate in the distinctive culture fostered by the Dom Polskis, Turnvereins, and Sokols embedded in those neighborhoods.

The onset of the Great Depression tended if anything to reinforce the importance of the neighborhood, particularly in hard-hit ethnic, racial, and religious communities. With millions of families finding themselves in difficult circumstances and with public-sector social safety nets no more than embryonic, neighborhood institutions and solidarity became critical to both individual and group survival. As one historian writes, "New York's Jewish neighborhoods eased both the generational transition and the economic hardships of the Depression years. . . . In working-class enclaves, where the Depression dealt its harshest blow, neighborhood support networks preserved Jewish morale and offered critical material aid. While middle- and upper-class Jews seldom required the financial supports of their neighborhoods, Jewish residential clustering encouraged ethnic persistence for Jews at all economic levels."[33]

What was true for New York's Jewish communities was equally true for other racial and religious groups. But the Great Depression and World War II were also when, in the constant swing of the pendulum between community and individualism in American society, the idea of community was briefly in the ascendant. Within the framework of shared effort and sacrifice that characterized much thinking during the Depression and the war years, "the small-scale city neighborhood," in Looker's words, "sat close to the core of wartime understandings of American nationhood and purpose."[34]

In contrast to urban Black neighborhoods, which grew steadily from migration, becoming more and more crowded during the Depression and World War II, most white neighborhoods spent the Depression and war years in something of a time warp. While a steady trickle of people moved out and houses and other buildings became older, returning American troops after World War II found that their old neighborhoods had changed little from 1940 or, for that matter, from 1930. When those ex-soldiers started to establish their own households, though, they found that their neighborhoods had few vacant homes to offer them.

A decade of economic depression followed by wartime austerity had stifled housing production and discouraged more than routine maintenance and repairs in older housing. The 1950 census, which came after postwar production had already begun to ramp up significantly, found severe housing shortages in nearly every urban area in the United States. In cities such as Boston, Chicago, Cleveland, and Milwaukee rental vacancy rates were barely 1 percent. In Cleveland, a city with over 110,000 homeowners, there were barely five hundred units listed for sale that year. Ads placed in the *Los Angeles Times* from people seeking housing captured the desperation of many families:

> "No sympathy or charity. Wanted: Just a Home. Whatever you have to offer. We aren't perfect, just normal people. Veteran, wife and child. Won't you please call us?"
>
> "Have bride but no threshold. Newlywed couple without home. Please rent us a bungalow, apartment or house, furnished or unfurnished. Up to $50."
>
> "Refined Christian couple. Ex-Army officer & wife. College grads. Want house or apt. Permanently employed. Best local references. No children or pets."
>
> "It's the usual tale! But being a returned veteran I do want a home so my wife & I (no children or pets) can be together again. I'm sick of hotels & discouraged no end."[35]

As two historians have written, "Veterans returned to 'no vacancy' signs and high rents. As late as 1947, one-third were still living doubled up with relatives, friends, and strangers. American family life was on hold."[36]

The year 1950 was a pivotal moment in the history of the American urban ethnic neighborhood. For writer and broadcaster Ray Suarez, 1950 was the "last full cry of urban America": "The teeming ethnic ghettos of the early century had given way to a more comfortable life," he writes, "with religion and ethnicity, race and class still used as organizing principles for the neighborhood. The rough edges of the immigrant 'greenhorns' were worn smooth, and a confident younger generation now entered a fuller, richer American life. . . . [I]t was the ghetto, yes, but made benign by assimilation."[37] Yet the signs of change were already visible, and by the end of the 1950s the process of change was already well under way. Within the next decade many neighborhoods that had flourished for generations disappeared, while others began an inexorable process of transformation. The reasons were complex, multifaceted, and impossible to pin on a single cause, as some people have tried to do, such as white flight, urban renewal, or the interstate system. In the next chapter, we will try to disentangle the threads.

THE AMERICAN URBAN NEIGHBORHOOD UNDER SIEGE, 1950–1990

In his observation with which the last chapter closed, Ray Suarez put his finger on an important part of the story. With little immigration since the early 1920s and the experience of World War II still vivid, the younger native-born generation was far more "American" than their immigrant parents or grandparents. They may have enjoyed the close ties and networks of the neighborhoods they grew up in, but they didn't need them as much. They were comfortably at home in the wider American world and expected more from it than their parents or grandparents.

For many such people, the old neighborhood may have been comfortable, but it was also confining. Moreover, it was crowded, usually a little shabby, and had few homes for sale. People wanted larger homes, and they wanted new ones. The burgeoning single-family subdivisions that dotted the suburban landscape appealed far more than the central cities. Levittown, which rose from Long Island's potato fields, was replicated on the outskirts of every major American city. From 1950 to 1960, St. Louis County, which surrounds the city of St. Louis on three sides (the other being the Mississippi River), almost doubled its housing stock, building nearly one hundred thousand new dwellings. As one mover told Suarez many years later, "people our age at that time wanted to buy houses, and there just weren't any houses available in the city of St. Louis. So they all moved, and bought homes out in the county. . . . We bought our first home on the GI Bill, that's the way everyone was going then."[1]

Mortgages by the two key federal lending agencies, the Federal Housing Administration (FHA) and the Veterans Administration (VA), requiring little or no down payment fueled the suburban exodus. That exodus, however, was largely limited to white families partly because far more white urban families had the means to buy the new suburban houses but also because of overt racial discrimination by not only developers but also by government through the rules imposed by the FHA and the VA. White flight and suburbanization were about race but at the same time, however, they were not just about race.

The 1950s marked the onset of what came to be known as "the urban crisis." Its most visible manifestation was the flight of white families from central cities. White families began to leave cities in large numbers soon after the war, whether or not those cities' Black populations were growing either in the city or their neighborhood. As economist Leah Boustan has written, for "urban whites, most of whom never interacted with a Black family, leaving for the resource-rich suburbs was an economic calculus, one that was accelerated by the steady stream of poor migrants, both white and Black, into central cities."[2]

Although Boston and Pittsburgh saw little Black in-migration during the 1950s, the white population in both cities dropped by over 15 percent between 1950 and 1960, more than in Chicago and Philadelphia although less than in St. Louis and Detroit, both of which lost nearly one-quarter of their white population during the same decade.[3] All in all, thirty-two cities with populations over 100,000 saw their populations decline from their 1950 peak in the following decade, as shown in table 4.1. These thirty-two cities, which contained over 18 million people, or roughly 1 out of every 8 Americans, lost 1.2 million people. They were a roll call of urban America. Nearly all those who left were white.

Suburbanization tended to blur differences between different white ethnic and religious communities while widening the racial divide. The families who bought in the new subdivisions generally came from all white ethnic backgrounds, linked less by ethnic identity than by their shared identity as young couples with common aspirations to a distinct middle-class way of life. As William H. Whyte wrote at the time in *The Organization Man*, the suburbs "have become the second great melting pot."[4]

The new suburbs were distinct neighborhoods in important respects, and the new suburbanites threw themselves with determination into the process of turning them into good neighborhoods. "There was something compulsive about it, something too intense to be natural," Ehrenhalt writes. "Those people not only shared lawnmowers and cooked dinner for each other but joined and volunteered for clubs and social organizations with an energy that seems in retrospect to have bordered on the manic."[5] Eventually, as we will discuss in chapter 13, these suburbs of the 1950s would evolve into something very different.

TABLE 4.1 Cities over 100,000 population that lost population from 1950 to 1960

CITY	1950 POPULATION	1960 POPULATION	N CHANGE	% CHANGE
Providence, RI	248,674	207,498	−41,176	−16.6
Milwaukee, WI	871,047	741,324	−129,723	−14.9
Boston, MA	801,444	697,197	−104,247	−13.0
St. Louis, MO	856,796	750,026	−106,770	−12.5
Scranton, PA	125,536	111,443	−14,093	−11.2
Trenton, NJ	128,009	114,167	−13,842	−10.8
Fall River, MA	111,963	99,942	−12,021	−10.7
Pittsburgh, PA	676,806	604,332	−72,474	−10.7
Reading, PA	109,320	98,061	−11,259	−10.3
Buffalo, NY	580,132	523,759	−56,373	−9.7
Detroit, MI	1,849,568	1,670,114	−179,454	−9.7
Hartford, CT	177,397	162,178	−15,219	−8.6
Jersey City, NJ	299,017	276,101	−22,916	−7.7
Newark, NJ	438,776	405,220	−33,556	−7.6
New Haven, CT	164,443	152,048	−12,395	−7.5
Somerville, MA	102,351	94,697	−7,654	−7.5
Minneapolis, MN	521,718	482,872	−38,846	−7.4
New Bedford, MA	109,189	102,477	−6,712	−6.1
Camden, NJ	124,555	117,159	−7,396	−5.9
Washington, DC	802,178	763,956	−38,222	−4.8
Hoboken, NJ	50,676	48,441	−2,235	−4.4
Cleveland, OH	914,808	876,050	−38,758	−4.2
Rochester, NY	332,488	318,611	−13,877	−4.2
Albany, NY	134,995	129,726	−5,269	−3.9
Philadelphia, PA	2,071,605	2,002,512	−69,093	−3.3
Canton, OH	116,912	113,631	−3,281	−2.8
Syracuse, NY	220,583	216,038	−4,545	−2.1
Chicago, IL	3,620,962	3,550,404	−70,558	−1.9
Baltimore, MD	949,708	939,024	−10,684	−1.1
Utica, NY	101,531	100,410	−1,121	−1.1
Youngstown, OH	168,330	166,689	−1,641	−1.0
Cincinnati, OH	503,998	502,550	−1,448	−0.3

Source: Decennial Census, Bureau of the Census.

Meanwhile, back in the cities, migration was turning into white flight. Continued **Black** in-migration was combined with sweeping changes to the physical fabric of older cities driven by urban renewal and the interstate highway system. Neither initiated the flight to the suburbs, but both combined to magnify its extent and exacerbate its effects well beyond what might have otherwise been the case.

The Federal Government and the Destruction of Urban Neighborhoods

The story of the federal role in the decline of the cities and the rise of the suburbs has been told elsewhere but is worth reexamining in light of its effect on urban neighborhoods.[6] When the housing market collapsed during the Great Depression of the 1930s, the federal government created the FHA to revive mortgage lending by providing federally backed insurance to lenders. If a mortgage approved by the FHA went into default, the FHA would buy it from the lender, making the lender whole. The FHA was an elegant solution to the crisis of the time, as it established the thirty-year fixed-rate low–down payment home mortgage as the American norm and, at little expense to the public purse, led to a dramatic expansion of homeownership. It did so, however, in a racially discriminatory fashion.

In order to evaluate the potential risk of default of individual home mortgages, the FHA relied heavily on the work of economist Homer Hoyt, who became principal housing economist at the FHA soon after its founding in 1934. Given the pervasive racial and cultural assumptions of the time, it is unlikely that the FHA's practices would have been radically different had Hoyt never existed. The central role he played and the intellectual firepower he brought to selling his ideas, however, makes him worthy of our attention.

Hoyt's view of neighborhood change, which was reflected in FHA mortgage underwriting, can be summarized in three principles:

1. *Single-use neighborhoods are preferable to mixed-use neighborhoods.* The segregation of land uses into separate use districts fostered by zoning was a positive value, as was low residential density. Thus, low-density suburban areas characterized by detached single-family homes were most favored.
2. *Newer neighborhoods are preferable to older neighborhoods.* Reflecting neighborhood life cycle theory, Hoyt wrote that "it is well recognized that residential land values are at their peak when a neighborhood is new and that they gradually decline as the neighborhood reaches maturity and approaches old age."[7] Thus, the FHA made it far easier to obtain mortgage insurance on new compared to existing homes and all but impossible to obtain long-term financing for houses in need of rehabilitation in older neighborhoods.
3. *Homogeneous neighborhoods are preferable to diverse neighborhoods.* Hoyt warned that it was in the "twilight zone, where members of different races lived together[,] that racial mixtures tend to have a

depressing effect on land values."[8] Based on this principle, the FHA *Underwriting Manual* recommended against the introduction of "inharmonious racial or nationality groups" into existing neighborhoods or new developments, and encouraged the use of restrictive covenants in real estate deeds barring Blacks and often Jews and Asians from "invading" white neighborhoods.

While the federal government did not create racial segregation, through the FHA it "exhorted segregation and enshrined it as public policy."[9] Parenthetically, although FHA practices are often characterized as being based on the so-called redlining maps, those maps were prepared by a separate federal agency, the Home Owner's Loan Corporation, and the two agencies had little to do with each other.

By following Hoyt's principles, the FHA effectively denied older neighborhoods, particularly Black neighborhoods, adequate mortgage capital while making mortgages available to racially segregated developments in the emerging suburbs. After the war when Congress created the VA, which offered returning veterans mortgages with no down payment, the new agency adopted the FHA's underwriting criteria, further extending the reach of Hoyt's ideas.

As historian Kenneth Jackson sums it up, "the main beneficiary of the $119 billion in FHA mortgage insurance issued in the first four decades of FHA operation was suburbia, where almost half of all housing could claim FHA or VA financing in the 1950s and 1960s."[10] The behavior of private-sector lenders was much the same. In either case, it became far more difficult for people to qualify for mortgages in older mixed-use and more diverse urban neighborhoods. These practices continued overtly until President John F. Kennedy's 1962 executive order barring racial discrimination in FHA lending, although many argue that they continued informally to varying degrees until enactment of the Fair Housing Act six years later and perhaps even after that. Their prevalence during these critical years in the postwar transformation of American life is a major reason for the magnitude of the wealth gap between white and African American households in the United States today.

The decline of cities had been a federal concern since the 1930s, when observers had first called attention to the beginnings of urban population loss.[11] When prominent city planner Harland Bartholomew pointed out in 1940 that "decentralization of American cities has now reached the point where the main central city, at least, is in great jeopardy," he was but one of many voices calling for a concerted federal strategy to address what were increasingly being seen as the two incipient crises of the city: the decline of the city as a center of business, commerce, and industry and the spread of slums and blight.[12]

The latter term, adapted from its historic use to describe plant diseases, came into widespread use in the 1930s and, like so much else in midcentury urban thinking in America, emerged from the work of the Chicago School. New Deal figures often drew explicit parallels between urban slum conditions and disease; as prominent New York City progressive Joseph McGoldrick put it, "we must cut out the whole cancer and not leave any diseased tissue."[13] The trope of urban blight was juxtaposed against the seductive modernist vision of cities by planners and architects such as Le Corbusier, whose 1920s Radiant City plans envisioned shiny new cities with housing, commerce, parkland, and highways each in their own rationally organized place with light and fresh air for all.

The economic gap between central cities and their suburbs grew wider and the calls for action more insistent after World War II. Those calls were answered with the urban renewal program, enacted in the 1949 Housing Act, with the dual goals of helping older cities reverse their decline and providing "a decent home and suitable living environment for every American family." With its commitment to increase the supply of affordable housing and remove dilapidated slum housing, urban renewal had broad bipartisan support as well as the support of the nation's African American leaders. Robert Weaver, later appointed as the first secretary of the Department of Housing and Urban Development (HUD), became "urban renewal's most prominent advocate," stating in one speech that "the major achievement of urban renewal is that it has restored hope for older cities and worn out neighborhoods."[14] As historian Steve Conn writes, "For this generation of liberals, urban renewal was an example of positive action from the federal government, the Civil Rights Act in bricks and mortar."[15]

It was a generous program. In 1956, the federal government appropriated $3.23 billion for urban renewal, equal to roughly $30 billion in 2020 dollars, or roughly ten times recent annual appropriations for the Community Development Block Grant program. Urban renewal funds were difficult to turn down. The federal government provided two-thirds of the cost, while local governments could provide the other one-third in many ways, including staff salaries, land contributions, and public works projects.

The program was based, however, on a premise that was not only faulty but also in retrospect almost perverse: that urban decline could be halted by making the cities more like the suburbs. That meant clearing large tracts of land for large-scale development, whether downtown office buildings or public housing projects; demolishing thousands of "obsolete" buildings; and widening streets, laying out highways, and building parking garages to make the city more automobile-friendly. Reflecting the pervasive belief in neighborhood life cycles, the all but universal premise was that obsolete neighborhoods needed to be demolished and rebuilt from scratch.

Urban renewal respected no race, creed, or ethnicity. Many white ethnic neighborhoods faced the wrecking ball, such as Chicago's Halsted Street and

Boston's West End, from which three thousand largely Italian American families were displaced. But African American neighborhoods were the hardest hit. Even in cities where the great majority of urban renewal's victims were white, Black families were still disproportionately impacted. In 1960, "only" 32 percent of the families displaced by urban renewal in Boston were Black, but only 9 percent of that city's total population was Black. In Baltimore, 89 percent of those displaced by urban renewal between 1951 and 1964 were Black.[16] Black novelist James Baldwin summed up widely held feelings in one memorable sentence: "Urban renewal is Negro removal."[17]

Suffering from the worst housing conditions, often strategically close to downtowns and with a largely disenfranchised population unable to challenge powerful political and business interests, neighborhoods of color became frequent targets of urban renewal. In 1957, three out of every four families displaced through urban renewal were Black or Puerto Rican.[18] Overall, an estimated total of 500,000 households were displaced by the urban renewal program over its life, or 1.6 million to 2 million people.[19] Of these, close to half were probably displaced from Black neighborhoods. In Chicago alone by 1966, 14,000 Black families had been displaced or were slated for relocation.[20]

The Mill Creek Valley urban renewal project in St. Louis was typical (figure 4.1). West of downtown, Mill Creek Valley in the 1950s was a long-standing Black community of nearly twenty thousand persons. Housing conditions were bad; a 1947 study had found that on one out of three blocks, all or nearly all the buildings were substandard. Many still relied on outdoor privies. The physical conditions of the area served as the city's justification for urban renewal, although its central location was implicitly understood to be a key reason. The city received $23 million ($225 million in 2020 dollars) from the federal urban renewal program. Voters overwhelmingly approved a $10 million bond issue for the local share of the project cost. Demolition began in 1959, and by 1965 the last resident was removed.

While Mill Creek Valley looked like a "slum" to middle-class St. Louisans, it was in many ways the heart and soul of Black St. Louis. The area contained 839 businesses and institutions, including 42 churches and 13 hotels, many Black-owned, and a Negro Baseball League stadium seating ten thousand. The neighborhood was home to well-to-do professionals and businesspeople living side by side with working-class and poor households. Although much of its housing was seriously deficient and its residents were mostly poor, it was a real community and as much of a haven from the wider world as any immigrant enclave.[21]

Most civic leaders in St. Louis saw Mill Creek Valley not as a viable community but instead as an obsolescent area in need of modernization. They saw it as an embarrassment that greeted visitors to St. Louis when they arrived at Union Station and a blight that needed to be eradicated. And so it was. Most families

FIGURE 4.1.   St. Louis mayor Raymond Tucker (at right) and civic leader and bond issue chairman Sidney Maestre looking out over the Mill Creek Valley area slated for demolition, 1956

(Photograph courtesy of Missouri History Museum)

ended up in segregated Black neighborhoods north of Delmar Boulevard, increasing the pressure on Black households already in those areas to move northward into then-white neighborhoods. For decades after the land was cleared, Mill Creek Valle was known as "Hiroshima Flats" for its vast expanses of vacant land. Even today most of the area remains a bleak landscape of 1970s and 1980s commercial and industrial buildings surrounded by parking lots, although in what might be seen as having ironic overtones, it also contains the campus of Harris-Stowe State University, a historically Black university.[22]

As urban renewal accelerated during the 1950s, it was joined by a program that arguably had even more pernicious effects on cities in general and urban neighborhoods in particular. The interstate highway program, which began construction in 1956 following enactment of the Interstate Highway and Defense Act, was the single largest federal infrastructure investment in American history.[23]

The original plan called for about six thousand miles of the forty-one thousand–mile interstate system to pass through urban areas, dictating that highways would be cut through densely populated city neighborhoods, eminent domain would be used to take properties, and thousands of structures would be bulldozed to make way for ribbons of concrete.[24] Low-income neighborhoods were often chosen as highway routes, in part to reduce land-acquisition costs and in part to complement the activities taking place simultaneously through urban renewal.[25]

With the federal government initially providing 90 percent of the cost of the new highways, states found it all but impossible to resist the program. Rights-of-way, sometimes far wider than needed, cut vast swaths through crowded neighborhoods. In Detroit, the right-of-way of the Chrysler Freeway, I-375, with service roads on either side, is 350 feet wide, greater than the length of a football field, only one-third of which was occupied by the highway itself. Barely a mile west of downtown Detroit, the intersection of I-96 and I-75 sprawls over forty acres, obliterating the equivalent of six to eight city blocks. Highways cut through many neighborhoods that had been spared by urban renewal. I-81 destroyed Syracuse's largely Black 15th Ward, cutting the city's heart in half, while I-375 obliterated what was left of Detroit's Black Bottom after much of it had already disappeared through urban renewal (figures 4.2 and 4.3).

From Quiescence to Neighborhoodism

Poorly situated to challenge local elites' strong support for these programs and with little experience of organized advocacy, the initial neighborhood response to both urban renewal and the highway program was one of quiescence. As these programs continued to devour urban neighborhoods, however, the response shifted from quiescence to activism, ultimately leading to a national revolt against freeways and urban renewal. While it was too little too late for most neighborhoods, the neighborhood revolt presaged the neighborhood movement of the 1970s and the growth of today's community development networks.

The first neighborhood revolt against highways erupted in San Francisco in 1956, where plans to cut a highway through the western part of the city triggered such heated neighborhood opposition that the Board of Supervisors ultimately voted to cancel the project outright.[26] Challenges to urban expressways increased in the mid-1960s as expressway projects were blocked in New York City, Boston, Baltimore, New Orleans, and a host of other cities.[27]

Successful opposition to highway projects, however, was almost always the product of middle-class or business interests with access to the corridors of power. Jane Jacobs's successful fight to block the cross-Manhattan expressway, that would have sliced through Greenwich Village and Lower Manhattan, mobilized an alliance of affluent professionals with robust political connections, while in the Bronx, lower-income Jewish residents protested Robert Moses's

FIGURE 4.2. Hastings Street before highway construction in its 1940s heyday as the center of Detroit's Black community

(Photograph courtesy of Detroit Historical Society)

FIGURE 4.3. Hastings Street after construction of I-375 in the 1950s

(Photograph courtesy of Detroit Historical Society)

Cross-Bronx Expressway to no avail. In New Orleans, affluent French Quarter residents and business leaders blocked the riverfront expressway, but despite opposition, an elevated highway cut through the middle of Tremé, the heart of Black New Orleans.

Fewer successful protests derailed urban renewal projects compared to interstate highways, perhaps because middle-class and affluent neighborhoods were far less likely to be in the path of urban renewal projects. The urban renewal program was ultimately done in not by grassroots pressure but by the growing elite consensus that the program, despite its great cost and devastating physical impact, had done little to revive central cities. By the time Robert Weaver became HUD secretary in 1965, he had long ceased to be an advocate for the program. In the end, the differential outcome of neighborhood revolts reflected race- and class-based power relations and political influence, an implicit contradiction that bedevils the neighborhood movement to this day.

The 1960s was an age of social ferment. Activism was part of the vocabulary of the time. The 1960s was also when poverty became a public issue, leading to the war on poverty legislation of 1965. A lasting legacy of this era was the community development corporation (CDC), nonprofit organizations dedicated to improving a specific neighborhood or cluster of neighborhoods. CDCs grew in part out of the war on poverty, specifically the program known as the Community Action Program, which has been called "the largest, most systematic neighborhood organizing project ever tried."[28]

The Community Action Program bypassed city governments, seen by many of the planners of the war on poverty as indifferent to low-income and minority neighborhoods, and provided funds instead directly to local community action agencies with a mandate to foster "maximum feasible participation" of the residents of the low-income neighborhoods where they were located. Community action agencies often became vehicles for Black or insurgent political activism, leading many mayors to feel that the federal government was funding their enemies. At their behest, Congress reined in the agencies with the 1967 Green Amendment, giving local governments the power to decide who would be eligible for community action funds. Many community action agencies eventually evolved into CDCs.

The initial impetus for CDCs came from Senator Robert Kennedy after his famous walking tour of Bedford-Stuyvesant in February 1966. Ten months later, he announced a plan to create CDCs that would "combine the best of community action with the best of the private enterprise system."[29] These corporations would focus on economic development, giving local residents and businesses a stake in and substantial control over their activities. Kennedy authored legislation that created the Special Impact Program within the war on poverty to provide grant support to CDCs, initially funded at $25 million (roughly $200 million in 2021 dollars). CDCs received direct federal funding through the Special Impact Program and successor programs until the late 1970s. Encouraged by federal and foundation support, particularly the Ford Foundation, the number of CDCs steadily grew during the late 1960s and the 1970s. A 1994 survey found that of 534 organizations nationally identified as CDCs at that point, 39 had begun in the 1960s and 172 in the 1970s.[30] We will return to CDCs and their role in neighborhood change later in this chapter.

By the 1970s, a neighborhood movement with its roots in highway and urban renewal battles was reaching critical mass. "Neighborhood" gave resident empowerment an ideological dimension grounded in Catholic social theory and the neighborhood ethnic identity rhetoric of the time.[31] Presenting itself as flowing from American traditions of local democracy, self-reliance, and community, the neighborhood movement promoted the idea that many, if not most, of society's problems could be fixed by empowering neighborhoods. We call this ideology of neighborhood empowerment "neighborhoodism."

From the very beginning, neighborhoodism suffered from deep and ultimately unresolvable internal contradictions. The rhetoric of neighborhood empowerment masked fundamental conflicts over race, ethnicity, and social class as well as over the relationship between neighborhoods and government. While arguably it was never a coherent movement, for a brief period, perhaps helped by its ambiguous rhetoric, empowering neighborhoods became a potent political symbol resonating with both sides of the national political divide.

In the 1976 presidential campaign, both Jimmy Carter and Gerald Ford stressed the preservation of urban neighborhoods, privileging local voluntary initiatives over top-down government programs. Once elected, President Carter appointed Monsignor Geno Baroni, a prominent proponent of neighborhoodism, as Assistant Secretary of HUD for Neighborhood Development, Consumer Affairs, and Regulatory Functions. Although Baroni helped move the Community Reinvestment Act into law later that year, most of his initiatives foundered on the harsh budgetary realities of the late 1970s. The same was true of the National Commission on Neighborhoods, charged by Congress in 1977 to "investigate the causes of neighborhood decline" and "recommend changes in public policy so that the federal government becomes more supportive of neighborhood stability."[32] Although the commission delivered a voluminous report with over two hundred recommendations, its deliberations were riven by internal conflict, and it had little or no effect on public policy. The remaining years of Carter's term were dominated by other issues, and the presidency would soon pass into very different hands.

While it may have appeared that whites and Blacks, middle class and poor, liberals and conservatives, could work together under the big tent of neighborhoodism, the idea that neighborhood empowerment can solve deeply rooted societal problems was doomed by its contradictions. In Ronald Reagan's 1980 presidential campaign, "neighborhood" was no more than gauzy rhetoric, part of the five-word litany "Family, Work, Neighborhood, Peace, Freedom" that had become an organizing theme of his speeches.[33] Using neighborhoods to evoke an earlier era when people took care of each other locally without incursions from federal bureaucrats, Reagan turned the ambiguous symbol of neighborhood empowerment into a cudgel against federal programs.

While the brief shining moment of "neighborhoodism" as an ideological movement died with Reagan's election, efforts to build stronger neighborhoods that emerged under its rubric continued under new policy paradigms. Before turning to those paradigms, however, we need to look at the changes in neighborhood conditions and the federal response to those changes that were taking place during the 1960s and 1970s.

Neighborhood Change during the "Urban Crisis" Years

Urban renewal and highways, along with suburbanization, further destabilized an already struggling urban organism. Overcrowded Black neighborhoods were bulldozed, their residents dispersed. With few suburban options available to them, Black families began to move into those parts of the cities that had previously been barred to them, often neighborhoods where much of the white population was already leaving or predisposed to leave.

Whether white flight was inevitable and the extent to which it was spurred or exacerbated by blockbusting and similar practices has long been debated. The outcome, however, is well known. Millions of white families picked up and left urban neighborhoods beginning in the 1950s with this trend accelerating through the 1970s, particularly after the urban riots of the 1960s (figure 4.4). By the time white flight slowed around 1980, Chicago had lost over half of its 1950 white population, or 1.6 million residents, and Detroit lost nearly three-quarters, or 1.1 million residents. Meanwhile, undermined by urban renewal, highway construction, and finally the outward movement of the Black middle class, the solid Black neighborhoods of the immediate postwar years became a thing of the past.

While the rapid turnover of urban neighborhoods was itself destabilizing, compounded by the pernicious effects of blockbusting, a further destructive change was the creation of a seemingly permanent reservoir of vacant houses in cities such as Detroit and Philadelphia. While there are many reasons for the rise in vacant properties in the heart of America's older cities, it all begins with

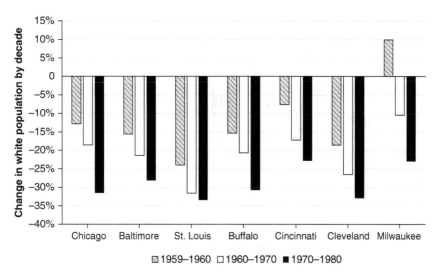

FIGURE 4.4. Percent change in white population in major cities by decade, 1950–1980

(Authors' work based on decennial census data)

a simple arithmetical reality: during the "urban crisis" years from 1950 to 1980, far more people left the cities than came in (figure 4.5). Leah Boustan calculated that "each black arrival led to 2.7 white departures."[34]

Cities in the 1950s were overcrowded, with few vacant homes available to buy or apartments to rent. By 1960, however, the construction of new housing had relieved the housing shortage, and an adequate supply of vacant homes was now available for home seekers. After 1960, continued net out-migration began to create a glut of urban housing. This was a new urban phenomenon. From the earliest years of American urban history through the 1950s, slum housing may have been dilapidated or unsafe but was always occupied. For the first time in American urban history, the excess of vacant urban housing became a major public issue.

Housing vacancy is a product of urban decline but it is also a *cause* of decline, creating spillover effects that extend into its surroundings that can lead to reinforcing loops of continuing abandonment. Strong links between vacant properties and negative neighborhood effects have been well established. Two studies of vacant properties in Philadelphia nearly a decade apart came to similar conclusions, with the latter study finding that the presence of a vacant property could reduce the value of properties on the same block by up to 20 percent and the earlier study finding that the reduction was $3,500 to $7,500.[35]

Vacant properties are also associated with crime, violence, and health problems. A recent study in Philadelphia found a strong relationship between the

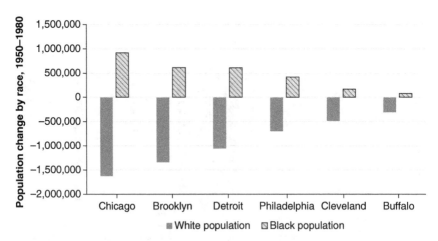

FIGURE 4.5.   Black in-migration and white out-migration in selected cities, 1940–1980

(Authors' work based on decennial census data)

presence and number of vacant properties and reported aggravated assaults on the same block, with the risk of violence increasing as the number of vacant properties rose.[36] A comprehensive review of research on health conditions found that vacant lots and abandoned buildings could negatively affect mental health and rates of chronic illness, sexually transmitted diseases, stunted brain and physical development in children, and unhealthy eating and exercise habits.[37] Studies have also linked abandoned buildings and vacant lots to "the breakdown in social capital—crucial to a community's ability to organize and advocate for itself."[38]

Although the urban renewal program was not formally abolished until 1974, it was fading by the mid-1960s, stung by public opposition and the growing evidence of its harmful effects and its failure to slow, let alone reverse, the tide of urban decline. With the creation of the new Department of Housing and Urban Development (HUD) in 1966, federal policy began to shift. In a reversal of the policies that guided the FHA for decades, Phillip Brownstein, the new undersecretary of HUD in charge of the FHA, informed FHA staff that "stimulating a flow of mortgage funds into the inner city, yes even into the slums, for the transfer of houses, for rehabilitation, and for new construction, is an FHA mission of the highest priority" and that a home loan application "should not be rejected simply because it involves poor people, or because it is in a portion of the city you have been accustomed to rejecting or red-lining for old-fashioned, arbitrary reasons."[39] From then through the early 1970s the federal government

TABLE 4.2 Principal federal housing and neighborhood assistance programs, 1964–1974

PROGRAM	YEAR	DESCRIPTION
War on Poverty/Office of Economic Opportunity	1964	Multifaceted program to reduce poverty, including preschool education, job training, community action, Job Corps, VISTA volunteers, and more
Public education support	1965	Grant program for school districts with large numbers of low-income students
Model Cities	1966	Targeted program for comprehensive neighborhood revitalization
Section 312 housing	1966	Low-interest rehabilitation loans for property owners (mainly homeowners) in targeted areas
Section 236 housing	1968	Low-income rental housing developed by private developers with federal mortgage subsidy
Section 235 housing	1968	1% federally subsidized mortgages for low-income home buyers
Community Development Block Grant	1974	Block grants to local governments for community development activities, including housing rehabilitation and social services
Section 8 housing	1974	Federal housing subsidies for low-income renters, including tenant-based subsidies for private-market housing and project-based subsidies to support new construction and rehabilitation

created an array of new programs to improve housing and neighborhood conditions, largely aimed at lower-income urban communities. The most important of these programs are shown in table 4.2.

Except for the Model Cities program and the modest Section 312 program, these initiatives were all mean-tested programs designed to either improve housing conditions or deliver social services to lower-income households. While those are important social policy goals, they were unlikely to improve neighborhoods. Means-tested housing projects, with some exceptions, have a poor track record in improving the neighborhoods in which they are built, while programs that raise the economic level of people living in distressed neighborhoods as often as not lead them to move out of those neighborhoods rather than improving the neighborhoods themselves.

Of these programs, the Section 235 program is most widely recognized to have done more harm than good to many urban neighborhoods. Few federal housing programs have had better intentions, poorer design, and worse execution. Although its goal of turning a million low-income families into homeowners was an admirable one, it was initiated with little awareness of the many pitfalls to such a strategy and implemented by FHA offices under pressure for quick results and little preparation for the job, often by the same people who only a few years earlier had been enforcing racial segregation in suburban subdivisions and denying loans in low-income communities of color. The program collapsed in the early 1970s under the weight of massive defaults and widespread misrepresentation and fraud by brokers, appraisers, contractors, and FHA officials, leaving behind a trail of nearly one hundred thousand empty houses and a host of destabilized neighborhoods.[40] This outcome was far more than unfortunate, since a well-designed, well-executed program to expand lower-income homeownership at that point might well have stabilized many neighborhoods that subsequently declined.

The Model Cities program was meant to be very different. Seen by Weaver as the centerpiece of HUD's new direction, it sought to link physical improvements, social services, antipoverty initiatives, and community participation in targeted neighborhoods in carefully selected cities. The program was hobbled from the beginning, however, by a mismatch between intentions and reality. It was initially envisioned as a narrowly targeted, carefully coordinated program to direct significant new HUD resources along with funds from existing programs in HUD and other federal agencies into neighborhoods in no more than 50 cities. Mayoral pressures, however, led to the program expanding from 50 to 150 neighborhoods, while a lukewarm Congress cut the program's appropriation. Once begun, conflicts over strategy and priorities and the inherent conflict between the two pillars of community participation and centralized coordination of multiple programs magnified the disparity between the program's ambitions and its limited reach. As two contemporary observers noted, "the contradictions between the strategies, inherent in the legislation, were not resolved in the regulations. Instead, they were crystallized, and the mixture of myth and truth in each strategy, as well as the contradictions, went unchallenged."[41] The Model Cities program was quietly closed down in 1974 after five years of operation.

The Model Cities program clearly failed in its larger goals of neighborhood transformation despite the possibility of individual success stories such as the South Bronx, where some credit the program with having jump-started that neighborhood's revival.[42] No systematic evaluation of the program's outcomes was ever done, although a 1973 study commissioned by HUD found that while "Model Cities proposed to effect a significant change in the quality of life of selected American cities within the short span of five years[,] . . . [t]oday, some six years after initiation of the Model Cities program, it is clear that the goal of a significant improvement in the quality of life of selected urban neighborhoods has not yet been attained."[43] A recent University of Michigan student thesis compared the 1970–2000 trajectories of Model Cities neighborhoods in ten cities to surrounding neighborhoods, finding no meaningful difference.[44] While no more than suggestive, this is consistent with our observations.

Given the Model Cities program's limited resources and built-in conflicts and the powerful social and economic trends working against older cities and their neighborhoods, it may have been unreasonable to have expected significant results. The program, however, suffered from a more fundamental failure; namely, to the extent that it had an underlying basis in a theory of neighborhood change, that theory was fatally flawed. That flaw can be summed up succinctly. Rather than seeing neighborhoods as entities with their own distinct dynamics qua neighborhoods, the designers of the program saw them as simply the sum of the individual conditions of the people living in the neighborhood. In other words, they believed that if they could improve the conditions—health, education, housing, employment, and so forth—of the people living in the neighborhood, neighborhood revival would inevitably follow.

The Model Cities strategy was additive. For example, if improvements to the local public school and the construction of new low-income housing are each positive goods, then simultaneously providing both will be that much more beneficial, since not only will each deliver some benefit, but the (presumed) synergy between the two will also act as a multiplier of those benefits. While this may be true for individual beneficiaries, it is at best questionable in terms of its neighborhood impact. Neighborhood conditions are clearly affected by the social and economic condition of their residents, but they are far more than those conditions. The Model Cities program did not recognize any factors driving neighborhood change beyond the sum of the individual conditions of its residents. The role of market factors was not even considered, and while citizen participation was an important part of the process, it focused entirely on eliciting resident involvement in the design of housing and social programs and perhaps on energizing sluggish municipal bureaucracies rather than building community cohesion or social capital.

Those elements were not part of the program designers' thinking, nor, as far as we can tell, were they raised by contemporary critics of the program. Neither protagonists nor critics possessed a theoretical framework or vocabulary to enable them to understand neighborhood dynamics in ways that would make it possible to design neighborhood strategies that could alter neighborhood trajectories. Neither the work of the Chicago School nor that of Homer Hoyt, or neighborhood life cycle theory, with which many of those involved may have been familiar, were of any use. All of them were overwhelmingly deterministic and even fatalistic in their premises, offering no insights about how to strengthen a struggling neighborhood by working with its residents rather than, as in the urban renewal model, clearing them out and replacing them with others.

In essence, the only model the planners of the Model Cities program had to work with was the social work model growing out of the settlement house movement of the early twentieth century and from which the public housing advocates of the New Deal emerged. The model was based on the idea of individual uplift, and the premise that changes to individual conditions, or physical improvements to the environment, could change neighborhood level social conditions, as epitomized by a widely distributed New Deal public housing poster (figure 4.6). It was not until the mid-1970s that new theories of neighborhood change began to emerge that offered a theoretical basis for community-based neighborhood revitalization.[45]

While the dominant urban narrative was one of decline amid growing poverty, unemployment, and vacant housing, a less visible yet parallel process of change was also taking place. Although white flight took a toll on the cities' previously stable working-class and middle-class neighborhoods, they did not disappear. These neighborhoods, sometimes dubbed "middle neighborhoods," continued to exist but were diminished in number and extent. Some were white ethnic neighborhoods such as The Hill, the Italian neighborhood in St. Louis. Often, however, they went through racial transformation but remained intact, as working-class and middle-class African American families seeking better housing conditions took advantage of the space left by white flight to leave the overcrowded, segregated Black ghettos and move into neighborhoods from which they had previously been excluded. These neighborhoods became and remained for decades thereafter Black neighborhoods of largely middle-class character. Such neighborhoods emerged in almost every large American city, including Lee-Harvard in Cleveland, Penrose in St. Louis, Overbrook in Philadelphia, and South Shore, the neighborhood where Michelle Obama grew up, in Chicago. They represent a far more important part of American neighborhood history than has been acknowledged. In chapter 11, we discuss their history and the daunting challenges they face today.

Morning in America and Continued Urban Decline

At the governmental level, the 1980s represented a fundamental change in course. While the erosion of government's role as a would-be solver of social problems had already begun, it took on a far more prominent ideologically charged role under Ronald Reagan. In his 1981 inaugural address Reagan delivered the famous line "Government is not the solution to our problem, government is the problem." Under the previous Carter administration, the erosion of government activism had taken on an apologetic, almost sub-rosa character. To the extent that HUD evinced concern with urban conditions and neighborhood decline during the

FIGURE 4.6. New Deal poster: Housing as a driver of change in social conditions

(Source: Library of Congress)

1970s, that came to an end. The Reagan administration's approach to urban policy reflected in *The President's National Urban Policy Report* of 1982 was that "urban America would improve and prosper only if the Reagan economic and federalism reforms succeeded. Thus, US urban policy, such as it is, exists only as derivative of these larger, more comprehensive domestic initiatives."[46] As Robert Beauregard writes, "through most of the 1980s the discourse on urban decline virtually disappeared. Dominant was revival, revitalization, renascence and rediscovery."[47]

Attention shifted from neighborhoods to downtowns and to a view of government as a facilitator for private investment rather than a force for social change. Intellectual ballast for that role was provided by Harvard political scientist Paul Peterson, who wrote in his influential 1981 book *City Limits* that "policies and programs can be said to be in the interest of cities whenever the policies or programs maintain or enhance the economic position, social prestige, or political power of the city, taken as a whole," and that those policies should be "limited to those few which can plausibly be shown to be conducive to the community's economic prosperity."[48]

Fueled by generous depreciation allowances, investment flowed into downtowns after the end of the 1981–1982 recession. Glass-walled office buildings, malls, and waterfront festival marketplaces mixing retail, entertainment, and recreation, inspired by the Rouse Corporation's successful projects in Boston and Baltimore, began to rise from the ground. Mayors, their cities still reeling from the fiscal shocks of the 1970s, became cheerleaders for developers rather than advocates for social and policy change.

The sight of gleaming new downtown towers and shopping malls obscured the fact that most of the nation's older cities were still losing population. Despite the rhetoric of revival in the media discourse paralleling Reagan's "morning in America" rhetoric, the overall trajectory of urban neighborhoods was still sharply downward, while early signs of decline were appearing in many of the suburbs that had been the promised land for so many only thirty years earlier. Despite the publicity given gentrification, a term that was popularized in the 1970s, it was vanishingly rare. Few neighborhoods that were already areas of concentrated poverty in the 1970s escaped poverty in the 1980s.

Crime and homicide rates increased during the 1980s—in some cities gradually and in others precipitously—in tandem with the crack epidemic. That increase was particularly great in Washington, D.C., as shown in figure 4.7, which also shows how significantly crime has dropped since the 1990s. Although crime increases affected entire cities, their effect was most palpable in high-poverty neighborhoods. As Patrick Sharkey, paraphrasing Elijah Anderson's classic study of street life in Philadelphia's ghetto, *Code of the Street*, wrote, "the dominant feature of public life in Philadelphia's poorest neighborhoods was neither homelessness nor drug abuse nor prostitution; it was violence."[49] And as Ta-Nehisi Coates described in his memoir of growing up in Baltimore, "when crack hit Baltimore, civilization fell."[50]

As Sharkey points out "much of what we know about urban poverty is based on a set of classic studies carried out between the early 1980s and the mid-1990s, when

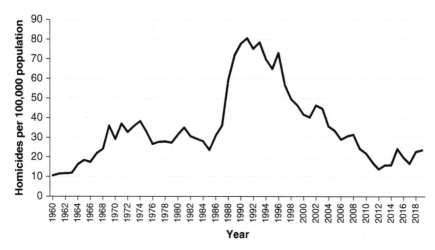

FIGURE 4.7.   Homicide rates in Washington, D.C., 1960–2019

(Authors' work based on Federal Bureau of Investigation Uniform Crime Reports data)

violence was extremely high or rising quickly."[51] Coupled with the inevitable media attention, that violent era still conditions our perception of urban reality, although that reality has changed much for the better despite worrisome evidence of some reversal since the onset of the COVID-19 pandemic.[52] The years of violence weakened the social networks that had previously existed in many low-income communities, further undermining Black families already destabilized by poverty. This led to stresses in many Black middle-class neighborhoods, rendering those neighborhoods less able to withstand the destructive pressures that would arise after 2000.

During the 1990s many things began to improve. The crack epidemic waned and with it much of the violence. The community development movement grew along with a new paradigm for neighborhood change, as we discuss in the next part of this chapter. More significantly, economic growth coupled with the expansion of the Earned Income Tax Credit raised the incomes of millions of lower-income families, while in many of America's hardest-hit cities the income gap between white and Black households narrowed and poverty declined.

The urban renascence media euphoria of the early 1980s had given way by the 1990s to a more measured perspective, and the growing economic polarization and social disparities of the cities had begun to gain recognition. As the millennium neared, moreover, the beginnings of an actual "return to the city" that had been predicted since the early 1970s were becoming visible, harbingers of large-scale change that would become apparent in the next decade with powerful effects in many urban neighborhoods. The 1990s ended on a note of cautious optimism for the future of America's older cities and their neighborhoods.

The Rise of a New Community Development System

Although federal funds were slashed under Reagan, CDCs continued to be established. The 1994 survey found that an additional 263 CDCs formed during the 1980s, more than doubling the total around the United States.[53] More important than the absolute number of CDCs, though, was the emergence of a new multilayered community development support system. By the end of the 1980s, a collection of programs and initiatives had gelled into a new policy paradigm for neighborhood intervention, replacing the federally driven paradigm of the 1960s and 1970s. Instead of programs run by public agencies, the new policy paradigm created tools administered by different agencies that could be combined with each other by local actors in multiple ways.[54] Three notable changes characterized the new neighborhood strategy framework: networked nonprofitization, privatization, and devolution. While this framework has shown its ability to tailor activities to local conditions and leverage private investment, its strengths come with many often-overlooked weaknesses. We will discuss this framework here and then pick up the discussion of CDCs and their role in neighborhood change later in chapter 9.

Networked Nonprofitization

Through the 1970s, neighborhood-based activities in American cities received direct government support that went to entities such as community action agencies created for the express purpose of receiving and spending federal funds and to other organizations, including many citywide or regional social service providers. The CDC, an independent neighborhood-based entity, was a newcomer to the neighborhood scene.

The 1980s saw CDCs not only take on the central role in neighborhood change but also become embedded in a national network, including the National Congress for Community Economic Development trade association and national and regional support organizations known as intermediaries. Given the simultaneous trends toward privatization and devolution, the intermediaries played and continue to play a key role in connecting community development organizations to one another and to critical resources while providing technical assistance and acting to varying degrees as a voice for community development organizations on the national scene.

The three principal national intermediaries are the Local Initiatives Support Corporation (LISC), Enterprise Community Partners, and NeighborWorks America. The first two, notably, were top-down initiatives driven by foundations and corporations. LISC was created in 1979 under the aegis of the Ford Foundation, while Enterprise Community Partners was established in 1982 by James Rouse, a wealthy shopping center developer "to see that all low-income people have the opportunity for affordable housing and to move up and out of poverty."[55] NeighborWorks, by contrast, grew from local efforts, reflecting how community development has often advanced by sharing successful local efforts across the nation. The story of how it emerged is instructive.

Dorothy Richardson was a homeowner in Pittsburgh's Central North Side neighborhood. In the mid-1960s, concerned about what she saw as her neighborhood's decline, she began organizing her neighbors to put pressure on City Hall and on the city's banks, which had largely written off her neighborhood. In 1968 she and her neighbors formed Neighborhood Housing Services (NHS) of Pittsburgh, raising $750,000 in grants, persuading local lenders to contribute to a loan fund for property improvements, and lobbying the city to enforce housing codes and improve neighborhood schools and parks. As described in a 1976 *New York Times* article, the NHS's approach was "to contain and reverse neighborhood blight by throwing every known preservationist remedy into a small area on the edge of spreading deterioration."[56]

The model that Richardson created through trial and error quickly caught on. In 1970 the Federal Home Loan Bank Board sponsored the Neighborhood Reinvestment Task Force, which promoted the NHS model of neighborhood-government-bank partnerships nationally. By 1975 there were forty-five NHS partnerships across the country, and in 1978 Congress created the Neighborhood Reinvestment Corporation, which became NeighborWorks in 2005, to support the burgeoning NHS network.

Intermediaries such as NeighborWorks work through local partnerships. LISC has established offices in thirty-five cities, where it supports local community development initiatives. NeighborWorks has 240 CDC partners in its NeighborWorks Network. Regional or local intermediaries also exist, of which one of the most notable is Cleveland Neighborhood Progress, funded by two major local foundations to complement the efforts of the national intermediaries. The central role of intermediaries reflects the pressures of the second element, privatization, in the neighborhood policy framework.

Privatization

Neighborhood policy prior to 1980 was largely a function of federal grant programs. To be sure foundations played a role, most notably the Ford Foundation's 1961 Gray Areas program, which piloted many of the programs that became the war on poverty. After 1980, however, the balance shifted to private actors.

In some respects, this was the culmination of a long-term trend. Since the mid-1960s the public housing program had been de-emphasized in favor of programs through which low-income housing was built by for-profit or nonprofit developers, including the 1974 Section 8 program under which low-income tenants received vouchers to live in privately owned rental housing. Still, all these programs were based on funds appropriated by Congress and administered by the federal government.

A major shift toward the privatization of public resources was the increasing substitution of tax incentives for direct grants, reflected most visibly in the Low-Income Housing Tax Credit (LIHTC) program, the single most important vehicle for developing affordable rental housing in the United States since its enactment in 1986. The LIHTC finances roughly 100,000 housing units each year, for a total of 3.23 million units by 2018.[57] The LIHTC program raises private equity for the construction or rehabilitation of low-income rental housing by providing credits to wealthy investors and large corporations, which they can use to offset their federal tax obligations. The investors receive tax credits for ten years, while the housing must be occupied by low-income households for fifteen years.[58]

While LIHTC is a tool for building affordable housing rather than a neighborhood revitalization strategy, it has become widely used by CDCs in part because the program allows them to collect generous developer fees they can use to fund other operations. Their dependency on the program, however, has problematic implications. The design of the LIHTC program incentivizes siting developments in high-poverty neighborhoods, often areas with a surplus of private housing renting at levels similar to or even below the rents in LIHTC housing, while disincentivizing mixed-income developments.

From an institutional perspective, LIHTC is radically different from the traditional federal grant program. The LIHTC program exists not as an appropriation but instead as language in the Internal Revenue Code. Responsibility for allocating the credits is delegated to state housing agencies, which received allocations based on their state's population. Once a developer has received an allocation for a project from the state, the developer must find an investor to buy the credits by investing equity in the project. Since the equity that can be raised through sale of the credits is often not enough to cover the full cost, the developer may also have to raise additional grant or loan funds from lenders, foundations, or state and local governments. Perhaps the most important role of both LISC and Enterprise Community Partners as intermediaries has been that of matchmakers between nonprofit developers and large corporate buyers of LIHTC tax credits.

Federal tax credit programs have proliferated, as can be seen in table 4.3. All of these programs have two clear downsides. First, they are inherently less efficient. They cost more than direct grants in terms of federal treasury outlays rela-

TABLE 4.3 Federal tax credit programs affecting urban neighborhoods

FEDERAL TAX CREDIT	YEAR ESTABLISHED	FEDERAL AGENCY RESPONSIBLE	ELIGIBILITY	ADMINISTERING AGENCY
Historic preservation	1977	Department of the Interior	Certified historic properties	Department of the Interior and state historic preservation offices
Low-income housing	1986	Internal Revenue Service	Low-income housing projects	State housing finance agencies
Brownfields	1997	Environmental Protection Agency	Environmentally contaminated sites	US Environmental Protection Agency
New Markets	2000	Department of the Treasury	Economic development projects in distressed areas	Community development entities certified by the US Treasury
Opportunity zone	2017	Internal Revenue Service	Designated low-income census tracts	None

tive to the amount of funds that go to the housing project or neighborhood improvement activity, since they must provide private investors with enough profit to entice them to participate. Second, they are more complex and challenging to implement than grant programs. As a result, projects financed with tax credits, in addition to investor profits, are burdened with large fees to the lawyers, accountants, and consultants who assemble the complex deals, along with the intermediaries themselves. Housing advocate Chester Hartman described these programs as "feeding the sparrows by feeding the horses."[59] In the final analysis, the best argument that can be made in favor of tax credits over grant appropriations is that they tend to shelter the program from the annual appropriation process, thus keeping the program going despite unfavorable shifts in political winds. While that is true enough and important to the program's beneficiaries, it is questionable as a basis for public policy.

Until recently, however, each tax credit program was targeted to a specific and beneficial social or economic objective, and one can argue that despite weaknesses in these programs, their overall effect has generally been positive. One cannot say that of the most recent tax credit, the Opportunity Zone program, which was part of the Federal Tax Cuts and Jobs Act of 2017. Individuals and firms that invest in projects in Qualified Opportunity Zones, which are largely low-income areas but include some contiguous non–low-income areas, receive significant breaks on capital gains taxes, substantially increasing the return on their investment.[60]

The attractiveness of the Opportunity Zone program to investors is not in doubt. The benefit to the affected neighborhood is more questionable. While almost a third of the residents of opportunity zones are below the poverty level, many of the zones have clearly been designated by the states as places where significant investment opportunities exist and where the presence of low-income people is at most incidental, as in one zone in the heart of downtown Portland, Oregon, and an oceanfront zone in West Palm Beach, Florida, home to a superyacht marina.[61] Moreover, there is no requirement in the law that the investment benefit low-income households; indeed, the law does not even require public reporting of Opportunity Zone investments. A program designed to direct investment into low-income communities with no accountability and no provisions to ensure that the communities and their residents get any benefit from the investment is hardly likely to improve distressed neighborhoods or their residents.

Devolution

Finally, policymaking toward neighborhoods has also been decentralized. Devolution, the transfer of public-sector decision making from the federal government to states and localities, has become the norm. Categorical or project grants have been largely replaced by block grants, such as the Community Development Block Grant and HOME Partnerships, which cities receive based on a formula and which give local government discretion over how the funds are used within the broad parameters of federal law. While several grant programs were created by the Clinton administration, including Empowerment Zones and Homeownership Zones, they were one-shot programs rather than ongoing commitments. The only exception was HOPE VI, a program designed to dismantle distressed public housing projects and replace them with privately developed and operated mixed-income housing.

An argument can be made that the federal pullback has motivated state and local governments to increase their role. There is some truth to this. As federal funds have declined, state and local spending has increased, although it is hard to tell by how much since published data conflates funds originating with state and local government with federal pass-through funds. Some states have enacted low-income housing and historic tax credit programs designed to piggyback on the respective federal programs. State and local housing trust funds have also proliferated, collectively generating almost a billion dollars from dedicated sources of revenue in 2016.[62] Although seemingly a large amount, in terms of the total demands on those trust funds it is barely more than trivial.

All three trends reflect the rightward shift in national politics and the demands of a neoliberal economic model. Block grants are popular with local elected officials of all political stripes. As David Erickson put it, "giving local communities the tools to help themselves is wildly popular with liberals and conservatives alike."[63] Reflecting on the great variety of tax credit projects around the nation, Erickson concluded that "the decentralized program showed how it could be all things to all people, which helps explain why so many members of Congress—across the political spectrum, from large and small cities—found it an easy program to defend and promote."[64] Nonprofitization also has distinct political advantages, as conservatives can support CDCs as examples of do-it-yourself local self-reliance preferable to government handouts.

Clearly, the new community development policy system has political advantages. But is it good policy? In many respects, the community development field has converted a political necessity into a policy virtue. Its advocates argue that the new decentralized tool-based policy system is more flexible and adaptive than any top-down policy process could ever be. By moving from government to "governance" (voluntary collaboration), they argue, the new system can meld the advantages of the public, private, and nonprofit sectors while ensuring equity through federal regulations requiring that programs target low-income households and disadvantaged neighborhoods. The private sector fosters efficiency and consumer responsiveness, while the nonprofit sector brings civic engagement and local knowledge, ensuring that projects reflect neighborhood needs and concerns. The transition to the new paradigm has been compared to the shift from routinized manufacturing to flexible specialization.[65] Instead of a cookie-cutter, mass-

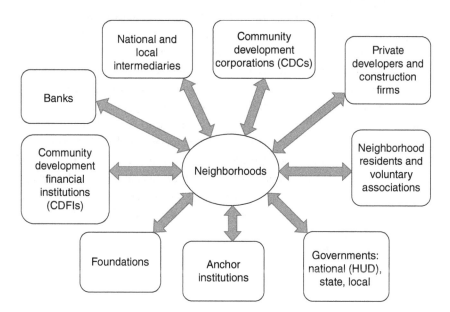

FIGURE 4.8. Participants in the community development system

production approach to housing, as in the large public housing projects of the 1950s and 1960s, the new system emphasizes customized production adapted to the specific needs of each community.

This decentralized tool-based system, which has been called network governance, requires coordinating a dizzying array of actors (figure 4.8). It raises the collective action problem: that is, how to voluntarily gain the cooperation of multiple self-interested actors to achieve a common objective. In the absence of governmental coercion, advocates argue that the collective action problem can be solved by the accumulation of social capital, or trust.[66] As each project brings together different actors who work together to achieve success, over time successful collaboration builds greater trust and enhanced collaboration across the entire system. Shared norms about what goals should be pursued and how the work should be done emerge, while social capital constrains self-regarding behavior and channels action in public-regarding directions.

That is an idealized vision, but the tool-based system of network governance does have strengths. If, as we argue, neighborhoods can only be understood in the context of local and regional conditions, then decentralization of decision making is a rational strategy. Network governance offers the promise of treating neighborhoods as dynamic, multifaceted systems. Conceptually, it is difficult to argue against local community development systems based on collaboration and trust. Of course, collaboration and trust are often harder to achieve and sustain in practice than in principle.

Faith in the virtues of a decentralized tool-based housing and community development system has become widespread, often framed in contrast to top-down bureaucratic inflexible government programs, which are frequently caricatured as the product of insensitive bureaucracies forcing unwelcome programs down the throats of resisting communities. But network governance has significant weaknesses. Above all, it has added a new layer of inequality. Cities and neighborhoods with sophisticated local community development networks are in a strong position to take advantage of the array of policy tools, while cities and neighborhoods lacking those networks, which is more often true of smaller cities and poor neighborhoods, are generally left out in the cold. In chapter 9 we revisit CDCs along with other key agents of neighborhood change in today's cities, exploring how well the system actually works for inhabitants.

THE POLARIZATION OF THE AMERICAN NEIGHBORHOOD, 1990–2020

As with any far-reaching economic or demographic change, no one can pin down exactly when and where it began, but at some point during the 1990s, something important started to change in American cities. Despite having been all but given up for dead since the 1960s and 1970s, cities came back to life, a couple at first, a few more after the arrival of the new millennium, and still more after the end of the Great Recession. Without understanding that change, it would be impossible to understand the state of neighborhoods in America today.[1] While we will drill down into many of the subjects covered in this chapter later, this chapter will provide an overview and context for much of the rest of this book.

By the 1990s, the United States was looking very different from what it had looked like in the 1950s. Twenty-five years after the immigration reforms of 1965, the wave of immigration that followed was making the United States an increasingly diverse country, with large and growing Asian and Latinx populations. New immigrant neighborhoods of Bangladeshis in Detroit, Salvadorans in Los Angeles, and Cambodians in Philadelphia had begun to emerge.

Birth rates had declined, and families were smaller. In the 1950s America was a land of young, married, child-raising couples. Over the following decades as the share of families raising children dropped, the number of single people, both young and old, grew. There were fewer children and more older people. The nation's economic distribution shifted, leading to what has been called the hollowing out of the middle class. The young married couples of the 1950s were part of a large middle class that encompassed not only a growing professional and managerial class but also most of the large unionized blue-collar industrial workforce.

By the 1990s that middle class was shrinking, a decline that has continued to this day. Both of these shifts have had powerful implications for American neighborhoods, driving revival in some but undermining long-standing vitality in others.

Although racism remained a powerful barrier, African Americans were far more dispersed across cities and metropolitan areas than before. While disproportionate numbers still lived in segregated areas of concentrated poverty, those depopulated areas were a far cry from the once-vibrant ghettos such as Chicago's Bronzeville and Detroit's Black Bottom. More African Americans lived in the suburbs, and racially mixed neighborhoods were no longer the rarities they had been in the 1960s and 1970s.

The economic underpinnings of America's cities were radically different from those of the 1950s. While Americans still made things, they made fewer and fewer things in the nation's older cities. The industrial behemoths that had dominated cities such as Pittsburgh and Cleveland, driving their economies and employing most of their residents, were gone, leaving vacant hulks to remind people of what once had been. By the end of the century a new economy, variously described as a knowledge economy, a creative economy, or a service economy, rooted in the growth of universities and medical centers, the so-called eds and meds sector, had begun to rise in its place. By the mid-2010s, Pittsburgh boasted more jobs in education and health care than it had in factory jobs fifty years earlier. The well-paying working-class jobs that were lost when the factories closed, though, were gone forever.

The growth of the new urban economy was paralleled by another shift that has been dubbed the "march of the millennials."[2] In a trend that began in the 1990s but accelerated after the start of the millennium, young people began to flock to the nation's older cities, not all young people but specifically members of the one-third of their generation with four-year college degrees. While during the 1990s they moved mainly to coastal cities such as Boston, New York, San Francisco, and Washington, D.C., after 2000 many started to move to formerly industrial cities of the East and the Midwest such as Baltimore, Pittsburgh, and St. Louis, homes to major universities and research-oriented medical centers. In Philadelphia, the number of people ages twenty-five to thirty-four with a BA or higher degree more than doubled between 2000 and 2016, reversing that city's long-term population decline. By 2019, nearly one out of four Washington, D.C., adult residents were young people between the ages of twenty-five and thirty-four with a BA or higher degree.

While much of the millennial migration was driven by people seeking the diverse mixed-use environments that were emerging in downtowns and in gentrifying neighborhoods, two other factors were critical. First, the growth of the eds and meds economy and its spin-offs meant that growing numbers of suitable jobs for college graduates were available in the same cities that offered the settings they sought; and second, the decline in urban crime and violence that began in the 1990s increased the appeal of urban areas as a place to live and even as a place to raise a family for a growing number of households. Washington, D.C., went from being the so-called murder capital of the United States in the early 1990s to a glittering playground for millennials in barely two decades.

While the much-celebrated "back to the city" movement was real, it was limited. Many young well-educated people were moving to the cities, but most others were not. Outside a small number of magnet cities such as San Francisco and Washington, D.C., the effects of the new in-migration tended to be felt only in small parts of the city, mostly in downtowns and a few adjacent neighborhoods, along with neighborhoods bordering amenity-rich areas such as Baltimore's Inner Harbor or near the city's major universities and medical centers. Urban downtowns, where few if any people had lived since the late nineteenth century, were becoming upscale residential neighborhoods, epicenters of the youthful migration to the cities. From downtown Detroit to Chicago's Loop, developers were converting empty 1920s office buildings into apartments, along with new restaurants, fitness centers, and other facilities catering to the affluent young.

Not only were many other parts of the same cities seeing little or no revival, but many urban neighborhoods were actually declining, often more so than during preceding decades. The cities were becoming increasingly polarized places, and the onetime working-class and middle-class neighborhoods of earlier years, many of which had survived decades of urban decline, were increasingly endangered. African American communities were most at risk, as many once-solid Black working- and middle-class neighborhoods stumbled, undermined by the aging of the generation that created those neighborhoods in the 1960s and 1970s, the wave of subprime mortgages and foreclosures, and the decision of growing numbers of young Black families to seek suburban alternatives.

The urban revival was often exaggerated and overhyped. Contrary to some urbanists' predictions, the suburbs showed no signs of withering away. Their fundamental fallacy was to see the relationship between urban revival and suburban growth as a zero-sum proposition rather than recognize that two distinct processes were taking place side by side. Even as the cities drew new affluent residents and billions in investment, suburbs continued to grow, sprawling farther and farther away from the center.

Although almost every age group other than the millennial generation was still showing net outward movement from central cities, suburban sprawl was furthered less by direct urban out-migration and more by outward movement from within the suburban ring. Cleveland State's Tom Bier, in his research on home buyers in northeastern Ohio in the 1980s and 1990, was struck by "the extent of movement *up* in price to a newer, larger house, and the extent of movement *outward* by suburban residents, and not just outward but *from the suburb where they had been living.*"[3]

The upward and outward dynamic of intersuburban migration led to shifts that paralleled those taking place in the central cities: a growing divergence of rich and poor places and a hollowing out of the middle. Many suburbs prospered, including many of the original nineteenth-century railroad suburbs, with their commuter trains to the central city and their compact, walkable downtowns. New Jersey railroad suburbs of New York City such as Montclair and Morristown drew affluent in-migrants as upscale restaurants and specialty stores opened in their downtowns and modest one- and two-story structures were replaced by upscale apartment buildings.

Other suburbs, however, were showing strain, particularly many of those built in the first wave of suburbanization after World War II. By the mid-1990s, young families who had settled in inner-ring suburbs with such exuberance in the 1940s and 1950s had either moved on to bigger houses elsewhere or begun to succumb to the challenges of age. Their homes were showing their age too and were far less appealing to new middle-class families than they had once been to their parents or grandparents.

Many inner-ring suburbs of America's reviving cities began to turn into what might be called a secondary poverty belt, such as north St. Louis County outside the city of St. Louis and southern Cook County outside Chicago, a subject we discuss in further detail in chapter 13. Park Forest, a Cook County suburb profiled in William H. Whyte's classic *The Organization Man* as the archetypal dynamic neighborhood-focused middle-class community of the 1950s, is struggling today.[4] As the town's mayor observed in 2014, "few would have envisioned the day in Park Forest when one of its churches would operate a food pantry that feeds approximately 350 local families per week[,] . . . and who would have believed that one day it would be necessary for Habitat for Humanity to renovate Park Forest homes that had gone into foreclosure?"[5]

The middle has not disappeared. America's suburbs still contain many good yet unpretentious neighborhoods occupied by people with middling incomes, but they are fewer, and many are vulnerable to a future recession, just as many proved vulnerable during the foreclosure crisis and recession of 2007–2009. We will discuss those events, which were a watershed for hundreds of urban and suburban neighborhoods, later in this chapter.

The early suburbs contained fairly coherent neighborhoods. Indeed, a 1978 study found that urban and suburban residents held remarkably consistent perceptions of their neighborhoods as existing within defined spatial bounds.[6] One wonders, however, whether the same can be said for many of the sprawling ex-urban McMansion suburbs that have proliferated in the last few decades. This is not a trivial question. As we discussed earlier, areas in which the population density is so low as to all but preclude any significant informal interaction between neighbors might not be considered "neighborhoods." But given the pervasive nature of neighboring behavior, it is certainly possible that alternative forms of what one might call "quasi-neighboring" or less spatially defined behavior, perhaps organized around schools or local government issues or even through social media, may play an important social role in these communities. This would be a worthy study for some enterprising future ethnologist.

The partial reurbanization of America and the simultaneous revival of the cities and expansion of the suburbs triggered levels of neighborhood volatility not seen since the explosive "urban crisis" years of the 1960s and 1970s. Across urban America, neighborhoods were changing, often seemingly overnight. That process came to be symbolized by the term "gentrification," which since 2000 has become a widely used and equally widely contested shorthand for neighborhood change. Ironically, as we will discuss later, in many, perhaps most, American cities gentrification remains a relatively rare phenomenon compared to neighborhood decline and the relative immobility of concentrated poverty neighborhoods. Although perhaps seen as almost a synonym for neighborhood change, in reality it is but one of many forms that neighborhood change takes.

Patterns of Variation

The rise of the gentrification discourse raises an important issue. In the years preceding the 1930s Great Depression, nearly all cities were growing. From the 1950s through the 1980s, conversely, nearly all cities outside the Sunbelt were declining. Since the 1990s, though, different cities and their neighborhoods have followed wildly different trajectories. Since neighborhood trajectories are strongly driven by larger citywide and regional forces, it is worth spending some time talking about the divergent trends driving American cities.

In the 1960s and 1970s the "urban crisis" was an all but universal reality in the nation's older cities. When Jeanne Lowe wrote *Cities in a Race for Time* in 1967, she looked at five cities as paradigms of distress: New York, Philadelphia, New Haven, Pittsburgh, and Washington, D.C.[7] Today, Washington and New York are appropriately seen as belonging to a separate class of thriving magnet cities, while Pittsburgh has recently been widely hailed as a model of urban revival. Boston and Washington, two cities that lost much of their population during the late twentieth century and were seen at the time as deeply distressed,

are now growing at a rapid pace while drawing thousands of affluent newcomers. Similarly, it was in Seattle—today the archetype of the booming tech city—
where the notorious "will the last person . . ." billboard went up in 1971
(figure 5.1)). Things have changed since then. Since 2010, Seattle's population has
been growing by about thirteen thousand people per year (figure 5.2).

Pittsburgh has come close to stabilizing its population but has yet to begin
growing back, while the 2020 census found that Cleveland and St. Louis are still
seeing sustained population loss. Simple statistics about population growth or
decline, however, miss an important area of divergence among American cities.

A different lens through which the divergent trends of American cities and
their neighborhoods can be seen is that of the "influx of wealth," or the in- or
out-migration of more versus fewer affluent households. When we look at America's cities through this lens, we find that most fall into four distinct types, as
shown in figure 5.3. For purposes of this exercise, we have defined "wealth" and
"upper income" broadly as those households earning at least 125% of the national
median income, or roughly $72,000 per year or more in 2016. Key features of
the four city types can be summarized as follows:

- Sunbelt cities, such as Phoenix, Dallas, Fresno, and Las Vegas, are seeing
  net in-migration across all income levels, but most in-migrants are lower-
  and middle-income households, reflecting both the generally lower wage
  levels of these cities' job base and the relative affordability of their housing
  stock. Between 2000 and 2016, Dallas added 55,000 low to middle-income
  households but fewer than 6,000 upper-income households.
- Magnet cities, such as Seattle, San Francisco, Boston, and Washington,
  D.C., are seeing large-scale in-migration of upper-income households
  coupled with smaller net out-migration of low- and middle-income
  households, reflecting the rapid growth of well-paying jobs in those
  cities as well as the high cost of housing, making it increasingly difficult
  for lower-income households to remain in the city. From 2000 to 2016,
  Washington, D.C., added 47,500 affluent households and Seattle nearly
  64,000.
- Reviving legacy cities, such as Baltimore, Pittsburgh, and Philadelphia,
  are seeing small net in-migration of upper-income households but equal
  or greater out-migration of low- and middle-income households. While
  the growth in affluent households reflects the strength of the knowledge
  economy in these cities along with a few areas that offer the amenities
  attractive to young professionals, the outflow of less affluent households
  is largely a response to continued neighborhood decline rather than

FIGURE 5.1. Seattle then and now. The famous Seattle "Turn out the lights" sign, 1971.

(Photograph courtesy of Greg Gilbert/The Seattle Times)

FIGURE 5.2. Seattle today.

(Photograph by Google Earth © Google 2022)

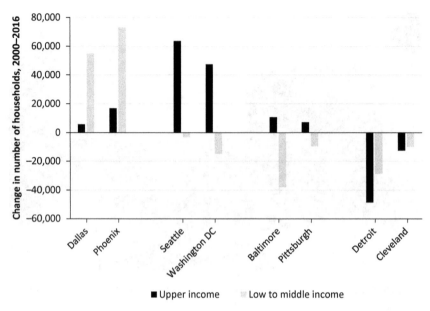

FIGURE 5.3. Who's moving in, who's leaving: Net household change by income in American cities, 2000 to 2016

(Authors' work based on decennial census and American Community Survey data)

price pressures or gentrification and reflects the availability of affordable suburban alternatives.

○ Struggling legacy cities, including Detroit, Cleveland, and smaller cities such as Akron and Dayton, have a net outflow of households at all income levels, reflecting the continued economic weakness of these cities as well as the many affordable suburban alternatives. Between 2000 and 2016 Detroit lost 48,500 affluent households, over half of all affluent households in the city in 2000. The rate of decline in Detroit's upper-income population has slowed more recently, suggesting that a reversal of that decline might be in the offing.

These trends powerfully affect neighborhood trajectories. While gentrification in its most common meaning of more affluent households moving into lower-income neighborhoods is a limited phenomenon in many Sunbelt cities, the steady influx of middle-income families fosters greater neighborhood stability than in many cities elsewhere in the United States. In contrast to older cities, though, where neighborhood identities were often fostered by resident identity or traditional boundaries, Sunbelt neighborhoods are often the product of developers' decisions and seemingly arbitrary subdivision boundaries but for all that are no less real. Where subdivisions are bordered by open-space areas—nonresidential areas such as shopping malls or industrial parks—or arterial roads, those features often create clearly defined neighborhood boundaries tending to promote neighborhood identification, as can be seen in figure 5.4 from Garland, Texas, a suburb of Dallas. The City of Garland actively promotes neighborhood identity and engagement through many programs and initiatives.[8]

In magnet cities such as Seattle and Washington, D.C., however, gentrification is a powerful driver of neighborhood change. The sheer number of affluent households seeking to live in these cities and the inability of developers to keep up with demand mean that large parts of the city are under intense demand pressure. Rising house prices, which spill over even to distressed areas where few affluent in-migrants are moving, put increasing pressure on lower-income households throughout the city.

By contrast, gentrification in cities such as Baltimore and St. Louis affects only a handful of the city's neighborhoods. In Baltimore those neighborhoods cluster in the shadow of downtown, around Johns Hopkins University, or near the city's Inner Harbor. Meanwhile, the decline of once-vital working-class neighborhoods and the stagnation of areas of concentrated poverty affect far more of the city and in their separate ways are far more destructive of their residents' hopes of living in a good neighborhood than gentrification, which arguably provides some benefits to some if not all long-term residents.

The net out-migration of affluent households from Detroit and Cleveland does not mean that no gentrification is taking place in these cities; net out-migration, after all, does not mean that there is no in-migration, only that those leaving exceed those moving in. Detroit's downtown is changing as 1920s office towers are repurposed and restored to become home to an affluent young population, as is Midtown around the Detroit Medical Center and Wayne State University, while more modest change is visible in a handful of small residential enclaves such as Corktown. But the influx has been modest, covering at most 5 percent of the city's land area, compared to the continued outflow from the city's other residential neighborhoods.

It is a safe bet that if one asked a typical educated layperson today what the major form of neighborhood change in American cities has been over the past couple of decades, the answer would almost certainly be "gentrification." But that answer would be wrong. The reality was portrayed by a 2019 study of neighborhood change from 2000 to 2016 by a University of Minnesota research team. Some of their findings are worth highlighting:

- The most common form of American neighborhood change, by far, is poverty concentration. About 36.5 million residents live in a tract that has undergone low-income concentration since 2000.

FIGURE 5.4. Neighborhood borders in Garland, Texas

(Overlay by Bill Nelson on Google Earth base map © 2022 Google)

- Low-income residents are invariably exposed to neighborhood decline more than gentrification. As of 2016, there was no metropolitan region in the nation where a low-income person was more likely to live in an economically expanding neighborhood than an economically declining neighborhood.
- On net, far fewer low-income residents are affected by displacement than concentration. Since 2000, the low-income population of economically expanding areas has fallen by 464,000, while the low-income population of economically declining areas has grown by 5,369,000.
- Nonwhite residents are far more likely to live in economically declining areas. In 2016, nearly 35 percent of black residents lived in economically declining areas, while 9 percent lived in economically expanding areas.[9]

Joe Cortright of the City Observatory, who looked at the long-term trend from 1970 to 2010, wrote that "while media attention often focuses on those few places that are witnessing a transformation, there are two more potent and less mentioned storylines. The first is the persistence of chronic poverty. . . . *The second is the spread of concentrated poverty: three times as many urban neighborhoods have poverty rates exceeding 30 percent as was true in 1970* and the number of poor people living in these neighborhoods has doubled."[10]

What is going on? As Cortright suggests, two separate things. First, poor neighborhoods—those areas where poverty has been highly concentrated since the 1970s or 1980s—are stuck in place. They rarely move out of poverty, whether through gentrification, self-help, or any other mechanism. And the poorer they are, the less likely they are to see any change. Second, many neighborhoods that were not poor a few decades ago or even ten years ago have become poor neighborhoods.

St. Louis fits this picture closely. In 1970, only 16 out of 106 census tracts in St. Louis were concentrated poverty areas where 30 percent or more of their residents had incomes below the national poverty level. By 2017 there were 44 out of 106, almost three times as many. Some of this change took place in the 1970s and 1980s, years of devastating urban decline. But among low-poverty (under 20 percent poverty rate) neighborhoods in St. Louis in 1970 that became high-poverty (over 30 percent) neighborhoods by 2017, almost half (9 of 20) did not become high-poverty neighborhoods until after 2000, after the urban revival was well under way.

Even more distressing, urban middle-income neighborhoods that have become high-poverty neighborhoods since 2000 are disproportionately African

American. Chicago's South Shore is a case in point. While to the casual observer it still looks like a pleasant collection of classic Chicago bungalows and medium-size apartment buildings, by 2017 over one-third of the population lived below the poverty level, and 20 percent of the housing units were vacant. That story was repeated not only across Chicago but also in Detroit, Cleveland, and any of the other cities where African American families had moved into middle-class neighborhoods vacated by their white residents in the 1960s and 1970s, sustaining them over the following few decades.

Meanwhile, the few neighborhoods in these cities that gentrified were most often white or racially mixed urban working-class neighborhoods. Indeed, in a reality at odds with the popular narrative, the neighborhoods most likely to gentrify, particularly in cities where the influx of wealth is still modest, are neither Black nor severely distressed but instead are predominantly white or racially mixed, still intact working-class neighborhoods. We looked at the income trajectories of Chicago's middle-income neighborhoods between 2000 and 2017 by their racial configuration (figure 5.5).[11] While upward movement into a higher income range is not necessarily evidence of gentrification, it is a precondition of gentrification. The data is telling. Most predominantly white neighborhoods stayed the same or moved up, while most predominantly Black neighborhoods moved down. We will explore this further in chapter 10.

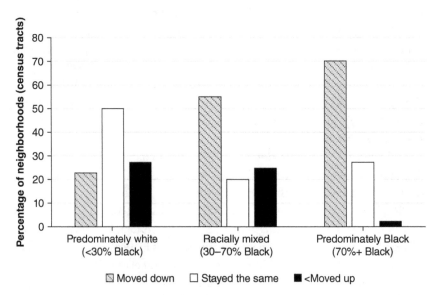

FIGURE 5.5. Trajectories of middle-income neighborhoods in Chicago by racial configuration, 2000 to 2017

(Authors' work based on decennial census and American Community Survey data)

The decline of so many urban neighborhoods since the 1990s reflects many different factors. Demographic trends were working against them. The houses in these neighborhoods were aging, as were many of their owners. The continuing fiscal problems of older cities were leading to either higher taxes, declining public services, or both. For younger would-be home buyers the suburbs beckoned, with their promise of newer houses, better schools, safer streets, and lower taxes.

But in addition to what may be called systemic problems, many urban neighborhoods were hit hard by the foreclosure crisis of 2006 and 2007 and the Great Recession that followed in its wake. We discuss that crisis and its effects below, along with some thoughts on the COVID-19 pandemic that was raging as this was being written, and whether it may have similarly destabilizing neighborhood effects.

The Foreclosure Crisis, the Great Recession, and the COVID-19 Pandemic

During the first years of the twenty-first century it appeared to many observers that housing markets in older cities had turned a critical corner. Millennials were moving into reviving neighborhoods and downtowns, more and more people were buying homes, and house prices, even in distressed neighborhoods, were rising to unprecedented levels. The trends in three New Jersey cities are shown in table 5.1. It was hard at first to understand what was going on. All three cities were and still are struggling. As racially and ethnically diverse, mostly working-class and lower-income cities, none were gentrifying by any reasonable definition at the time or since. Although all three were close to New York City, none was showing economic growth that might support house price increases of 15 percent to 20 percent per year. Observers could not understand what mysterious phenomenon had triggered this amazing change.

It turned out that it was not particularly mysterious. It was a classic real estate bubble, driven above all by the subprime lending boom that began in the late 1990s and blew up in the new millennium. Although the number of books that have been written on the subject would fill a large bookshelf, it is useful to summarize here.[12] The problem began with what many in the lending industry saw as a reasonable, even creative idea. Mortgage lending had always been based on a simple "either you qualify or you don't" model. There was one body of criteria, and if you met them you received what was sometimes called a "prime" mortgage. If you failed, you received no mortgage. As automated underwriting gradually replaced loan officers' judgment during the 1990s, a new idea emerged.

TABLE 5.1   Sales prices and mortgage volumes in New Jersey Cities, 2000–2006

	ELIZABETH, NEW JERSEY		NEWARK, NEW JERSEY		PATERSON, NEW JERSEY	
	MORTGAGES	SALES PRICE	MORTGAGES	SALES PRICE	MORTGAGES	SALES PRICE
2000	797	$141,000	1,358	$118,000	856	$128,000
2002	812	$167,000	1,580	$146,000	945	$161,000
2004	1,351	$270,000	2,439	$208,000	1,573	$235,000
2006	1,538	$375,000	3,208	$300,000	1,810	$340,000

Source: Home Mortgage Disclosure Act.

Rather than treat lending as a yes/no proposition and disqualifying subprime borrowers, why not provide those borrowers with mortgages but adjust the interest rate upward to reflect the higher risk they represented? That way, more people could become homeowners, and the increased business would bolster the financial sector.

In theory this might have worked if lenders had rigorously assessed risk and adjusted terms to reflect it properly. We say in theory because that assumes that the underwriting models were based on enough reliable data to match the increased risk of each subprime borrower with the right interest rate, a highly doubtful assumption. It was never really tried. Instead, at a time when vast amounts of money in the global financial markets were looking for profitable places to land, and with mortgage securitization passing the risks on to unsuspecting third parties, it turned into a lending frenzy best summed up in the famous line from one subprime lender: "If you had a pulse, we give you a loan. If you fog the mirror, we give you a loan."[13]

Lenders came up with increasingly exotic mortgage products, such as the so-called NINJA (no income, no job, no assets, no problem) loans and loans with "teaser rates," low discounted interest rates for the first two years, rapidly rising to untenable levels thereafter. With lenders indifferent to borrowers' incomes, property values, or the relationship between the two and seemingly willing to refinance any loan, a bubble emerged. This description is an oversimplification but captures the essence of the story. The ensuing bubble caused prices to sky-rocket in Newark, Elizabeth, and hundreds of other cities across the country.

The bubble burst starting around 2006. This led to the Great Recession, triggered by the meltdown in financial institutions including such storied names as Bear Stearns and Lehman Brothers. The results can be seen in the post-2006 trajectories of mortgage originations and sales prices in the same three cities, shown in figure 5.6 and 5.7. From 2006 to 2012, the number of home purchase mortgages in the three cities fell from nearly 6,600 to under 1,000. While mortgages have

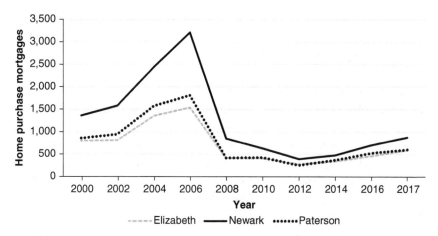

FIGURE 5.6. Home purchase mortgage originations in three New Jersey cities, 2000 to 2017

(Authors' work based on Home Mortgage Disclosure Act data)

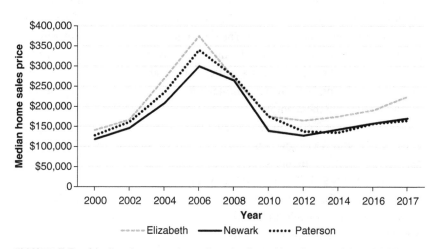

FIGURE 5.7. Median house sales prices in three New Jersey cities, 2000 to 2017

(Authors' work based on New Jersey State Treasury and Boxwood Means/PolicyMap data)

since recovered modestly, they are still less than one-third of what they were at the height of the bubble. House prices collapsed. By 2012, they were less than half of what they had been in 2006 and only slightly higher than in 2000, when the feeding frenzy began. Although they too have picked up slightly, as of 2020 they had not regained more than a small part of the postrecession loss.

What happened in Newark, Paterson, and Elizabeth happened across the United States. But not everywhere, of course. Booming cities such as Portland and Denver experienced little more than a hiccup before prices began to rebound, fueled by sustained economic growth and a homebuilding industry that consistently lagged behind demand. Today, the median house price in Portland is 50 percent above its bubble peak and in Denver more than double. House prices in affluent suburban areas around the country have not experienced comparable explosive growth but have generally recovered their losses. The same is largely true of many Sunbelt cities that were hit hard by the foreclosure crisis; the median Los Angeles house price hit $555,000 in 2006, dropped to $311,000 by 2011, rose to $644,000 in 2017, and was over $700,000 by 2020. Predictions that Las Vegas and Phoenix would turn into sunbaked counterparts of Detroit and Cleveland were soon proven wrong, monuments to the pitfalls of prediction and certain writers' premature rush to judgment.

The collapse of the real estate bubble devastated millions of homeowners, who lost their homes and with them the greater part of what little wealth they possessed. It also destabilized thousands of neighborhoods and communities, which lost homeowners and saw their housing stock fall into the hands of speculators or into vacancy and abandonment. The protracted mortgage foreclosure process in many states led to many houses being abandoned by their owners well before the lender had taken title, making matters worse, as did the customary lender practice of evicting both owners and tenants from houses on which they had foreclosed, leaving them empty.

While the federal government created the Neighborhood Stabilization Program, which gave local governments and nonprofit organizations funds to acquire, rehabilitate, or demolish foreclosed properties, it was a piecemeal effort that received only $7 billion spread thinly across the country over the four years of the program. This was a trivial amount in a nation where millions of properties were going into foreclosure. To put it in perspective, between 2009 and 2012 private investors and speculators invested roughly $25 billion in buying foreclosed properties in the Las Vegas area alone, an area containing less than 1 percent of the nation's population.[14] Research on the Neighborhood Stabilization Program strongly suggests that whatever individual properties may have benefited from the program, it had no significant effect in changing the trajectory of neighborhoods destabilized by foreclosures.[15]

Neighborhood effects varied both in the extent to which house prices, and real estate activity generally, crashed when the bubble burst and in the degree of recovery since then. Two types of neighborhood stand out as being hardest hit in both respects, as can be seen in table 5.2, which shows price change from

TABLE 5.2   Uneven Recovery in Chicagoland

			MEDIAN SALES PRICE			
COMMUNITY TYPE	CITY	NEIGHBORHOOD	2007	2011	2017	% CHANGE 2007–2017
Central city	Chicago	Citywide	$269,000	$140,000	$239,000	−11
	Upscale and gentrifying	Lincoln Park	$485,000	$348,000	$775,000	+60
		Wicker Park	$488,000	$420,000	$575,000	+18
	Middle-income and struggling	Chatham	$239,000	$55,000	$81,000	−66
		South Shore	$195,000	$25,500	$52,500	−73
Struggling South Cook suburbs	Harvey		$88,000	$14,650	$23,000	−74
	Markham		$112,000	$30,000	$36,000	−68
	Park Forest		$110,000	$39,750	$44,095	−60
Stable West and North suburbs	Bensonville		$255,000	$113,000	$220,000	−14
	Des Plaines		$277,000	$165,000	$237,000	−14
	Morton Grove		$366,000	$202,500	$295,000	−19

Source: Compiled using data from PolicyMap.

2007 to 2017 for a cluster of urban neighborhoods and suburban municipalities in the Chicago metropolitan area.

The region's stable, affluent suburbs west and north of the city and the city of Chicago on average saw significant decline after the onset of the crisis—typically 40 percent to 50 percent—but recovered strongly. By 2017, while prices were still below their bubble peaks, they were within 10–20 percent of those peaks. The city of Chicago trend, though, averages wildly divergent neighborhood outcomes.[16]

Upscale and gentrifying city neighborhoods saw less decline and much stronger recovery. Today, prices in both gentrifying Wicker Park and upscale Lincoln Park are well above their bubble peaks. Conversely, struggling middle neighborhoods on the city's south side saw greater declines and less recovery. Today, prices in both Chatham and South Shore are far below their peaks. Both are predominantly Black middle neighborhoods.

The picture is similar in the struggling suburbs of southern Cook County, much of which were built during the 1950s and populated during the era of white flight. Not only did their prices collapse when the bubble burst, but they also have seen virtually no price recovery since hitting rock bottom around 2011. If anything, their current market conditions are even more dire than those of the city's hard-hit middle neighborhoods.

This picture reflects two distinct but related patterns. The first is subprime lending. The targeting of communities of color by subprime lenders has been thoroughly documented.[17] With homeownership rates much lower than in white communities, those neighborhoods offered lenders a large pool of potential

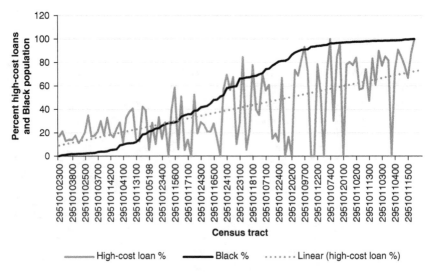

FIGURE 5.8.   Race and subprime lending in St. Louis, 2005

(Authors' work based on Home Mortgage Disclosure Act data and decennial census data)

buyers, many of whom were unsophisticated about homeownership and mortgages. Black communities were targeted through influential intermediaries. As
one Wells Fargo loan officer testified, the bank "had an emerging-markets unit
that specifically targeted Black churches, because it figured church leaders had
a lot of influence and could convince congregants to take out subprime loans."[18]
Figure 5.8 shows the relationship in 2005, at the height of the bubble, between
the racial composition of census tracts in St. Louis and the percentage of high-
cost home purchase mortgages, a proxy for subprime mortgages. Seventy-five
percent of all mortgages made in the city's predominantly Black middle census
tracts that year were high-cost loans, compared to 29 percent in the rest of the
city.

The neighborhoods that became ground zero for subprime lending were not
the most heavily disinvested ones but rather the ones that were one step up on
the economic ladder: predominantly Black middle neighborhoods inside central cities and lower-priced inner-ring suburban communities. Those neighborhoods also had many older homeowners with equity in their homes who were
convinced to refinance with subprime mortgages. These were often so-called
cash-out refinancings whereby the new mortgage was substantially larger than
the one being refinanced, providing the owner with a cash windfall. However
valuable that may have been to many financially strapped owners, it wiped out
their home equity, all but ensuring that when the bubble burst their position
would be untenable.

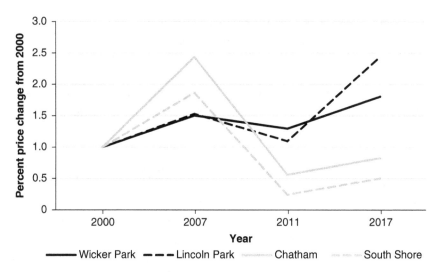

FIGURE 5.9. Percent change in house sales prices in four Chicago neighborhoods, 2000 to 2017

(Authors' work based on Zillow/PolicyMap data)

The result was rapid, unsustainable house price increases in those neighborhoods and subsequent collapse. Figure 5.9 compares the two Chicago Black middle neighborhood tracts with the two upscale/gentrifying neighborhood tracts from table 5.2 in terms of the percentage rise and fall in prices from 2000 to 2017. Prices rose faster in percentage terms in the middle neighborhoods but dropped much faster when the bubble burst. When that happened, both long-term owners and recent buyers found out almost overnight that their equity had disappeared and that they were "underwater," meaning that the value of their property was less than the amount of their mortgage. This, multiplied by the hundreds of similar neighborhoods around the United States, was the principal reason for the drastic erosion of Black wealth in recent years. Black homeowners in a single census tract of the hundred or so in St. Louis lost $35 million in home equity between 2008 and 2016.[19]

The end of the bubble set off a cascade of destabilizing effects. Millions of homes whose owners were unable to either make escalating payments or refinance went into foreclosure. As the banks took and resold the properties, the new buyers were most often absentee investors taking advantage of discount prices offered by the banks. From 2000 to 2018 the number of homeowners in the South Shore tract dropped by 28 percent and in the Chatham tract by 47 percent. While many of the new landlords were responsible owners, others capitalized on the depressed prices of the houses to milk them for a few years and then walk away. Vacant properties more than doubled in both areas between 2000 and 2018.

Meanwhile, many of the remaining homeowners left, losing confidence in the neighborhood and feeling helpless to undo the destruction taking place.

The continuing crisis of Black middle neighborhoods and of inner-ring suburbs is discussed further in chapters 11 and 13. Most of these neighborhoods have never fully recovered from the trauma of 2007–2009 despite a decade of steady national economic recovery since then. As we write this, though, in the midst of the COVID-19 pandemic, it inevitably raises questions about the potential effect of the pandemic on the future trajectory of urban and suburban neighborhoods after the immediate health effects have passed.

Obviously, it is impossible to know the answer at this point. The steps taken to manage the pandemic have led to a severe recession, and while the economy is recovering strongly, the nature of the recovery has prompted a dangerous level of inflation. Even if the recovery is sustained and inflation is brought under control, however, there is reason for substantial concern for those neighborhoods that were already struggling before the onset of the pandemic.

First, the restrictions imposed by the pandemic meant that thousands of businesses closed, putting their employees out of work. The effect was widespread unemployment; although it abated to some extent during the summer and fall of 2020, it was still high early in early 2021. While massive federal aid, culminating in the American Rescue Plan enacted early in 2021, has mitigated much of the hardship associated with mass unemployment, millions of families are still struggling.

The effect of economic hardship on people's housing conditions is straightforward. Many homeowners have been unable to make mortgage payments, while many renters, particularly low-income renters with little or no financial cushion, have been unable to pay their rent. As of mid-November 2020, the US Census Bureau reported that more than one out of five tenants, including more than one of four tenants earning under $25,000 and nearly one out of three Black tenants, were behind on their rent.[20] Recognizing the importance of keeping people in their homes during the pandemic, the federal government and most states imposed moratoria on evictions. The federal moratorium ended in mid-2021, while state moratoria ended early in 2022.

Rent arrearages place not only the tenant but also the landlord at risk. Many landlords, particularly the small mom-and-pop landlords who own most of the one- to four-family properties in lower-income areas, lack the cash reserves to absorb large amounts of rent arrears before having difficulty themselves making mortgage payments or paying property taxes. Federally funded emergency rental assistance programs will benefit many tenants and landlords, but at this point it is impossible to tell how many and how that will address a problem potentially affecting millions of tenants.

It is unknown how many tenants will eventually face eviction. Much will hinge on the extent to which cities and states will be able to quickly get the large amounts of federal funds into the hands of tenants and landlords. As of this writing at the beginning of 2022, the money is indeed getting into their hands, but it is becoming clear that it is far from enough. In the meantime, some tenants will probably work things out with their landlords. That number may be large, because some landlords may prefer to forgive rent arrears and retain a tenant who resumes rent payments rather than evict the tenant and face the uncertainty as well as the short-term loss of finding a new tenant. Landlord behavior is likely to vary with the strength of the local housing market; in a strong market, some may perceive the benefits of eviction as outweighing the risks, especially if it offers an opportunity to increase the rent. In the final analysis, however, widespread evictions and landlord insolvency, which can lead to deferred maintenance and potential abandonment, are potentially significant neighborhood destabilizing events over and above the personal hardships they create.

Foreclosures can have comparable effects, but for a variety of reasons they are not likely to be as great a problem, at least on a national level, as rental arrears. As with rental arrears, a variety of state and federal mortgage forbearance measures have been put into effect during the pandemic. As they end, however, a wave of foreclosures comparable to that of the foreclosure crisis appears unlikely. First, many lenders have already indicated that assuming the owner resumes payment, arrears will be added to the end of the loan term rather than coming due immediately. Second, in contrast to 2008 when millions of homes became underwater, housing prices have been rising steadily in most areas since 2020. As a result, most homeowners will have not only equity but also strong expectations of future appreciation, both of which they will want to preserve. Finally, most homeowners have deeper financial cushions than renters. Nationally, as of mid-November 2020, less than 1 percent of homeowners were in arrears on mortgage payments.[21] Despite this the risk of foreclosures exists particularly in neighborhoods such as the Black middle neighborhoods discussed earlier, where both homeowner equity and expectations may be lower.

The third issue is the extent to which the pandemic has and will continue to affect small businesses. Small businesses, particularly those serving lower-income communities and those owned by people of color, are highly vulnerable to business downturns. Many businesses have closed due to the pandemic, and the risk that many will not reopen or, if they do, will fail to recover and subsequently close is high. A Federal Reserve study estimated that two hundred thousand more businesses than usual closed during the first year of the pandemic, disproportionately concentrated in the restaurant, service, and retail sectors.[22] All of these not only employ large numbers of lower-wage workers but also represent a large share of the commercial activity in neighborhood-level commercial districts. Large numbers of permanent business closings in those areas will destabilize neighborhoods by reducing the incomes of many neighborhood residents and by undermining neighborhood anchor districts.

The effect of these factors will not fully become clear for some time. As we saw with the foreclosure crisis and the Great Recession, the long-term effects of the pandemic are likely to be uneven. Lower-income neighborhoods and their residents, especially areas with high shares of lower-income renters, however, may experience far worse effects than more affluent ones.

Closing Note

In later chapters we drill down into each of the different trends and dynamics we have touched upon in this chapter. But they raise many troubling concerns about the future of the American neighborhood. The first, as reflected in the effects of the foreclosure crisis, the Great Recession, and the COVID-19 pandemic, is the fragility of many neighborhoods and their susceptibility to exogenous shocks. Over the period covered in this chapter neighborhoods have suffered two such shocks, one of which is still ongoing as this is written, with profoundly destabilizing effects. Fragility is closely tied to economic conditions and race, the latter reflecting the extent to which the us housing market is racially divided, over and above its economic stratification.

Although the effect of the COVID-19 pandemic will gradually wane, it would be foolish to believe that there will be no future shocks. By their nature, shocks of this sort are what Nicholas Nassim Taleb has dubbed "black swans," events that cannot be predicted yet can be expected to happen periodically.[23] We cannot anticipate what the next black swan will be, whether it will be another pandemic, an economic crisis, an effect of climate change, or something that we cannot even imagine at this point. What we can anticipate is that shocks will happen and will affect the lives of people, their cities, and their neighborhoods in unpredictable ways. If both history and current experience are a guide, unless we fundamentally change the way we think about neighborhoods and what we do to help build their resilience, future crises will disproportionately harm lower-income people and their neighborhoods.

A second and even more fundamental question is whether the good neighborhood is becoming an elite good. The last two decades have seen an increasing pattern of neighborhood polarization, with elite gentrification existing side by side with increased concentrated poverty and the decline of middle neighborhoods. We are not suggesting that the decent yet unpretentious working-class or middle-class neighborhoods that formed such a central part of the American physical and social environment a few generations ago no longer exist. They do, but the evidence suggests that they are fewer than they once were, particularly in the urban areas where they were once the norm.

As millions of well-paying blue-collar jobs have been lost and economic inequality has grown, the middle class has shrunk. The neighborhood effects of that hollowing out have been exacerbated by the process of "economic sorting" described by Bischoff and Reardon in which neighborhoods are becoming increasingly homogenous economically, with more rich neighborhoods, more poor ones, and fewer in the middle.[24] Both trends have eaten away at the universe of middle-income good neighborhoods. In older Rust Belt cities such as Chicago, the number of middle-income neighborhoods dropped by over one-third from 2000 to 2017. Even in Phoenix, which has seen a steady influx of middle-income households, the number of middle-income census tracts dropped by 10 percent. While we believe that a poor neighborhood can be a good neighborhood, such neighborhoods face daunting challenges. The question of whether we as a society can address those challenges and restore the opportunity for more people to live in good neighborhoods still remains to be answered.

NEIGHBORHOODS AS MARKETS

Neighborhoods mean many different things to people, but one fundamental feature of every neighborhood is its role as a market, that is, an economic system "that allows buyers and sellers to exchange any type of goods, services and information."[1] Within any neighborhood, the properties that are offered for purchase or lease constitute the goods being offered in the market. The buyers (or lessors) are anyone who wants to live, own property, or conduct a business in the neighborhood. Indeed, to the extent that one thinks of a neighborhood as a physical or geographic entity, one could even argue that a neighborhood is a market, no more no less.

Clearly, that is not the case. But while people may think of neighborhoods in emotional or social ways, much of what we care about when we think of neighborhoods is based, in ways that may not always be immediately visible, on an underlying foundation of housing market activity, on choices people make about where they want to live, and on their willingness to make a financial as well as emotional commitment to that place. People make those choices for reasons, and neighborhoods compete with each other to be chosen. As traditional forces that may have once sustained neighborhoods independent of market considerations—such as ethnic identity or attachment to a particular institution such as a factory, church, or social club—have waned, people's decisions to live in one area rather than another are increasingly driven by market-based choices. This chapter explores how neighborhood markets work, what drives them, and how they affect the complex package of conditions that drive neighborhood change.

Earlier we discussed the extent to which neighborhoods are a feedback system. The market is a central part of that system, reflecting the constant flow of information from buyers, sellers, and intermediaries that is the essence of any market. In contrast, however, to economists' idealized notion of a self-correcting system of balancing feedback loops that naturally heads toward equilibrium, the complex behavioral nature of neighborhood markets, along with exogenous factors affecting neighborhoods such as migration and economic restructuring, means that they experience reinforcing feedback loops tending toward disequilibrium and instability. Thus, the natural state of a neighborhood is not stability but change. While change can often be positive, it can also be destabilizing and ultimately threatening to the sustainability of good neighborhoods.

The strength or weakness of the neighborhood housing market, reflected in the extent to which individuals choose to live in that neighborhood rather than elsewhere, may be the single most important factor determining the neighborhood's overall vitality or weakness. When people make an affirmative choice to move into a neighborhood, they are then likely to behave in ways that enhance the neighborhood's vitality. If people live in a neighborhood, however, because they lack choices and leave if they gain the means and ability to do so, that neighborhood's social cohesion and vitality are far more likely to deteriorate rather than improve. Put differently, a good neighborhood is far more likely to exist when the people who live there choose to remain and the people who move in do so by choice rather than for lack of affordable alternatives. Those choices are, more often than not, market choices.

When more people choose to live in a neighborhood, the area's real estate market becomes stronger. Increased real estate market strength—reflected in strong housing prices, a steady volume of sales, and a healthy rate of appreciation over time—in turn leads to important changes in the way property owners behave. In a strong or improving housing market, both homeowners and landlords are more likely to invest in their properties, contractors are more likely to rehabilitate vacant properties or build new infill housing on vacant lots, and tax delinquencies and foreclosures will be rare. Residents who see their neighborhood improving are likely to be more attached to the area and more likely to remain even if they have the means to leave. Upwardly mobile homeowners will be more likely to stay in their present homes or buy new homes in the neighborhood rather than move out, while renters looking to become homeowners will be more likely to buy in the neighborhood rather than elsewhere.

This does not mean, of course, that having a strong or rising residential market ensures a good neighborhood that benefits all its residents. While real estate change can trigger positive change in a neighborhood, this is not a guarantee, nor are its outcomes necessarily all positive. Higher housing costs, particularly when they are spurred by regional housing shortages or speculation rather than enhanced quality of life, can undermine the social fabric that gives a neighborhood its vitality, triggering changes—such as reduced affordability and greater residential overcrowding—that may reduce rather than improve residents' quality of life. Even where the higher costs reflect improvement in the area's quality of life, prices that rise too rapidly may render the area unaffordable to less affluent longtime residents.

Market Forces and Market Actors

A neighborhood is affected by exogenous and endogenous market forces and by market actors, the entities that participate directly or indirectly in the market. The principal forces affecting neighborhood housing markets are shown graphically in figure 6.1.

Neighborhoods exist in citywide and regional contexts. A neighborhood in Buffalo, in a region that has lost population and where economic growth is modest, will have a significantly weaker neighborhood market than a neighborhood identical in all significant respects in New York City, even though both neighborhoods may be in the same relative position in their respective markets. Thus, a dilapidated house located in the Washington, D.C., Anacostia neighborhood, a house that requires considerable work to be livable located in a neighborhood

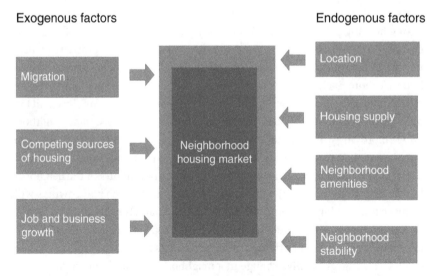

FIGURE 6.1. Principal forces affecting neighborhood housing markets

where household incomes are only modestly above the poverty level, was listed at Zillow in January 2020 for $300,000 "as is."[2] The same house in Detroit would probably be slated for demolition.

In addition to regional demographic and economic trends, neighborhood markets are affected by competition from other neighborhoods offering similar features across the region. Few neighborhoods, particularly in large metros containing hundreds of distinct neighborhoods, are unique. While some neighborhoods may be able to carve out distinct market niches within their region by offering a particular configuration of features that appeal to a distinct segment of the market, such as artists or gay couples, such examples are rare.

In contrast to markets for many other products such as toasters and T-shirts, where the transaction involves relatively few significant actors beyond the buyer, the seller, and a key market intermediary such as Walmart or Amazon, many different actors in addition to buyers and sellers play significant roles in neighborhood housing markets. While home buyers and sellers, for example, are direct market actors, neighborhood community development corporations and local government agencies, although not directly engaged in buying or selling, can be indirect market actors because they act in ways designed to affect the market or that inadvertently affect the market. Similarly, when lenders historically redlined certain neighborhoods, they were behaving as market actors, albeit malign ones, since their refusal to participate in those neighborhoods' markets deprived the neighborhoods of a critical element needed to make their market work. The principal market actors are shown in table 6.1. The first four categories in the table are transactional actors; in other words, they are directly engaged in the buying and selling transactions that in the literal sense constitute the market. While the roles of buyer and seller are straightforward, as are for the most part those of the parties we refer to as "transaction entities" such as brokers and appraisers, the role of lenders and other capital providers is more complex.

Neighborhood markets cannot function without third-party capital. Access to adequate capital in the form of mortgage loans to home buyers, investors or buyers of commercial properties, home improvement loans, construction and bridge loans to developers, loans to businesses for fit-out and equipment, and lines of credit to small businesses and contractors are the essential fuel needed to make possible the transactions that sustain a well-functioning market. The public and private entities that exist to provide these resources act as gatekeepers for capital access, thus determining whether a well-functioning market can exist. In the past when many lower-income and African American neighborhoods were redlined, meaning that lenders no longer provided capital for transactions in those areas, their real estate markets withered, with devastating effects to both the quality and quantity of housing in those areas. Capital access on reasonable terms is

TABLE 6.1 Neighborhood market actors

	CATEGORY	ROLES OR ACTIVITIES
Transactional actors	Buyers[a]	Home buyers
		Residential renters
		Residential property investors
		Commercial property investors
		Business lessors
	Sellers[a]	Property owners
	Financial intermediaries	Lenders
	Real estate transaction entities	Providers of public financing and subsidies
		Realtors, brokers, agents, appraisers, title companies, and lawyers
Environmental actors	Developers and contractors	Providers of additional housing supply[b]
	Business operators	Providers of goods and services to residents and others
	Public sector	Maintenance of infrastructure
		Provision of public services and facilities
		Provision of discretionary assistance
		Code enforcement and other regulations
		Maintenance of public safety
		Public education
	Nonprofit sector	Community development corporations
		Social service, education, and health care providers
		Religious and fraternal organizations
	Anchor institutions	As direct market participants[c]
		As service providers and employers
	Resident organizations	Neighborhood organizations, block organizations, and specialized organizations (such as community gardens)
	Residents	As investors in their properties
		As neighborhood actors

Notes:

[a] These terms are used in the generic sense to refer to all actors who participate either on the buy side or the sell side of market transactions.

[b] Developers can be for-profit or nonprofit entities and include many community development corporations, which, however, often carry out other market-influencing activities.

[c] While not their principal function, anchor institutions, such as hospitals and universities, often intervene in markets directly either by buying or selling real estate in proximity to the institution or by providing financial assistance to employees to purchase homes in nearby neighborhoods.

particularly important to home buyers. While absentee property investors often have access to nontraditional sources of financing such as hard money lenders, home purchases are largely dependent on the availability of mortgage financing.

Home-purchase mortgages are the tip of the capital iceberg. Homeowners and landlords need loans to repair and upgrade their properties, while homeowners benefit from home equity lines of credit for debt restructuring, higher education, or starting a small business. Small developers, who play a critical role in expanding neighborhood market supply by rehabilitating dilapidated properties and building new ones, need short-term financing for acquisition, predevelopment costs, and construction. Finally, commercial loans to acquire a property or a business and purchase equipment and inventory and lines of credit to manage uneven operating cash flows are needed to sustain a viable neighborhood retail and services base.

While banks and other lenders are generally seen as the key financial players, the role of government in setting the ground rules for capital access is a significant one. Many home-purchase mortgages, particularly in lower-income neighborhoods, are made through the Federal Housing Administration (FHA), which provides federal guarantees for mortgage loans. In Baltimore, nearly 60 percent of all home-purchase mortgages in census tracts in the lower half of the city's income distribution in 2018 were government-insured, compared to 30 percent in the upper half and 18 percent in the top quartile.[3] The federal government also creates a secondary market for mortgages through Fannie Mae and Freddie Mac, infuses loan capital into the banking system through the network of federal home loan banks, and establishes the regulatory framework for lending through a maze of seemingly overlapping government agencies, including the Federal Reserve System, the Office of the Comptroller of the Currency, and the Consumer Financial Protection Bureau.

While capital access is rarely a problem in affluent neighborhoods, it has long been an issue in lower-income neighborhoods with lower property values. During the years following the foreclosure crisis, the imposition of stricter underwriting standards for borrower credit scores and property appraisals led to a sharp drop in credit access in many struggling neighborhoods already hard hit by subprime lending, foreclosures, and the Great Recession. While not the only factor, credit constraints significantly contributed to the fact that many of these neighborhoods had not recovered ten years after the end of the recession.

Part of the reason for inequitable capital access is the multiplicity of "gatekeepers," any one of which can potentially block access to capital for any individual buyer and, by extension, to the neighborhood as a whole. In chapter 4, we discussed how from the 1930s to the 1960s the FHA and private lenders effectively made many older urban neighborhoods off-limits for mortgage borrowing and excluded African American families from growing suburban neighborhoods. Long after the Fair Housing Act had made overt racial discrimination illegal, informal practices such as racial steering by real estate agents, in which buyers were only shown houses in areas that fit the agent's idea of racial suitability, continue to affect neighborhood housing markets and distort buyers' housing choices.[4]

More recently, attention has focused on the role of real estate appraisers as market gatekeepers, particularly with respect to their role in undervaluing properties in Black neighborhoods.[5] Appraisals, which represent an estimate by a presumably trained analyst of the "true" market value of a property, play an important and often underappreciated role in capital access, since the appraisal determines the amount that a lender is willing to lend on a property, typically some percentage—most often 80 percent—of that value.[6] Thus, if the price agreed upon by the buyer and the seller is significantly higher than the value set by the appraiser, the lender will only lend 80 percent of the lower amount, thus requiring the buyer to come up with far more cash equity than he or she had anticipated or may have available. In low-value areas, a low appraisal may lead a lender to refuse to lend at all on the grounds that the value of the property, which is collateral for the mortgage loan, is too small to justify the loan. Although we believe that low values in Black neighborhoods are more a function of structural racism in home-buying decisions and that much of the seeming bias in appraisals reflects this reality rather than being driven by the appraisal process itself, it is an important example of the power of relatively invisible gatekeepers to influence neighborhood capital access.

Environmental actors collectively create the larger environment within which the neighborhood market operates. Their influence can be direct, as with developers who build houses to add to the area's housing supply, or indirect, in the way the quality of public services or infrastructure can influence buyer and seller perceptions and behavior.

The principal reason that environmental actors play such important roles is that while on its face the essence of the market appears to lie in individual property transactions, it is in fact a market for neighborhoods. The market for individual properties is interwoven with and dependent on the market for the neighborhood. People may not literally buy neighborhoods, but when they buy a house they are buying a share in a neighborhood, something that most buyers fully understand. Environmental actors may not define the features of the individual properties being bought and sold but instead define the features that make up the character of the neighborhood, which determine the core neighborhood values that we characterize as amenities and stability, which in turn largely drive consumer decisions.

We now turn to the question of how neighborhood features affect the choices made by prospective consumers of a neighborhood. We will focus on the residential market, which is far more central to the dynamics of most neighborhoods than the commercial market, and for reasons we discuss below will emphasize the home buyer market.

Consumer Choice and Neighborhood Markets

Markets are based on the principle of consumer choice. Just as consumers pick cars or Cuisinarts, prospective homeowners and tenants pick neighborhoods, albeit usually for more complicated reasons. Before exploring those reasons, however, we need to place the idea of consumer choice in context.

A world where all consumers have equal choices and equal information and where nonmarket forces, including laws and public policies, play little or no role is a fantasy. While neighborhood markets can be considered free markets in the strict sense that they are largely open to all comers and provide for relatively open bargaining between buyers and sellers, consumer preferences are both influenced and constrained by many factors, beginning with income and wealth and including economic, social, psychological, cultural, and racial factors, as well as by public policies and regulations, all filtered through each consumer's often irrational and biased perceptions along with uneven, inconsistent access to information. Neighborhood choice can be expressed in a quasi-mathematical formula as follows:

$$\text{Neighborhood choice} = \frac{(\text{preferences} - \text{constraints})}{(\text{perceptions} + \text{information})}$$

Constraints on choice, both formal and informal, are powerful. Some are a function of the market itself, such as the limits on choice imposed by a working-class family's modest income and wealth. Others are exogenous to the market and often pernicious. An African American family that might have chosen to buy a home in Levittown on Long Island in 1950 would have been unable to do so because of the racial restrictions imposed by FHA underwriting. Seemingly neutral or benign governmental action such as building codes, which define building standards and thus set the de facto minimum cost of properties, and zoning codes, which limit the variety of housing types that can be constructed in different areas, further distort the market.

Public actions influence or constrain housing choices but do not determine them. This is an important distinction. FHA policies limited which families could get mortgages to buy in Levittown but did not determine who wanted to live there. Similarly, although construction of the interstate system may have accelerated suburbanization around American cities, the fact that the interstate system was authorized in 1956 and largely built in the 1960s, well after the onset of mass suburbanization, should make clear that it did not cause suburbanization.[7]

The combination of FHA lending practices (which prioritized new suburban development over existing urban neighborhoods and enforced racial segregation in suburban subdivisions), urban renewal and the construction of interstate highways through the hearts of American cities had a traumatic effect on preexisting urban neighborhoods, disproportionately affecting lower-income and African American neighborhoods.[8] While these programs and practices ended by the 1970s, they left lasting scars.

It would be a serious error, however, to see the fate of urban neighborhoods since then as having been determined by those policies and practices. The collapse of once-vital Black neighborhoods such as Bronzeville was tragic, but many more factors were involved including the exodus of the Black middle class to areas that had been opened up by white flight as well as the loss of Chicago's industrial base. Ironically, had suburban developments such as Levittown been open to Black home buyers from the beginning, the exodus from traditionally Black neighborhoods and from the cities in general might well have been even faster and more traumatic in their ultimate effect on urban neighborhoods.

Both consumer choices and neighborhoods are segmented. Consumer preferences vary, with some predictability based on such factors as household type and size, especially the presence of children; age and stage in life cycle; and somewhat less predictably, lifestyle or cultural preferences. They are also segmented by race, most notably reflected in the racially driven reluctance of white home buyers to buy in predominantly Black neighborhoods.[9]

Neighborhoods are similarly segmented by whom they appeal to most strongly; the preference of highly educated millennials for dense central-city downtowns can be contrasted with the preferences of child-raising couples for neighborhoods of detached single-family houses, with or without white picket fences. Research on consumer segmentation has become quite sophisticated. The market research firm Claritas has developed what it calls its PRIZM model, which divides all American households into sixty-eight distinct categories oriented along social group and life stage group axes and given catchy names such as "Aspiring A-listers" and "Campers & Camo."[10]

However much the PRIZM model may strike some as overkill, it recognizes that preferences are cumulative rather than distinct; in other words, a couple with small children may be looking for a neighborhood of single-family houses, but their educational level, their cultural and lifestyle preferences, and even their political orientation will progressively narrow their preference to a subset of such neighborhoods.[11] The extent to which such a particular couple can act on their preferences, of course, will depend on not only whether a neighborhood meeting their criteria exists but also their income and assets.

A healthy neighborhood should have housing options for both homeowners and renters. There are major differences, however, between the decision-making process of home buyers and renters as well as in their impact on neighborhood conditions. Unfortunately, in some circles this often seems to be translated into a simplistic and misguided "homeowners good, renters bad" echo of *Animal Farm*. Much of the difference between home buyers and renters lies in the disparity in stability of tenure. The typical homeowner remains in the same dwelling for far longer than the typical renter. In Indianapolis the median homeowner has lived in the same dwelling for twelve years, the median renter for twenty-one months.[12]

A second factor is the difference in incomes. Homeowner incomes are typically much higher than those of renters, giving them far more choices in the market. In Atlanta, the median household income of homeowners is over $98,000 compared to not quite $39,000 for renters. Given typical rents and sales prices in the Atlanta area, a median home buyer could afford the great majority of houses for sale in the area in 2020, while a median tenant would have far more limited options. Furthermore, the transaction costs and "stickiness" of homeownership are far greater than for rental tenure. Down payments and closing costs are a far greater expense than security deposits, while the effort needed to exit homeownership is so much greater that some researchers believe that homeownership has a significant negative effect on labor market mobility.[13] This makes the stakes that much higher for home buyers.

The upshot is that home buyers, with a wider range of options as well as the intention to remain in place for an extended period, tend to give greater weight to nonpecuniary factors with respect to both the house and the neighborhood, while renters, with fewer choices, tend to focus more narrowly on simply finding a unit they can afford and a landlord who will accept them.[14]

These dissimilarities translate into significant differences in the relative impact of homeowners and tenants on neighborhood conditions. A vast body of research on the effects of homeownership consistently shows significant effects on social capital and collective efficacy; social and behavioral factors, particularly youth behavior and outcomes; and property maintenance and improvement.[15] This is not to suggest that the presence of renters in reasonable numbers has a negative effect on a neighborhood per se but rather that their presence does not appear to trigger the positive features associated with homeownership.[16]

Although home buyers may have more options than renters, for most their choices are still constrained. In addition to the obvious constraints imposed by a buyer's limited income and cash resources for down payments and closing costs, constraints can be imposed by racial or ethnic characteristics or by cultural or psychological factors. While overt discrimination by race or ethnicity is now illegal, informal discrimination persists in the form of racial steering by real estate agents and discriminatory lending behavior, including steering to more expensive mortgage products and disparate loan-denial rates. With respect to cultural or psychological issues, the line between constraints and preferences tends to become fuzzy. For example, the desire of a newly arrived immigrant family to live in an immigrant enclave is arguably more than a preference; it is a constraint imposed by that family's psychological and cultural support needs. The tendency of such enclaves to dissolve over time unless replenished by a flow of new immigrants represents a process by which those constraints are removed and households are thus increasingly able to act on their personal preferences.

In the final analysis, all consumers are looking for the best match between neighborhood characteristics and their preferences within the boundaries established by their constraints. In the course of their search, they make explicit or implicit trade-offs between different neighborhood features. Specifically, they are looking to match their preferences with four distinct neighborhood features: supply, location, amenities, and stability and risk. The first two are relatively straightforward, but the other two raise more complex issues.

Housing Supply

The most fundamental issue for home buyers is whether a neighborhood contains homes that meet their criteria with respect to price, size, features, and condition. A family with children will look for a house or apartment with multiple bedrooms as well as ample space for children's activities, while most families will look for a house or apartment that requires relatively little work on their part to render it livable. The market for fixer-uppers or "handyman's specials" is a small one, outside a handful of up-and-coming hipster neighborhoods in large cities. In contrast to neighborhood criteria such as stability and amenities where a prospective home buyer's preferences often tend to be relatively general and often based on limited or unreliable information, preferences for the home itself tend to be much more specific although constantly subject to renegotiation in light of price and other constraints.

Location

Location preferences can be defined as proximity or ease of access to places important to the members of a home buyer's household, particularly workplaces. Consumers vary widely, however, in their tolerance for extended journeys to work or, alternatively, in their preference for or dependence on public transportation. A significant share of the residents of low-income urban neighborhoods rely on public transportation for their work trips and may be reluctant to move to an area that lacks access to public transportation even if they could afford to do so. Conversely, price affects locational decisions, particularly in high-cost regions; the real estate adage "drive till you qualify" reflects the reality that neighborhoods close to the most important destinations, particularly in strong market cities such as San Francisco and Seattle, tend to be unaffordable to most buyers. As a result, buyers may trade off longer commutes for housing quality or affordability.

Amenities

Just as prospective buyers vary in their preferences for location and housing, they also vary in the amenities they look for in a neighborhood. In contrast, however, to the relatively easily defined features of the former, amenities tend to reflect less explicitly held subjective preferences. To one child-centric source, neighborhood amenities are simply "the presence or absence of sidewalks, parks/playgrounds, and recreation centers."[17] Conversely, a study that focused on older adults defined amenities as the proximity of food retail, community-serving retail, services, and civic and community facilities.[18] Amenity and stability elements, discussed immediately below, are often conflated, as in a *Forbes* article that lumps factors such as low crime rates and pride in homeownership together with others such as outdoor activities and proximity to public transportation as "what makes a neighborhood truly great."[19]

From a market perspective, amenities are those elements in a neighborhood which are perceived by a prospective buyer as making it a more desirable or appealing place to live. What those are will vary from buyer to buyer. They can be as straightforward as easy access to parks or the presence of a mature tree canopy along residential streets or as intangible as neighborhood character or identity. They are highly subjective and influenced by a wide range of family and individual characteristics such as age, child-rearing status, activity preferences, cultural values, race and ethnicity, and social class.

Features of a neighborhood that may be seen as amenities by some individuals may be irrelevant or even negative factors to others, particularly in a neighborhood that contains a heterogeneous mix of residents. It is important, however, not to conflate amenities in the market sense with what are often treated as neighborhood "assets" in the community development world.[20] While there are many features of a neighborhood that may be seen as assets by people who live in the neighborhood, including services such as senior centers and health clinics and "third places" such as barbershops and taverns, those amenities may not be perceived as meaningful or relevant by people making home-buying decisions.

Stability and Risk

While the role of neighborhood amenities in consumer choice links concrete realities such as a park or a light rail stop with subjective preferences, the role of neighborhood stability, which arguably may be the most important of all elements affecting neighborhood choice, is heavily grounded in perceptions and in the interpretation of often ambiguous information.

Stability is not meant in the literal sense of indefinitely remaining the same. All neighborhoods change, upwards, downwards, or sideways. We define neighborhood stability as the perception that the neighborhood is and is likely to remain (or become) a good place to live and is therefore a sound place in which to make both a financial and a psychological investment. Kahneman and Tversky's prospect theory, illustrated in figure 6.2, underlies the importance that we place on this aspect of neighborhood choice.[21] That theory, vastly oversimplified, holds that when people make important decisions, the fear of loss significantly out-

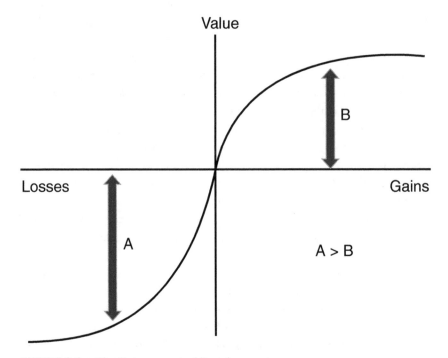

FIGURE 6.2. The Kahneman and Tversky curve

(Authors' work based on Kahneman and Tversky prospect theory)

weighs the hope of gain. This is particularly powerful when applied to the home-buying decision, which for most American families represents their most significant financial investment as well as a significant personal and emotional commitment. Applied to neighborhood choice, this theory suggests that prospective buyers will be driven to avoid what they perceive as negative features of a neighborhood, since those features increase the risk of loss, both with respect to the financial as well as the hedonic utility of their investment.[22] We find this argument compelling. It helps explain the importance of crime, race (to white buyers), and school quality in the home-buying decision.

On its face, the importance given to school quality in the home-buying equation would appear to be self-evident, reflecting the value that parents place on the education of their children. On closer examination, that assumption is placed in question by the fact that most American households today do not have school-age children. Only 22 percent of all American households contained school-age children in 2017, many of whom did not go to public schools, while according to the National Association of Realtors, 70 percent of home buyers in 2018 did not have school age children in the home.[23] The number does not change greatly if one adds households with preschool children to the number of school-centric households.

The importance of school quality, however, is more than adequately explained by the role of school quality as a proxy for neighborhood stability and for the probability of house value appreciation.[24] It is arguably the single most powerful positive element within the cluster of features that constitute neighborhood stability, as in most respects stability is perceived as the absence of negative features.

The most obvious negative feature is crime, in particular violent crime. The role of both the reality and the perception of crime in driving neighborhood decline has long been recognized.[25] Perceived disorder, in terms of both visible social disorder (public drinking, prostitution, vandalism) and physical disorder (graffiti, debris, broken streetlights), are closely related to perceived crime and affect neighborhoods similarly to actual criminal activity.[26] A prospective buyer's perception of disorder can also be triggered by different visual stimuli observed while walking or driving through a neighborhood, ranging from prominent features such as the presence of abandoned buildings or trash-strewn vacant lots to details such as tall chain-link fences in front yards, bars on ground-floor windows, or sagging porches. Neighborhoods, like homes, can have or lack so-called curb appeal.

While crime and disorder are realities, perceptions of crime and disorder are filtered through implicit values and biases, particularly implicit racial bias. Research studies have found that white subjects perceive neighborhoods with large Black populations as being more dangerous, independent of actual crime levels, and that their perceptions of neighborhood disorder are strongly affected by their perception of the share of Black residents in a neighborhood.[27] Another study found that white respondents shown a series of images of identical neighborhood scenes rated the neighborhoods significantly lower on a scale of neighborhood conditions when the people in the pictures were Black than when they were white.[28]

The persistence of underlying racial bias means that white home buyers—who still make up the great majority of home buyers in most areas—although increasingly open to buying homes in racially mixed areas, remain highly unlikely to do so in predominantly Black neighborhoods, usually not even looking at those neighborhoods in the course of their home search.[29] This in turn contributes significantly to the market weakness of many predominantly Black middle-class neighborhoods, since in most parts of the United States the Black home buyer pool is not large enough to fully absorb the supply of housing in those neighborhoods. This problem, which is reflected in and magnified by the appraisal issues noted earlier, has grown in recent years as a result of the increasing tendency of Black home buyers to buy in suburban or racially mixed neighborhoods rather than in traditionally Black urban middle-class neighborhoods.[30] In the final analysis, large numbers of white home buyers continue to perceive Blackness per se as a risk factor leading to decisions to avoid buying in predominantly Black neighborhoods.

Stability and amenities are not fixed properties of neighborhoods. They are the product of the interaction of many factors in which public policies, particularly those of local government, play important roles. How local governments allocate their resources to provide public services, build or maintain publicly owned facilities, enforce housing codes, address vacant abandoned properties, and support the work of community-based organizations all affect a neighborhood's quality of life and how it is perceived by both the residents of the neighborhood and those who might contemplate moving there.

The interactions between the functions performed by the many different units of local governments with one another and with nongovernmental actors, such as resident organizations and neighborhood-based institutions, are not only complex but also powerful in their implications for an area's vitality, quality of life, and market strength. Regrettably, few cities appear to be aware of the importance of these interactions or, if they are aware, they appear to be willing or able to develop a more systematic focus on using public policy as a tool to nurture good neighborhoods.

Finally, change, while inevitable, is itself a potential destabilizing factor whatever the nature and direction of change. Healthy neighborhoods have coping mechanisms. As Jane Jacobs wrote in *The Death and Life of American Cities*, a healthy neighborhood is one "that keeps sufficiently abreast of its problems so it is not destroyed by them."[31] Neighborhood coping mechanisms, however, can be overwhelmed by too much happening too soon. As Rachel Woldoff points out in her ethnographic study of change in an urban neighborhood, the intensity of destabilization is related to the pace of change.[32] An isolated problem such as a foreclosure or the appearance of graffiti on one brick wall can be assimilated. At some point, however, if the problems mount, neighborhood resilience can break down, and reinforcing cycles of decline can emerge.

Information Channels

Perceptions and information are intimately related. No one has perfect information about the market, while most people fail to even come close. The process by which individuals gather information about neighborhoods is strongly colored by emotion and implicit bias and constrained by time pressure. Information channels may reinforce prior biases or introduce new but often unspoken biases of their own. While the ways individuals conduct house searches and evaluate alternative neighborhood options, particularly since the explosion of internet house and neighborhood information searches, have not been extensively studied, some key dynamics of the process can be described.

Websites such as Zillow and Realtor.com have broadened the search process, but most home searches still rely heavily on informal networks, including the process by which they select the real estate agent through whom they ultimately buy their home.[33] Most white buyers get their information from other white people, and most Black buyers get their information from other Black people. As Marie Krysan found, white buyers almost universally work with white real estate agents, and the great majority of Black buyers work with Black real estate agents.[34] Over half of the buyers found their real estate agents through social networks. Once a buyer has selected a real estate agent, that agent subsequently becomes the buyer's principal source of information.

Because so much of the home-buying process is grounded in buyers' perceptions and mediated through the selective channel's buyers use to obtain the information that drives those perceptions, it is hardly surprising that neighborhood marketing, where neighborhoods use websites, social media, and other tools to increase potential buyers' awareness of the neighborhood and present neighborhood information in a positive light, has become widespread. This is particularly true of urban neighborhoods, where all but the strongest neighborhoods are likely to suffer from an implicit suburban bias with respect to both perceptions and information flow.

A good example of such efforts is that of the Grandmont Rosedale Development Corporation in Detroit. If a prospective buyer has heard of the neighborhood and

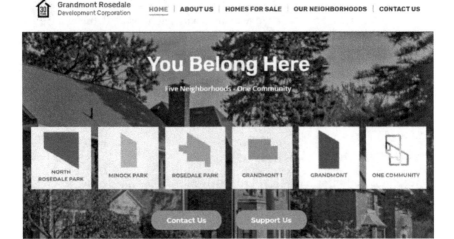

FIGURE 6.3. Home page of the Grandmont Rosedale Development Corporation website

turned to the web to find more information, the corporation's website is the first one that appears in a Google search of "Grandmont-Rosedale Detroit." The home page, which appears when one clicks on that listing, makes an immediate appeal (figure 6.3).

The City of Baltimore along with local foundations and corporations has created a nonprofit entity called the Live Baltimore Home Center to market the city's neighborhoods to both home buyers and renters.[35] The organization, which is professionally staffed and maintains a storefront in a prime downtown location, pursues an impressive array of activities to connect people to Baltimore's neighborhoods and help them become homeowners, including promoting the availability of mortgages, down payment assistance, and other support.[36]

Information combined with previously held values and biases drives neighborhood perceptions, perceptions drive neighborhood reputations, and to a large degree reputations drive markets. Perceptions, reputations, and markets can change relatively quickly, however, when new information begins to circulate through the system, supplanting previous information. A previously shunned neighborhood can become desirable, while a previously well-regarded neighborhood can come to be seen as a place to avoid, although the mechanisms by which this happens are not fully understood. The role of changed neighborhood narratives, which can go viral at least within a community or region, is likely to be particularly important.[37]

Quantifying Neighborhood Markets

The foregoing discussion was qualitative, focusing on the behavior and perceptions of the participants in the residential home-buying market. Those behaviors and perceptions drive outcomes that can be used to measure the market strength or weakness of any neighborhood. Three key variables are the most important: home sales prices, home sales volume, and distribution of sales between home buyers and investors. Each of these three variables, which correlate strongly with one another, says something about the character of the neighborhood housing market. Combined, they add up to a meaningful picture of the market.

The significance of sales prices is intuitively obvious. As a general rule, the stronger the neighborhood's market, other things being equal, the higher the price the houses in the neighborhood will command.[38] If that price, however, is driven by speculation rather than reasoned home-buying decisions or if, despite high prices, the number of sales is too few to absorb the available housing supply, it may have different meanings than when conditions are otherwise. As a general rule, however, high sales prices correlate positively with sales volumes and negatively with the percentage of sales to investor buyers.

While most people understand that if prices are too high or rise too quickly that can be problematic for households that are priced out of the market, it is not as widely understood that prices being too low is also a problem. What "too low" means may depend on the context. As a general proposition, prices are too low if they are significantly below replacement or restoration cost, that is, the cost to either construct a similar house de novo or restore a vacant dilapidated house to sound, livable condition. Where prices are below restoration cost, the gap between the two is often referred to as the "market gap" or in some cases the "appraisal gap." In essence, what this means is that if a derelict, abandoned house in a neighborhood would cost $90,000 to restore to sound, livable condition but its market value restored would only be $60,000, that house has a market gap of $30,000.

The market gap discourages contractors or developers from acquiring and restoring vacant properties or building infill houses on vacant lots and also discourages property owners from investing in upgrading or renovating occupied properties without scarce public subsidies. Thus, the market gap not only hastens deterioration of the existing housing stock but also, in the absence of expensive public intervention, can lead to growing numbers of vacant abandoned properties, undermining neighborhood property values and quality of life.[39]

Moreover, low prices below replacement cost make little or no contribution to increasing affordability for lower-income home buyers and for renters. Almost any family with enough stable income to consider homeownership can afford a house at or above the replacement cost in many urban neighborhoods outside hot market cities. Given mortgage interest rates in effect in 2021 and typical property tax rates, a family earning as little as $30,000 can afford to buy a house priced at or above $120,000, while few households earning less than $30,000 are credible candidates for homeownership. While this picture has shifted somewhat since the run-up in house prices that began in 2020, and the sharp increase in mortgage interest rates more recently, it is still largely true.

While in the weakest markets house prices can drop to where they are little more than the transaction costs, rents do not behave similarly. Landlords need to cover operating costs, taxes, insurance, reserves, and a reasonable return on their investment. If they cannot rent their properties for whatever amount that might be, rather than reduce the rents, which would result in an ongoing loss of income, they are likely to abandon the properties.[40] Extremely low sales prices in distressed neighborhoods, rather than leading to lower rents, often have a counterproductive effect on landlord behavior. Realizing that by cutting costs to maximize net cash flow they can generate enough income to show a profit on their initial investment in a few years even if the property is worthless by that point, unscrupulous landlords milk the property, often walking away in the end.[41]

Sales volume, seen as a ratio between the number of properties on the market at a given point or over a given period and the number actually purchased, may be even more important.[42] Since the actual number on the market is difficult to establish, it is much simpler to use a well-established real estate rule of thumb that annual turnover in the residential market under normal market conditions is typically around 7 percent of the housing stock.[43] Annual turnover in the existing home market from 1999 through 2015, except for a brief period from 2003 to 2005 when the market badly overheated, has consistently remained between 5 percent and 9 percent.[44] Sales volume, understood this way, is a more meaningful measure of market activity than the popular "days on market" metric used by the real estate industry.

An annual sales volume of 5 to 9 percent therefore is a proxy for a healthy turnover rate, that is, a rate at which the number of new home buyers is sufficient to replace the number of homeowners whose homes come on the market during the year. We call this the "replacement range." If the sales volume is significantly below that range, it is likely that there are not enough buyers to absorb the supply. That condition at a minimum impairs homeowners' mobility and, if combined with house prices below restoration cost, is likely to trigger property disinvestment and abandonment.[45]

An area with sales volumes within the replacement range is also likely to have sales prices above restoration cost, as the relationship between the two measures is close. Figure 6.4 shows that relationship by census tract in Baltimore. Of fifty-eight census tracts in the lowest two sales price quintiles in the city, from 2016

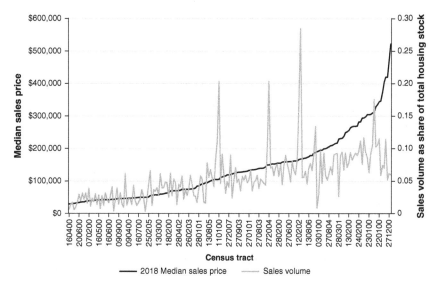

FIGURE 6.4.   The linear relationship between sales volume and median sales price by census tract in Baltimore, 2018

to 2018 only three had average sales volumes above the minimum replacement range level, and twenty-five had sales volumes below 2 percent, suggesting that the probability of a house coming on the market in those census tracts finding a buyer might be less than the probability of the house ending up abandoned. In chapter 12 we discuss how the phenomenon of low demand, as illustrated by sales volumes below the replacement rate, is an important factor in the post–Great Recession decline of urban Black middle neighborhoods.

In contrast to the first two measures in figure 6.4, where reasonably accurate data can be obtained from public records in most US cities, few public agencies track whether the buyer is planning to live in the house or not, and if they did, there is no reason to believe that the data would be reliable. Estimating the percentage of investor buyers relies on using one of a number of proxies, of which the best is to compare the address of the property in the property records with the address to which the property tax bills are sent, the inference being that where they are the same the owner lives in the home.[46] CoreLogic assumes that absentee buyers are those where the zip code of the address to which the tax bills are sent is different from that of the property, which most probably understates the percentage of absentee buyers in low-value areas, since many small mom-and-pop investors live close to the properties they buy.[47]

While a home buyer's decision to buy reflects a long-term psychological as well as financial commitment to the neighborhood, an investor's decision is a

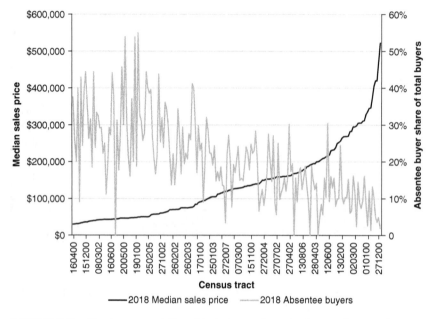

FIGURE 6.5. The inverse relationship between investor buyer share and median sales price by census tract in Baltimore, 2018

short-term purely financial one; that is, "will I make enough money from this property, either from cash flow or capital gain on resale, to justify the purchase?" Thus, a high home buyer share is a signal of market strength as distinct from exploitative or extractive buying. As is true of sales volumes, the percentage of investors in the market is strongly related to sales price except that the relationship is an inverse one, as shown in figure 6.5. Although the overall relationship is strong, there is much more variability on this measure at the lower end of the market than is true of sales volumes, suggesting that some low-priced neighborhoods may still be seeing some not insignificant home buyer activity.

Summing Up

We introduced the idea of neighborhoods as feedback systems in chapter 2. At this point we can expand that discussion by looking at the specific elements in the feedback system that is the neighborhood market and how the interaction of elements in that system leads to market change. The most fundamental condition of neighborhood markets, as is true to varying degrees of all markets, is that they are dynamic. With rare exceptions, which are usually found at the highest and lowest ends of the market, all neighborhood markets change and can do so far more quickly than many neighborhood actors or local governments can anticipate or assimilate. The process of change can be summarized as a process by which information about existing conditions or specific short-term changes alters neighborhood actors' perceptions, leading to changes in behavior, which in turn change neighborhood market conditions; as conditions change, information about change continues to affect perceptions and behavior in an ongoing feedback loop. This is shown in summary graphic form in figure 6.6.

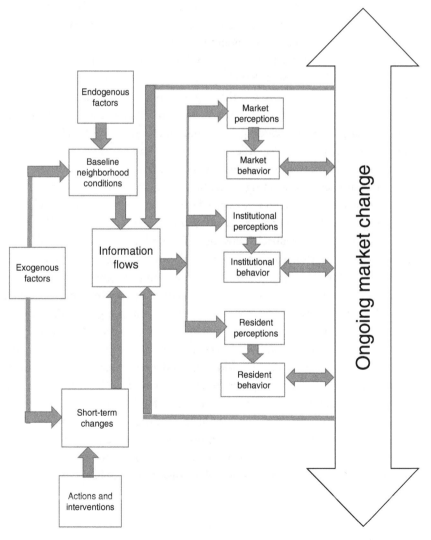

FIGURE 6.6. Extending the model of neighborhood change

Information flows are the critical element in the feedback system. At any given point, people's perceptions of the neighborhood are driven by the information they have, accurate or not, about neighborhood conditions. When a specific change takes place in a neighborhood, which can be triggered either by changes in exogenous conditions or by a specific intervention such as the removal of a neighborhood eyesore or the restoration of a neighborhood park, information about that change enters the system, which in turn acts on the perceptions and behaviors of internal (homeowners, tenants, landlords) and external (home buyers, investors, realtors) neighborhood actors. More people may buy homes, prices may rise, and more existing property owners may invest in their properties.

Short-term changes may not lead to ongoing market change. Whether they do depends first, on information about the change entering the system and, second, on how the market actors respond to that information. In practice, it will also depend on the nature of that change and on the way the change interacts with the underlying conditions of the neighborhood where it takes place, a series of complex relationships not shown in figure 6.6, that is already complicated enough. Many changes, including many that some actors hope will lead to systemic change, do not lead to market change. Even if new information enters the system, the salient market actors may simply shrug it off if the information confirms or reinforces their existing perceptions of the neighborhood rather than changing them or if they do not consider the information credible or significant.

Once sustained market change has begun to take place, however, that process creates a series of feedback loops that affect both the behavior and the perceptions of neighborhood actors. That process can take place slowly or quickly. Exogenous factors are as important or more so than endogenous ones in determining the pace of neighborhood change. In cities such as New York and Seattle, both of which are seeing sustained in-migration of high-earning young people and households, once a neighborhood has been characterized as a desirable place for such people to live, market conditions can change dramatically overnight. Conversely, in St. Louis and Cleveland, even though the information message may be identical, change will be far slower because the inflow of people using that information to make market choices is far smaller.

As we explore the many dimensions of neighborhood change that are characteristic of today's urban and suburban neighborhoods, we will revisit the elements of this feedback system and in the final chapter of this book further deepen our analysis to begin building a more robust theory of neighborhood change.

NEIGHBORHOODS IN AN ERA OF DEMOGRAPHIC CHANGE AND ECONOMIC RESTRUCTURING

In the previous chapter, we discussed how neighborhood markets are segmented; that is, any given neighborhood is likely to appeal to some groups, defined by income, life cycle, or many other variables, more than others. While neighborhoods are not internally homogenous, their diversity tends to be bounded although within fluctuating parameters. In the heyday of the immigrant ethnic neighborhood early in the twentieth century, neighborhoods tended to be relatively ethnically homogenous but highly diverse by income, age, and household type. Today as ethnic boundaries have become less meaningful for much of the American population, people sort themselves into neighborhoods more around income, education, life cycle, household type, and, increasingly, lifestyle and even political or ideological orientation.

The role that segmentation plays in driving neighborhood dynamics points out the importance of understanding underlying demographic, social, and economic factors. Change over time in the American population based on almost any demographic or economic measure, such as the number of married couples raising children or the years between college graduation and first marriage, directly affects neighborhood change. Some neighborhoods may find themselves overwhelmed by demand from growing demographic groups, while others, vacated by elderly homeowners, find no takers and suffer from housing vacancy and abandonment.

The extent to which the United States has changed since 1960, a good starting point, is striking. In 1960 two-thirds of American households were married couples, with most raising children. If you were not part of a married couple, you were probably single and lived in an apartment, a rooming house, or a single-room occupancy hotel. Eighty-nine percent of the nation's population was classified as "white," and barely 5 percent had been born outside the United States. In 1960 nearly two-thirds of American families could be considered middle income, earning between 50 percent and 150 percent of the national median income. The white, native-born, middle-class, married couple household, with or without children, is no longer the norm in American society. We have become a much more diverse and divided society. As many commentators have pointed out, we have also become increasingly segmented by tastes, lifestyles, and behavior.

This chapter explores how American society has changed in the past sixty years and how those changes are in turn driving neighborhood change. We will look at demographic, racial and ethnic, and economic changes and briefly sketch some of the contours of the cultural, ideological, and technological changes taking place over the same period. All of these changes present new challenges for building or maintaining good neighborhoods that can serve as wellsprings of economic mobility and social cohesion.

The Rise of the Millennials and the Decline of the Traditional Family

The United States of the 1960s was a nation of families and above all married couples. As table 7.1 shows, in 1968 nearly three-quarters of American households were married couples. Most were raising children, and of those who were not, most would be raising children in the future or had finally seen their youngest child leave the home. Men and women married far younger and had shorter life expectancies than today. In 1956 the median age for first marriage in the United States was 22.5 for men and 20.1 for women, while life expectancy was 67 years for men and 73 years for women. For most Americans, life included only brief passages through two phases that people today see as extended stages of adult life: independent adult life before marriage and life as active empty nesters before transitioning into old age. Both phases have become important drivers of neighborhood change.

The Disappearing Traditional Nuclear Family

Urban and suburban neighborhoods from the late nineteenth century until well past the mid-twentieth century, as we describe further in chapter 12, were designed for a world of couples raising children. Among those couples, stay-at-

TABLE 7.1 Distribution of households in the United States by type and presence of children under age 18 in 1968 and 2018

	1968		2018	
HOUSEHOLD TYPE	NUMBER (000)	% OF HOUSEHOLDS	NUMBER (000)	% OF HOUSEHOLDS
Married couples	43,291	71.6	57,848	45.2
With children under 18	25,481	42.2	22,334	17.4
Families with male head	1,209	2.0	5,887	4.6
With children under 18	431	0.7	2,723	2.1
Families with female head	5,332	8.8	14,897	11.6
With children under 18	3,192	5.3	7,790	6.1
All child-rearing households	29,109	48.2	32,847	25.6
Single individuals	10,710	17.7	33,518	26.3
Other nonfamily households[a]	NA	NA	7,914	6.1
All Households	60,444	100	128,063	100

Source: 1968 data from Current Population Survey; 2018 from 1-year American Community Survey.
[a] Nonfamily households, other than single individuals, were not recognized at that time as a distinct category. While undoubtedly there were some households in the 1960s that today would be placed in this category, their numbers were small and were probably included by the Census Bureau in one or another of the family categories.

home mothers were the norm. In 1950, only 12 percent of mothers with preschool children were part of the labor force. Much of the energy of those young mothers of the 1950s went into sustaining neighborhood life. As Ehrenhalt writes, "the feelings of safety and familiarity that existed for those growing up . . . were in part created by mothers who stayed home and knew more about what teenagers were up to than the teenagers wanted them to know."[1]

Those days are long gone. Less than half of American households today are married couples, and fewer than half of them are raising children; fewer than one in five households are married couples with children under age eighteen in the home. By 1985, over one-third of mothers in married couples with preschool children were in the labor force; today, nearly two-thirds are. In most child-rearing couples today both husband and wife work, but barely one-quarter of American households of any type are raising children. From being the dominant household type, married couple families have become simply one of many different forms of household, none of them dominant in the sense that any one defines the social framework for American neighborhoods. For many of the growing number of other households, the traditional single-family neighborhood today is a poor fit for their needs, their capabilities, or their aspirations.

These shifts have been most pronounced in the nation's central cities (table 7.2). More families have left, and more single people have moved into cities compared

TABLE 7.2 Distribution of households by type in three cities in 2017

HOUSEHOLD TYPE	WASHINGTON, DC	CHICAGO	PITTSBURGH
Married couples	25.1%	32.5%	28.3%
With children under 18	9.6%	13.4%	8.4%
Families with male head	3.5%	5.1%	3.4%
With children under 18	1.4%	1.9%	0.7%
Families with female head	13.8%	15.2%	11.3%
With children under 18	6.1%	7.2%	6.0%
All child-rearing households	17.1%	22.4%	15.0%
Single individuals	45.2%	37.4%	43.4%
Other nonfamily households	12.4%	9.9%	13.6%
All Households	100%	100%	100%

Source: 2017 1-year American Community Survey.

to less urban places. Nearly half of all the households in Washington, D.C., are single individuals. Only one out of four are married couple households, and fewer than one in ten are married couples raising children. Both Washington and Pittsburgh have far more nonfamily households, including unmarried couples living together and people in a variety of informal sharing arrangements. This may not quite be the "childless city" bemoaned by some commentators, but their characterization is not too far from the mark.[2]

The flow of urban families with children to the suburbs in search of a better life is well known, from the first waves of suburbanization even before World War II, the white flight of the 1960s and 1970s, and today's Black flight as thousands of middle-income African American families follow in their white counterparts' footsteps.[3] The second trend, while widely publicized, is often poorly understood: namely, the influx of young people, often categorized as the millennial generation, into central cities. Since the significance of this influx for the future of cities and their neighborhoods is arguably even greater than that of the shift in household types, we will explore it and chart its parameters in some detail.

The March of the Millennials

Although to refer to all young people moving into cities as the millennial generation is imprecise, it is not an inappropriate shorthand.[4] The pace of in-migration picked up notably as that generation, born between 1981 and 1996, began to come of age after 2000, especially since 2010. While some writers have argued that the migration is overstated, they fail to recognize that it is not all millennials who are disproportionately moving to central cities but specifically those millennials who have at least a four-year college degree and not to all cities in equal numbers. One of the authors has previously called this group the "young grads."

Table 7.3 shows the change from 2000 to 2018 in the number of young people aged twenty-five to thirty-four by education level for eight American cities: three magnet cities, three reviving midwestern cities, and two Sunbelt cities. In looking at table 7.3, one should bear in mind that in 2018, 36 percent, or slightly more than one-third of people aged twenty-five to thirty-four overall in the United States, had a BA or higher degree and made up only 5 percent of the population of the United States as a whole. From 2000 to 2018, the number of young people with a BA+ degree grew by 416,000 in these eight cities, accounting for almost half of their total growth; in Boston and Washington, D.C., they were over 60 percent of all growth, while in Chicago their number grew by over 100,000 while the city lost 177,000 people overall. In every city, the increase in young grads was greater from 2010 to 2018 than during the previous decade.

Meanwhile, the number of young people without BA degrees in these cities was dropping; indeed, if one leaves out San Antonio and Phoenix, the decline was well over 100,000. Those two cities show quite a different picture from the magnet and midwestern cities. In the latter, growth in young grads is their principal source of population growth, and they are becoming a disproportionately large share of the population. In the Sunbelt cities, their numbers are growing, but slowly; they make up only a small share of total population growth, and their share of the population is below the national average.

The growth of young grads in cities such as Washington and Seattle, where they now make up nearly one out of every four adult residents, has powerful implications for these cities' neighborhoods. They are largely single or if not are in informal relationships. In Washington, D.C., only 7 percent of people ages twenty-five to twenty-nine were currently married in 2018. While they may at some point marry, raise children, and start looking for a single-family house, that day may be years off. In the meantime, they are much more likely to seek out neighborhoods that offer what sociologist Terry Nichols Clarke calls a "scene," centers of "entertainment, consumption and amenities."[5]

The in-migration of young grads is the strongest factor driving the conversion of historically nonresidential downtown areas such as Washington Avenue in St. Louis and Old City Philadelphia into residential neighborhoods and the gentrification of residential areas close to downtown or to major employers, anchor institutions, and amenities. Figures 7.1 and 7.2 show areas with concentrations of young grads in Baltimore in 2000 and 2018 (areas where 20 percent or more of the population is twenty-five to thirty-four years of age and 50 percent or more of the population have BA or higher degrees). From a few small pockets around the Inner Harbor and a small area three miles to the north adjacent to

TABLE 7.3 Change in population age twenty-five to thirty-four by educational attainment for selected cities from 2000 to 2018

CITY	CHANGE 2000–2010			CHANGE 2010–2018			CHANGE 2000–2018		
	ALL	BA+	WITHOUT BA	ALL	BA+	WITHOUT BA	ALL	BA+	WITHOUT BA
Boston	2,794	14,317	-11,523	45,482	41,705	3,777	48,276	56,022	-7,746
Washington, DC	25,259	31,704	-6,445	37,145	37,903	-758	62,404	69,607	-7,203
Seattle	3,940	11,486	-7,546	5,315	54,052	-2,737	55,255	65,538	-10,283
Chicago	-18,235	4,764	-67,999	30,092	53,011	-22,919	11,857	102,775	-90,918
Columbus	8,257	6,658	1,599	39,674	27,662	12,012	47,931	34,320	13,611
Pittsburgh	2,570	4,941	-2,371	11,653	14,869	-3,216	14,223	19,810	-5,587
Phoenix	6,630	5,118	1,512	47,396	29,889	17,507	54,026	35,007	19,019
San Antonio	24,765	1,096	12,669	56,832	21,213	35,619	81,597	33,309	48,288
Eight Cities		136,084	-80,104		280,304	39,285		416,388	-40,819

	PERCENTAGE OF 25–34 WITH BA+		25–34 WITH BA+ SHARE OF TOTAL POPULATION		25–34 WITH BA+ AS SHARE OF GROWTH 2000–2018
	2000	2018	2000	2018	
Boston	52	70	11	18	62
Washington, DC	51	74	9	18	62
Seattle	55	75	12	19	45
Chicago	36	54	7	11	NA[a]
Columbus	39	47	8	10	25
Pittsburgh	42	64	6	13	NA[a]
Phoenix	21	29	4	5	12
San Antonio	22	28	3	5	10
					45

Source: Decennial Census, 2014–2018 Five-Year American Community Survey.
[a] These cities lost population during this period.

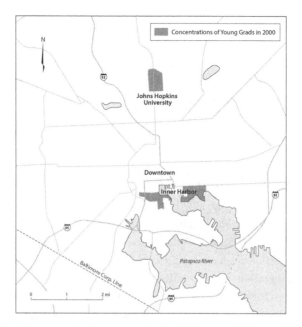

FIGURE 7.1. The spread of young grads in Baltimore, 2000 to 2018. Young grad concentrations in Baltimore in 2000.

(Source: PolicyMap, adapted by Bill Nelson)

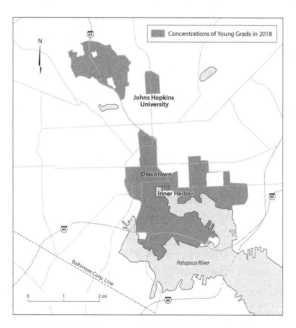

FIGURE 7.2. The spread of young grads in Baltimore, 2000 to 2018. Young grad concentrations in Baltimore in 2018.

(Source: PolicyMap, adapted by Bill Nelson)

Johns Hopkins University, young grads have spread to occupy much of central and northern Baltimore, around the harbor, and throughout downtown, where thousands of residential units have been created from old office buildings, as well as north and west of the Johns Hopkins University campus. The spread of young grads matches almost precisely the locus of gentrification in Baltimore.

Aging and the Empty Nest

The US population is aging, albeit less rapidly than in countries such as Japan and Italy, driven by declining birth rates and increasing life expectancy and only partly offset by immigration. While increases in life expectancy have stalled in recent years, birth rates have continued to decline. Meanwhile, the size of the baby boom generation, roughly half of whom were over age sixty-five in 2020, will continue to fuel an increase in the elderly population for the next decade. At least partly for that reason, the rate of increase in the elderly population has accelerated since around 2000. While from 1960 to 2000 the number of people over age sixty-five in the United States grew by an average of 450,000 to 500,000 per year, since 2000 it has been growing by 800,000 per year.

In contrast to the decline in child-rearing families and the rise in college-educated young people, both of which disproportionately affect central cities, the aging of America has a different spatial impact. While some individual urban neighborhoods are seeing growing elderly populations, the greatest impact of the aging trend is visible in rural and small-town America and within metropolitan areas in what can be called an "aging zone," concentrated in the inner-suburban ring around central cities largely corresponding to the first generation of post–World War II suburbs. That ring is clearly visible in the Philadelphia area in figure 7.3, along with the area inside the city known as the Far Northeast, the last part of the city to be developed during the late 1940s and 1950s and demographically similar to the inner-ring suburbs outside the city's borders. The darkest shading shows census tracts where 25 percent or more of the population is over age sixty-five, an elderly population share close to that of Japan, where the current figure is 28 percent. Similar aging clusters exist in most older American metropolitan areas.

The aging of the American population is likely to have unpredictable effects on the neighborhoods where older adults live or to which they may move. While some older people do indeed migrate to the Sunbelt, that is far from a universal tendency as a 2011 report summed it up. "Although the myth persists that older adults move *en masse* to the Sunbelt states once they retire, the overwhelming evidence is that older adults prefer to 'age in place' in their existing homes and communities."[6] Most elderly people do not move, while many who do move will

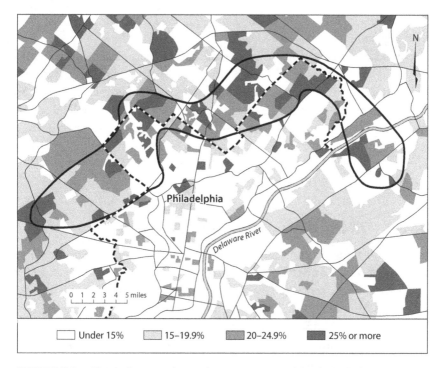

FIGURE 7.3.   Naturally occurring retirement communities in Philadelphia and its suburbs (percentage of population over age 65)

(Source: PolicyMap, adapted by Bill Nelson)

remain in the same community or region. As a result, many towns and neighborhoods, such as those in figure 7.3, are coming to be referred to as Naturally Occurring Retirement Communities or NORCs. The concentration of older people in these areas is changing not only the demand for public facilities and social services, prompting many creative innovations around the country, but also the social dynamics of these neighborhoods.

The empty nester phenomenon is somewhat different. As baby boomers' children have grown up and the boomers have reached their fifties and sixties largely active and healthy, their choices have become a major concern of pundits, demographers, and developers. Dozens of reports and blog posts have appeared on the effects of this generational downsizing and on empty nesters' purported return to the cities. In all of this it is difficult to separate, in Nate Silver's phrase, "the signal from the noise."[7] The much-heralded return of empty nesters to the cities appears largely anecdotal or promotional, supported by little quantifiable evidence. That is not to say that it is not taking place at all; the anecdotes are likely to signify something. While there is undoubtedly some movement of empty nesters into central cities, as a factor in urban neighborhood change its effects are modest compared to those of the Young Grads.

That may change. The sheer number of baby boomers makes them a significant wild card in terms of their influence on future neighborhood trends in both urban and suburban America. At the same time, one should not assume that all or even most of the members of that generation are the affluent, well-educated, and worldly couples portrayed in the media. Most are not college graduates and lack either the means or the inclination to move into a condo in Philadelphia's Center City or a row house near Baltimore's Inner Harbor.

Race, Ethnicity and Immigration

As we discussed in chapter 3, urban neighborhoods in the early twentieth century were largely defined by ethnic and racial identities. Most were dominated by a single white ethnic community, while after the end of World War I almost every city saw a distinct African American ghetto emerge, defined by legal restrictions and social constraints. The great majority of white ethnic neighborhoods gradually disappeared in the years after World War II. While the assimilation of the native-born children and grandchildren of the immigrant generation drove much of their demise, it was hastened by the end of mass immigration. The number of immigrant arrivals in the United States dropped from over eight million in the first decade of the twentieth century to fewer than seven hundred thousand in the 1930s, while from 1930 to 1970 the number of foreign-born residents in the United States dropped by nearly one-third, from fourteen million to under ten million, and their share of the population dropped from 15 percent to 5 percent.[8]

This was the product of the 1924 Immigration Act, which had established draconian immigration quotas based on the national origins of the historic population of the United States. Under that law, for example, between 1946 and 1950 only slightly more than 1,000 people were admitted each year from the entire Asian continent.[9] In 1960, 89 percent of the population was classified as "white" and almost all the remaining 11 percent was classified as "Negro," in the terminology of the time. Only 0.5 percent of the population fit into neither category, while there were so few Latinx immigrants from countries other than Mexico that the US Census Bureau did not even bother to classify them by country of origin, putting them all into a single "other Americas" category.

In 1965 Congress passed the Immigration and Nationality Act, also known as the Hart-Celler Act, abolishing national quotas. Although proponents played down the possibility that the bill would have a significant impact on immigration

TABLE 7.4   Race and ethnicity in the United States, 1960 and 2018

1960		2018	
CATEGORY	%	CATEGORY	%
White	89	Non-Latinx white	60
		Latinx (see note)	18
Black	11	Black or African American	13
Other	<1	Asian	6
		Other (including two or more races)	3

Source: Data for 1960 from 1969 Statistical Abstract, and 2018 data from Population Estimates, US Bureau of the Census.
Note: In 2017 about 65 percent of Latinx respondents identified themselves racially as "white," while about 26 percent identified themselves as "other."

flows or the demographic makeup of the country, few bills before or since have had such a fundamentally transformative effect on American society. The Hart-Celler Act turned the United States into a multinational, multiethnic nation.

Table 7.4 compares the racial and ethnic composition of the United States today to that of 1960 but that table barely begins to hint at the diversity of the American population. Roughly 10 percent of American Black people are African and Caribbean immigrants, while the Asian umbrella includes not only large numbers of people from China, Korea, India, and the Philippines but also some from virtually every Asian nation. The Census Bureau breaks down America's fifty-six million Latinx residents into twenty-four separate subcategories and even then finds that over one million fail to fit into any category. Nearly 14 percent of the nation's population are foreign-born, only slightly fewer than at the historic peak nearly a hundred years ago.

The Black population in the United States is more spatially dispersed than in the 1950s. In contrast to that era, however, when Black ghettos housed an economically diverse population with rich, middle-class, and poor rubbing elbows, today's Black population lives in far more economically homogenous although still often racially distinct clusters.[10] The vibrancy of neighborhoods such as Bronzeville and Black Bottom is a thing of the past. While many of those neighborhoods were destroyed by urban renewal or highway construction, as happened to Black Bottom in Detroit, it is unlikely that they would have survived the social and economic changes of the last sixty years intact.

The increase in immigration has led to a resurgence of ethnic neighborhoods. While the greatest change has been in the growth of Latinx communities, urban and suburban areas have both seen a proliferation of immigrant ethnic neighborhoods of every description. Since immigrants to the United States are highly diverse economically as well as racially and ethnically, their neighborhoods vary widely economically, with some immigrant communities being affluent, some poor, and some containing a mix of people of different economic levels.

Three large contiguous suburban townships in central New Jersey with a combined population of roughly 260,000 are now nearly 40 percent Asian or of Asian descent, with three-quarters of those from India (figure 7.4). As one writer describes Edison Township, "From indoor cricket to a Hindu temple, paan shops, *dosa* and *biryani* stalls, and saris in the store windows, this eastern U.S. suburban area could be an Indian municipality."[11] Oak Tree Road, known as "Little India," is a shopping district one and a half mile long that "attracts South Asian customers from Maine to Maryland."[12] The area is an affluent one; in 2017, the median income of Asian households in Edison was nearly $120,000.

Suburban enclaves as affluent as Edison tend to be the exceptions among immigrant neighborhoods, but an immense variety of neighborhood configurations have come into being. While immigration magnets such as New York City and Los Angeles have had immigrant neighborhoods for decades, in recent years similar neighborhoods have emerged in cities that had earlier lagged as immigrant destinations. A large predominantly Bangladeshi neighborhood known as Banglatown has emerged in Detroit, while in Dayton, Ohio, a refugee community of Ahiska Turks, an ethnically Turkish community originally from the former Soviet republic of Georgia, has moved to and revitalized the city's Old North neighborhood. Almost every American city has similar stories.

The greatest number of immigrant neighborhoods in the United States, however, are Latinx neighborhoods. From northeastern mill towns such as Lawrence in Massachusetts, Passaic in New Jersey and Reading in Pennsylvania, all of which are now majority-Latinx cities, to large cities or rural areas, few regions in the United States lack a strong Latinx presence. Again, their diversity is staggering. Dominican immigrants in Lawrence, Cubans in Miami, Tejanos along the Mexican border, and Salvadorans in Los Angeles are members of distinct cultures, only tenuously linked by a common language.

Researchers who have studied the spatial effects of immigration have found them to be generally positive, especially for older urban neighborhoods suffering from depopulation and disinvestment. As sociologist Robert Sampson, who has studied the subject closely, writes, "the evidence merits including immigration alongside other more dominant hypotheses for the nation's crime decline and its urban revitalization."[13] While Sampson cautions about drawing excessive generalizations, given the diversity of immigrant populations and their settings, he nonetheless finds strong relationships between immigration and crime declines, challenging current political rhetoric on the subject. At the same time, immigration has triggered localized conflicts, not only the highly publicized and often ideologically charged conflicts between the dominant non-Latinx

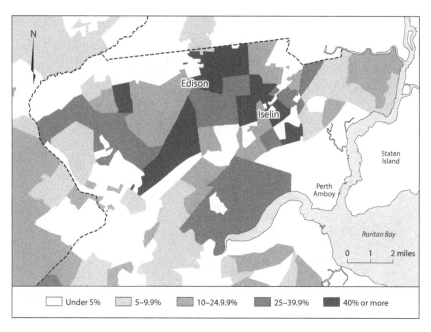

FIGURE 7.4.   The Indian American community of central New Jersey

(Source: PolicyMap, adapted by Bill Nelson)

white population and Latinx immigrants but also conflicts between Black and Latinx or other immigrant communities or between native Blacks and African or Afro-Caribbean immigrants.

Another issue is the staying power of immigrant neighborhoods. Just as the first wave of late nineteenth- and early twentieth-century immigrant communities gradually dissolved as their residents or their descendants assimilated into larger ethnically mixed communities, the same may be taking place, often at an accelerated pace, in more recently formed immigrant enclaves. As we discussed in chapter 3, the transition of the first generation of immigrants was often a two-step process: from the initial enclave to a less crowded, more outlying but still immigrant-focused neighborhood usually still within the central city, followed a generation later by the conjoined processes of suburbanization and assimilation. That first step is already taking place for many immigrant communities more quickly than in previous generations. Some of Detroit's Banglatown residents already see the neighborhood as a first-step community and aspire to earn enough money to move to the nearby inner-ring suburbs of Warren and Sterling Heights, where a Bangladeshi community is beginning to emerge.[14]

The suburbanization of Latinx communities in northern New Jersey, a major center of the nation's Latinx population, is clearly visible in figures 7.5 and

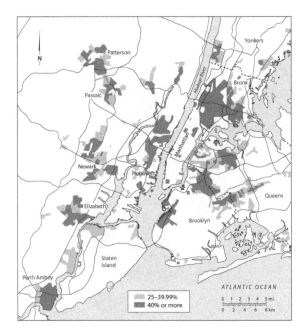

FIGURE 7.5. The suburban spread of the Latinx population in northern New Jersey in 2000

(Source: PolicyMap, adapted by Bill Nelson)

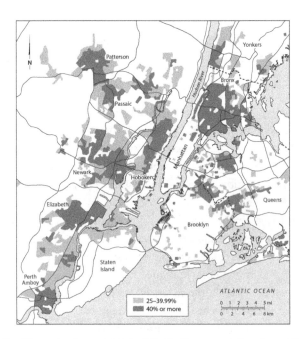

FIGURE 7.6. The suburban spread of the Latinx population in northern New Jersey in 2018

(Source: PolicyMap, adapted by Bill Nelson)

7.6. As late as 2000, large Latinx population were largely limited to a few central cities, including Newark, Elizabeth, Jersey City, and Paterson. By 2018 the Latinx community had spread beyond the central cities into their suburban neighbors, forming a nearly contiguous belt of high Latinx population density from the small majority-Latinx city of Perth Amboy (immediately east of the area of Indian population density mentioned earlier) to the inner-ring suburbs of Bergen County, over thirty miles to the north.

Whatever the future may hold, immigration has transformed hundreds if not thousands of American neighborhoods. The effects of this transformation, which vary dramatically based on the characteristics of the immigrant community and those of the larger community in which they have settled, are only beginning to be well understood.

Economic Trauma and Transformation

The last sixty years in the United States have seen economic transformations as potent and unsettling as the nation's demographic transformation. After nearly a hundred years during which America's economy was driven by manufacturing and its manufacturing sector was driven by heavy industry, led by steelmaking and the automobile industry, that era came abruptly to an end during the 1970s. Symbolically, at least, the end of that era has a date: September 16, 1977, known to this day in Youngstown, Ohio, as "Black Monday," the day when Youngstown Sheet & Tube shut down its Campbell Works. "Within the next 18 months," Salena Zito writes, "US Steel announced that the nation's largest steel producer was also shutting down 16 plants across the nation, including their Ohio Works in Youngstown, a move that eliminated an additional 4,000 workers in Youngstown."[15]

The number of manufacturing jobs in the United States peaked in 1969 at nearly 20 million, or nearly 30 percent of the nation's total nonagricultural workforce. While manufacturing is still an important part of the nation's economy, it commands a much smaller share. By 2019, the remaining 12 million industrial jobs made up only slightly more than 8 percent of the nonagricultural workforce. Jobs in the flagship steel and automobile industries have dropped from nearly 2.2 million in the 1960s to roughly 750,000 today. Moreover, factory jobs are not what or where they once were. Manufacturing has all but disappeared in historic centers of industry such as Pittsburgh, Philadelphia, and Cleveland. Factories are more likely to be found today in small cities or rural areas in the South and West and are far less likely to be unionized. Today only 1 out of 11 manufacturing workers in the United States are union members, compared to nearly half in the 1960s.[16]

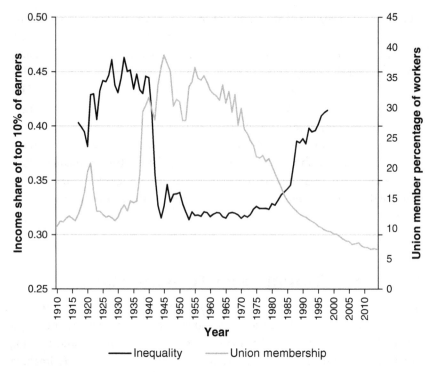

FIGURE 7.7. Private-sector labor union membership and income inequality in the United States, 1910 to 2010

(Courtesy of Emin Dinlersoz and Jeremy Greenwood)

During the decades following World War II, unionized factory jobs propelled millions into the middle class and into homeownership in either the central cities or their burgeoning inner suburbs. The relationship between declining union membership and increased income inequality is vividly depicted in figure 7.7. The loss of manufacturing jobs and the decline of industrial unions has had a devastating effect on many neighborhoods, particularly in industrial cities and even more so in smaller cities such as Youngstown or Flint, which have been unable to create a new export economy to replace their lost industrial base.

Innumerable neighborhoods in industrial cities were configured socially and economically around factory jobs, sustained by the wages that factory workers brought home. They were also, particularly in cities dominated by heavy industries such as steel and automobiles, organized socially around unions and workplaces. Industrial unions were not only a means by which workers improved wages and working conditions, but they were vehicles for social cohesion, for crafting individual and group identity, through such mundane things as picnics, clubs, and the role of the union hall as a neighborhood social center. Even in those few areas where unions, as economic organizations, still play an important role, the social function of the union has largely withered away. As Robert Putnam and Shaylyn Romney Garrett write in their book *The Upswing,* "the solidarity of union halls is now at most a fading memory of aging men."[17]

The growth of income inequality also meant that there were fewer and fewer middle-income households, a phenomenon aptly characterized as the "hollowing out of the middle class." As sociologists Sean Reardon and Kendra Bischoff have documented, this has been coupled with an increasing tendency of Americans to sort themselves by economic level, resulting in a decline in middle-income neighborhoods. Historically diverse by income and other social characteristics, the decline of middle-income neighborhoods has been even greater than the decline of middle-income households.[18] This decline has been particularly pronounced in urban areas, where the national trends have been exacerbated by continued outward middle-class migration as well as in recent years the concentration of more affluent households in small upscale or gentrifying enclaves.

In 1970 over half of all of Philadelphia's census tracts were middle income, meaning that their median income was between 80 percent and 120 percent of the citywide median. By 2018, the number had dropped to only slightly more than one-quarter. Conversely, in 1970 only 3 percent were either poor (under 50 percent of citywide median) or wealthy (over 200 percent); by 2018, that number had grown to nearly 20 percent.

The downward trajectory of the nation's middle neighborhoods will be discussed in detail in chapter 12. While many factors are contributing to their difficulties, they begin with the change in the economic makeup of the nation's households.

Sorting, Identity, and the Good Neighborhood

A major reason that people of diverse economic levels, occupations, and backgrounds could comfortably share neighborhoods fifty or sixty years ago was that in most other respects they were not that different. Social values, behaviors, and preferences varied little across the income spectrum. Moreover, whether or not one had a bachelor's or higher degree, which aside from race has become the dominant socioeconomic divide in America today, made far less difference in one's economic conditions, behaviors, and attitudes than it does today.

The wage premium for a four-year or higher college degree has grown steadily since the 1970s. Not only has the gap between individual earnings of college and high school graduates widened, but the income gap between households headed by a college graduate compared to those headed by a high school graduate has widened even more.[19] Today, the income of the average household headed by a college graduate is double that headed by a high school graduate. A household headed by someone with a professional degree, which includes not only lawyers and those with MBAs but also city planners and social workers, has an income on the average more than three times that of the high school graduate's household (figure 7.8). This disparity arises from three different factors that reinforce one another:

- The wages of college graduates have risen more quickly than those of people without a BA or higher degree, including those with an associate degree or some college;[20]
- Men and women with college degrees are increasingly likely to marry one another rather than marry someone without a college degree, thus concentrating high earners within the same households; and
- Once married, households made up of people with college degrees are significantly more likely than those without degrees to remain married rather than divorce or separate.

All of these reflect fundamental shifts from the 1960s and 1970s. A recent study found that by age forty-six, nearly 60 percent of people without a high school diploma and nearly 50 percent of those with a high school diploma or some college who had married at least once had divorced, compared to only 30 percent of college graduates.[21] Since married couples—with the potent economic benefits of

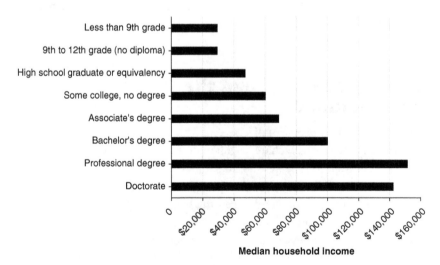

FIGURE 7.8. Educational attainment and median household income, 2020

(Bureau of the Census, Current Population Survey)

having two wage earners as well as significant child-rearing benefits over single parents—are more likely to be made up of two college graduates, they thus pass on the economic benefits of a college education to future generations. Nationally, in 2018, 89 percent of all children born to women with college degrees were born into an intact marriage, compared to only 54 percent of children born to women without a college degree. In urban areas the disparity was even greater. As journalist Claire Cain Miller has written, "Marriage, which used to be the default way to form a family in the United States, regardless of income or education, has become yet another part of American life reserved for those who are most privileged."[22]

These disparities extend to other behavioral realms. Only 8 percent of college graduates are regular smokers, compared to 27 percent of people with only a high school diploma. Sixty percent of college graduates exercise enough to meet the official standards for aerobic activity, compared to 37 percent of high school graduates.[23] Harder to quantify but readily visible are different preferences in style, food, recreational activities, and more based on educational attainment.[24] Whereas sixty years ago both factory workers and college professors would go to the same white tablecloth restaurant to celebrate a family milestone or social occasion, today their choices would be starkly different.

Political polarization has also increased, often corresponding to and reinforcing barriers created by economic or social class disparities. In a 2015 Pew survey, 49 percent of respondents with a BA or higher degree took largely liberal positions on public issues, compared to 26 percent of those with a high school diploma or less.[25] Since the 1990s, according to another Pew study, "Partisan animosity has increased substantially. . . . In each party, the share with a highly negative view of the opposing party has more than doubled since 1994. Most of these intense partisans believe the opposing party's policies 'are so misguided that they threaten the nation's well-being,'"[26] or as Putnam and Garrett pithily put it, "both Democrats and Republicans increasingly dislike, even loathe, their opponents."[27]

The partisan divide in the 2020 presidential election links both the educational and the racial divides, as the exit polls shown in figure 7.9 illustrate. Notably, the partisan gap between white and nonwhite (the data conflates Black, Latinx, and Asian) voters without college degrees is roughly double the racial gap for voters with college degrees. All these shifts are part of a larger picture with powerful implications for neighborhoods. In *The Upswing*, Putnam and Garrett present a mass of evidence to show how, after steady movement toward greater economic equality and communitarian values from the end of the nineteenth century to the 1950s and 1960s, those trends abruptly reversed as the nation turned from communitarian to individualistic values. As Putnam and Garrett put it, we went from a "we" society in the 1950s and 1960s to a measurably more "I" society today.[28]

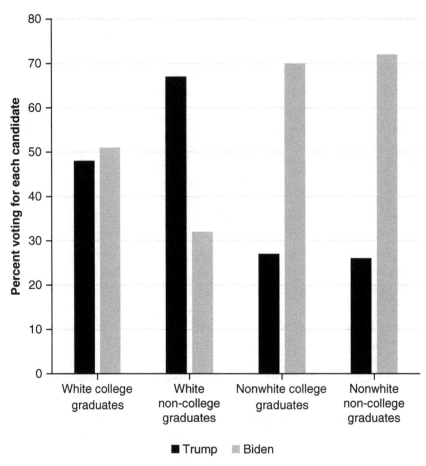

FIGURE 7.9. Voting in the 2020 presidential election by race and educational level

(Authors' work based on exit poll data reported in the New York Times, *November 3, 2020)*

An individualistic society focuses on the self and on its "identity," an idea that over the past fifty or so years has moved from a concept used in social psychology to perhaps the fundamental defining term of contemporary American society. Two prominent thinkers called attention to this shift in important books that appeared almost simultaneously at the end of the 1970s: Christopher Lasch in *The Culture of Narcissism* and Richard Sennett in *The Fall of Public Man*.[29] While coming from radically different disciplines and perspectives—Lasch was a part-Freudian, part-Marxist literary scholar, while Sennett was (and is) a less ideologically grounded social philosopher—they both identified the emerging preoccupation with the self as a threat to the forms of social engagement central to the communitarian ideal. Sennett focused on it directly, writing that "often against our own knowledge, we are caught up in a war between the demands of social existence and a belief that we develop as human beings only through contrary modes of intimate psychic existence."[30] While he does not address neighborhoods as such, he focuses on the role of civility, which he defines as "the activity which protects people from each other and yet allows them to enjoy one another's company," very much a paraphrase of the idea underlying the value of weak ties for good neighborhoods that we introduced in chapter 1.[31]

Identity challenges the premises of communitarianism in two distinct ways: first, as a focus on the self to the exclusion of others, and second, by focusing on group identity.[32] As Putnam and Garrett write, "the concept of 'identity' itself had begun to spread beyond developmental psychology to gender and racial identity in the 1970s and 1980s and to identity politics by the 1990s."[33] Sennett put his finger on the danger of this spread, writing of

> the perversion of fraternity in modern communal experience. . . . The narrower the scope of a community formed by collective personality, the more destructive does the experience of fraternal feeling become. Outsiders, unknowns, unlikes become creatures to be shunned; the personality traits the community shares become ever more exclusive; the very act of sharing becomes ever more centered upon decisions about who can belong and who cannot.[34]

Reinforced by the way in which the internet and social media have come to function as echo chambers for the "perversion of fraternity," the demands for ideological purity among insiders, the drawing of boundaries between insider and outsider, and the shunning or demonizing of those outside the boundaries have come to play an increasingly prominent role in contemporary American communal life.

At any level, a good neighborhood is fundamentally a communitarian project. The heyday of the white urban neighborhood and its emerging suburban counterparts was arguably the 1950s, the height of the "we" society. In many respects, American society has made important progress since then in terms of what "we" means. "We" today has brought LGBTQ people into mainstream America in ways that would have been unthinkable in the 1950s, has largely ended the paternalistic relegation of women to subordinate roles, and, although in far from adequate fashion, begun the process of incorporating America's Black population into the national polity.

This is important, even essential. But it raises many questions, particularly when coupled with the simultaneous focus on identity and especially with respect to race. First, these changes appear to resonate most powerfully, on the one hand, in the intimate settings of personal relationships and, on the other, in national legal and institutional frameworks and far less in the intermediate space of the neighborhood. It is telling that the propensity of white home buyers purchasing a home in a predominantly Black neighborhood has actually declined over the past decade from what was already a very low level.[35] Second, to what extent is much of the broadening of the mainstream yet another elite project, another reflection of the gap in attitudes and values between the highly educated, affluent minority and the less educated and less affluent majority of America's white population? This is a complex question, which we cannot answer in this book, yet the extent to which recent years have seen a reemergence of forums for openly racist discourse as well as the hardening of lines over a variety of social and cultural issues raises questions about the nature and extent of America's social transformation. As Putnam and Garrett observe, pointing out how much more significant Black economic and educational progress was from the 1940s through the 1970s than since, "a selfish, fragmented 'I' society is not a favorable environment for achieving racial equality."[36]

Nor, we must recognize, is it a favorable environment for sustaining or rebuilding good neighborhoods. At the same time, the picture is not entirely bleak. Immigrants have revived many urban neighborhoods, while other neighborhoods have been reinvigorated through the efforts of their residents and community development corporations. Although not without fostering conflict, the youth movement to the cities has given downtowns and many nearby areas new life, even in a city such as Detroit that not long ago was grist for apocalyptic media fantasies. Under the media radar, numerous urban and suburban neighborhoods continue to provide decent, if not manicured or elegant, places for people to live good lives and for their children to grow into successful adults. As the experience of the COVID-19 pandemic brought home for many people, being part of a neighborhood and being able to connect with others within a bounded physical space—not the virtual space of Zoom and Instagram—still matter. The good neighborhood is challenged, but it is not a lost cause.

THE CONTINUING YET CHANGING SIGNIFICANCE OF RACE

Race in the narrow yet powerful sense of white and Black is the pervasive fault line running through the heart of American society. To understand the role of race in neighborhoods and neighborhood change, though, we must confront a paradox: race is constant but is constantly changing. Race is like other divisions that influence the trajectories of neighborhoods, such as class and ethnicity, and yet completely different. Unlike any other divide in America society, the persistence and pervasiveness of race across history makes it a constant in neighborhood life. At the same time, neighborhood conditions and change are never only about race. Race interacts with other factors, creating complex patterns that vary across time and space. Race is no exception to our dictum that context matters.

Isabel Wilkerson's valuable book *Caste: The Origins of Our Discontents* describes how the concepts of race and caste are interwoven throughout American history, explicating the persistence and pervasiveness of race. Caste is the unseen foundation, the

> architecture of human hierarchy. . . . A caste system is an artificial construction, a fixed and embedded ranking of human value that sets the presumed supremacy of one group against the presumed inferiority of other groups on the basis of ancestry and often immutable traits. . . . A caste system uses rigid, often arbitrary boundaries to keep the ranks apart, distinct from one another and in their assigned places. . . . Race does the heavy lifting for a caste system that demands a means of human division.[1]

While clearly not exculpating or excusing racist behavior, this frame makes clear that one does not need to hold personal racist beliefs to have one's behavior guided by an invisible code of instructions structured by caste.

Up to a point, race has been a permeable construct in American society. Until relatively recently, full "whiteness," understood as an ideological construct that arbitrarily confers status and privilege, was seen as belonging only to Protestants of impeccably northwestern European ancestry. Gradually, though, Irish Catholics and then Jews, Italians, and other southern and eastern European peoples came to be seen as "white," as they are today. More recently, we argue, the same status is being granted to some members, but far from all, of what are generically referred to as Asian and Latinx people. Over time, we suspect, social whiteness will include progressively more so-called nonwhite people. Yet one constant persists in the social construction of race: Black people are excluded from whiteness. No matter how many Black individuals gain wealth, influence, or power, Black people continue to be excluded as a category because whiteness is defined in opposition to Blackness. That is the essence of the American caste system and the source of its recurring injustices.

While race as a caste system has been a constant in American society, how race plays out on the ground in neighborhoods has varied significantly across different historical periods and places. Efforts to explain the relationship begin, as is often the case, with the Chicago School of Human Ecology's invasion-succession model of neighborhood change under which, in the course of a neighborhood's life cycle, groups of progressively lower socioeconomic status "invade" a neighborhood, pushing out higher-status groups and leading to a progressive decline in the neighborhood's physical and social character. While the Chicago School's analysis was not racial per se, as most immigrant groups of any ethnicity were considered "invaders," it encompassed racial change. It was a short step from there to tipping point theory, the belief that once the percentage of Blacks in a neighborhood's reaches a certain point, the neighborhood inevitably tips to all-Black. That proposition, which came into vogue in the 1960s and 1970s, still dominates much of the literature on race and neighborhoods despite empirical evidence to the contrary.

Concepts such as tipping point theory reflect the way in which American society uses race as a way of defining space, distinguishing between white space and Black space, as discussed in recent books by sociologist Elijah Anderson and legal scholar Sheryll Cashin.[2] Not only have Blacks been historically unwelcome in white spaces, reflected in both overt racial discrimination and a host of small encounters and indignities, but whites stereotype Black space. As Anderson notes, "for many Americans, the ghetto is where the Black people live."[3] The corollary to this is that Black spaces—that is, neighborhoods where large numbers of Black people live, including well-groomed middle-class communities—are systematically devalued by white observers. As psychologist Courtney Bonham writes, "race is embedded not only in human bodies and social identities, but is etched into mental representations of physical structures."[4] She refers to this as the phenomenon making "middle-class Black space" invisible.

One would be foolish not to acknowledge this reality, yet as with everything having to do with neighborhoods, history and context matter. While we are not optimistic that the relationship between race and caste in America will change fundamentally anytime soon, we are more optimistic that under the right circumstances vicious cycles of neighborhood segregation and decline can be replaced by virtuous circles of neighborhood diversity and vitality. We believe that this process can be hastened by identifying and understanding the processes that have created both strong Black neighborhoods and stably integrated neighborhoods in American communities, which we strive to do in this chapter.

The Changing Context of Race and Neighborhoods

While varying degrees of racial segregation existed in nineteenth-century American cities, the social boundaries of the caste system were rarely translated into explicit geographic boundaries until about 1910, when the dominant white majority sought to formalize those boundaries using racial zoning. Reacting to the move by a Black lawyer and his family into a house in a white neighborhood in Baltimore, the city enacted an ordinance specifying that "no negro may take up his residence in a block within the city limits of Baltimore wherein more than half the residents are white."[5] The idea quickly spread to other cities but was invalidated by the US Supreme Court in 1917.[6] Not surprisingly, the court's objections were not to the principle of racial segregation but instead to the restrictions on private property rights that the ordinances imposed.

Shorn of the ability to use municipal ordinances to enforce racial segregation, at a time when the First Great Migration stimulated by World War I was leading to increased Black urban populations, developers and property owners turned to racial covenants to accomplish the same end. Covenants, also known as deed restrictions, are a legal device originating in English common law to limit the use of properties by incorporating restrictions into the deed to the property rather than relying on an external restriction such as a zoning ordinance. In principle deed restrictions are a neutral device and are widely used today to, for example, ensure that affordable housing developments remain affordable over time or that land preserved for farming is not subsequently developed or to regulate such mundane matters as fencing and home businesses. Covenants have a dark side, however. With the demise of racial zoning, they became the principal way that racial exclusion was enforced.

Reflecting the narrow construction of whiteness common at the time, the 1919 Minneapolis real estate ad shown in figure 8.1 featured the following restriction: "The premises . . . shall not at any time be conveyed, mortgaged or leased to any person or persons of Chinese, Japanese, Moorish, Turkish, Negro, Mongolian, Semetic [*sic*] or African blood or descent."[7] A 1928 covenant from Seattle barred occupancy "by any Hebrew or by any person of the Ethiopian, Malay or any Asiatic Race."[8] Ethiopian meant Black, Malay meant Filipino, and Hebrew meant Jew. While many covenants, such as those above, barred anyone not meeting full whiteness standards, such as Asians, all barred Black buyers and tenants.

The US Supreme Court upheld the validity of racial covenants in 1926, ruling that "the constitutional right of a Negro to acquire, own and occupy property does not carry with it the constitutional power to compel sale and conveyance to him of any particular private property."[9] From the end of World War I until the court reversed its position in 1948 and held that racial covenants were unenforceable as a matter of law, covenants barring Black families from buying or renting in newly built developments were commonplace.[10] According to an article cited by the US Commission on Civil Rights, "by 1940, 80 percent of both Chicago and Los Angeles carried restrictive covenants barring Black families."[11]

The end of racial covenants in 1948 did not mean the end of legally imposed segregation. Not only did the nation lack fair housing laws to bar private discrimination, but Federal Housing Administration and Veterans Administration mortgage lending policies, as described in chapter 4, ensured that as America suburbanized after World War II, the new mass suburbs would be all but completely restricted to whites. While a 1961 executive order by President John Kennedy ended overt discrimination in lending by federal agencies, discriminatory practices have continued even after passage of the 1968 Fair Housing Act banning discrimination in marketing, selling, and renting housing.

Even where discrimination in sales and rentals is not an issue, Black neighborhoods are bedeviled by other forms of racial discrimination and targeting. Redlining, as the practice of lenders and insurance brokers denying mortgages or policies to property owners in Black neighborhoods came to be known in the 1960s, has not disappeared. Indeed, redlining took a strange turn in the widespread practices of subprime mortgage lenders in the early 2000s. Instead of denying mortgages to Black (and Latinx) neighborhoods during the housing bubble years, in a practice that came to be known as "reverse redlining" lenders aggressively marketed subprime and other questionable mortgage

FIGURE 8.1. A racial covenant in a 1919 Minneapolis real estate advertisement

(Image courtesy of the Mapping Prejudice Project, University of Minnesota)

products in many of those same neighborhoods, with ultimately disastrous consequences.

Over half a century after passage of the 1968 Fair Housing Act, urban and suburban neighborhoods remain stubbornly segregated by race. According to studies that have tracked segregation at the neighborhood level across metropolitan areas, racial segregation has been decreasing but at a disappointingly slow rate.[12] Two common explanations for the persistence of segregated neighborhoods are that racial prejudice is alive and well but has simply gone underground and that whites shun Black neighborhoods not because they are Black but because they are poor. Neither explanation is compelling. Few white families buy in predominantly Black neighborhoods, whatever the incomes of their residents or the amenities the neighborhoods offer. At the same time, growing numbers of white buyers appear to be comfortable living in racially integrated neighborhoods, where the percentage of Black households is significant but generally less than a majority.

Any effort to isolate one cause of neighborhood segregation, however, distorts our understanding of neighborhood change. Race cannot be separated from economic class, as it is layered with perceptions of class. The engrained associations of class and race and their manifestations in physical space are equally important. Moreover, racial attitudes and economic interests do not shape neighborhood trajectories in a straightforward, linear process. Instead, these and other factors interact with each other in complex feedback processes influenced by specific historical and geographical contexts, resulting in neighborhood racial patterns that are more varied and complex than conventional wisdom suggests.

The widely held belief that racial tipping is inevitable creates a confirmation bias that inhibits our ability to recognize the diversity of neighborhood change patterns, including healthy Black neighborhoods and stably integrated neighborhoods. As we discuss later in this chapter, the racial tipping point hypothesis, first described by political scientist Morton Grodzins in the 1950s and elaborated by economist Thomas Schelling in 1971, is fundamentally flawed.[13] While segregation remains widespread, our analysis of racial change by census tract in St. Louis over nearly sixty years from 1960 to 2019 illustrates the diversity of racial dynamics. While the narrative of racial change leading to resegregation was largely true from 1960 to 1980, reflecting in part the traumatic effects of the rapid pace of both Black in-migration and white flight during those years, the picture shifted significantly from that point onward.

As figure 8.2 shows, the number of segregated Black census tracts (75% or more Black) leveled off after 1980, and the continued decline in segregated white tracts (less than 25% Black) through 2000 reflected an increase in the number

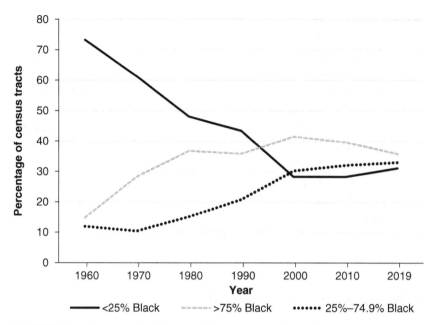

FIGURE 8.2.   Percent distribution of census tracts in St. Louis by racial configuration, 1960 to 2019

(Authors' work based on decennial census and American Community Survey data)

of racially mixed tracts. Since 2000, despite the traumas of the foreclosure crisis and Great Recession, the distribution of neighborhoods by race in St. Louis has remained roughly constant. Moreover, while the handful of racially mixed tracts in 1960 were not stably integrated but were in transition from white to Black, racially mixed tracts today are more stable. Two-thirds of the racially mixed tracts in 2019 had been integrated for twenty years or more.

St. Louis has not become an integrated city. Over two-thirds of the city's census tracts are still racially segregated, and the great majority of the city's Black population live in segregated neighborhoods. On the other hand, it is noteworthy that neighborhoods in which 20–50 percent of the population is African American are St. Louis's highest-value neighborhoods, with median house values nearly 25 percent higher than those in the city's predominantly white neighborhoods. These are typically the neighborhoods that St. Louis residents cite as gentrifying neighborhoods, a subject we discuss in chapter 10.

Neighborhood change and racial attitudes embody powerful feedback loops. Neighborhood life cycle theory, which along with tipping point theory perpetuated the stereotype that the arrival of Black families in a neighborhood is a prelude to racial segregation and neighborhood decline, continues to influence people's thinking. But times and conditions have changed. Even in St. Louis, with its well-deserved reputation as a racially divided city, spatial patterns of segregation and integration have become more complex and diverse in recent decades.[14]

Whether the experience of new patterns of racial diversity will significantly reduce racially motivated behavior and set in motion virtuous feedback effects remains to be seen. Moreover, even if conscious racial attitudes change, the unconscious identification of race and caste is likely to persist. That said, it is the exceptions to the racial stereotypes that best illustrate the complex dynamics of neighborhood change and offer insight into possible pathways to the future good neighborhood. In the next two sections of this chapter, we explore two key exceptions: good Black neighborhoods and stable integrated neighborhoods. Black suburban neighborhoods, along with the intersection of race, class, and political institutions in shaping them, are discussed in chapter 13.

The Good Black Neighborhood

The scholarly focus on concentrated poverty neighborhoods and the distress of the so-called Black underclass, along with the persistence of the racial stereotyping of "Black space," have caused both scholars and the general public to overlook the existence of vital, healthy Black neighborhoods.[15] Most Black families do not live in areas of concentrated poverty or abandonment. While many neighborhoods are segregated, many of them are also good neighborhoods, with well-kept homes, moderate levels of crime, adequate or better schools, and a community life rooted in churches and other third places, such as barbershops and beauty salons. While some are affluent neighborhoods, most are neighborhoods of working-class and middle-class families: factory workers, owners of small businesses, and public employees. They are middle neighborhoods.[16]

Even the most successful Black neighborhoods, however, are almost always at greater risk of destabilization than comparable white neighborhoods because of the inherent economic and social insecurity of Black people in American society and also because they are embedded in a larger geography of race that often places them adjacent to areas of concentrated poverty.[17] Other things being equal, this means that they will be more vulnerable to recessions and more exposed to crime and have access to less well-performing schools. Moreover, as we will discuss later, the resistance of white buyers to buying homes in largely Black neighborhoods means that they have difficulty sustaining enough market demand to replace departing homeowners.

The story of urban Black middle neighborhoods is closely tied to the story of white flight. As we discussed in chapter 4, as late as the 1950s middle neighborhoods, with scattered exceptions, were white neighborhoods. Racial discrimination still effectively confined the great majority of Black families, whatever their economic condition, to Black ghetto neighborhoods. With most ghetto housing owned by absentee landlords, the Black ghetto was a reservoir of pent-up demand for better housing and homeownership opportunities.

Beginning in the 1950s and through the 1960s and 1970s, millions of white families abandoned the cities for the lure of the suburbs. In every major city white flight exceeded Black in-migration, usually by a significant margin. For every Black person moving into St. Louis in the 1960s, four white residents left. It was during those years, with the wholesale depopulation of many urban neighborhoods, that cities first saw houses being abandoned en masse and large stretches of St. Louis's Northside and Detroit's East Side began to turn into the urban prairies that still haunt these cities today. Because of this depopulation, white flight is often mistakenly used as a synonym for neighborhood collapse. The real story is more complicated. True, vast numbers of whites left, and some neighborhoods did fall apart. But many neighborhoods did not fall apart. And in many cases when they did, it often had less to do with racial change than with parallel economic changes and predatory real estate practices.

The other important part of this story is rarely told. Middle neighborhoods continued to exist, although diminished in number and extent. In a few cases, they remained largely white neighborhoods. More often, they went through racial change but retained their economic and social strength as working- and middle-class Black families took advantage of the space left by white flight to leave their overcrowded and substandard housing behind and become homeowners in neighborhoods from which they had previously been excluded. In a little-recognized process largely obscured by dominant narratives of neighborhood decline and suburban growth, many formerly white middle-class neighborhoods in America's older cities that went through racial transition in the 1960s and 1970s became and remained for decades thereafter good middle-class Black neighborhoods.

The small northwest Detroit neighborhood of Crary–St. Mary's, named after the public school and parish church that bookend the area, was typical. Its homes were built from the later 1930s to the 1950s, an era of prosperity and rapid growth in Detroit. It was a middle-class community with solid although unpretentious brick houses set back from the street by generous front yards (figure 8.3). Up to 1970, its population was entirely white. That changed during the 1970s as its residents fled the city for the burgeoning suburbs. By 1980, Crary–St. Mary's was 84 percent Black. The skin color of the people living in the houses had changed, but little else did, as can be seen in table 8.1.

The Black newcomers were middle- or working-class families. They were homeowners whose incomes were similar to those of the people they replaced,

FIGURE 8.3.   Street in Detroit's Crary–St. Mary's neighborhood

(Google Earth © 2022 Google)

TABLE 8.1   Key indicators for Crary–St. Mary's, 1970–2000

	1970	1980	1990	2000
% Black population	1.8	84.7	95.1	96.9
% population below poverty level	3.7	11.4	15.8	13.4
% married couples with children under age 18 as percentage of all households	25.8	29.7	21.5	20.2
% owner occupants	82.3	79.1	73.2	74.6
% of dwelling units vacant	1.2	2.3	3.3	3.5

Source: Bureau of the Census, Decennial Census.

and they raised families. The number of married couples with children in the area actually increased from 1970 to 1980. Seen in the context of the decline of the Detroit economy and the demographic shifts changing the nation, Crary–St. Mary's remained highly stable through the 1980s and 1990s. At the end of the millennium, it was still a middle-class neighborhood. We will revisit this neighborhood and its subsequent trajectory in chapter 11.

Crary–St. Mary's had many counterparts in Detroit as well as in almost every other older city in America, including Lee-Miles in Cleveland, Overbrook in Philadelphia, and South Shore and Chatham in Chicago. The rise of the Black urban middle neighborhood in the 1960s and 1970s, the enactment of the 1968 Fair Housing Act, and the growth in Black homeownership during those decades are all related. The number of Black homeowners in the United States grew by over 40 percent during the 1960s; in Detroit alone, over fifty thousand more Black families became homeowners. By 1980, well over half of Detroit's Black families were homeowners. Most of the Black families who bought homes in Crary–St. Mary's during the 1970s were almost certainly first-time home buyers.

In *Black Picket Fences*, Mary Pattillo-McCoy documents life in a similar middle-class Black neighborhood on the South Side of Chicago she dubbed "Groveland." Groveland went from being entirely white in 1960 to 98 percent Black in 1980, but the homeownership rate never fell below 70 percent, and the educational levels of the neighborhood's adults actually increased.[18] Groveland embraced a Black cultural identity along with a fierce attachment to middle-class standards of property maintenance and decorum.

For more than a generation, these neighborhoods were the principal seedbed of the Black middle class in American cities as well as centers of community engagement and leadership. They were a haven for Black families, as veteran Chicago reporter William Lee wrote of his childhood neighborhood years later. "In my mind's eye, the South Shore of my youth was pristine. With its big old homes and apartments, four grocery stores and doctors' offices, South Shore had all kinds of residents—laborers, city workers, artists, businessmen and executives—raising their families side by side. A black child in the '80s could feel insulated from the trappings of urban life. It's where first lady Michelle Obama called home."[19]

Obama grew up in an apartment on the second floor of a brick bungalow in South Shore. As she writes in her autobiography *Becoming*, "Everything that mattered was within a five-block radius."[20] This included her church, her grandparents, Bryn Mawr Elementary School, and Rosenblum Park. When Obama lived there the neighborhood went through racial transition, going from almost entirely white in 1960 to 98 percent Black in 1980. Initially, despite rapid racial change, the neighborhood remained strong. As she writes, "in general, people tended to their lawns and kept track of their children."[21] Researchers have repeatedly shown that the first Blacks moving into white neighborhoods tended to have higher incomes than the whites they were replacing, and property values initially remained stable or actually increased.[22] As one detailed study of neighborhood change put it: "Upper middle-class blacks . . . are the leading edge of racial change."[23]

A crucial factor in creating and sustaining strong Black neighborhoods was and still is sufficient demand by Black home buyers. The rise of the Black middle neighborhood in the 1960s and 1970s was fueled by massive pent-up demand by families whose aspirations to homeownership had been blocked by racial segregation. Healthy neighborhoods need a steady supply of middle-class homeowners who can maintain their housing and be engaged in their neighborhood. Since few white families buy homes in Black neighborhoods, the market for Black home buyers is largely limited to the region's Black families. While this means that the opportunity space for good Black neighborhoods is greater in metropolitan areas with large Black middle-class populations, such as Chicago and Atlanta, that opportunity space only exists if enough of those Black middle-class buyers choose to buy in Black neighborhoods rather than in the larger number of racially mixed and largely white neighborhoods potentially accessible to them. The crisis of today's Black middle neighborhoods, which we will discuss in chapter 11, is in many respects the result of those buyers increasingly opting to buy elsewhere.

Good Black neighborhoods are not only less secure but also do not necessarily confer the same social and economic benefits on their residents as good white neighborhoods. Aside from the market implications of racial stereotyping, Black neighborhoods face additional challenges not faced by white neighborhoods. Black neighborhoods may face invidious behavior by lenders and insurance companies, while racial stereotypes may inhibit retailers from locating in their commercial areas. Their proximity to areas of concentrated poverty means that middle-class youths in those neighborhoods are more likely to be exposed to the temptations of the street and "fast money."[24] As Pattillo-McCoy sums it up, "Black middle-class neighborhoods like Groveland subsequently have more crime, fewer services and resources, less political clout, and less adequate schools than most white neighborhoods."[25]

For all their challenges, good Black neighborhoods are a useful corrective to what Mary Pattillo calls the "conundrum of integration," the assumption that integration is the only way to improve the lives of Black people, an assumption that stigmatizes Black communities and lifts up proximity to whites as a value in itself.[26] Racial integration is not an end in itself. But it is another way to achieve good neighborhoods.

The Successful Integrated Neighborhood

Traditional theories of neighborhood change have little room to accommodate the existence of stable racially integrated communities. Neighborhood life cycle theories and the ecological model of the Chicago School of Human Ecology both offered a deterministic view of race and neighborhood change. As the ubiquitous Homer Hoyt wrote in 1939, "the presence of even one nonwhite person in a block otherwise populated by whites may initiate a period of transition."[27] The theory of racial tipping points gave earlier theories a more scientific gloss.[28] Clearly influenced by the traumatic effects of white flight, which was taking place in American cities as they were writing, Grodzin, Schelling, and other tipping point theorists argued that whatever the preferences of the majority, if even a small percentage of white homeowners in a neighborhood do not tolerate the presence of Black neighbors and move out, that process will initiate a cycle of moves that ultimately leads to the neighborhood becoming entirely Black. That theory was summed up by the influential community organizer Saul Alinsky, who quipped that integration was merely the time "from the entrance of the first Black family to the exit of the last white family."[29]

These deterministic theories were a product of their time, detached from history and context. Even then, there were many exceptions. Some neighborhoods were racially diverse and remained that way over many decades. In 1990, 19 percent of neighborhoods in all metropolitan areas were racially diverse (defined as having Black populations between 10 percent and 50 percent), and over three-quarters of the census tracts that were racially diverse in 1980 remained that way in 1990.[30]

Since 1990, the number of stable integrated neighborhoods has steadily grown. A recent study found that the percentage of integrated Black-white neighborhoods that tipped and became racially homogeneous over two decades fell from 40 percent between 1970 and 1990 to only 20 percent between 1990 and 2010. Both white flight from integrated neighborhoods and white avoidance of such neighborhoods fell significantly after 1990.[31] The St. Louis analysis described earlier reinforces that point. Not only had most of the diverse census tracts remained that way for twenty or more years, but a large number had also seen their Black population share exceed 50 percent, only to gradually decline while retaining substantial Black populations over time. A carefully designed test of the tipping point theory concluded that "the 'tipping point' is closer to an urban legend than an unstable equilibrium that explains racial segregation."[32]

Arguably the single most blatant flaw in tipping point theory is its failure to understand the racial configuration and preferences of the pool of would-be home buyers eager to buy in a neighborhood. Although Schelling appears to know otherwise, his model all but assumes the existence of a nearly infinite pool of Black home buyers as well as all but universal white aversion of integrated neighborhoods, both egregious misrepresentations of reality then and even more so today. As discussed in chapter 6, since a predictable percentage of any neighborhood's homeowners regularly move, the neighborhood's racial configuration is ultimately determined by the racial mix of the pool of home buyers and renters. If that pool is dominated by one group or the other, eventually the character of the neighborhood will tip toward the group that dominates that pool, whether white, Black, or other. Assuming that 10 percent of white homeowners lack tolerance for Black neighbors but the Black share of the home buyer pool is also 10 percent, the neighborhood will remain stably integrated. Moreover, race is rarely the only factor driving decisions, while the effect of friction, the cost in both time and money to sell one house and buy another, acts as a further deterrent to flight. In retrospect, the urban crisis era of white flight and rapid racial transition was an extreme and dramatic moment in American history, unlikely to be repeated in the future.

That said, in America's racialized society long-term stable integration does not come easily. Racial determinants of behavior, whether systemic or individual, have a momentum that is difficult to overcome. The racialized perception of space affects housing searches, creating institutional barriers to the creation and maintenance of stable integrated neighborhoods. Maria Krysan and Kyle Crowder call the process by which segregation is perpetuated through racially divergent housing searches the "social structural sorting perspective."[33] The home search is not a rational process in which the buyer considers all the alternatives dispassionately and then chooses the one that maximizes their goals; rather, it is one that relies on heuristics to narrow the alternatives and simplify decision making. Krysan and Crowder point out that "residential moves are structurally sorted along racial lines, with individuals' perceptions and knowledge of residential options shaped by lived experiences and social interactions within a racially segregated social system. The racialized patterns of mobility and immobility that emerge from these structural conditions continually reproduce the system's segregated social and spatial structure."[34] As they note, for many white home buyers in the Chicago metropolitan area, the South Side is "a large, aggregated swath of sameness" that they do not even think to consider.[35] Most white buyers would probably say the same thing about the North Side of St. Louis or Cleveland's East Side. Similarly, many Black home buyers eliminate white neighborhoods from consideration because of their geographically constrained social networks and lived experiences as well as the not unrealistic fear that they will not be welcomed in such neighborhoods. While these factors make it more difficult to sustain integrated neighborhoods, recent experience nonetheless suggests that for many people factors other than race may be as important or more so. These factors in turn influence the likelihood that a neighborhood will be able to achieve stable racial integration.

The characteristics of regional housing markets affect the opportunity space for integrated neighborhoods. Stronger regional housing markets and higher home prices relative to incomes constrain home buyers' choices. In such a market, integrated neighborhoods may more often land on white buyers' radar. Another factor may be the size and configuration of Black settlement in the region. Massey and Denton suggest that the most problematic regions are those they call "hypersegregated," where much of a region's Black population "lives within large, contiguous settlements of densely inhabited neighborhoods that are packed tightly around the urban core."[36] A study of the Washington, D.C., suburbs found that distance from the Black population center was positively correlated with stable integration.[37] Beyond that, all the same factors that affect neighborhood choice everywhere come into play, including the character of the housing stock and neighborhood amenities such as public transit, open space, and proximity to downtown or major universities and medical centers.

While local actors can build a more appealing housing stock and stronger neighborhood amenities, structural factors are almost completely beyond the power of local actors. Structural or ecological factors, however, do not dictate outcomes but instead operate through perceptions and behaviors that can be influenced by local actors. As the authors of *Paths of Neighborhood Change* observe, "if ecological facts are overwhelming, it is because of the effect of these facts on the perceptions and actions of individual [residents] and corporate actors. In a neighborhood that goes up and down, it is ultimately the actions of these residents that make the outcomes real."[38] Residents can and do act to counter the structural factors driving resegregation. As Ingrid Gould Ellen observes, "almost every case study of diverse communities has identified an active community group."[39] Strong community organizations working for stable integration may not guarantee success but they increase the odds.

Neighborhood racial change or stability can become self-fulfilling prophecies. If people believe that their neighborhood will resegregate, it probably will. If they believe that it will maintain a stable racial mix, it most likely will. And the longer a neighborhood maintains a stable racial mix, the greater the likelihood that it will remain stable into the future. The challenge in racial change, as in all neighborhood change, is that it is subject to social contagion and rapid feedback effects. Change may be inevitable, but it need not be destabilizing. The challenge for local actors is to prevent the cascade of negative effects flowing from uncontrolled change. Examples of integrated neighborhoods from the urban crisis era can tell us a great deal about the ability of neighborhood actors to foster stability and virtuous cycles.

Local "fragile movements," as Juliet Saltman called them, for integrated neighborhoods grew out of the civil rights movement in the 1960s and 1970s as civil rights activists realized that history and institutional racism, more than legal barriers, drove residential segregation.[40] Just as affirmative action was necessary to overcome the historic burdens of racial discrimination in job markets, activists realized that affirmative steps were needed to overcome the historic legacy of segregated neighborhoods. Their efforts were typically implemented by suburban governments and neighborhood associations.

While many suburbs resisted racial integration, some welcomed it. Local governments in Oak Park outside Chicago, Shaker Heights in the Cleveland area, and University City west of St. Louis successfully fought tipping pressures, sustaining white and Black home buyer demand at levels that have maintained their racial balance, as shown in figure 8.4. Oak Park, Shaker Heights, and University City can be called intentionally integrated communities because they have intentionally used public policies to maintain stable integration or, as it is sometimes called, integration maintenance. Some policies were relatively uncontroversial, such as banning for-sale signs to counter blockbusting and requiring strict property inspections when homes changed hands to forestall their deterioration. Other policies designed to boost white housing demand, such as affirmative marketing and home buyer assistance programs targeted to white buyers but not Black buyers, were more controversial. Prompted by the NAACP, which enlisted the Reagan administration's Justice Department, federal courts in 1988 ruled that racial quotas designed to maintain neighborhood racial balance were unconstitutional.[41] Since then the courts have generally upheld local integration maintenance policies as long as they do not involve quotas.[42]

Early on, Shaker Heights banned for-sale signs to discourage panic selling and started an affirmative housing marketing program to encourage whites to buy in areas where they were underrepresented. Arguably more important, the community worked to maintain a high-performing school system, using busing and magnet schools to maintain a racial balance. An integrated municipality, however, may

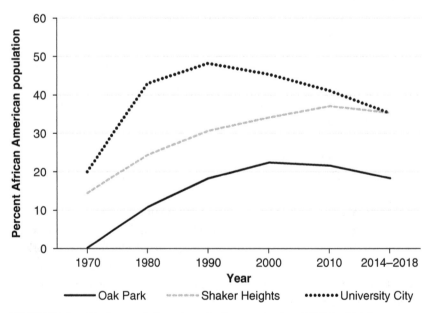

FIGURE 8.4. Black population share in three suburbs, 1970 to 2018

(Authors' work based on decennial census and American Community Survey data)

or may not also mean integrated neighborhoods. In Shaker Heights, the Black population share of individual census tracts ranges from 4 percent to 90 percent. Integration is much more granular in Oak Park, where no census tract has more than a 28 percent Black population and only two have less than 11 percent.

Saltman suggests that integration is not about intimate socializing but instead creating a pluralistic community, "meaning two or more diverse groups living peaceably in a common territory and sometimes joining in common effort."[43] Her argument is consistent with our stress on the importance of weak ties for bridging across social divides. Black and white residents of Shaker Heights, Oak Park, and University City have lived together for decades, sharing blocks and neighborhoods to varying degrees, rubbing elbows in shared public spaces, and working together in local government and civic organizations.

The task of maintaining stable racial integration in central city neighborhoods falls on civil society rather than on city government, for which integration maintenance is rarely a priority. A study of fourteen stable integrated communities in the late 1990s called them "one of the best-kept secrets of our nation."[44] We tell two stories of such neighborhoods here. West Mt. Airy in Philadelphia, a neighborhood that reached roughly two-thirds Black population in the 1980s and has been stable at roughly 50 percent white and 50 percent Black since 2000, and Vollintine Evergreen in Memphis, which has sustained a stable population that is about 60 percent Black and 40 percent white over the same period. Notably, both neighborhoods' proximity to high-poverty African American neighborhoods would have suggested to many that they were fated to tip racially and decline socioeconomically.

Located in northwest Philadelphia and surrounded by neighborhoods that are largely either white or Black, West Mt. Airy has strong amenities.[45] It is well served by public transit; bordered on two sides by green space, Fairmont Park and Wissahickon Gorge; and boasts a diverse, attractive, and increasingly competitive housing stock. Prices have risen steadily over the past decade, to about $400,000 during the first half of 2021, almost double the citywide median price.[46]

West Mt. Airy's success reflects the institutions its residents formed to sustain the community. Black families began moving into the area in the 1950s. Reflecting fears of possible panic selling, local churches and synagogues came together in 1959 to form West Mt. Airy Neighbors to support racial integration, persuading the Philadelphia City Council to pass an ordinance prohibiting solicitations and "sold" signs and limiting the number of for-sale signs.[47] West Mount Airy Neighbors is still active after more than sixty years. Known as the "PhD ghetto," West Mt. Airy has established a distinct market niche. The neighborhood's reputation as a diverse community has attracted like-minded people, including many Jewish and Black families of relatively high educational and socioeconomic status and strong progressive values, nurturing a vibrant civic scene. Weaver's Way, a food co-op founded in 1973 with nine thousand members today, manages two working farms and provides fresh food to a local shelter and schools. West Mt. Airy began early and built momentum. Historical momentum can support integration as well as segregation.

Constructed largely between 1922 and 1944, Vollintine Evergreen was one of the first trolley suburbs east of downtown Memphis.[48] As in West Mt. Airy, Black in-migration and real estate agents' block busting triggered panic selling in the late 1960s, leading to local church leaders forming the Vollintine Evergreen Community Association (VECA). Rather than taking a race-specific approach, however, VECA has focused on strengthening the neighborhood's quality of life. VECA remains active and engaged over fifty years after its founding. Indeed, the neighborhood itself is most often known today as "VECA" rather than the more cumbersome Vollintine Evergreen.

Vollintine Evergreen has many assets that VECA leveraged to attract residents. Its distinctive bungalow homes with large verandas, shown in figure 8.5, helped it to win designation as a National Historic District. Nearby Rhodes College serves as a neighborhood anchor, drawing home buyers. The neighborhood's most distinctive amenity, the V&E Greenline, is a testament to the extraordinary civic capacity of the community. In 1980 the Louisville & Nashville Railroad abandoned a line running through the heart of the neighborhood, which soon became an unsafe area and a dumping ground. Although the city refused to purchase the right of way, VECA organized volunteer clean-ups and tree plantings

FIGURE 8.5. Homes in Memphis's Vollintine Evergreen neighborhood

(Google Earth © 2022 Google)

while encouraging residents to walk and bicycle along its route. In 1997 VECA was able to purchase the right-of-way and created a separate volunteer-driven community corporation to maintain the Greenline. In 2019, four hundred people provided 4,300 voluntary hours of service to the greenway, which according to a 2012 survey is used by nearly sixty-five thousand people each year. Vollintine Evergreen has become a stable integrated community, attracting both white and Black families, in which houses in 2021 were selling for $200,000 to $300,000.

We are not suggesting that integrated neighborhoods such as West Mt. Airy and Vollintine Evergreen are the only way to build good neighborhoods for people of color or that intentional integration and quality-of-life maintenance are necessary for stable racial integration. They show, however, that racial tipping was not an inevitable outcome even at the height of the urban crisis era, let alone today. Moreover, they are stably integrated neighborhoods with significant Black populations. Integration is not always the "one-way street" that Stokely Carmichael criticized over fifty years ago, which assumes that the path to integration is one of small numbers of Black people joining much larger numbers of white people in white people's neighborhoods.[49]

Race and Neighborhoods in a Globalizing Nation

Sixty years ago when white flight and racial change were transforming America's cities and their neighborhoods, race was largely seen as binary. While the Black-white racial divide and the persistence of discriminatory behavior specifically directed toward Black people continue to play a powerful role in American society, as the United States moves toward becoming a majority-minority nation, race and ethnicity and their relationship to neighborhood trajectories have become more complex. Large and growing Latinx and Asian communities in American cities and suburbs have muddled the binary dynamic, adding a more complex Black-white-Latinx-Asian frame to the underlying Black-white racial dynamic.

Moreover, each of those generic categories is actually an umbrella term for groups that are divided into innumerable distinct racial and ethnic identities. A new generation of racially diverse neighborhoods is emerging, fostered not by integration maintenance strategies but instead by structural dynamics largely unrelated to intentional activity. Race continues to shape neighborhood trajectories, but it does so differently than in the past.

The restructuring of urban economies has changed cities' racial dynamics. The clustering of new economy jobs in downtowns and urban tech corridors, coupled with the "march of the millennials" described in previous chapters, has produced a pool of mobile, highly educated young people seeking a more "authentic" urban experience, many of whom see racial diversity as a part of that experience. Derek Hyra has described how the Black history of the Shaw–U Street neighborhood in Washington, D.C., was used as a marketing tool to stimulate housing demand.[50] Whether this is racial progress or crass commercialization, it would have been unimaginable a few decades ago. Each generation's racial attitudes are shaped by the collective memories of growing up in a distinct historical period. While the racial turmoil of the 1960s was traumatic for many people, as Jennifer Hochschild and her colleagues write, "the fading of the collective racial memory of the 1960's era, coupled with a new set of collective memories, new people and new experiences in the context of increasing racial and ethnic heterogeneity," have led to new more tolerant attitudes and practices among younger people.[51] Acting on these attitudes, young people have chosen to live in more integrated neighborhoods.[52] Racial attitudes may shape neighborhoods, but neighborhoods also shape racial attitudes.

New types of neighborhood are emerging. As one study notes, "neighborhoods where blacks and whites live in integrated settings alongside Hispanics and Asians represent a new phenomenon in the United States."[53] The authors call neighborhoods with minimum threshold numbers of non-Latinx white, Black, Latinx, and Asian residents "global neighborhoods." The increasing racial and ethnic diversity resulting from immigration is leading to more integrated neighborhoods. Zhang and Logan argue that the increase in diverse neighborhoods cannot be explained simply by the increase in the racial or ethnic diversity of metropolitan areas. Rather, it and is due in large part to "*process* changes that are driven by the transformation of intergroup relations and neighborhood dynamics."[54] One possible explanation of these changing racial dynamics is the buffering hypothesis, namely that the presence of Latinx and Asian populations provides a buffer between Black and white residents, making Black people less visible and less threatening to whites.[55] We are skeptical. Multiethnic neighborhoods have emerged in all sorts of contexts, including in metropolitan area that were initially mostly white or divided between Blacks and whites, suggesting that other factors are at work.

A further dimension is added by the growing suburbanization of America's Black families, a process that has accelerated markedly in the past decade.[56] In many metropolitan areas, Black suburban populations exceed those in central cities. The effects on segregation are mixed. While in many cases this process appears to be furthering diversity and integration, elsewhere, notably St. Louis County surrounding the city of St. Louis, it is leading to growth in both racial segregation and concentrated poverty, a phenomenon exacerbated by the county's political and institutional fragmentation, which we discuss in chapter 13.

It is important, however, not to overstate the rise in neighborhood diversity. At the same time that racial segregation has declined and new global neighborhoods have emerged, the number of nearly all-Black neighborhoods has grown while many white households continue to flee racial diversity. Perhaps the most disturbing trend is the increase in the number of Black concentrated-poverty neighborhoods, including many formerly Black middle neighborhoods, which have increased while racial diversity has grown in middle- and upper-income neighborhoods.

The new patterns of neighborhood racial diversity have built-in limitations. Diversity is indeed a crude statistical measure that obscures important details. With few exceptions, the presence of white households in racially diverse neighborhoods has had little effect on school segregation. Moreover, efforts to draw the children of affluent white in-migrants into public schools may end up creating stratified school systems rather than furthering either racial or social class integration.[57]

Other things being equal, more diverse neighborhoods appear to have weaker social ties than more homogeneous neighborhoods. Robert Putnam found that residents living in ethnically diverse neighborhoods reported lower levels of trust not only between groups but also among their own group, a phenomenon he called "hunkering down."[58] In other words, diverse urban neighborhoods may be statistically integrated but socially segregated. Derek Hyra found this in his study of Washington's Shaw–U Street neighborhood.[59]

In that neighborhood, however, racial diversity was overlaid with extreme economic inequality, something that is likely to reduce intergroup interaction. Lower-income residents of one racial or ethnic group are unlikely to have more than minimal social interactions with affluent, more educated residents of another. Indeed, diverse neighborhoods are often riven by class cleavages and fears of displacement by the less affluent, often as much social and political as physical displacement.[60]

While recognizing its roots in lived experience, we nonetheless question the widespread pessimism about the new diversity in urban neighborhoods. Given the less central role that neighborhoods play in the social and economic relationships of the twenty-first-century American city, to expect residents of widely varying racial, ethnic, and class backgrounds to form intimate social relations is not only unrealistic but also reflects a nostalgic yearning for a bygone era. It is likely to be enough that diverse residents develop weak ties, mingling in public spaces and learning to tolerate and respect each other's differences. Good neighborhoods can be an important source of bridging social capital without intimate ties.

All of this takes us back to the paradox with which we began this chapter: that race is an enduring constant in neighborhoods and is constantly changing.

The great majority of Latinx residents self-identify in the US census as white, and many of them may already be seen as white by the majority. While people of Asian origin are largely, in Canadian terminology, "visible minorities," that may not pose an insurmountable barrier to their being assimilated by the majority into whiteness, which may already be happening. Race as a social construct is constantly changing. As happened to many immigrant groups during the first half of the twentieth century, over time more and more groups leave minority status and become "white," with the sole exception of Blacks.

The resurgence of the Black Lives Matter movement in response to the 2020 murder of George Floyd suggests that the country has made little progress on race relations. In many respects that is true. Regarding neighborhood dynamics, however, we have come a long way from the white flight and resegregation that characterized so many communities during the urban crisis era. At that time, the Chicago School's model of neighborhood change and its corollary, the racial tipping point theory, seemed credible. Today, we can see both as artifacts of their distinctive moments in American urban history. The opportunity space for building good diverse neighborhoods has expanded. Nonetheless, race remains stubbornly persistent in the American psyche, while spatial polarization by economic condition and the income and wealth gap between Black and white households have grown even as urban revival, immigration, and millennial inmigration have led to new models of urban diversity. The urban crisis, with its fraught history of racial tension, has not disappeared but is now overlaid with a new set of historical forces.

9

AGENTS OF NEIGHBORHOOD CHANGE

To understand neighborhood change, it is essential to understand both intentional and unintentional processes. Most forces affecting neighborhoods lack intentionality; they are not guided by conscious efforts to bring about neighborhood change. As we discussed in chapter 6, markets may be the most powerful single force affecting neighborhoods. While they are to varying degrees shaped by intentional policies or decisions, they are largely the product of structural forces, such as migration trends, job growth or decline, and the features of the housing stock, that are often influenced by choices made decades or even hundreds of years earlier.

By contrast, local governments, community development corporations, neighborhood associations, and other agents of change engage in intentional actions to stabilize or revive neighborhoods, from small interventions such as miniparks and playgrounds to massive multimillion-dollar redevelopment projects. Even when they are the same actors as those who participate in the market transactions, they act differently when they are pursuing intentional change. As intentional actors, they are, or seek to be, agents of change.

Processes of neighborhood change are fragmented, variable, and unstable. While they share many common features, they operate differently in different cities and even in different parts of the same city. This is particularly true when we look at the network of intentional interventions and change agents that can be characterized as the neighborhood policy system. The complex and sometimes even chaotic nature of the neighborhood policy system raises questions of democratic accountability and equity, especially when important policy decisions are outsourced from government to nonprofits, whether massive anchor institutions or small neighborhood-based community development corporation (CDCs).

Although city government is not always the dominant actor in the neighborhood policy system, it is almost always a factor. While we have mentioned local government often in the preceding chapters, it is time to look at it directly and understand the ramifications of its unique multifaceted role in both sustaining and, unfortunately, sometimes undermining good neighborhoods.

The Many Roles of City Government

Over the past more than one hundred years, city governments in the United States have evolved into complex, multifaceted entities employing thousands of people whose work affects those who live in, work in, visit, or own property in the city, often in ways little appreciated by those who benefit or are harmed by them. The impact of city governments is often hidden by the fact that more and more of their functions are performed not through the city or general governmental entity but instead through a proliferation of special-purpose authorities created by state or local governments as well as governmental partnerships and contracts with private-sector actors.

When it comes to neighborhoods, local government affects their fate through three distinct systems: infrastructure and service delivery, regulation, and intentional intervention. Neighborhoods as we know them would be impossible without local government provision of essential (or desirable) public services and infrastructure. Cities build and maintain water and sewer systems, roads and bridges, street lighting, and public transit systems. They provide urban amenities, including parks, libraries, community centers, swimming pools, hiking, and biking trails. Local government, usually acting through independent boards of education, provide K–12 public education and often pre-K and community college education as well. Cities also provide the day-to-day services neighborhoods depend on, including police and fire protection, trash collection, and snow removal. Many local governments provide essential public health services such as inspecting restaurants and vaccinating children.

Local governments also exercise legal authority granted by the states to regulate many activities deemed as being relevant to the public health, safety, and general welfare.[1] Building codes set standards for construction, while zoning codes dictate what types of structures, of what dimensions, and for what uses may or may not be built. Housing and health codes dictate the standards for existing housing and the obligations of landlords to tenants. Local police enforce criminal laws, exercising broad discretion over which laws to enforce and in what fashion.

Decent public services and effective regulation are both critical elements of a good neighborhood. Good schools and public safety, both heavily dependent on local government, are consistently ranked among the most important factors, if not the most important factor, influencing people's satisfaction with their neighborhood or their desire to move into or remain in a neighborhood. Seemingly mundane matters such as whether a neighborhood's streetlights are working powerfully affect neighborhood quality. During Detroit's financial crisis, street lighting deteriorated so much in 2013 that a reporter wrote, "The darkness has created a sense among some residents that leadership has lost control long ago and that parts of the city have become an urban version of the Wild West. Forget about effects on property values, some residents say. They just want peace of mind."[2] By that point, at least half of the city's streetlights weren't working. Mayor Mike Duggan, who was elected at the end of 2013, made a commitment to have every streetlight in Detroit working again, a pledge that was realized by 2017.

We are not suggesting that effective governmental services by themselves can create good neighborhoods. Many other factors play equally important roles. But without the underpinning provided by an adequate level of local public goods and services and responsible regulation, those factors are unlikely to be enough. Decent governmental services are a necessary if not sufficient condition for good neighborhoods.

The resources available to local government to provide services vary widely. While some cities' finances are on firm grounds, many cities suffer from long-term structural fiscal stress, threatening their ability to provide the basic services neighborhoods need. A study of three hundred local governments found that 32 percent had to take drastic action to cope with fiscal stress after the Great Recession, including blanket reductions in employee salaries and significant cuts in services.[3] Hollowed out by cuts, few local public health departments were able to respond effectively to the COVID-19 outbreak.[4] While conditions gradually improved after the recession, many cuts have never been restored, especially in older Rust Belt cities with declining populations and weak economies, a reality brought home by Detroit's 2013 bankruptcy, the largest municipal bankruptcy in American history. Fiscally stressed cities find it challenging to provide basic city services, let alone fund targeted neighborhood development programs.

Given limited local resources, federal aid to cities has long been the principal source of funding for intentional policies to stabilize and revitalize neighborhoods, particularly through Community Development Block Grant Program, which not only enables cities to invest in distressed neighborhoods but also requires them to do so. As we noted earlier, however, Community Development Block Grant funding is down 75 percent in inflation-adjusted dollars from its peak in the late 1970s.

During the 1960s and 1970s, a generation of mayors portrayed themselves as champions of neighborhood empowerment. One of the first, Kevin White, was elected mayor of Boston in 1967 with the support of neighborhood groups opposing urban renewal. His successor, Raymond Flynn, elected in 1983, remained committed to a proneighborhood, affordable housing agenda until he left office in 1994. Rather than subsidize downtown developers, Flynn's administration imposed fees on large commercial developments to fund affordable housing. By 1993 those linkage fees had generated over $70 million, helping build ten thousand units of affordable housing.[5] Other proneighborhood mayors include John Lindsay in New York in the 1960s, Dennis Kucinich in Cleveland in the late 1970s, and Harold Washington, the city's first African American mayor, in Chicago from 1983 to 1987. These mayors emphasized neighborhood economic development, although they were rarely antibusiness, as was sometimes claimed.

By the 1980s, however, urban populism was widely seen as ineffective if not outright inappropriate. As we discussed in chapter 4, perhaps the most influential book on urban policy of the time, Paul Peterson's *City Limits*, argued that because city boundaries are permeable, putting cities in competition with one another, they must concentrate on enhancing their economic competitiveness.[6] Redistributive policies should be shunned, Peterson argued, since they attract poor people while generating no offsetting economic or political benefits for the city. It was only a short step from that logic to the conclusion that cities should not invest in poor or declining neighborhoods but instead should concentrate resources on strengthening downtowns and other high revenue-generating nonresidential areas while encouraging gentrification in nearby neighborhoods.

Besides shunning redistributive policies, according to Peterson, cities need to focus on developmental policies, incentivizing investment, and seeking out export industries to generate investment in the local economy, along with its attendant multiplier effects.[7] While few would dispute the importance of cities' efforts to build a new economic base to replace their disappearing manufacturing sector, it was a narrow focus that took many cities down unproductive paths, particularly when investments were driven by narrow interests of the cities' corporate partners rather than yielding sustainable economic growth.

Since the 1980s, cities and states across the nation have invested vast sums in corporate-driven downtown projects, most visibly in the forms of sports stadiums and convention centers, few of which generate returns commensurate with the sizable public subsidies they receive. Many are impressive structures, to be sure. Mercedes-Benz stadium in Atlanta, home of the National Football League's Atlanta Falcons, was completed in 2017 at a total cost of $1.5 billion, with taxpayers contributing over $700 million. Among other things, the stadium incorporates a four-story–tall stainless steel falcon, reputedly the largest freestanding bird sculpture in the world, and a retractable circular roof supposedly inspired by the Roman Pantheon featuring a pinwheel design consisting of eight translucent, triangular panels that open and close like a flower.

Although the argument for public subsidies for stadiums is that they generate jobs and economic growth, the research is overwhelming that the economic benefits of stadium subsidies are minimal if not nonexistent.[8] For the most part, professional sports franchises are not true export industries but instead are entertainment for metropolitan-area residents that displace dollars that would have otherwise been spent on alternative forms of entertainment, such as movies, bars, and restaurants. Public investments in stadiums are not developmental policies, in Peterson's terms; they are reverse redistributive policies that shift money from the mass of taxpayers to the wealthy owners of sports franchises.[9]

Notwithstanding the logic of Peterson's argument, the empirical evidence suggests that cities' ability to significantly influence their growth trajectory through public subsidies and incentives is severely limited. In his insightful 2016 book *City Power*, Richard Schragger challenges Peterson's thesis, which had all but become conventional wisdom. Calling the imperative for cities to focus on economic development a "false constraint," Schragger writes, "any claim that cities have transformed themselves through improved policies of capital attraction and retention is seriously overstated."[10] We agree. As we observed in chapters 4 and 5, cities have gone from economic free fall during the era of urban crisis in the 1970s and 1980s to enjoying new vitality in the downtowns, tech corridors, and gentrifying neighborhoods in the new century. This is primarily the result not of city policies but instead of the changing economic function of cities.

The new urban economy has also changed the old conflict between neighborhoods and downtowns that fueled the political appeal of urban populist mayors. Not only have downtowns themselves become neighborhoods, but many cities have come to view strong neighborhoods as conducive to economic growth in the new economy.[11] Investing in neighborhoods, especially those in and near growth corridors, is increasingly seen not as a distraction from development but instead as part of a larger economic development strategy. As a recent book on neighborhood politics put it, "The once-calamitous disregard of older neighborhoods has somewhat faded. . . . In the new postindustrial geography neighborhoods with market potential can readily become revitalization targets."[12]

City governments may be motivated to subsidize neighborhood development as part of an economic development strategy but less often for the sake of the people who presently live in them. Echoing Schragger, we contend that cities have relatively little power to shape their economic growth trajectories. They can support the efforts of, for example, a Johns Hopkins facility or the Cleveland Clinic to grow, create jobs, and draw revenues into the city, but they cannot create such entities, nor can they direct their efforts. This means that efforts to change the economic trajectory of cities are at best marginally effective. It also means, however, that cities can engage in efforts to improve the quality of life in neighborhoods and redistribute opportunity to those who have been left behind by the postindustrial economy *without undermining their economic prosperity*. To the extent that such efforts build human capital, they can have positive economic effects. The revitalization of the South Bronx in New York City, where city government partnered with CDCs, developers, and lenders, is an example of this. We will return to it after discussing the role of CDCs in neighborhood revitalization, picking up the networked governance thread from chapter 4.

The Promise and Pitfalls of CDCs

Community development corporations, nonprofit organizations dedicated to improving a specific neighborhood geography, can be distinguished, at least in principle, from the settlement houses and social service providers from which they sprung by their mission of not just providing services but also empowering residents to positively affect the trajectory of their neighborhood. This, of course, can lead them to take on multiple and often seemingly conflicting missions. How central CDCs are in the present and future of the American urban neighborhood is debatable. Most neighborhoods do not have CDCs, and the effect of many CDCs on their neighborhoods where they do exist, as we will discuss, is often limited. At the same time, we think they are important as much for their aspirations as for their accomplishments and as a distinct, and distinctly American, approach to fostering positive neighborhood change.

As figure 9.1 shows, CDCs can have multiple, seemingly contradictory, goals or missions. Critics argue that they cannot reconcile these tensions and end up embracing one end of the continuum at the expense of the other. Howard Husock, a prominent right-wing critic, argues that CDCs, by embracing community change over individual mobility, trap residents in debilitating dependency. "Rather than encouraging upward mobility and genuine self-reliance, the implicit message of the CDC movement to the poor is: Stay put and organize for government benefits. As a result, CDCs are bad for cities."[13] In "The Myth of Community Development," Nicholas Lemann argued that CDCs do not revive poor neighborhoods but instead only "gild the ghetto," providing better hous-

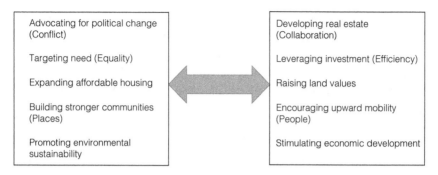

Advocating for political change (Conflict)	Developing real estate (Collaboration)
Targeting need (Equality)	Leveraging investment (Efficiency)
Expanding affordable housing	Raising land values
Building stronger communities (Places)	Encouraging upward mobility (People)
Promoting environmental sustainability	Stimulating economic development

FIGURE 9.1.   The multiple missions of community development corporations

ing and services for residents but offering little opportunity for residents to improve their lives and economic prospects.[14]

Reflecting these concerns, others have argued that it is preferable to invest in dispersal strategies rather than community development, helping people to move in search of better opportunities.[15] CDCs have been criticized for building expensive housing in segregated high-poverty neighborhoods, reinforcing economic and racial segregation and effectively giving suburbs a free pass to block construction of affordable housing in more integrated opportunity-rich environments.[16] Finally, CDCs are criticized for having drifted away from their mission of empowering communities, focusing instead on executing complex real estate transactions with professional staff "who often live outside the community and are more likely to emphasize the technical details of development over community empowerment."[17]

There is some truth to all these criticisms. CDCs are rarely successful at turning around concentrated poverty neighborhoods. They often build affordable housing projects in areas of concentrated poverty, racial segregation, and limited opportunity. Distracted by the demands as well as the financial rewards of real estate development, many have de-emphasized community organizing and empowerment. At the same time, we do not believe these tensions are inherently irreconcilable. The CDC model is not doomed to failure. Without shortchanging the daunting challenges, many CDCs have been successful at reconciling or at least managing these tensions and thereby becoming effective promoters of good neighborhoods.

Under the right conditions the multiple missions of CDCs can be complementary. The term "community development" itself suggests a potential synergy between strengthening community bonds and developing the local economy. Strengthening community connections, for example, can positively affect real estate values. People want to live and buys homes in neighborhoods with strong identities and a vibrant communal life. Extensive community engagement by

CDCs may slow down the development process, but strong buy-in from residents can lead to development projects that enjoy greater public acceptance and are more attuned to local design and public space preferences.

Measuring CDCs' impact is made difficult by their multiple objectives. A 2005 study by the Urban Institute sought to objectively measure CDC impact by focusing on the sole outcome of change in property values, arguing that "sales prices are the generally recognized proxy measure for many other indicators of neighborhood quality, such as crime and poverty rates, because these other aspects of neighborhoods are *capitalized* into the values of its properties."[18] The study was intentionally skewed toward finding impact by cherry-picking five neighborhoods having CDCs with "strong national reputations for effective community development work."[19] The researchers used sophisticated statistical techniques to isolate the impact of the CDC on single-family home values, controlling for characteristics of the target neighborhood, such as location near a park and well-performing schools, that could influence home prices. The results of the research were discouraging: in only two of the five neighborhoods (Denver and Portland) did property values in neighborhoods with a CDC outperform comparable low-income neighborhoods without a CDC. Moreover, the context of these neighborhoods raises serious questions about the definition of "success."

Tellingly, the two "successful" cases were neighborhoods in cities with strong real estate markets, including strong latent market demand for housing and retail services, as well as seriously undervalued assets, such as an underperforming commercial corridor or light rail stop. By improving neighborhood conditions and removing negative features depressing demand, the CDCs were effectively able to unlock that demand. Since 2000, not only had property values in Denver's Five Points neighborhood risen to where the median neighborhood sales price in 2017 was $420,000, but the median household income had tripled, and the Black and Latinx population share was cut in half from 79 percent to 39 percent.[20] In other words, Five Points gentrified.

That was not the CDC's goal—indeed, it has worked hard to preserve affordable housing—but most people would not call this successful community development. Improving a place can hardly be considered successful community development if many longtime residents were forced to move out. We are not saying that these CDCs are failures because property values increased, but we insist that rising single-family home values should not be the only yardstick for measuring success, nor should the absence of rising values automatically signify failure.

The Urban Institute study also examined Slavic Village Development in Cleveland, a strong CDC operating in a weak market. Once home to Polish and Czech immigrants, Slavic Village had experienced significant population loss and economic decline. Unlike Portland and Denver, however, Cleveland had been losing population, and the study found no "striking departure of prices . . . after the CDC intervention."[21] This is not surprising. Although the area has some assets, such as attractive parks, highway access, and a pedestrian-oriented retail center, Cleveland's housing supply outstrips housing demand, and outside of a handful of enclaves property values are consistently low. At the same time, as the study noted, "Slavic Village had built or restored more houses than any other CDC in Cleveland," without which the neighborhood "would have had 400 more vacant lots."[22] Given the negative effects of vacant housing on quality of life, this is noteworthy. The work of the Slavic Village CDC may well have resulted in a better quality of life for the neighborhood's residents but without measurably improving the market.[23]

Any effort to isolate the impact of CDCs on neighborhoods is problematic. As we have emphasized throughout this book, neighborhoods are complex systems with many factors operating simultaneously, generating complex feedback effects. CDC evaluations are plagued by what statisticians call the problem of "endogeneity," the idea that many of the outcomes of interest are systemically linked to the CDC itself. Neighborhoods with CDCs are typically among the most distressed in a city, reflecting the fact that CDCs are often formed in response to neighborhood decline. CDCs therefore are often located in neighborhoods with the most intractable problems. It is not surprising that a review of forty-eight foundation-funded comprehensive community initiatives in the 1990s found that they improved the well-being of individual residents but did not produce population-level changes, such as reductions in neighborhood poverty rates.[24]

Often, CDCs cannot move the needle on housing values or poverty rates, but research has shown that they can build community ties and improve the quality of life in low-income neighborhoods. Another study surveyed residents of three neighborhoods served by CDCs in Newark, Boston, and Minneapolis, comparing responses on housing satisfaction, safety, and community building to responses by residents of similar neighborhoods without a CDC.[25] Residents of neighborhoods with a CDC were more satisfied with their housing, and two out of three of these neighborhoods showed improvements in real and perceived neighborhood safety compared to the non-CDC neighborhoods, though the overall crime victimization rate was still high by national standards. In two of the cities, CDCs were able to "have *measurable* effects on the social fabric of their neighborhoods."[26] Consistent with our emphasis on the importance of weak ties, CDC activities nurtured casual connections, not close ties or friendships. These connections help the neighborhood feel safer and build informal social controls that limit crime. More recently Patrick Sharkey and his colleagues have reinforced this point, showing that the presence of neighborhood-based nonprofits, including CDCs, significantly contributed to the stunning drop in violent crime rates beginning in the 1990s.[27]

An impressive example of a successful partnership between city government and CDCs is the South Bronx in New York City.[28] In the 1970s and early 1980s, the South Bronx was a poster child for urban decline and neighborhood decay, drawing visits by Presidents Jimmy Carter and Ronald Reagan. But it was not just a political prop. It had frighteningly high rates of violent crime, in an extreme manifestation of the crime wave that swept American cities from the 1970s to the 1990s, along with widespread arson and property abandonment. During the 1970s alone, the population of the Bronx dropped by three hundred thousand, or 21 percent.

The area's rapid decline set the stage for a remarkable partnership between local government, CDCs, and other players in the system we call networked governance. By 1979, New York City had taken possession of over 100,000 units of vacant and occupied housing after the owners failed to pay their property taxes, giving the city control over valuable assets that could be leveraged for neighborhood renewal.[29] In 1985, Mayor Ed Koch announced what came to be known as the city's Ten-Year Plan for Housing, which led the city to spend $5.1 billion between 1987 and 2003 to rehabilitate 173,961 vacant and occupied housing units; over 75,000 of the new or rehabilitated units were in The Bronx alone. In some sections of the South Bronx, over 30 percent of all housing units in the area were assisted.[30]

The city's control of the housing inventory and its access to capital were necessary but not sufficient conditions for success, which also required the active cooperation of CDCs, intermediaries, private developers, and banks. Using city funds, groups such as the Mid-Bronx Desperadoes and Banana Kelly rehabilitated thousands of housing units. A closer examination of one section of the South Bronx, Hunts Point–Longwood, shows the dramatic results. During the 1970s this neighborhood hemorrhaged population, losing a jaw-dropping 63 percent of its residents in one decade (figure 9.2).[31] With crime, drugs, and gangs rampant, the urban fabric was in shreds. Everyone who could do so had left.

Today, Hunts Point–Longwood provides rich soil for growing good neighborhoods. The population has rebounded and crime has plummeted. In 1990 there were forty-four murders in the area; in 2021 there were eleven. Robbery and burglary are down by similar amounts.[32] The streets are full of people, and the major retail corridors, such as Southern Boulevard and Prospect Avenue, are bustling. A vibrant food scene includes Caribbean, Mexican, Central American, and West Indian restaurants. In 2018, the vacancy rate was only 1.6 percent. While prices of the few owner-occupied houses in the neighborhood are high, by New York City standards the neighborhood is affordable. Ninety percent of the neighborhood's households are renters, and most rents are affordable to working families thanks to the presence of 6,188 subsidized housing units.[33] In short, Hunts Point–Longwood is in many respects a cluster of good neighborhoods, benefiting from

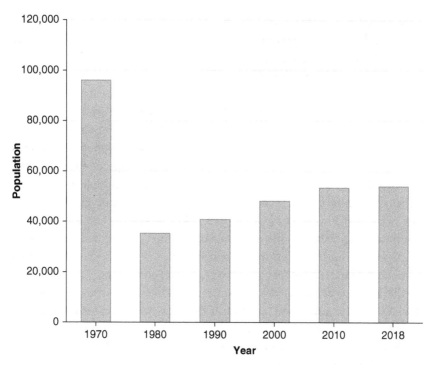

FIGURE 9.2.   Population change in Hunts Point–Longwood, 1970 to 2018

(Authors' work based on decennial census and American Community Survey data)

excellent subway service connecting residents to job-rich areas in New York City while remaining relatively affordable to working-class families.

It is important to acknowledge, however, that good neighborhoods cannot solve the problems of poverty and economic inequality. Many families in Hunts Point–Longwood are still struggling. In 2018 median incomes were only 40 percent of citywide levels, and the poverty rate was more than double the citywide rate. Many children in the local public schools still perform well below grade level. While rents are affordable by New York standards, in 2018 one-third of the households were "severely rent burdened," meaning they paid more than 50 percent of their income for housing, leaving little for other necessities such as food, clothing, and transportation.[34] Life is far better for the poor residents of the South Bronx than when the area was in free fall, but it is far from perfect. Good neighborhoods can improve the quality of life for poor households and help them stretch their limited budgets but do little to address the underlying problems caused by poverty and poorly paid jobs.

The success of the South Bronx and its CDCs is inspiring but not easily replicated because it benefited from conditions that few cities can match. New York

City is a global powerhouse with unusually strong job and housing markets. The city has also been a magnet for immigrants, propelling the demand that filled the South Bronx's vacant apartments and vacant lots. By the early 2000s, a remarkable 60 percent of New York City's population were immigrants or their children. The city's strong housing market enabled New York City to borrow billions of dollars for housing supported by rents from Battery Park City, a planned development built on Hudson River landfill in Lower Manhattan through a public-private partnership. In most other cities, agents of neighborhood change must work with fewer resources and under far less advantageous circumstances.

The ability of CDCs to grapple successfully with their multiple missions also depends on their organizational capacity, which is wildly uneven. A 2008 survey found that 10 percent of CDCs have 125 or more full-time staff members but the median CDC employs only 7.5 staff members. One-third had 4 or fewer employees.[35] This highlights the challenge facing CDCs trying to navigate the complex demands of network governance. In the South Bronx, a national intermediary, the Local Initiatives Support Corporation, provided ten CDCs in New York City with training and technical assistance, with strong financial support from the city. According to Alexander von Hoffman, during the ten years of the city's housing program, "the number of viable CDCs in New York City grew from a handful to over a hundred."[36]

Most CDCs do not have the advantages of New York City's strong housing market and the Local Initiatives Support Corporation's capacity-building efforts. Successful CDC performance is both expensive and complex, and the unevenness in the distribution of CDC resources is likely to lead to uneven neighborhood outcomes. Few funders cover operating costs, the basic glue of any organization. One of the most successful CDCs pursuing a multifaceted mission is the Youngstown Development Corporation in Youngstown, Ohio. Although its leadership and strategic thinking are exemplary, a critical underpinning of its success is the fact that a local foundation has made a long-term commitment to providing the organization with a core of general-purpose operating funds. Elsewhere, in order to keep their staff paid, many CDCs find themselves chasing grants for specific projects regardless of whether those projects address community needs or priorities.

CDC operating shortages can be addressed by real estate development. Successful Low-Income Housing Tax Credit (LIHTC) projects yield generous development fees. A completed one hundred-unit LIHTC apartment project, for example, may yield a CDC $2.5 million to $4 million in fees with few strings attached, providing flexible funds for future operations. As a result, CDCs, especially in weak housing markets, often prioritize the development of LIHTC projects; while they provide better-quality housing for residents, they often cannibalize limited demand for existing housing and increase vacancy elsewhere in the area, exacerbating racial and poverty concentration.[37]

Local CDC-centered network governance systems vary tremendously across the nation. Almost every older city in the country has at least one CDC, but the number and strength of CDCs varies widely. Cleveland has some of the strongest and most active CDCs and one of the most vigorous systems of network governance in the nation.[38] Local foundations have spent millions of dollars building CDC capacity, funneling their funds through a local intermediary, Cleveland Neighborhood Progress. Skilled professionals move back and forth between CDCs, government, foundations, and intermediaries, all of which builds trust, essential to the community development system. Few cities can point to anything comparable. At the same time, it is not clear that Cleveland's sophisticated community development network has resulted in significantly better market outcomes for the city's neighborhoods, although they undoubtedly improved the quality of life in many neighborhoods.

In the final analysis, it is difficult to reach a conclusion about how effective CDCs are at building and sustaining good neighborhoods. CDC impacts need to be evaluated in context and along multiple dimensions, without any romantic illusions that they can rebuild local economies or address underlying issues of poverty and inequality. With their grassroots connections and local knowledge, CDCs embody our theme that context matters. Even the strongest CDCs, however, cannot by themselves turn around neighborhoods characterized by concentrated poverty and housing abandonment that lack the assets found in Denver's Five Points. But too often the concept of turning around is defined as rising real estate values. If CDCs bolster social connections, address crime through community policing, and improve the quality of life for people who live in disinvested neighborhoods, as we discuss in chapter 12, this may be more important.

Anchor Institutions and Private Corporations as Agents of Change

The mission of CDCs is to sustain and rebuild neighborhoods. The mission of local government is, broadly speaking, to provide for the general welfare of the people who live, work, and do business in the city, a mission that generally includes at least sustaining and at times rebuilding neighborhoods. That both should be agents of neighborhood change is logical and arguably inevitable. At the same time, there are other institutions whose central mission is far removed from fostering neighborhood change but that have become engaged as agents of neighborhood change for various reasons.

With all such institutions a question inevitably arises: To what extent is their engagement with a neighborhood a means to achieve some goal connected with their central mission, and to what extent is it intended to benefit the neighborhood? It is not that those goals are inherently in conflict; indeed, the involvement of universities or medical centers in nearby neighborhoods is usually driven by a conviction that those goals are congruent. Yet, the institution may define neighborhood benefit differently than its neighbors or have different priorities than they do.

The story of the Cincinnati Center City Community Development Corporation (3CDC) is instructive. Created by Cincinnati's major corporations with the strong support of city government, 3CDC's mission is to "strengthen the core assets of downtown by revitalizing and connecting the Central Business District and Over-the-Rhine."[39] Over-the-Rhine is a mixed-use neighborhood immediately adjacent to downtown Cincinnati dominated by historic mid-nineteenth-century architecture. Once home to German immigrants, it declined after World War II and was subsequently largely abandoned to the point where most buildings were empty and its population was less than 20 percent of its postwar peak. The interventions of 3CDC have resulted in dramatic change to the area, but it is hard not to conclude that for 3CDC, Over-the-Rhine was more a real estate opportunity based on its proximity to downtown than an opportunity to rebuild a neighborhood socially or economically on behalf of its residents. While receiving many plaudits, 3CDC's activities have also spawned controversy.[40]

The most prominent members of this cluster of agents of change are large educational and medical anchor institutions. Many of America's larger older cities are home to important universities and medical centers, legacies of their industrial heyday and the generosity of their industrial barons. In 1873, philanthropist Johns Hopkins endowed a university and hospital in Baltimore that pioneered medical education and public health research. Today, Johns Hopkins University's medical complex is among the largest in the world and by far the largest force in Baltimore's economy. It epitomizes what have come to be known as anchor institutions, "institutions that, by reason of mission, invested capital, or relationships to customers or employees, are tied to a certain location."[41] Anchor institutions have a strong stake in the future of the neighborhoods around their campuses.

Prior to World War II, urban universities and medical centers, while valuable local assets, tended to be relatively small and largely self-contained, with little impact on either the local economy or their surrounding neighborhoods.

After the war, the expansion of health care and higher education resulted in dramatic growth of these institutions. Controlling for inflation, the United States spent twenty-five times as much for health care in 2014 as it did in 1950, although the population of the country only doubled. Medical research, which is concentrated in a handful of major centers such as Johns Hopkins, increased by fifty times. From 1965 to 2014, university enrollment grew from six million to over twenty million. Education and health care have become the dominant economic sector in most cities, with anchor institutions as the dominant employers. In 2018, the education and health care sectors made up 38 percent of all jobs in Philadelphia and 37 percent in Baltimore, not counting thousands of jobs in tech spin-offs and support services.[42] Even in cities with highly diversified economies, such as Los Angeles and Seattle, health care is the largest single employment sector.

In the urban crisis years, urban universities and hospitals were rarely viewed as benefactors by their neighbors. Landlocked in dense urban areas and under intense pressure to expand, they often found themselves on a collision course with their neighbors. Moreover, while anchor institutions were expanding, many of the neighborhoods around them were struggling under the weight of white flight, poverty, and crime.

The weakness of cities' real estate markets and the antiurban tenor of the times meant that anchor institutions had little interest or incentive to foster residential or retail growth in surrounding neighborhoods. Instead, universities and hospitals worked with city governments to acquire and clear adjacent blocks or entire neighborhoods, using eminent domain and federal dollars to create increasingly self-contained complexes. Amendments to the urban renewal laws in 1961 allowed university and hospital development expenditures to count toward local matching requirements for federal urban renewal grants, giving city governments a strong incentive to partner with them. A history of the University of Pennsylvania's urban renewal efforts noted that it "gave urban universities nationwide a virtual blank check to ally with local redevelopment authorities to clear swaths of city blocks for institutional expansion and commercial redevelopment in campus areas—largely at federal expense."[43] Universities, always somewhat insular, grew more so. The fortress-like architecture of urban universities and hospitals of the time, with windowless brick or stone walls facing city streets, reflected their state of mind. In order to wall themselves off from rising crime and decay, streets were closed and barriers were put up to create policed, landscaped campus oases with their own cafeterias, bookstores, and theaters.

In the mid-1960s, the University of Pennsylvania was the driving force behind a $100 million urban renewal project that leveled twenty blocks in Philadelphia's Black Bottom neighborhood to build the nation's first inner-city technology center, displacing thousands. A few years later the university displaced another 1,220 people in the Hamilton Village neighborhood to build a "so-called Super Block, including a stretch of looming concrete high-rise dormitories."[44] In New York City, Columbia University purchased ninety-two buildings in surrounding neighborhoods between 1962 and 1968, displacing 6,800 mostly African American and Puerto Rican residents.[45] As universities continued to expand, neighborhood opposition grew, often with the involvement of students inspired by the protest movements of the 1960s. In 1968, plans to take public parkland to build a gymnasium for Columbia University blended with anger over its involvement in the Vietnam War to fuel student protests and occupations of university buildings.

By the 1990s both urban conditions and attitudes toward city living had begun to change, however, creating the possibility of a different relationship between anchor institutions and their neighbors. Urban crime had begun its remarkable decline. Students and young professionals had begun to seek out pedestrian-friendly, mixed-use urban neighborhoods. Rather than being a burden, universities and hospitals began to realize, their urban location could become an asset they could leverage to recruit students and staff. Instead of turning their backs to the city, they began to embrace their urban location, breaking down the barriers between campus and city. Often working with private developers, they began reaching out into surrounding neighborhoods, making the transition from enclaves to anchors.[46]

As nonprofit institutions, universities and most hospitals have obligations that reinforce their anchor mission. Although they benefit from local public services, such as police and fire, they do not pay local real estate taxes. Recognizing this problem and under increasing local government pressure, some hospitals and universities have agreed to make payments in lieu of taxes to local governments. While Yale only pays taxes on about 3 percent of its $3 billion in real estate to the City of New Haven, mostly on its retail properties, it makes a substantial payment in lieu of taxes to the city, recently increased to $21.5 million per year from 2022 on.[47]

Some nonprofit hospitals also make payments in lieu of taxes, while in exchange for their tax exemption the Internal Revenue Service requires tax-exempt nonprofit hospitals to provide community benefits. A 2021 New Jersey law requires nonprofit hospitals to pay a "community service charge" equal to $3 per bed per day to the municipality.[48] The 2010 Affordable Care Act goes a step further, requiring nonprofit hospitals to include in their mission services to the urban communities where they are located.

To encourage community outreach by universities, in 1994 the Department of Housing and Urban Development established the Office of University Partnerships, which made grants to universities working to create partnerships with

local communities. Land-grant universities have broadened their mission beyond agriculture to fund urban extension agents who bring university resources
to local communities. Finally, universities are increasingly embracing service
learning, the idea that students can learn by directly engaging with community
problems. Many service-learning projects take place in communities neighboring college campuses.

The University of Pennsylvania was one of the first major institutions to embrace an anchor mission. Both the university and its much larger medical complex are in West Philadelphia, just east of Center City across the Schuykill River
(figure 9.3). Relations between the university and the surrounding community

FIGURE 9.3.   The city of Philadelphia

(Map by Emily Blackburn)

had long been hostile, reflecting fallout from the university's urban renewal efforts years earlier. Under Judith Rodin, who became the university's first female president in 1994, things began to change. Over the next ten years, Rodin led the university's efforts to build bridges with the community and revive nearby neighborhoods, concentrating on the smaller area within West Philadelphia known as University City. To leverage its investment, the University of Pennsylvania brought eleven major institutions together in 1997 to form the University City District, a not-for-profit entity funded by institutional contributions. More recently, while the university has maintained its commitment, much of the leadership linking the academic world to the West Philadelphia community has shifted to Drexel University, which has played an increasingly important role since John Fry, who had worked under Rodin at Penn, became Drexel's president in 2010. Key elements in the strategy have included:

- Neighborhood safety and physical improvements: These include safety ambassadors (unarmed officers who report crime and track public hazards), streetscape improvements, enhanced street lighting, extra park maintenance, and an inexpensive shuttle service.
- Local procurement and hiring: The University of Pennsylvania began to direct more contracts and purchases of goods and services to minority-owned companies in West Philadelphia. Between 1996 and 2003 the university tripled its contracting with local businesses, from $20.1 million to $61.6 million.[49] By 2009 an estimated 26 percent of its contracts went to minority- and women-owned firms, and approximately 35 percent of all construction workers on its projects were women or minorities.[50]
- Public school partnership: The University of Pennsylvania took the lead in creating a new K–8 public school in University City, run through a collaboration of the school district and Penn's Graduate School of Education. Opened in 2001, the Penn Alexander School has been highly successful both educationally and as a driver of neighborhood change.
- Real estate development. The University of Pennsylvania has invested heavily in retail development in University City, including a thirty thousand–square-foot Barnes and Noble superstore that doubles as the university bookstore, a Hilton Hotel, art galleries, a yoga studio, a bakery, and restaurants along the 40th Street corridor. By 2004 the university had invested $170 million in these retail developments, attracting another $370 million in private investment.

The University of Pennsylvania has been accused of gentrifying the area, making it unaffordable for low-income families and people of color.[51] The catchment area for the Penn Alexander School, which includes about 30 percent of University City's population, has experienced rising median household incomes and soaring home values. From 1998 to 2011, house values inside the school's catchment area increased at more than double the rate of the rest of University City and four times the rate of the city as a whole.[52] A 2018 article in the *Philadelphia Inquirer* was headlined "The Penn Alexander Effect: Is There Any Room Left for Low-Income Residents in University City?"[53]

The remainder of University City has experienced trends that also look like gentrification. Crime is down, home values are up, and the streets are alive with upscale retail activity. From 2000 to 2019 University City's Black population dropped by about a third, while per capita incomes rose at more than twice the rate of inflation. At the same time, however, more than a third of the population of University City lives below the poverty line, and per capita income still lags significantly behind the city.[54] Given the appeal to today's young adults of walkable urban neighborhoods with attractive older homes, much of this change would undoubtedly have happened without the intervention of the University of Pennsylvania and its partners, although probably at a slower pace and without many of the child-rearing families drawn by the Penn Alexander School. Moreover, the rest of West Philadelphia appears to have seen little benefit from the anchor initiative. From 2000 to 2019 the population of the rest of West Philadelphia fell steadily, and the poverty rate increased from 25.6 percent to 31.3 percent.[55] The "eds and meds effect," as it might be called, drops off rapidly with distance.

The University of Pennsylvania's anchor strategy has made it possible for University City to become an island in the city with enhanced public goods and services. The university and its partners fund the University City District, which provides additional police services, sanitation, lighting, landscaping, and public transit, similar to the many business improvement districts that have been established in urban downtowns, typically funded by a surcharge on district property owners' property tax bills. While the value of such entities to those funding them is manifest, it is equally clear that they create a two-tiered municipal governance structure, with wealth—in the form of anchor institutions or corporations—funding enhanced services in select neighborhoods while other neighborhoods languish.

A further issue in anchor initiatives is democratic accountability. Rodin writes that the University of Pennsylvania did not turn to CDCs to manage the process because "they lack sufficient organizational capacity reliably to lead and manage a complex, long-term reinvestment effort."[56] This is undoubtedly true. There are few CDCs anywhere that could match the University City initiative in terms of its comprehensive nature and sustained strategic investment over decades. Yet, this is remote from the network governance model of community development. The University of Pennsylvania, the University of Pennsylvania

Medical Center (Philadelphia's largest employer), and Drexel do not just participate in the networks; they dominate them.

Carolyn Adams makes a compelling case that third-sector organizations in
Philadelphia, such as the University of Pennsylvania, have effectively replaced the
city as planner for University City and similar inner-city neighborhoods and are
largely insulated from public scrutiny.[57] While a case can be made that the transformation of University City has benefited the city of Philadelphia as a whole, the
decisions about the future of the area were made neither by the city nor area residents. Instead, they were mostly made by a handful of major, mostly tax-exempt,
institutions for which neighborhood change was first and foremost about sup-
porting their missions as institutions, not as neighborhood change agents. The
lofty language of their mission should not obscure the effective absence of government with its decision-making processes, however inadequate, grounded in
representative democracy.

Although it is among the most sophisticated and comprehensive, the University City venture is but one of many similar eds and meds–led neighborhood
change initiatives around the United States. In Detroit, a similar effort spear-
headed by a cluster of institutions including Wayne State University and the Detroit Medical Center led to the creation of University Cultural Center Inc. in
1976. Now known as Midtown Detroit Inc., it has had a transformative effect on
Detroit's Midtown and New Center neighborhoods. In a usage more meaningful perhaps than intended, its dynamic long-term executive director Susan Mo-
sey is widely known as the "mayor of Midtown."

A similar venture was launched by a cluster of institutions in Cleveland including Case Western Reserve University and University Medical Center, which
has dramatically changed the University Circle area on that city's east side. A
major concern today of University Circle Inc. is how to create linkages to nearby
lower-income neighborhoods to enable their residents to benefit from their proximity to the University Circle area. A more modest but more democratic initiative is the Northside Urban Partnership in Syracuse, where St. Joseph's Hospital,
a large community hospital rather than a major research institution, partnered
with neighborhood residents, religious institutions, and a regional nonprofit,
CenterState Corporation for Economic Opportunity, to pursue the community's revitalization. Ironically, it is likely that St. Joseph's smaller size and more
limited resources prompted it to form such a partnership rather than attempt to
exert direct control over the future of the Northside neighborhood.

Anchor institutions, particularly the great universities and medical centers
in cities such as Philadelphia, Cleveland, and Detroit, bring valuable assets that
can potentially provide benefits well beyond the neighborhood scale. The University of Pittsburgh Medical Center is the largest private-sector employer in

Pennsylvania, and its potential to create opportunities, through training, jobs, purchase of goods and services, and contracts to the disadvantaged residents of the city and region is immense. Yale University has provided generous subsidies to enable over one thousand of its employees to buy homes in selected New Haven neighborhoods while underwriting the New Haven Promise, a program that pays the college tuition of graduates of New Haven's high schools.

Whether anchor institutions become neighborhood change agents in a larger, more meaningful sense depends on their ability to address two challenges. The first is how to extend their resources beyond their immediate surroundings into disinvested neighborhoods of color farther from the institutions themselves. In Cleveland, University Circle Inc. is grappling with this question but still searching for an answer. A second challenge is how to truly collaborate with neighborhoods. A case study of the relationship between the University of Pittsburgh and the Oakland neighborhood is subtitled "From Conflict to Cooperation, or How the 800-Pound Gorilla Learned to Sit With—and Not on—Its Neighbors."[58] The disparity in resources and power between the residents of disadvantaged urban neighborhoods and an institution such as the University of Pittsburgh is so immense as to be all but unbridgeable. In the absence of a strong role for local government or a strong neighborhood organization willing and able to negotiate from a position of strength with anchor institutions, one is left relying on nothing but the institution's goodwill. History suggests, to paraphrase the prophet Jeremiah, that it is little more than a broken reed.

The same challenges apply to for-profit developers that present themselves as community or neighborhood builders, of which a good example is the St. Louis–based firm McCormack Baron Salazar (MBS). Over nearly fifty years MBS, probably the largest developer of affordable housing in the United States, has built more than twenty-two thousand units largely in urban and often distressed neighborhoods. While MBS bills itself as "the nation's leading for-profit developer, manager and asset manager of economically-integrated urban *neighborhoods*," that is a misnomer.[59] The MBS strategy is very different from the CDC model, which attempts to build on the fabric and assets of a neighborhood. MBS goes into an existing low-income neighborhood, often a dilapidated public housing project, tears it down, and then builds an entirely new affordable housing or mixed-income community from scratch. According to one estimate, only about 20–30 percent of the original residents make it back into the new community.[60] The requirements that MBS establishes mean that "the most motivated and stable residents move to the new community," with the rest ending up in traditional, less desirable, public or private housing elsewhere.[61]

MBS does extensive community engagement with the residents of its units, but the fact is that as a for-profit developer beholden to investors and shareholders, its imperative is not just to lead but also to control any environment in which it has a financial stake. Any dilution of that control in the interest of true neighborhood engagement puts the corporation's core investments at risk. To its credit, MBS raises funds for wraparound services that are run by a spun-off nonprofit, Urban Strategies, but these services are done *for* residents, not *by* them.

We are reluctant to criticize MBS. It is extraordinarily successful at competing for federal grants and obtaining financing, and its developments are generally well designed, safe, healthy, and well maintained; it is rare to see graffiti in an MBS development. For the original residents who get to come back, it is undoubtedly a positive step. As often as not, however, MBS "neighborhoods" are self-contained enclaves within larger urban neighborhoods, with little relationship to their surroundings. Indeed, they are generally owned entirely by MBS and branded with new names to distinguish themselves from the surrounding neighborhoods.

The Challenge of Equity and Accountability

The foregoing discussion has brought out some of the strains as well as the potential in the networked governance model. The shift from a government-led model to a tools-based policy system that relies on iterations of public, private, and nonprofit partnerships may have increased flexibility and engaged new actors, but it has also created new problems of equity and democratic accountability. It is fundamentally competitive, bringing some of the features of a market into a setting historically seen as one driven by social benefit. The neighborhoods with the strongest CDCs, or the greatest proximity to a major anchor institution, are able to compete more effectively and get the most attention. And while some CDCs may be models of grassroots democracy, many are far from representative of their neighborhoods. Their boards are likely to contain well-connected bankers, lawyers, or anchor institution executives—and for good reason, since their business model is driven by access to capital and political resources. For all the good work CDCs do, they are not a solution to the challenges of inequity and uneven access to resources that bedevil urban neighborhoods.

The issues become even more troubling when we turn to anchor institutions and private corporations. Reflecting the neoliberal ideology of the past few decades and driven by their severe fiscal constraints, cities have made a devil's bargain with those institutions and corporations. In return for their investment of capital in the city's neighborhoods, local governments have effectively ceded large parts of the city to those entities' control, in the end further fragmenting the city's social, economic, and political structures. While anchor institutions and large corporations bring extraordinary resources of both money and talent to community development, they often deploy these resources in ways that prioritize their corporate or institutional agendas over conflicting resident agendas. And while they may in theory be part of a networked system, the power imbalance between them and the other players in the system, in the absence of a strong and effective public sector, is so great that instead of a networked system, power has simply shifted from one base to another. That base, moreover, lacks political legitimacy or accountability to justify its exercise of power outside its core mission.

DECONSTRUCTING GENTRIFICATION

If there is a single word that has come to encapsulate the popular understanding of neighborhood change in the second decade of the twenty-first century, it is "gentrification." While a powerful force driving neighborhood change in a handful of hot market and magnet cities such as San Francisco and Washington, D.C., gentrification has affected far fewer American neighborhoods elsewhere than many believe. Just the same, it has come to play a dominant role in the neighborhood conversation, obscuring equally if not more important trends moving neighborhoods in the opposite direction. We will look at some of those trends, particularly the widespread decline of traditional urban and suburban middle-income neighborhoods, in later chapters.

Building on our earlier discussion, particularly in chapters 5 and 7, this chapter will explore gentrification as a form of neighborhood change: why, how, and where it takes place and how it affects the neighborhoods that are gentrified as well as the lives of the residents of those neighborhoods. In this chapter we look at gentrification as not only an economic phenomenon but also a social phenomenon, deeply embedded in racial and cultural dynamics, as well as a political phenomenon, reflecting the unequal power dynamics of the contemporary American city. Finally, we discuss what all this means in the context of the future of urban neighborhoods and the concept of the good neighborhood. We begin, however, with a short historical overview of the term "gentrification" and the phenomenon, which of course long precedes the term itself.

The term "gentrification" was coined by British sociologist Ruth Glass in the introduction to her 1964 book *London: Aspects of Change*, where she describes, in language worth quoting at length, how

> one by one, many of the working-class quarters of London have been invaded by the middle classes—upper and lower. Shabby modest mews and cottages . . . have been taken over when their leases have expired and have become elegant expensive residences. Larger Victorian homes, downgraded in an earlier or recent period[,] have been upgraded once again. . . . Once this process of "gentrification" starts in a district, it goes on rapidly until all or most of the original working-class occupiers are displaced, and the whole social character of the district is changed.[1]

Glass was not the first to notice or name the process she described, which goes back hundreds if not thousands of years. Scholars have identified similar trends in Roman Britain and Roman North Africa, while Friedrich Engels coined the term "[to] Haussmann" to describe such processes, after the notorious rebuilder of Paris.[2] Jane Jacobs characterized similar processes as "unslumming" in her seminal *The Death and Life of Great American Cities*.[3] Glass, however, coined the term that would take on a life of its own.

In that one paragraph, Glass identified all of the features that became part of how gentrification is most widely understood: a series of transformative processes taking place in lower-income or working-class neighborhoods resulting from an influx of more affluent households. These processes may include physical changes to the housing stock through rehabilitation and reconfiguration, increases in the value of the housing, displacement of the neighborhood's previous residents, and changes to the neighborhood's social or cultural character. In short, it is about spatial or neighborhood change; moreover, it is about one particular type of neighborhood change. Gentrification has nothing to say about the processes by which those Victorian homes were previously downgraded, only about the process by which they are now being upgraded.

Glass's term began to catch on in the 1970s, putting a name to the emerging phenomenon that was sometimes called the "back to the city" movement.[4] That movement, which first appeared in such places as Park Slope in Brooklyn and Capitol Hill in Washington, D.C., prompted both scholarly interest and an early wave of antigentrification and antidisplacement political and organizing activity calling for public action to prevent displacement. While their efforts prompted a number of federally funded studies during the late 1970s, the Carter administration ultimately rejected calls for action, concluding not unreasonably that the "population and economic trends" represented by such efforts "are far too small to slow significantly or to reverse the movement to the suburbs and the loss of economic activity by central cities."[5]

Much of the initial wave of gentrification—which, as President Jimmy Carter's Department of Housing and Urban Development officials recognized, was a trickle compared to the flood of people, jobs, and businesses fleeing the central cities at the same time—petered out in the 1980s. While changes took hold in some neighborhoods, "islands of renewal in a sea of decay," as Brian Berry called them in 1985, other areas to which so-called urban pioneers had moved in the 1970s quietly reverted to their previous state, little changed if at all by the brief flurry of activity.[6] This was particularly true outside of the handful of places such as San Francisco that were already beginning to draw significant numbers of generally young, generally white, highly educated people before the end of the millennium.

The pace of gentrification appears to have significantly picked up steam after 2000. After slowing down briefly during the foreclosure crisis and the Great Recession, it gained renewed strength once the recession was over. Both scholarly interest in gentrification and its visibility in the popular media have also skyrocketed since 2000. A search of Google Scholar by year for published books and articles with "gentrification" in the title found that from an average of fewer than one hundred per year prior to 2000, the number grew to two hundred per year from 2005 to 2009 and to over five hundred per year from 2015 to 2019.

Far more important than the proliferation of scholarly articles and papers is the extent to which gentrification has come to dominate the broader conversation about neighborhood change. Indeed, it is fair to say that in most American cities today, the gentrification discussion is not so much part of the public discussion of neighborhood change as it is the entire conversation. Moreover, as it has spread it has taken on an increasingly confrontational quality, instilling guilt and defensiveness among those characterized as gentrifiers and anger among those opposing gentrification, spilling over into episodes such as London's 2015 Cereal Killer demonstrations. As described in *The Guardian*, "Hundreds of protesters attacked a cereal cafe in east London on Saturday night, daubing the word 'scum' on the shop window and setting fire to an effigy of a police officer. Riot police were called in to defend the Cereal Killer Cafe in Shoreditch after it was targeted by a large crowd of anti-gentrification activists carrying pigs' heads and torches."[7]

While the entire idea of a store selling artisanal cereal at £6.50 for a large bowl (including one variety called Unicorn Poop that contains "buttery fruity rings & flakes with freeze-dried marshmallows & served with bubblegum milk") is at one level more than a little ridiculous, the story nonetheless raises important questions.[8] Many, however, seem at most only tangentially related to the phenomenon Ruth Glass described over fifty years ago. We will try to deconstruct those questions later in this chapter. In the end, though, any discussion of gentrification, particularly in the framework of this book, must be about neighborhood change.

The Drivers of Gentrification

What exactly do we mean when we refer to gentrification? In its most well-known form, it is as Glass described: the movement of more affluent people into a less affluent residential neighborhood, resulting in upgrading of the housing stock and higher housing costs and potentially over time displacing those she referred to as the "original working-class occupiers."[9] Picking up on this theme, radical geographer Neil Smith, perhaps the most prominent writer on gentrification during the 1970s and 1980s, distinguished between gentrification and redevelopment, writing in 1982 that gentrification was "the process by which working class residential neighborhoods are rehabilitated by middle class homebuyers, landlords and professional developers, . . . [while] redevelopment involves not rehabilitation of old structures but the construction of new buildings on previously developed land."[10] Today, however, most people would probably agree that other forms of neighborhood change or neighborhood formation, including not only the conversion of downtown office buildings and industrial lofts to residential use but also what Mark Davidson and Loretta Lees have called "new-build" gentrification,[11] or the construction of new housing in previously vacant and underutilized urban areas, should also be considered forms of gentrification. The common denominator of all of these is the movement of a distinct "gentrifier" demographic into urban space, changing existing neighborhoods and forming new ones.

Thus, at one level the central driver of gentrification can be seen as the emergence of what can be considered a demographic of gentrifiers, a critical mass of people who share the desire, resources, and ability as well as a sense of what they are looking for in a neighborhood to gentrify urban space, that is, to transform it in the ways that have come to be known as gentrification. That is a critically important part of the picture but only one part. To understand how gentrification has become a significant phenomenon, it is necessary to understand how gentrifiers are formed, why their destination is the central city rather than elsewhere, and how gentrifiable housing and neighborhoods come into being.

As we examine these three questions, it is essential to keep the context in mind: neighborhood change is a constant, and gentrification is a form of neighborhood change. Gentrification is not a phenomenon that somehow exists outside the larger pattern of constant neighborhood flux. Neighborhoods move up, down, up and then down, or vice versa. Both the earlier downgrading of Glass's large Victorian homes and their subsequent upgrading were part of that same fundamental flux. Within that framework, however, gentrification is a distinct and important form of neighborhood change, if not quite new at least new in its scope and significance. It would be well worth analyzing even if it played a far less important role in contemporary American urban life and neighborhood discourse than it does.

In some respects, the question of who are the gentrifiers is the simplest of the three. As we discussed in chapter 7, gentrification of American cities has been overwhelmingly driven by the influx of young well-educated adults, often referred to as the millennial generation. While much media attention has been given to the movement of older empty nester households to urban neighborhoods, there is little evidence that they make up more than a small part of the universe of gentrifiers, although their greater affluence makes them a popular media subject as well as highly attractive to developers. Canadian geographer Markus Moos has suggested that the phenomenon be renamed "youthification."[12]

One factor that contributed to the higher rate of gentrification since 2000 than during the preceding decades was the extent to which the younger cohort grew nationally. While their numbers increased by less than two million from 1982 to 2000, they increased by over five million from 2000 to 2018. As the cohort grew, an increasing share of them moved to central cities. As both Pittsburgh's and Baltimore's total population continued to decline, the number of adults aged twenty-five to thirty-four with a BA or higher degree in both cities more than doubled. Today, one out of four adult residents in Boston and Washington, D.C., and nearly one out of five in Pittsburgh is twenty-five to thirty-four years old with a college degree.

Underlying the phenomenon of gentrification are the major transformations in the US economy that have taken place over the past fifty or more years. As many have written, the economic function of cities in the developed world has shifted from production to consumption, a change that was particularly jarring for cities that had historically been centers of industrial production. As they lost manufacturing jobs, cities grew jobs requiring education and specialized skills, most often concentrated in health care and higher education, the so-called eds and meds sector, although some cities developed distinct specializations in other sectors. Financial sector jobs grew in New York City, and tech jobs grew in Seattle, while in Washington, D.C., a large and highly diverse body of well-paid high-skill jobs grew in the myriad businesses, think tanks, and associations that sought to benefit from proximity to the federal government.

The shift from production to consumption and the growth in high-wage, high-skill employment at the same time as the cohorts of young educated adults were growing meant that their purchasing power was that much greater. This was also true of investment capital generally, the extent and availability of which grew steadily during the 1990s and early 2000s. While this purchasing power and capital needed an outlet, it was far from foreordained that so much of it should flow into the cities or take the forms it has taken.

Before exploring why it did so, it is important to reiterate a point made earlier; namely, far from all of the available capital and purchasing power that is being invested in growth and development is going into the cities. While more has gone into the cities since 2000 than in the two previous decades, as revival and gentrification take place in the cities, the suburban ring around those same cities continues to expand, and large numbers of working-class and middle-class people, today as often African American as white, continue to leave the central cities for suburbia. Gentrification is but one of many simultaneous processes of neighborhood change taking place in twenty-first-century America and, for all its political visibility, far from the most prevalent one, again outside a handful of highly visible magnet cities.

At the same time as they were growing high-skill white-collar jobs, however, the cities were becoming more attractive destinations for in-migrants in other ways. They were becoming safer. After peaking in the early 1990s, violent crime began to drop across the United States, a drop that was experienced in most major cities.[13] From 1995 to 2018, the number of murders dropped by 56 percent in Washington, D.C., even as its population grew by over 20 percent. Urban amenities began to flourish, ranging from reclaimed waterfronts to music and theater venues and restaurants. More and more cities became, in sociologist Terry Nichols Clark's phrase, "entertainment machines" or, in Michael Sorkin's more dismissive phase, "theme parks."[14] Cities increasingly became places where wealth was spent rather than created, growing by providing the services and amenities sought by a consumption-oriented society. All of these trends were part of a single interactive process in which safety, amenities, job growth, investment, and the in-migration of young college graduates have built on one another in reinforcing causal loops.

Amenities, which can be a scenic waterfront or a cluster of theaters and restaurants such as Cleveland's Playhouse Square, are not merely the product of consumption demand but are themselves generators of demand, drawing people with money to spend and wealth-creating skills to cities. A critical part of this is what Clark calls the "scene."[15] When enough amenities cluster in one area to form a critical mass, they create scenes. Scenes draw people together to share activities, participate in a distinctive shared atmosphere, and define their identities by sharing the scene with other like-minded people. Scenes also offer young unattached people the greatest opportunity to make friends and identify potential romantic partners.

Many factors contribute to drawing young people to these cities, but the presence of a "scene" is a critical element. Millennials, who set the pace for urban revival, cluster in areas that offer the amenities that most resonate with their interests and lifestyle. These areas have not only restaurants, cafés, and music venues but also greater transit accessibility and high density as well as lively mixtures of different activities on the same block or even in the same building. In that light, it is not surprising that the reinvention of historically nonresidential downtowns, with their high density and transit connectivity, as largely residential mixed-use areas is a prominent feature of the urban revival. While the underlying reasons for their preferences may be unclear, their desire for these amenities and the value of a critical mass of amenities in creating a mutually reinforcing cycle of amenity growth and in-migration are unquestionable.

The increased attractiveness of the cities paralleled and undoubtedly reinforced a growing tendency among educated young people to want to live in cities. While recent research found little difference in the 1980s between the migration patterns of people aged twenty-five to thirty-four compared to older age groups, those patterns began to shift significantly in the 1990s.[16] Since 2000 the young grads have made up a disproportionate share of urban in-migrants, with their numbers in some cities outweighing the simultaneous out-migration of everybody else.

By highlighting the role of the educated young in-migrants in gentrification, we are taking sides in a debate that was triggered by Neil Smith in a 1979 article titled "A Theory of Gentrification: A Back to the City Movement by Capital, not People," which has since been frequently quoted and reprinted.[17] The same article propounded the "rent gap" hypothesis, which we discuss below. Writing from a more or less classical Marxist perspective, Smith sees both the disinvestment in declining areas and the reinvestment in gentrifying ones as being driven by the flow of capital. The relationship between people and capital, however, is more complex and more interactive.

While such theoretical formulations tend to treat people as passive beings blindly following larger forces beyond their control or knowledge, individual agency needs to be taken far more seriously as a factor in gentrification. Indeed, the evidence on the ground suggests that most often people precede capital into a neighborhood; namely, the initial stages of gentrification are driven by a series of discrete individual decisions to buy or rent in a particular lower-income neighborhood, using modest financial resources cobbled together from various sources and often following on the emergence and diffusion of a narrative about the neighborhood.[18] Creating an upscale neighborhood housing market is an incremental process, beginning slowly and, if successful, gradually gathering speed. Capital follows people, often first in the form of small developers, rehabbers, and flippers and only gradually later, typically after the newly upscale market character of the area has begun to solidify, by corporate and institutional investment in the form of large multifamily, commercial, or mixed-use developments.

Although a few early gentrification projects were fueled by public money, most prominently perhaps Philadelphia's Society Hill, into which the city sunk millions in urban renewal funds, direct intervention by government today to initiate gentrification is rare. The initial stages of gentrification may indeed catch local planners by surprise. Once gentrification of a neighborhood has begun, however, local government may step in to help move it along by providing amenities such as park or streetscape improvements or selling city-owned land to developers; more rarely, cities may implement measures to discourage displacement or keep existing low-income housing from being lost.

That leaves perhaps the most complex question of all: why certain neighborhoods gentrify while others do not. Here, much of the scholarly literature is not only not helpful but even misleading, most notably Smith's well-known rent gap hypothesis, which has become a staple of academic analysis of gentrification. The rent gap hypothesis begins with the incontrovertible proposition that the capital initially invested in many neighborhoods, principally in the form of the neighborhood's housing stock, is often devalued over time by a series of forces, some arguably neutral but others malign, such as landlord milking, redlining, and abandonment. Smith then argues that

> as filtering and neighborhood decline proceed, the rent gap widens. *Gentrification occurs* when the gap is wide enough that developers can purchase shells cheaply, can pay the builders' costs and profit for rehabilitation, can pay interest on mortgage and construction loans, and can then sell the end product for a sale price that leaves a satisfactory return to the developer. The entire ground rent, or a large portion of it, is now capitalized; the neighborhood has been "recycled" and begins a new cycle of use.[19]

Reduced to its essence, this is a roundabout restatement of the obvious proposition that in a market economy such as the United States, property is only redeveloped, reused, or recycled when someone has a good financial reason for doing so, period. As an explanation for gentrification, however, it is worthless, as numerous scholars have pointed out again and again, including Robert Beauregard, who wrote in 1986 that "the 'rent gap' argument provides only one of the necessary conditions for gentrification and none of the sufficient ones."[20] Subsequent critiques by other scholars have been far more devastating.[21]

We would not mention the rent gap hypothesis were it not for its continued prominence in the literature and even more for the fact that it has led, in ways perhaps not necessarily intended by Smith, to two widely held but fundamentally erroneous ideas about why and how places gentrify. The first fallacy is that the greater the rent gap, the more likely gentrification is to happen, and the second is that gentrification is an inevitable outcome of decline. While neither proposition is remotely supported by evidence on the ground, both are alive and well in the popular literature and in the politics of gentrification.

To be sure, it is reasonable to assume that for gentrification to take place somebody has to believe that the potential value of a property is or will become greater than its current value, though even that proposition is far from universally true, as witnessed by the restoration of lofts and industrial buildings by artists driven by lifestyle rather than economic reasons. But even assuming that it is usually true, it is not a sufficient condition, as Beauregard points out. As we noted earlier, the great majority of urban neighborhoods have not gentrified; moreover, the neighborhoods that have been most devalued, and thus in theory have the greatest hypothetical rent gaps, are usually the last to gentrify if they ever do.

Gentrification is not a random phenomenon, landing anywhere property values are low enough. Moreover, while the extent of gentrification in any one city may depend on the size of demand in that city, which corresponds to the influx of wealth we discussed in chapter 5, aggregate demand tells us nothing about where within the city gentrification will take place. In cities other than a handful of particularly hot markets, gentrification is both limited and selective. A few neighborhoods gentrify, but most do not.

In contrast to gauzy theoretical formulations, solid empirical research can help identify which neighborhoods are more likely and which less likely to gentrify. Research has identified three features of urban neighborhoods that appear to be most important in establishing the likelihood of them gentrifying. All are logical enough, although one may initially appear to be counterintuitive.

The first and most powerful factor is location. Simply stated, an area that is adjacent to a strong high-value neighborhood or to a particular amenity or center of activity such as a body of water or major university is more likely to gentrify than one that is not. Indeed, that proposition can be put more strongly in the reverse: if an area is not close to such a neighborhood, amenity, or center of activity its likelihood of gentrifying is extremely small, not zero perhaps, but exceptions are vanishingly few. Two rigorous studies have found that location in this sense is the single strongest predictor of whether a neighborhood will gentrify.[22]

In Philadelphia, gentrification moved in linear fashion from Society Hill southward into Queen Village and Bella Vista, northeast from Old City into Northern Liberties and Fishtown, and from the University of Pennsylvania into West Philadelphia. In Baltimore, it has pushed eastward along the Inner Harbor from areas first redeveloped in the 1970s and 1980s into Canton, Fells Point, and Patterson Park as well as south and northwest from downtown and south and west from the Johns Hopkins University campus into Remington, Hampden, and Woodberry and east into Charles Village.

The second factor is a largely intact neighborhood fabric, that is, that the original built texture of homes and other structures that make up the neighborhood is still largely intact even though much of it may be deteriorated and in need of repair or rehabilitation. This is in contrast to heavily disinvested urban neighborhoods, where abandonment and demolition have replaced the traditional neighborhood fabric with a "perforated" one characterized more by vacant lots and abandoned buildings. This distinction is harder to quantify than location but not difficult to identify. Figures 10.1 and 10.2 show streets in two Baltimore neighborhoods, both initially developed with all but identical row houses but with vastly different textures today.

The precise nature of the fabric is less important. Location and cost factors being equal, it is more likely that a neighborhood of historic houses with superb architectural details will gentrify than one with more ordinary houses, but architectural or historic distinction are not conditions of gentrification. All of Baltimore's gentrifying neighborhoods are row house neighborhoods, but some are grand and historically or architecturally significant, while others are more modest and of no particular distinction, such as the Hampden neighborhood shown in figure 10.1. As distinct from large-scale redevelopment, where large numbers of vacancies are an opportunity, large numbers of vacant buildings and vacant lots are a deterrent to small-scale individual rehabilitation and home-buying efforts by individuals who by and large want to become part of a neighborhood—at least as an intact physical entity—rather than a patchy, fragmented environment.

The third factor is possibly counterintuitive. In much of the popular discourse, gentrification is seen as targeting African American neighborhoods, as exemplified in one blogger's comment: "This definition [of gentrification] says nothing about skin color but *the overwhelming majority of the time*, this plays out along the lines of white and black. The white people move in, and the Black people are moved out."[23] In fact, gentrification on the ground tends to avoid such areas. This proposition has been well documented by research in cities as diverse as Chicago, New York, Philadelphia, St. Louis, and Baltimore.[24] A recent study of Baltimore found 110 "gentrifiable" (that is, not upper income to begin with) predominantly Black census tracts in 2000, of which only 4 had gentrified by 2017; by contrast, 18, or nearly half of the 40 predominantly white gentrifiable tracts, were gentrifying.[25]

This does not mean that no gentrification of Black neighborhoods is taking place in those cities or elsewhere. Black neighborhoods are gentrifying, but their numbers are small compared to the effect of gentrification on white—and, in

FIGURE 10.1. Two Baltimore neighborhoods. Intact texture in gentrified Hampden

(Google Earth © 2022 Google)

FIGURE 10.2. Perforated texture in ungentrified Park Circle.

(Google Earth © 2022 Google)

Chicago, Latinx—working-class neighborhoods, at least until the latter neighborhoods have been "used up." The perception that gentrification targets Black neighborhoods has been fostered by the fact that in a few highly visible cities, most notably Washington, D.C., the only "gentrifiable" neighborhoods were Black ones, while in New York City gentrification in a small number of Black neighborhoods such as Harlem and Bedford-Stuyvesant has been most visible, notwithstanding the evidence mustered by Timberlake and Johns-Wolfe that gentrification in New York has been more extensive in white working-class neighborhoods.[26]

This phenomenon also undercuts the widely expressed belief—a fundamental part of Smith's rent gap hypothesis—that neighborhoods need to decline greatly before they can be gentrified. While it may be true of some gentrifying neighborhoods, it is not usually true; the most common gentrifying area is a white working-class neighborhood, which may at one point have been a more affluent area but may have long been a more or less stable, albeit modest and low-priced, neighborhood. The late nineteenth-century tenements of Hoboken, New Jersey, which are today condominium apartments selling for upwards of $500,000, were built for and remained rudimentary housing for working-class immigrants and their descendants until that small city's proximity to Manhattan led to its gentrification beginning in the 1970s. Similarly, Hampden in Baltimore was another long-standing white working-class neighborhood until its proximity to Johns Hopkins University made its modest row houses attractive to people with ties to the university.

Given that gentrifiers for the most part are likely to be white, the pattern of racial avoidance is sadly predictable from the racialized history of America's neighborhoods and white home buyer behavior. As we discussed in chapter 8 on race, white home buyers are significantly less likely to buy—or even look at—homes in predominantly Black neighborhoods, and whites are more likely to perceive a neighborhood as being dangerous if it is predominantly African American. Behavioral economists have found that people consistently place a greater premium on avoiding risk than on pursuing gain. Thus, from the perception of the initial group of white gentrifiers, who are already accepting what they consider to be not insignificant risks by moving into a neighborhood that has been devalued by the market, race becomes an added risk factor they could be expected to avoid if possible. While this reasoning is speculative, it is a credible explanation for a well-documented and widespread phenomenon.

The foregoing discussion has illuminated why and to some extent how gentrification happens. It leads to the even more complex question of what gentrification means; what it means in the larger context of neighborhood change and what it means for both the gentrifiers and particularly for the people who live in a neighborhood that is undergoing gentrification. That in turn raises further questions about gentrification as a social and political issue, questions that transcend the spatial frame of the gentrifying neighborhood. Much of this, however, begins with the question of the relationship between gentrification and displacement.

Gentrification and Displacement

Much of the opposition to gentrification has centered around the issue of displacement of longtime residents by more affluent newcomers. The idea of people being pushed out of communities that they and people like them may have occupied for years through no fault of their own except for not having enough money is understandably distasteful to any reasonable person. Reports of landlords in rapidly gentrifying areas in New York City and San Francisco forcing longtime tenants out of their apartments through unethical or illegal means are even more abhorrent.

Beyond the visceral, anecdotal level, however, there are many questions about the actual relationship between gentrification and displacement, beginning with what we mean by the term "displacement." The term has many meanings, fraught with implications for our understanding both of gentrification and its social effects. Dissecting the different forms of what may be considered from various perspectives to be displacement is not an effort to downplay the human distress and conflict associated with gentrification; instead, understanding the differences may help us think of better ways to minimize that distress.

Even as one attempts to dissect these terms, it is important to keep in mind the extent to which they are seen through the lens of not merely today's events but also history. In that respect, the most important history is that of the federal urban renewal and interstate highway construction programs, which displaced—in the starkest, most literal sense of the term—well over half a million American households during the 1950s and 1960s. As discussed in chapter 4, a disproportionate share of these households were people of color, largely African Americans. Hundreds of Black neighborhoods were eradicated or eviscerated.

The urban renewal wave ebbed during the late 1960s. The program itself was abolished in 1974, by which time the interstate highway system was largely in place, but the memory of displacement and destruction of neighborhoods remained present, as it does today. As psychiatrist Mindy Fullilove writes in her book *Root Shock*, "the howl of pain that went up with the first bulldozers has grown and deepened."[27] Those memories, layered over with decades of further indignities, make up the collective memory of America's urban Black population and are an ever-present subtext to any discussion of gentrification. As we look at displacement, we recognize that while it is important to interrogate the term critically, it is equally important to understand the social and historical context in which it exists and that the dispute over displacement is far more than a technical one.

Displacement as used in media and political discourse is (at least) three distinct and often conflated phenomena. We will refer to them as physical displacement, replacement, and dislocation, or cultural (and political) displacement. Physical displacement and replacement are most often conflated. It is not unusual to find studies that measure the change in a particular group's population before and after a neighborhood has been gentrified and define any decline in that population as displacement; thus, if there were one hundred Black renter households in an area in 2000 and fifty in 2018, they conclude that fifty were "displaced."[28] We find that assumption questionable. We have no idea why they left. If a family leaves a house or apartment for personal reasons—job change, desire for a larger (or smaller) dwelling, and so on—unrelated to changes in neighborhood conditions and is replaced by a different type of family, however defined, is that displacement?

In 1978, Grier and Grier laid out a more rigorous definition of physical displacement. Displacement occurs "when any household is forced to move from its residence by conditions . . . which (1) are beyond the household's reasonable ability to control or prevent; (2) occur despite the household's having met all previously imposed conditions of occupancy; and (3) make continued occupancy by that household impossible, hazardous or unaffordable."[29]

Thus, if a tenant has been paying rent reliably but the landlord raises it to a level where she can no longer afford to do so and subsequently evicts her for nonpayment of rent, that is displacement and, depending on the circumstances, may be attributable to gentrification. We also argue, although the Griers would disagree, that if a poor tenant paying over half of her income to rent a house in a low-income neighborhood loses her job, cannot pay her rent, and is evicted as a result, that too is displacement. Her poverty and the low wages she is earning are both conditions beyond her control. That type of displacement, however, has everything to do with poverty and a great deal to do with the structural cost of even modest housing but rarely anything to do with gentrification.

While it is easy to measure gross demographic change over time, it is far more difficult to measure physical displacement in the sense used by Grier and Grier, or any similar definition, and determine how much of it to attribute to gentrification. Thus, much of the research is based on more or less crude proxies or anecdotes, usually with ambiguous or misleading results. Pulling together what we can say about this, the evidence suggests that in most places, physical displacement is not widespread. The principal exceptions may be hot neighborhoods

in hot market cities, such as parts of Brooklyn and San Francisco, where both
the pressure and the pace of gentrification are unusual by comparison to most
cities and where the economic rewards to unscrupulous landlords, developers,
and others from pushing people out may be considerable. By contrast, little evidence of systemic displacement in this sense has been found in connection with
gentrification in other cities.[30]

Whether widespread or sporadic, displacement in the sense of deliberate practices that unjustly and adversely affect the well-being of vulnerable families and
individuals should not be acceptable. State and local governments should take action to minimize displacement and hold anyone acting inappropriately to account.[31] Replacement, on the other hand, is much more ambiguous and complex.

While physical displacement results from an intentional action, replacement,
which is much more common in gentrifying neighborhoods, is often a facially
neutral, impersonal market outcome. Assume that a low-income Black tenant
moves out of a house in a gentrifying neighborhood for reasons unrelated to gentrification. Once the house is vacant, the landlord rents it to a more affluent
white tenant or sells it to a white home buyer. This is in fact a process that often
takes place in gentrifying neighborhoods, reflecting the reality that renters in
the United States turn over exceptionally often. In many cities, the average
length of a tenant's tenure is only around two years.

This process will result over time in a significant decline in the number of
low-income tenants in a gentrifying neighborhood and, if it is a largely Black
neighborhood with mostly white gentrifiers, in a significant decline in the number of low-income Black tenants without anyone directly displaced, solely as an
outcome of market forces. If all of those seeking rental housing in a neighborhood are low-income Black households, the number of low-income Black tenants in that neighborhood will remain the same or grow. If the pool of prospective
tenants changes and gradually includes more households who are white, the
number of Black tenants will gradually decline. If, as is likely, some landlords
may prefer to rent to white rather than economically similar Black tenants or,
worse, actively discriminate against prospective Black tenants, the number of
Black tenants may decline even faster. But their number will decline even with
no disproportionate rent increases and *no* racially discriminatory or preferential behavior by landlords.[32] In a study of gentrification in Baltimore, Mallach
found that although the number of Black households in gentrifying neighborhoods declined, the number of white low-income households declined far more;
for every Black household replaced, five low-income white households were replaced.[33] The underlying dynamic of change can be racially neutral.

At its most fundamental level, this process of replacement is an inevitable
product of not only neighborhood change but also the larger processes of de-

mographic and social change. Just as neighborhood change is a constant, the process of replacement—economic, demographic, social, racial, ethnic, lifestyle, and so on—is the principal means by which all neighborhood change, not just gentrification, takes place.

Replacement may be inevitable, but that does not mean it is painless. Many forms of neighborhood change involve pain or loss to varying degrees. In gentrifying neighborhoods, the pain of replacement, with the pain of past displacements always present, may be compounded by the fact that some families who may have hoped to find a new dwelling within the same neighborhood are forced to move to an unfamiliar neighborhood. While in some cities—St. Louis being one—they may find no less affordable housing a few blocks away, in others such as Seattle and Washington, D.C., they may have to move a considerable distance, ending up with higher housing costs compounded by higher commuting costs. That, of course, is not as much about their neighborhood's gentrification as it is about the lack of affordable housing in the city and its region.

Paralleling replacement is the effect of gentrification on those who remain in the gentrifying neighborhood, a phenomenon often referred to as cultural displacement. A household in a gentrifying neighborhood may still be living in the same house or apartment in the physical sense, but as the neighborhood changes around them, the familiar place they know is being replaced with something different, perhaps even alien or hostile, with different faces, values, stores, sounds, and smells. A place that people once thought of as their territory is no longer theirs.

This can take many forms. It can be the shock of seeing a familiar barbershop or bodega turn into a wine bar or bicycle repair shop or experiencing social pressure from new residents with new norms of neighborhood behavior. As one longtime resident of a changing St. Louis neighborhood plaintively asked an interviewer, "Why can't we do what we do? Why can't we put chairs outside our houses?"[34] Changing norms and standards can lead to conflict, which can escalate when governmental authority enters the picture as when police are called over noise issues or an elderly longtime homeowner's sagging porch becomes the subject of a code enforcement complaint by the new neighbor in the expensively restored house next door.

At one level, it can reasonably be argued that all nontrivial neighborhood change may create some degree of cultural displacement. Rachel Woldoff, in her ethnographic study *White Flight, Black Flight*, poignantly describes the sense of cultural displacement experienced by middle-class Black homeowners as their neighborhood became increasingly populated by lower-income Black tenants and the neighborhood's culture changed.[35] The juxtaposition of two or more groups of people in the same neighborhood with significantly different norms for appropriate neighboring activity and public behavior, unless mediated through mutually agreed-upon guidelines for coexistence, can be profoundly de-stabilizing to both the neighborhood as an entity and the individuals who make up that neighborhood. The particular ways in which different groups may vary—race, ethnicity, income, age, and many other factors—are likely in the final analysis to be less significant than the mere fact of difference.

That said, there is a profound difference between cultural displacement as a generic reality of neighborhood change and that experienced or feared by lower-income Black residents in neighborhoods currently or potentially affected by the influx of affluent white households. When race and income are juxtaposed in the context of gentrification, they combine the two most pervasive fault lines in American society: the economic gap between haves and have-nots and, even more, our culture's Black-white racial divide. Those fault lines are also about power, not so much political power in the conventional sense, although that is also true, but rather about the power to influence one's environment. For that reason, cultural displacement, as has been expressed by many African American observers, is far from a trivial concern.[36] Moreover, it reflects the extent to which gentrification, while at one level simply another form of neighborhood change, is also about power and its antithesis, powerlessness.

Gentrification and Power(lessness)

While gentrification is one of many forms that neighborhood change can take, it differs fundamentally from other forms of change in that it is also implicitly about power, about the imbalance of power between those with more and those with less money, particularly when that imbalance is also racial, between Black and white. While the inoffensive white couple that buys a row house north of Patterson Park in Baltimore may not think of themselves as wielding power, their power is em-bodied in their greater income or wealth than that of their neighbors. While that is true up to a point under any circumstances, it is greatly magnified by the white-Black imbalance of power and status that pervades American society.

This power imbalance underlying gentrification has become a flashpoint for people in urban Black neighborhoods, whether or not their neighborhood is un-dergoing gentrification today or may do so in the future. It reflects, as reporter Jake Flanagin writes, "the utter and complete lack of control the poor and the nonwhite have in where they are permitted to live."[37] Thus, any thoughtful Black advocate understands that if their neighborhood were to be targeted by gentri-fication, they would be faced with a force they would be largely powerless to in-fluence. Even if the likelihood of gentrification in a particular African American neighborhood may be remote, the fear is magnified many times over by the underlying powerlessness of its residents. This was brought home by an anecdote told to one of the authors by our colleague Paul Brophy, who was teaching a graduate seminar at Washington University in St. Louis. A young African American student in the class was clearly unhappy with much of Brophy's presentation and finally made his point directly. "Listen, professor. When you talk about gentrification, you talk about numbers, about incomes and house prices and such. When *we* talk about gentrification, it's about powerlessness."[38]

The rent gap hypothesis, which can be read to assert that disinvestment is a preamble to gentrification, provides intellectual ballast for these fears. While far more African American neighborhoods in the United States have declined or remained poor and disinvested in recent decades than have gentrified, the gentrification discourse has become as much or more about the lack of investment in distressed African American neighborhoods as it is about investment or displacement in those neighborhoods. Along those lines, one of the authors reported from a focus group on gentrification he and his colleagues organized in St. Louis that "when [asked to talk] about economically improving neighborhoods, [Black] participants repeatedly pivoted to talk about economically declining neighborhoods."[39] Or as Stephen Danley and Rasheeda Weaver put it in a recent study of Camden, New Jersey, "residents fear gentrification in part because they have been physically excluded from development."[40]

At some point, however, the rhetoric of gentrification disconnects from spatial change and connects instead to the continuing economic and political dispossession of urban African American communities. That shift is encouraged by the increasingly explicit racialization of the popular gentrification discourse, as reflected in Ta-Nehisi Coates's blunt language: "'gentrification' is but a more pleasing name for white supremacy, is the interest on enslavement, the interest on Jim Crow, the interest on redlining, compounding across the years, and these new urbanites living off of that interest are, all of them, exulting in a crime."[41] Black blogger Hopewell puts it even more strongly. "Gentrification is a battle for physical spaces in cities but in the ultimate sense, a fight to maintain white power and dominance in America. . . . To control cities is to maintain white power, even in an emerging majority-minority America. Gentrification is war and black people sit in the crosshairs."[42] To these and other writers, the term "gentrification" has gone far beyond Ruth Glass's initial definition in order to stand for the larger ways in which the racial power imbalance operates, or is perceived to operate, in contemporary America.

The imbalance of power is a pervasive facet of urban reality, disproportionately affecting those marginalized by both their race and their social class. Its role in gentrifying lower-income neighborhoods is only one of the ways in which it operates. Thus, it seems logical to extend the use of the term "gentrification" to the ways in which those power imbalances perpetuate the disadvantages of those cities' heavily disinvested communities—few of which in cities such as Detroit and St. Louis have any likelihood of undergoing spatial gentrification—and blight the dreams of those cities' low-income residents, particularly those marginalized by both race and class. This is true whether or not they live in neighborhoods that are being gentrified, in the classical use of the term.

While the power imbalance is real and the outrage justified, there is danger in layering so much additional meaning onto the term "gentrification." First, it obscures other neighborhood changes taking place in the same cities, particularly neighborhood decline, affecting the lives of far more low-income and working-class Black families than gentrification, as we discuss in chapter 11. Second, it can lead to opposition to almost any kind of investment designed to revive or stabilize struggling and disinvested neighborhoods and improve living conditions for the families living there. As progressive housing advocate Rick Jacobus has written, "The way most people talk and think about [gentrification] seems to create a black hole of self-doubt from which no realistic strategy for neighborhood improvement can escape."[43] Since it is unlikely that a new term will be coined in the foreseeable future to distinguish between the many things that currently coexist uneasily under the gentrification umbrella, local leaders need to be aware of the paralyzing and polarizing effects of the "g-word" and find other ways to talk about neighborhood change.

The Meaning and Sustainability of Gentrification as Neighborhood Change

Looking at gentrification in the context of change over time, it can be understood as a distinct version of neighborhood change simultaneously incorporating economic change, generational change, lifestyle or cultural change, and sometimes, although less often, racial transition. While most other neighborhood change processes may embody one or two of these changes, few if any represent such a wholesale change in a neighborhood's social configuration. These shifts are shown graphically in figure 10.3.

Philadelphia's Fishtown and Northern Liberties neighborhoods are historically white working-class neighborhoods northeast of Center City that have largely gentrified since 2000. From 2000 to 2018, the share of adults with college degrees in the census tract straddling the two neighborhoods grew from 31 percent to 65 percent, from roughly equal to the national share to well above it.[44] The share of adults aged twenty-five to thirty-four increased from 18 percent to 49 percent, more than triple the national share. The tract median household

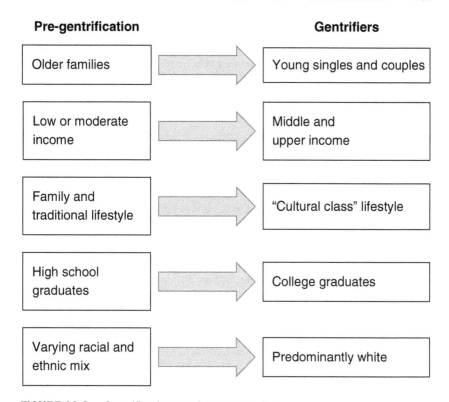

FIGURE 10.3. Gentrification as change over time

income more than tripled. Over the same period, the share of children under age eighteen dropped from 21 percent to 11 percent.

The phenomenon of gentrification, with its simultaneous juxtaposition of youth, affluence, education, and childlessness and their attendant lifestyle, has spawned a strikingly new type of neighborhood with no real precedent in urban history.[45] As such, it forms a rich and still largely untapped area for research into the distinct dynamics of the gentrified neighborhood, but its distinctiveness also reflects its inherently problematic nature over and above the vexatious issues of displacement and power discussed earlier in this chapter.

One problematic issue, of which gentrification can be seen as both symptom and cause, is the increasing spatial, economic, and racial polarization of cities and their neighborhoods. As we discussed in chapter 7, for many decades the United States has been characterized by not only a diminishing middle class but also increasing social and economic sorting. Over these years people have organized themselves into increasingly homogenous neighborhoods, of which gentrification may be the most visible manifestation. As a result, gentrification also has become the most potent symbol of the growing polarization of the cities. As the number of middle-class neighborhoods shrinks, cities are characterized by increasing disparities of wealth and poverty, investment and neglect. While affluent young people move into some neighborhoods with distinct locational or other assets, both Black and white working-class and middle-class people continue to leave the cities for the suburbs.

For all the controversy over how gentrified neighborhoods come into being, they can make a credible case for being good neighborhoods, as we have defined the term earlier. But many do so at a price of being "good" solely for a population that is so highly stratified at so many levels that it excludes the great majority of the city's population from effectively sharing in its benefits. That said, it must be recognized that there are pronounced variations among gentrifying neighborhoods. The trajectory of gentrification in still-struggling, slow-growth cities—such as St. Louis where, as one of the authors has shown, substantial lower-income populations continue to live in gentrifying neighborhoods long after the process of change has taken place—is a world apart from that in hot markets where the influx of youth and wealth is far greater.[46] In the former, a not unreasonable case can be made that the remaining less affluent residents of these neighborhoods benefit from the change in their neighborhood's economic and social environment, offsetting whatever cultural displacement they may also feel. This is particularly true if they are homeowners and able to gain significant equity from their home's appreciation. The extent to which those gains offset the losses is likely to be a matter for each individual to assess rather than something that can readily be generalized.

A second issue has to do with the sustainability of the gentrified neighborhood. Young people invariably grow older. Not quite as invariably but generally, young people also partner one another and often have children, which they raise together or separately. In the course of these changes, their behavioral preferences often shift. What then happens to neighborhoods whose existence is predicated on so many factors that are distinct to a particular moment in an individual's life cycle? Are these neighborhoods sustainable, or do they carry within them the seeds of future decline?

Obviously no one knows, and the answer is likely to vary from city to city and neighborhood to neighborhood. The answer seems to hinge, however, on two critical variables: the extent to which neighborhoods see an ongoing influx of young grads to replace those who age out, as it were, from these neighborhoods and the extent to which gentrified neighborhoods evolve toward a broader demographic mix over time.

Regarding the former, demographer Dowell Myers has argued that the cities are at what he calls "peak millennial" and that the demand for urban living by this demographic will decline over the coming decades.[47] While Myers's thesis received a good deal of media attention, it has been heatedly contested by others particularly Joe Cortright of City Observatory, who argues the contrary, concluding that "the urban wave we've experienced starting in the 1990s and *accelerating in the past decade* wasn't propelled by generational growth so much as by a growing preference for urban living by young adults."[48] Even assuming Cortright to be accurate in the near term, however, the pronounced decline in fertility and child-rearing in the United States over the past decade or more, coupled with possible shifts in urban preferences perhaps affected by the aftermath of the COVID-19 pandemic, could validate Myers's thesis in the longer term.

An alternative future for gentrifying neighborhoods is to evolve into neighborhoods that come to resemble other neighborhoods in having greater household diversity in terms of age and household characteristics, particularly with respect to child-rearing. A good example of such a neighborhood is Brooklyn's Park Slope, one of the handful of 1970s gentrifying neighborhoods that has become increasingly diverse in terms of age and household type over time, albeit still overwhelmingly white and wealthy. In essence, from a demographic and economic standpoint, Park Slope has evolved to become a typical upscale neighborhood, while retaining a few vestiges of a onetime radical counterculture such as the famous Park Slope Food Coop. The likelihood of gentrifying neighborhoods evolving in similar manner is likely to be a product of how much they offer amenities that are perceived as desirable by households at different life cycle stages, especially attractive school options for child-rearing families, and how much the current generation of gentrifiers retain their preference for higher-density urban living as they age.

In the end, over the coming decades any given neighborhood could move in any direction, remaining a youth-oriented neighborhood, evolving into a more conventional upscale neighborhood, or falling backward and declining economically. How those three options are distributed across American cities will be affected by not only neighborhood conditions and characteristics but also large-scale economic, demographic, and cultural trends. At the same time, more neighborhoods are likely to experience gentrification pressures. How many more, however, is an open question. Although to some gentrification may appear to be a wave of seemingly infinite scale, it is inherently limited by economic and demographic constraints. The number of young people as well as empty nesters and others with both the resources and the inclination to gentrify neighborhoods is not infinite. When we look back at the period from 2009 to 2019, it is important to remember that this was a decade of both sustained overall economic growth and equally sustained disproportionate income growth in the upper segments of the distribution, both factors conducive to gentrification. The future may be very different.

THE CRISIS OF THE URBAN MIDDLE NEIGHBORHOOD

Exactly what an urban middle neighborhood is may not be susceptible to precise definition. One writer has described these neighborhoods as "traditionally . . . the heart of American cities[,] . . . the neighborhoods where working- and middle-class citizens live; raise families; pay taxes; send their children to school; go to church, synagogue or mosque; and shop at the local grocer."[1] While most families today may no longer shop at the local grocer, the description still rings true. In the final analysis, middle neighborhoods are where those who make up the middle of the American income spectrum typically lived. Through most of the twentieth century, such neighborhoods, first in urban centers and then in the early postwar suburbs, made up the greater part of American cities and suburbs. While diminished from their heyday, they still make up a significant percentage of American neighborhoods. Their continuing survival is key to giving the American middle class the chance to live in a good neighborhood.

The Rise and Fall of Middle Neighborhoods

The typical urban middle neighborhood as it emerged during the second half of the nineteenth century and the early twentieth century, outside of a cluster of cities in the Northeast, was a neighborhood of single-family homes.[2] While American cities of that vintage had a central core made up of their downtowns, their major universities and medical centers, and a handful of immediately proximate residential areas, that central core typically covered 5 percent or less of its land area. The rest was made up of single-family residential neighborhoods dotted with the factories, rail yards, and similar features that sustained the cities' historic industrial economy. Even today, except for publicly subsidized lower-income rental housing projects, large apartment buildings outside the central core are rare.

The image of the early twentieth-century urban neighborhood as a tenement neighborhood is wildly misleading and reflects the extent to which images of New York City—truly only Manhattan—dominate our perceptions of that era. Even after decades of attrition, today over 90 percent of all the residential structures in Baltimore and Philadelphia and over 80 percent in Cleveland are single-family homes. In Baltimore and Philadelphia, these houses are usually brick row houses, while in midwestern cities they are more often detached houses, occasionally brick but usually wood frame.

Either way, these neighborhoods were and still are in ecological terms monocultures of single-family homes, like fields in which only a single crop is planted. This can vividly be seen in figure 11.1, an aerial view of part of Cleveland's West Side. Block after block of houses were dotted with scattered convenience stores and crossed at intervals by wider streets along which the neighborhood's main commercial activities were concentrated. As middle neighborhoods were recreated in the suburbs during the years following World War II, they followed a

FIGURE 11.1.   The single-family monoculture on Cleveland's west side

(Google Earth © 2022 Google)

similar model, fashioning a lower-density version of the urban neighborhood based on the automobile rather than the pedestrian.

The people who lived in these houses were of varying economic levels and cultural backgrounds, but in an era when marriage and child-rearing were all but universal norms, almost all were couples who married early and would spend most of their lives together raising children. The physical form of these neighborhoods reflected their social role. Families had the privacy of a separate home and a small backyard but at the same time were close enough to one another to encourage walkability and neighborliness. The commercial streets with their grocers, butchers, bakers, and taverns were rarely more than a short walk away, a necessity in the preautomobile era. Children walked to the neighborhood public school or the parochial school attached to the neighborhood parish church. Some neighborhoods clustered around factories, where most of the neighborhood's men worked. In other neighborhoods, jobs were only a streetcar ride away.

The urban middle neighborhood's heyday was from the 1920s through the 1960s, driven by the increasing acculturation and prosperity of the nation's immigrants as they moved out of their enclaves, as we described in chapter 3, and by the economic mobility made possible by the unionization of industrial work. It was an overwhelmingly white phenomenon. While many Black breadwinners also saw their wages grow, racial discrimination gave them few options to move into the new neighborhoods being built around them. By the 1950s, when middle neighborhoods were at their height and unbeknownst to most residents teetering on the edge of traumatic change, most families in American cities were middle income in the sense of having a family income fairly close to the city-wide median. In 1970, well after many neighborhoods had begun to decline, nearly two-thirds of the census tracts in St. Louis and over half in Baltimore were middle-income tracts.[3]

There were many gradations among middle neighborhoods. Those built around factories tended to be modest working-class neighborhoods, with smaller and plainer houses. Others, where white-collar wage earners took streetcars to downtown jobs, often had larger houses, often with more decorated doorways or cornices. But blue- and white-collar families lived side by side in most neighborhoods and shared similar lifestyles. They shopped in the same stores, attended the same churches, sent their children to the same schools, and shared largely common values and aspirations.

Although rooted in a substratum of racial discrimination and grounded in seeming moral certainties that are widely questioned today, the urban middle neighborhoods of the 1950s can nonetheless be seen as good neighborhoods. These neighborhoods worked well for the people who lived in them, fostering both strong and weak ties. As Ray Suarez writes about the suburbanites who left them behind in his elegiac *The Old Neighborhood*, "people talk about the close-ness, the intimacy of the old neighborhood. . . . We knew each other then."[4] We do not want to paint them in too rose-colored hues. They could be stifling and intolerant, and by the end of World War II, as we've mentioned, they were often shabby and crowded. But no neighborhood is idyllic, and for the most part they worked well.

Again, these were, with scattered exceptions, white neighborhoods. The major-ity of Black families in the 1950s, whatever their economic means, were still effec-tively confined by racial discrimination to Black ghetto neighborhoods. Although many of these neighborhoods had many of the features of good neighborhoods, with vital shopping districts and strong networks of social clubs and community organizations, they shared appalling housing conditions, as Thomas Sugrue writes about Detroit. "Blacks were entrapped in the city's worst housing stock, half of it substandard, most of it overcrowded. They lived in overwhelmingly Black neigh-borhoods, a reflection of the almost total segregation of the city's housing market. Detroit's Black population had doubled between 1940 and 1950, but the pool of available housing had grown painfully slowly."[5] With almost all housing owned by absentee landlords, the Black ghetto was a reservoir of pent-up demand for better housing and the opportunity to become a homeowner.

Although the first wave of mass suburbanization began in the 1950s, the greatest changes took place in the 1960s. The demographic changes that we de-scribed in chapter 7 were beginning to undercut the traditional family patterns that were in many respects the raison d'être of middle neighborhoods at the same time that millions of white families were abandoning the cities for the lure of the suburbs. During that decade, the white populations of cities plummeted. And between 1960 and 1980, as the baby boom shifted to the so-called baby bust, the number of child-rearing married couples in cities fell rapidly.

White flight is often mistakenly used as a synonym for neighborhood de-cline; indeed, some see the history of urban neighborhoods in the 1960s and 1970s as a simple racialized story of invasion and succession: "Blacks moved in, whites moved out, and the neighborhood fell apart." As we discussed briefly in chapter 4, the actual story is more complicated. True, vast numbers of whites left, and some neighborhoods did fall apart. But many neighborhoods did not fall apart. And in many cases when they did, it often had less to do with racial change per se than with parallel economic changes and predatory real estate practices.

While overcrowding, defined as more than one person per room, was wide-spread in America's older cities immediately after World War II, most older cities soon transitioned from a painful housing shortage to an equally problematic hous-ing surplus. Part of this was due to large-scale construction of new housing—mostly single-family homes and garden apartments—in central cities. From 1950 to 1960, New York City added over 350,000 units and Chicago over 120,000. In one decade, Milwaukee increased its housing inventory by nearly 25 percent. As a housing shortage changed to a housing surplus, the threat to middle neighborhoods shifted from overcrowding and congestion to vacancy and abandonment. The vacancy rate in the ten largest cities increased from 1.8 percent in 1950 to 6.8 percent in 1980. It was during those years that cities first saw houses being abandoned en masse, and large stretches of Northside St. Louis and Detroit's East Side begin to turn into the derelict near-prairies that still exist today.

Another important part of this story, however, is rarely told. Middle neighborhoods continued to exist, although diminished in number and extent. In a few cases they remained largely white, frequently ethnically homogeneous neighborhoods such as The Hill, the St. Louis Italian neighborhood that was the birthplace of iconic mid-twentieth-century baseball star Yogi Berra. Often, however, they went through racial transformation but experienced far less social or economic change as working- and middle-class African American families took advantage of the space left by white flight to leave their overcrowded and substandard ghettos and move into neighborhoods from which they had previously been excluded. In a little-recognized process largely obscured by dominant narratives about neighborhood decline and suburbanization, many formerly white middle-class neighborhoods in America's older cities that went through racial transition in the 1970s became and remained for decades afterward good Black middle-class neighborhoods, as we described in chapter 8. Many of those neighborhoods, however, are under threat today.

Middle neighborhoods, white, Black, Latinx or mixed, still accommodate 25–40 percent of the population of most older cities and arguably a larger share of many regions' inner-ring suburbs. As such, if only by the significance of their numbers, their future matters greatly to the future of the American neighborhood. There are, however, strong reasons that middle neighborhoods matter over and above the significance of their numbers.

Middle Neighborhoods as Spaces of Economic, Racial, and Ethnic Diversity

Twenty-first-century American cities are often described as a "tale of two cities," reflecting a well-justified concern over their economic and racial polarization. Yet, in many respects they may be more aptly seen as a "tale of three cities," with middle neighborhoods representing a third, often overlooked, intermediate environment that sustains much of what is left of their historic economic diversity. Middle neighborhoods fall between the poles of wealth or gentrification

TABLE 11.1 Households in Baltimore middle neighborhoods by income range, 2016

INCOME RANGE	PERCENTAGE OF ALL HOUSEHOLDS
0–$15,000	17.3
$15,000–$24,999	12.3
$25,000–$35,000	10.7
$35,000–$49,000	15.3
$50,000–$74,999	18.7
$75,000–$99,999	9.8
$100,000+	12.6

Source: 2012–2016 Five-Year American Community Survey.

and poverty or disinvestment. They remain rooted in the single-family home and the school and still house working- and middle-class families.

Middle neighborhoods tend to contain a more diverse economic mix than wealthy and poor neighborhoods, both of which are increasingly economically and demographically homogenous. As table 11.1 shows, in the seventy-one tracts with tract median incomes in 2016 between $35,000 and $55,000 in Baltimore, at most 20 percent of the households living in those tracts actually have incomes in that range; the incomes of the people who live in these tracts are evenly distributed across the entire range from under $15,000 to over $100,000. These tracts, taken as a group, have retained the mixed-income character of the traditional urban neighborhood, itself an important value. The social benefits of mixed-income communities, although hard to quantify, are real and significant.

From a racial standpoint, the picture is more complex. Most middle neighborhoods tend to be predominantly white, predominantly Black, or, in cities such as Chicago with large Latinx populations, predominantly Latinx. At the same time, more are racially diverse than either poor or wealthy neighborhoods. One-third of middle neighborhoods in both Baltimore and Philadelphia have Black population shares between 20 percent and 70 percent.

Middle neighborhoods represent a reservoir of economic and racial diversity in cities that are still racially segregated and becoming increasingly economically polarized. Middle neighborhoods are more likely to preserve the weak bridging social ties we discussed earlier as characteristic of good neighborhoods, enabling their residents to share public spaces with people who are different from them. People from different backgrounds and different economic levels may not become friends but can learn to get along with one another, cutting across the tribal boundaries that characterize so much of American life today.

Middle Neighborhoods as Places of Opportunity

A healthy city offers both residents and in-migrants diverse housing opportunities as their economic and family conditions change. Without viable middle neighborhoods, many cities would not be able to provide those opportunities. Instead, they would be dominated by distressed areas, which are rarely the choice of those who live there, or upscale and gentrifying areas, which are out of reach of many working-class families and in many cases do not offer the family-oriented environments that child-rearing families seek. As individuals and families living in distressed urban neighborhoods move up economically, building skills and finding better jobs, middle neighborhoods have traditionally been the places to which these individuals and families moved to improve their living conditions, just as late nineteenth-century immigrants to New York City moved to Harlem and the Bronx from the Lower East Side and Chicago families left Halstead Street's tenements for that city's bungalow neighborhoods.

During the 1960s and 1970s, formerly white middle neighborhoods became places of opportunity for middle-income Black families. These neighborhoods represented a vast improvement in living conditions over the ghetto areas where they had lived, not to mention being the best available option in that segregated era. A neighborhood is only a place of opportunity for upwardly mobile families, however, if they see it as a meaningful improvement over the neighborhood they want to escape. If the central city's middle neighborhoods are seen as less desirable in their housing conditions and the quality of life they offer compared to suburban alternatives, they will be bypassed. That is widely happening today. Loss of that market in turn hastens their decline, making it into a self-fulfilling prophecy.

Middle neighborhoods provide a particular opportunity for immigrants, whose presence can add vitality and entrepreneurial energy to a city. The Ironbound neighborhood, where over half of the residents are foreign-born, mostly from Latin America, is Newark's most vibrant neighborhood, and Ferry Street is its most vital commercial artery. Other legacy cities can point to immigrant communities, such as Bangladeshis in Detroit and Cambodians in South Philadelphia, who have enriched the city's social fabric, strengthened its economy, and helped stabilize once-struggling neighborhoods.

Middle Neighborhoods as an Urban Asset

Middle neighborhoods represent a massive investment in urban housing and infrastructure. This investment is made up of not only millions of homes, from single-family homes to large apartment buildings, but also streets and sidewalks, sewer and water systems, parks and playgrounds, school and community buildings, churches and synagogues, and commercial and industrial buildings. Although most of this housing and infrastructure is fifty to over a hundred years old, it is still usable if often needing repair or modernization. Over and above the physical infrastructure, many middle neighborhoods retain a social fabric—albeit often frayed—of neighborhood-based institutions and organizations. Much of this investment is at risk today, along with their large share of the city's tax and economic base.

The value of strong middle neighborhoods to their cities, however, goes beyond their fiscal worth. They have traditionally housed a disproportionate share of the pool of engaged citizens, the people who serve in public office, on nonprofit boards, and become involved with the city's parks and schools, particularly among cities' Black populations. Vital middle neighborhoods, moreover, can remain places of opportunity for upwardly mobile urban families and immigrants and potentially accommodate much of the nation's population growth over the coming decades in ways likely to be not only more cost-effective but also more environmentally sustainable than the continued outward expansion of metropolitan areas.

Middle neighborhoods, however, are threatened. In strong market cities such as Boston and Washington, D.C., the threat may come from upward pressures of gentrification but far more often comes from the downward pressures of decline, out-migration, and disinvestment.

The Forces Threatening Middle Neighborhoods

Both the number and stability of middle neighborhoods, particularly in central cities, have been undermined by many of the large societal and economic forces discussed in chapter 7 as well as forces specific to their physical and locational characteristics.

Middle neighborhoods have been hardest hit of all neighborhoods by the growth of income inequality and the hollowing of the middle class, the declining number of middle-income families, and the growth in economic sorting that has led to increasing numbers of rich and poor urban and suburban neighborhoods. Since many middle neighborhoods were sustained by the growth of the unionized industrial workforce, they have been further undermined by the decline of manufacturing, particularly in the older cities of the Midwest and Northeast, and the plunge in union membership, both of which began in the 1970s and accelerated in the 1980s. Having been created as places where families reared children, their market has been further depleted by demographic shifts that have led to fewer child-rearing families and more single individuals and nonfamily households. Those shifts have only been offset to a limited degree by immigration, which has replenished the demand pool for some but relatively few middle neighborhoods.

Those forces would have been enough to threaten the vitality of middle neighborhoods without any contributing local factors. The effect of the national forces, however, has been reinforced by distinctive local forces disproportionately affecting these neighborhoods as well as by public policies, often seemingly neutral in intent but malign in effect.

The Character of the Housing Stock

The single-family homes that make up most middle neighborhoods vary by size, architectural character, materials, and other features. They share, however, one overarching feature: they are old. Moreover, regardless of age, they often poorly fit today's housing market preferences. Since the 1960s, little new housing has been built in most of these areas. Ninety percent of the single-family homes in Cleveland and in Pittsburgh predate 1960, while in most inner-ring suburbs, 75–90 percent of the single-family homes were built before 1970. Although a handful of older homes have been rehabbed or updated, they make up a minute share of the total housing stock.

This housing does not appeal to many of the single individuals, childless couples, and people in informal living arrangements who make up much of the demand for urban housing today. While those few neighborhoods with distinctive architectural or historical character or that are close to downtown or major institutions, such as Shaw in St. Louis and Allentown in Buffalo, may draw them, most middle neighborhoods lack those features.

Most older houses in these neighborhoods have not been upgraded or modernized to any significant degree, while many suffer from major deferred maintenance and repair needs. This situation has severe consequences for middle neighborhoods by undermining potential housing demand. Even in areas where people may want to live, most prospective buyers, especially buyers with children, prefer a home that they can move into with no more than cosmetic improvements, and few have either the will or the money to take on significant upgrading. Without a major infusion of capital in the coming years, much of the housing in middle neighborhoods is at risk of deteriorating further, potentially to the point of no return. The increase in vacancies in many middle neighborhoods suggests that this may already be happening.

Loss of Homeowners

A substantial body of research has made a compelling case for strong associations between homeownership and many of the factors driving neighborhood stability and vitality, even after controlling for income and other potentially confounding social and economic variables.[6] Homeowners are more likely to vote and be actively engaged in neighborhood affairs than either renters or investors. They are more likely to invest in improving their homes and yards in the ways that make them visible neighborhood assets, contributing to the neighborhood's curb appeal. Increasing homeownership is likely to increase both neighborhood property values and neighborhood stability, while a decline in homeowners is likely to have the opposite effect. These differences in part reflect the greater stability of tenure and lower turnover associated with homeowners but are likely to include a psychological effect associated with ownership per se.[7]

The number of homeowners has dropped sharply in older city neighborhoods since 2000. The median middle neighborhood in Baltimore lost 23 percent of its homeowners from 2000 to 2016. There are many reasons for the erosion of homeownership in middle neighborhoods, beginning with the decline in middle-income demand reflecting the demographic shifts described earlier. That is not the only factor, however. Many middle neighborhoods, particularly those occupied by Black and Latinx families, were targets of opportunity for subprime lenders and impacted by subsequent foreclosures. As homeowners lost their homes and lenders subsequently resold them to investors, they went from owner occupancy to absentee ownership. More recently, impediments to home buying such as the increase in student debt and the reluctance of lenders to make mortgages for lower-priced homes, particularly to home buyers with less than pristine credit, have been recognized although not yet fully addressed by banks and policymakers.

The loss of homeownership in middle neighborhoods has significant negative consequences. Loss of the residential stability and community engagement more typical of homeowners than of renters is likely to damage these neighborhoods, particularly in light of the extreme economic insecurity of the lower-income renters likely to replace homeowners in struggling middle neighborhoods. Moreover, particularly in neighborhoods where house sales prices are severely depressed relative to rent levels, absentee landlords are not only unlikely to make the capital investment necessary to maintain aging housing stocks but also may actively milk their properties, disinvesting in them to focus on short-term cash flow.[8]

The decline in homeownership in middle neighborhoods is widely coupled with a decline in sales prices, particularly in communities that experienced a housing bubble during the years prior to 2006–2007. The combination of fewer homeowners and lower house values has led to massive loss of wealth by middle-income homeowners, particularly in Black middle neighborhoods. A recent study of St. Louis Black middle neighborhoods found that in a single census tract, homeowners lost over $35 million in home equity between 2008 and 2016.[9]

Location, Location, Location

Location assets are a particularly important factor in driving neighborhood market opportunities. As we noted in chapter 10, compelling research has found that the single most important factor predicting upward market change in a struggling area is its proximity to a strong neighborhood. Other factors likely to affect demand for housing in a neighborhood include proximity to reviving downtowns and major universities or to major well-maintained and actively used parks and water bodies, such as Baltimore's Inner Harbor and St. Louis's Tower Grove Park. While the sheer magnitude of housing demand may push higher-income buyers in magnet cities such as Seattle and Washington, D.C., into neighborhoods that lack proximity assets, in other cities where a smaller pool of home seekers can choose from a wide variety of neighborhoods and housing types, places that lack these assets are at a severe competitive disadvantage.

Most middle neighborhoods, particularly Black middle neighborhoods, lack significant locational assets. They were built for families for whom the neighborhood's own amenities such as schools, churches, and retail stores within walking distance were far more important in an era when jobs—particularly industrial jobs—were more widely dispersed across the city than they are today. Many of the Black middle neighborhoods that emerged in the 1960s and 1970s were neighborhoods of quasi-suburban character in the outer reaches of the central city, distant from what subsequently became the city's locational assets.[10] Either way, middle neighborhoods are often at a locational disadvantage.

Public Policy

While it would be unreasonable to claim that public policies at the state, federal, or local levels are the cause of the forces undermining middle neighborhoods, there is little question that through laws, regulations, and practices public policy can play a powerful role in either exacerbating or mitigating many of those forces. Those policies need not be explicitly directed at middle neighborhoods. Most are not neighborhood-specific; indeed, many negative middle-neighborhood impacts can be seen almost as collateral damage arising from policies enacted or pursued for completely different reasons.

A prime example is the extent to which public policy actively encourages middle-class housing demand to spread farther out beyond the boundaries of central cities and inner suburbs. As geographer Thomas Bier found in his study of the Cleveland metropolitan area, from 1960 through 2010 a total of 623,000 new housing units were created within the metropolitan area, while the number of households increased by only 336,000.[11] With little in-migration to central cities in recent years other than the young grads moving into a handful of prime locations, this vast oversupply undermines the market for the rest of the city.

Public policy drives this process through many channels: the fragmented structure of local governments and school districts within metropolitan areas, the absence of regional bodies empowered to manage the pace or location of development, the extensive public subsidies for roads and other infrastructure essential for development at the ever-expanding urban perimeter, and fiscal laws and regulations that put central cities—and increasingly inner suburbs—at a competitive disadvantage. In some states including Ohio, those provisions are openly antiurban. Ohio law provides tax advantages for people and firms moving from (mostly urban) cities to (suburban and rural) townships and in the allocation of state funds for road and highway maintenance.[12] The pervasive presence of exclusionary zoning particularly in more affluent outer suburbs, despite some modest reforms in a few states such as New Jersey and Massachusetts, continues to limit residential options for lower-income households and increase poverty concentrations in central cities and inner suburbs.

The home mortgage tax deduction, in addition to its pernicious macroeconomic effects, undermines older neighborhoods in two ways, first by creating a premium for buying larger and more expensive homes and second by allowing interest on home purchase mortgages to be deducted but not interest on home improvement loans. Similarly, decisions made by the Federal Reserve and the Clinton administration and then the Bush administration not to regulate speculative new mortgage products emerging in the late 1990s and early 2000s contributed greatly to the destabilization of hundreds of middle neighborhoods through subprime lending and the wave of foreclosures that followed. As with many other policies, these decisions disproportionately damaged Black and Latinx neighborhoods.

Joseph McNeely and Paul Brophy make the case that the neighborhoods movement that emerged in the 1970s, as we described in chapter 4, led to policies and programs designed to support middle neighborhoods.[13] The Community Reinvestment Act has been a force for positive change in many areas, while state-level historic tax credit programs that provide incentives for home buyers fixing up houses in designated historic districts have helped revive some neigh-borhoods, notably in Baltimore.[14] The neighborhoods movement soon dissipated as federal policy pivoted from neighborhoods to the growing problem of home-lessness. Many public-sector programs, however, including means-tested subsi-dized housing programs, provide little benefit to middle neighborhoods and may even work to their disadvantage.

This discussion could be further extended, but the salient point is that public policies, usually without explicit intention to affect middle neighborhoods, play a significant role in sometimes mitigating but more often exacerbating the chal-lenges faced by those neighborhoods. As we will discuss in the next section, the greatest challenges are faced by the subset of middle neighborhoods whose resi-dents are predominantly Black.

The Disproportionate Decline of African American Middle Neighborhoods

In chapter 8 we discussed the Detroit neighborhood of Crary–St. Mary's, which went through racial transition in the 1970s and became a strong African Amer-ican neighborhood. It was still a stable middle-class neighborhood in 2000. The median household income in 2000 was $38,325 (roughly $60,000 in 2021 dol-lars), 30 percent above the citywide median and close to the countywide median. Vacant homes were few, the poverty rate was low, the homeownership rate was high, and the share of households that were married couples with children was only slightly below the national level of 24 percent.

By 2010 conditions had changed dramatically, a change that has continued particularly with respect to the increase in vacancies and the decline in home-ownership (table 11.2). By 2017, the area's median household income had dropped to $31,805, a 44 percent decline in real income adjusted for inflation. In only a

TABLE 11.2   Key indicators for Crary–St. Mary's, 2000–2017

	2000	2010	2017
% population African American	96.9	97.0	93.2
% population below poverty level	13.4	30.3	31.4
% households that are married couples with children under age 18	20.2	10.9	7.4
% owner occupants	74.6	70.1	60.0
% of dwelling units vacant	3.5	10.3	21.6
Total population	10,087	8,231	7,393

Source: 2000 Decennial Census, 2006–2010, and 2013–2017 Five-Year American Community Survey.

FIGURE 11.2. Vacant houses in the Crary–St. Mary's neighborhood

(Google Earth © 2022 Google)

few years, Crary–St. Mary's had changed from being a stable middle-class neighborhood to becoming a more thinly populated area struggling with high vacancies and concentrated poverty (figure 11.2).

Trends are similar in Black middle neighborhoods in Chicago, Cleveland, St. Louis, and many other cities. Neighborhoods that had been relatively stable for decades and were still vital communities in 2000 had lost ground with respect to social, economic, and housing market indicators by 2018. Table 11.3 shows the aggregate change in key indicators for predominantly Black (80 percent or more Black) middle neighborhoods in six older American cities. While the conditions vary from city to city, with Baltimore's Black middle neighborhoods faring considerably better than those of Detroit and Cleveland, all lost ground. This does not mean that every neighborhood lost ground; indeed, in each city a few remained stable, and a handful may have even revived or gentrified. But the great majority followed a downward trajectory, gentle in Baltimore and steepest in Detroit and Cleveland.

By contrast, predominantly white (under 30 percent Black) tracts in the same cities showed much more varied trajectories. While some declined, quite a few gentrified, and most stayed roughly the same. Figure 11.3 compares trajectories of Black and white middle neighborhoods in Baltimore. Nearly half of all white middle neighborhoods moved upward. These neighborhoods made up the great majority of that city's gentrifying neighborhoods.

Table 11.4 shows aggregate change for predominantly white and predominantly Black middle census tracts from 2000 to 2018. Relatively few white

TABLE 11.3 Change in key neighborhood indicators for Black middle neighborhoods in six cities, 2000–2018

	% CHANGE IN NUMBER OF HOMEOWNERS	% CHANGE IN NUMBER OF CHILD-RAISING MARRIED COUPLES	% CHANGE IN NUMBER OF VACANT HOUSING UNITS	% CHANGE IN POPULATION	% CHANGE IN MEDIAN HOUSEHOLD INCOME IN CONSTANT DOLLARS
Baltimore	–16	–45	+53	–7	–12
Chicago	–20	–48	+121	–19	–31
Cleveland	–30	–70	+162	–23	–41
Detroit	–35	–69	+269	–28	–41
Milwaukee	–18	–33	+84	–8	–29
Philadelphia	–14	–50	+51	–5	–21

Source: 2000 Decennial Census, 2006–2010, and 2014–2018 Five-Year American Community Survey.

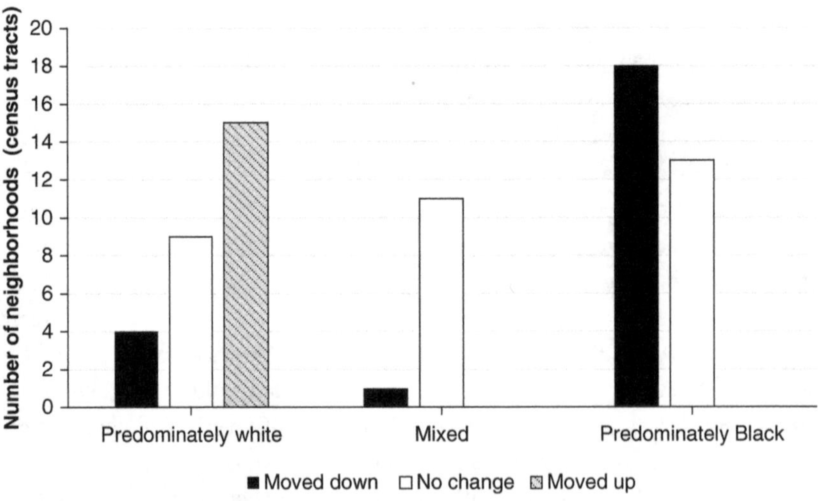

FIGURE 11.3. Trajectories of Baltimore middle neighborhoods by race, 2000 to 2018

(Authors' work based on decennial census and American Community Survey data)

middle neighborhoods, outside of Baltimore, actually gained ground, yet in every city, with respect to every indicator, white neighborhoods fared better, or at least less poorly, than Black neighborhoods in the same city.

There is a profound historical irony to this phenomenon. During the urban crisis years as cities generally were on a sharp downward trajectory, Black urban middle neighborhoods remained oases of relative stability. As the cities began to

TABLE 11.4 Percent change in key indicators for predominantly white and predominantly Black middle neighborhoods in six cities, 2000–2018

	% CHANGE IN POPULATION		% CHANGE IN NUMBER OF CHILD-REARING MARRIED COUPLES		% CHANGE IN NUMBER OF HOMEOWNERS		% CHANGE IN MEDIAN HOUSEHOLD INCOME (IN CONSTANT DOLLARS)	
	WHITE	BLACK	WHITE	BLACK	WHITE	BLACK	WHITE	BLACK
Baltimore	+4	−7	−3	−45	−7	−16	+41	−12
Chicago	−4	−19	−26	−48	+5	−20	−8	−31
Cleveland	−3	−23	−44	−70	−19	−30	−32	−41
Detroit	−7	−28	−13	−69	−21	−35	−37	−41
Milwaukee	+8	−8	−12	−33	−1	−18	−11	−29
Philadelphia	+12	−5	−16	−50	−6	−14	0	−21

Source: 2000 Decennial Census, 2006–2010, and 2014–2018 Five-Year American Community Survey.

revive in the new millennium with waves of in-migration and investment, these same neighborhoods began to lose ground. While many neighborhoods were subject to stresses and strains well before 2000, more and more Black middle neighborhoods were overwhelmed by their problems after 2000, creating vicious cycles of decline. Understanding why this is happening is critically important to addressing the challenges to good urban neighborhoods as well as the role race plays in the making and unmaking of those neighborhoods.

All the larger economic and demographic changes described earlier disproportionately undermined Black middle neighborhoods. With Black workers often "last hired, first fired," they have a weaker toehold on middle-class status. Often subject to overt or covert racial discrimination, they were more deeply affected by the regional economic decline and loss of industrial jobs that began in the 1970s and continued into the new millennium. Patterns of social stress and economic insecurity exacerbated by the invidious position of African Americans in the larger society and economy can destabilize Black middle neighborhoods in ways that do not affect their white counterparts.[15]

These neighborhoods gained little from the post-2000 urban revival. In city after city revival was concentrated in a few small areas, which rarely included any of the city's Black middle neighborhoods. Relatively few of those neighborhoods' residents benefited from the new jobs created in the downtowns or at the universities and medical centers, while they suffered disproportionately from the continuing erosion of manufacturing and other blue-collar jobs. By 2000, these neighborhoods were already highly vulnerable to internal and external pressures.

One of those pressures, which affected nearly all Black middle neighborhoods, was the often traumatic generational shift that became apparent around the new millennium. In 2000 homeowners in these neighborhoods were still often the founding generation, people who had moved there in the 1960s and 1970s as young families and formed the social and organizational core of these neighborhoods. By 2000, however, they were no longer young, and their children had largely grown and moved away. As was also true of their white counterparts in the postwar suburbs, they were beginning to age out and die or move away. The generational shift both increased the need for home buyer replacement and eroded neighborhood social capital, rendering it less capable of withstanding the shocks that came with the foreclosure crisis and the Great Recession.

Race, however, plays a much more explicit role in what came after. The first factor destabilizing the Black middle neighborhood was the rise of subprime lending at the end of the twentieth century and the resulting wave of foreclosures that followed. We discussed this traumatic episode in American economic history in chapter 5 but will focus here on its long-term effect on Black middle neighborhoods, which were ground zero for the wave of foreclosures that struck American neighborhoods.

These neighborhoods, which were already struggling with speculative pressures as well as the aging of their founding generation of home buyers, were ground zero for subprime lending. Not only did many new buyers in those neighborhoods have subprime or other toxic mortgages, but many existing homeowners refinanced their homes with equally toxic cash-out loans. Subsequent foreclosures, combined with the loss of jobs and income from the recession and increasingly stringent mortgage requirements imposed after the bursting of the bubble, all contributed to a collapse of the housing markets in Black middle neighborhoods. In Crary–St. Mary's, where 80 percent of all the mortgages made in 2005 were subprime loans, the median home price dropped from $92,000 in 2006 to $13,000 in 2011, while the number of sales fell by one-third. In a telltale sign, the number of home purchase mortgages went from 118 in 2006 to zero in 2011, indicating that the great majority of the 2011 buyers were not families planning to move into these homes but rather investors or speculators looking to rent out the homes, make a quick killing for a few years, and move on.

Increasing crime and disorder, deteriorating public schools and public services, and indifferent bureaucracies all helped drive out Black middle-class households, while the affordability of many suburbs offered alternatives even for families of modest means. All of these factors were exacerbated by the targeting of subprime lending to Black as well as Latinx neighborhoods. Many homeowners lost their homes and were forced to move, while others, as foreclosures increasingly destabilized the neighborhoods and residents faced increasing disorder in their midst that they felt powerless to change, concluded that flight was the only rational response.[16]

This part of the story, if not as well known as it should be, has been well documented. What is less well known is what came afterward. Neighborhoods of all kinds took substantial hits during the foreclosure crisis and the Great Recession, including white middle neighborhoods in the same cities and new subdivisions in the Sunbelt. And yet, as the national economy slowly recovered and the national housing market revived, Black middle neighborhoods—with few exceptions—remained stuck. Figure 11.4 compares sales price trends for white and Black middle neighborhoods in Cleveland from 2000 to 2019. From 2000 to 2012, prices in the two clusters rose and fell in lockstep, rising until 2006 and falling from 2007 to 2012. From then on, however, their fortunes diverged. The white neighborhoods began to recover, and by 2019 sales prices were back to their 2000 level. Sales prices in the Black middle neighborhoods barely budged during the same period, remaining stubbornly stuck at little more than half their 2000 level. For those neighborhoods, the recession has never really ended.

This is the critical question: not why these neighborhoods declined but why they have not revived. To explain this, we must take a closer look at these neighborhoods' housing markets. The story of Black middle neighborhood decline over the past decade is in large measure a story of housing markets and highlights the role of the market factors discussed in chapter 6 in sustaining or undermining good neighborhoods. Like most such stories, it has a racial dimension but is not just about race. It is about who is buying homes and, even more so,

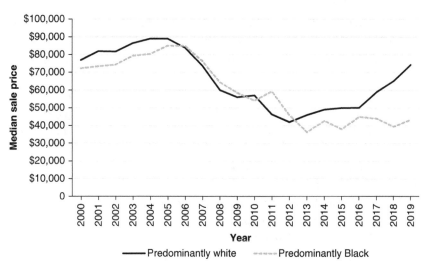

FIGURE 11.4. Sales price parallelism and divergence by race in Cleveland middle neighborhoods, 2000 to 2019

where they are buying them, which raises important questions about what people look for when they choose a neighborhood.

The decline of Black middle neighborhoods has been driven in part by the out-migration of middle-class families but more so because they are not being replaced by new middle-class homeowners. Too few people are buying homes in urban Black middle neighborhoods to replace the homeowners who leave. Although the share of Black home buyers nationally is smaller than it should be, this shortfall is not primarily a function of an overall shortage of Black home buyers.

Black home buying in the United States, after dropping sharply during the foreclosure crisis and the Great Recession, has rebounded strongly since then. Nationally, home purchase mortgages to Black home buyers, after hitting a low of 118,000 in 2011, rose to 284,000 by 2019.[17] But far fewer of those Black home buyers are buying in traditionally Black urban neighborhoods. In 2005, 307 Black home buyers took out mortgages to buy homes in Cleveland's Black middle neighborhoods. In 2018 the number was 73, less than a quarter as many, and over half of those 73 mortgages were in the Lee-Miles neighborhood, which may be Cleveland's last remaining stable Black middle neighborhood. Compared to fifteen or twenty years ago, today's Black home buyers in Cleveland and elsewhere are far more likely to buy in the suburbs than the central city. In 2019, only 350 mortgages were made to Black home buyers in Cleveland, but 1,500 were made to Black home buyers in the surrounding Cuyahoga County suburbs. Inside the city, they are more likely to buy in racially mixed than predominantly Black neighborhoods than in the past.

In chapter 6 we discussed the concept of replacement, that is, the key function of a steady flow of new home buyers to replace those homeowners who leave for the normal life cycle reasons (aging, employment, and mobility). By comparing the number of homeowners to the number of new buyers, we can calculate the actual replacement rate and compare it to the replacement range, the ratio of new home buyer purchases or purchase mortgages to the pool of existing owners needed to ensure that adequate replacement is taking place.

While Black middle neighborhoods in Baltimore and Chicago are seeing some revival of home buying, although not quite enough, Black neighborhoods in St. Louis, Cleveland, and Detroit are seeing far too little home buying to sustain their housing markets. The number of mortgages made to Black home buyers in 2018 in Cleveland's Black middle neighborhoods was less than 1 percent of the 8,411 homeowners living in those neighborhoods. What that means is that when the time comes to sell their homes, only a small percentage of homeowners in Cleveland's Black middle neighborhoods have any realistic possibility of finding a new homeowner to take their place. In some cases, their home may be bought by an investor, but often it will find no buyer, and eventually be abandoned. It is therefore not surprising that from 2000 to 2018, Cleveland's Black middle neighborhoods lost 30 percent of their homeowners, and their average vacancy rate had risen to above 20 percent. The median sales price in these neighborhoods in 2019 was under $40,000, less than half of what it had been in 2005.

Weak home buyer demand is not the cause of the challenges that Black middle neighborhoods are facing. On the contrary, it is a product of those difficulties, accumulated over many years. Once sustained weak demand takes over, however, it can create a vicious cycle that perpetuates continued disinvestment, destabilization, and the out-migration of those who can afford leave, as shown in figure 11.5. For that reason, stabilizing these neighborhoods will require breaking that cycle and restoring healthy home buyer demand.

One cannot fault Black home buyers for deciding to move to the suburbs. Where people move is rarely driven by ideological goals and far more by concrete desires to further their families' well-being. Black home buyers are buying elsewhere, perhaps with regrets, because they believe that other areas better meet those desires. Any effort to revive urban Black middle neighborhoods must acknowledge and address the reasons they have become less attractive than their suburban and more racially mixed counterparts. What this means comes out

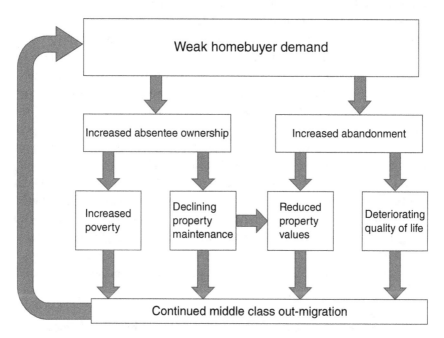

FIGURE 11.5. The vicious cycle of weak home buyer demand

clearly from focus groups held by Detroit Future City, an advocacy organization that has called attention to this issue:

> When asked about middle-class neighborhoods and what the middle class found desirable, focus group participants were consistent in describing these characteristics: cleanliness, well-maintained homes, low vacancy and blight, high rates of home ownership, adequate public safety, and access to a range of quality amenities and services, including good schools. Focus group participants also seized upon the costs of living in the city and what they believed was discouraging middle-class residents from staying or moving to Detroit. Among the deterrents were familiar themes such as high insurance and tax rates, struggling schools, blight and vacancy, and a lack of retail amenities.[18]

To this we would add the expectation of reasonable appreciation in the value of one's home over time.

Race is never far from the surface. As we discussed in chapter 8, white home buyers mostly confine their housing searches to white communities, while African Americans consider communities with a wide variety of racial compositions. Thus, while the small regional Black demand pool is dispersed across all the region's neighborhoods, little of the much larger white demand pool reaches Black areas. This reflects the apparent reality that, as studies by Courtney Bonam and her colleagues have found, middle-class Black space is "invisible" to white people. "The asymmetry in racial stereotype content shapes class perceptions, which spread to a more holistic set of trait perceptions, ultimately operating to dampen perceivers' willingness to live in . . . the same house when it is located in a Black, versus White, neighborhood. This gap in avoidance and devaluing of the Black versus White neighborhood house is present at both class levels, but is greater when the house is objectively middle-class versus lower-class."[19] In essence, as a report in *Slate* on Bonam's research put it, the typical white buyer "is almost incapable of assigning middle-class status to houses in Black neighborhoods."[20]

The data bear this out. Only 1 percent of white home buyers in St. Louis in 2018 bought homes in the roughly 40 percent of the city's census tracts that were 75 percent or more African American. Roughly one-quarter of those buyers bought homes in a single census tract near the affluent, largely white Skinker-DeBaliviere area. This is not a trivial concern, because it perpetuates racial segregation and also because the pool of potential Black home buyers in most cities is not large enough to sustain all the traditionally Black middle neighborhoods. Those neighborhoods emerged at a unique moment in time when massive pent-up Black homeownership demand needed an outlet. While Black home buying has returned to respectable levels nationally and in a few cities such as Atlanta and Indianapolis, in many other cities it remains well below the minimum level needed to sustain current Black homeownership rates.

Black home buyers typically make up a much smaller share of most cities' demand pool than the city's share of existing Black homeowners. With Black neighborhoods competing with neighborhoods throughout the metro area, a neighborhood that can attract only a small number of buyers out of an already small pool is at an inherent disadvantage. With their supply of homes far exceeding the demand, those homes will command lower prices than similar homes in white or more racially mixed neighborhoods that are not invisible, in Bonam's terminology, to the white home buyer market, while their market weakness means that they will also have more difficulty recovering from shocks such as the foreclosure crisis and the Great Recession as well as the potential future effects of the COVID-19 pandemic. David Rusk has called this the "segregation tax."[21]

The simultaneous spatial shifts in Black home buying and the decline of so many Black middle neighborhoods pose a version of the classic people versus place dilemma. Those shifts are undermining those neighborhoods. Their inability to replace their homeowners destabilizes them, perpetuating declining house values and loss of homeowners' equity and wealth, leading in turn to deterioration in the neighborhoods' quality of life and opportunity. At the same time, those buying elsewhere can reasonably be seen as making rational decisions on behalf of themselves and their families. Every legacy city metro offers many neighborhoods, both within the central city and in nearby suburbs, where available indicators suggest that public safety, school outcomes, and house price appreciation are all materially better than in many of the Black middle neighborhoods in those same cities. While house prices are often higher in these destination neighborhoods, they are not so high as to prevent middle-income households from buying those houses. This might suggest that public policy should simply allow these processes to take their course and see Black middle neighborhoods in much the same way many people viewed the immigrant neighborhoods that made up large parts of American cities a hundred years ago after the immigrants had moved on: as areas that served a particular purpose during a particular historical era but, once that purpose was no longer relevant, could evolve or decline as market forces might dictate.

We do not support that position. Parallels between today's Black experience and the earlier white immigrant experience are at best seriously flawed. Strong but anecdotal evidence suggests that the decision to leave neighborhoods such as Crary–St. Mary's is often undertaken reluctantly and with misgivings. These neighborhoods mattered to the people who left and still matter to those who remain. As Diane Richardson, a resident of one such Philadelphia neighborhood, told reporter Sandy Smith. "'This community means so much to me. I love where

I live. I work to keep it up. I don't want it to decline. . . . If there are foreclosures, we need help from the city to resolve the issue and get new people in. To take us to the next level.'"[22]

What Richardson and many others are saying is both important and relevant. The Black experience is fundamentally different from the immigrant experience. The likelihood that Black households will assimilate more or less seamlessly into the so-called melting pot, becoming effectively invisible as has happened over time, albeit not without strains, to white immigrant communities, is not a realistic possibility in today's America. Race matters. Healthy, vital Black neighborhoods have an important social function. As Detroit advocate and blogger Lauren Hood states, "Detroit needs not just places, but whole neighborhoods, where black people feel welcome—it's essential to our emotional and mental well-being. Safe black space is where black people are free from judgment. Free to be loud in conversation, laughter, music, and dress. Free to gather in large groups and not be perceived as a threat. Free to talk openly about race and not be classified a separatist or race-baiter. Free from profiling. Allowed to be seen and acknowledged."[23]

As long as race plays anything resembling the role that it currently plays in American society, such spaces will continue to be important. Clearly, one can argue that they do not have to be these particular spaces, but to relinquish spaces that have performed that role ably over an extended period in return for an uncertain, unpredictable future seems at best foolish, at worst dangerous.

These neighborhoods' role goes beyond this. As Chicago reporter William Lee points out, "the loss of the black middle class deprives their communities of their skills, tax revenue, and political clout while also robbing a younger generation of desperately needed role models."[24] Urban Black middle neighborhoods have been central to the formation of today's Black middle class, wellsprings of Black civic, political, and cultural engagement in the cities of which they have been a part. They also represent a body of valuable fixed assets, including homes and businesses as well as parks, schools, and other community institutions and a reservoir, albeit shrinking, of Black wealth.

The potential loss of these neighborhoods takes on particular significance in light of the changes taking place in American cities. The shift from manufacturing to eds and meds as their principal urban economic base has led to the cities' workforce becoming increasingly made up of suburban commuters, and the migration of a young, well-educated, and largely white generation to the cities is redefining historically nonresidential downtowns and nearby areas as new types of upscale urban neighborhoods. These changes have increasingly polarized cities along mutually reinforcing spatial, economic, and racial lines. We suggest that a city that is spatially polarized between rich (or at least well-to-do) and poor (or near poor), especially if that polarization is not only economic but also racial, is socially problematic and most probably unsustainable. The continued survival and vitality of Black middle neighborhoods in cities such as Baltimore and Detroit is perhaps the most important bulwark against this polarization and for a more equitable future for our cities.

The Middle Neighborhood Opportunity

The urban middle neighborhood, which flourished from the 1920s through the 1960s, with all its faults, was a cohesive community, strong in social capital, that enveloped its residents in a comfortable, although to some constricting, web of relationships. After World War II, the locus of the good middle neighborhood for many shifted in part to the suburbs. Millions of white families moved into Levittowns and Park Forests, where they adopted a car-oriented version of the middle neighborhood, as we discuss in chapter 13. In the central cities, hundreds of thousands of Black families who had been effectively barred from most neighborhoods and were still barred from most suburban developments took advantage of white flight to create their own middle neighborhoods. In all cases, while the middle neighborhood had little room for the poor, one did not have to be wealthy to enjoy its not insignificant benefits. They were homes for the blue-collar or white-collar family, whether Black or recent immigrants. Good places to raise children, they were conveyer belts of upward mobility.

Although fewer than they once were and often threatened, middle neighborhoods are still a valuable source of good neighborhoods in our cities and suburbs. As noted earlier, 25–40 percent of most legacy cities' populations live in middle neighborhoods. They are more likely to be racially and economically diverse than both poor and wealthy neighborhoods. Many middle neighborhoods have valuable assets such as solid older housing, walkable retail nodes or corridors, good parks, and decent schools, but they are often undervalued by the marketplace.

Middle neighborhoods are a significant challenge for both central cities and their inner-ring suburbs but have tended to fall into a policy blind spot, attracting far less media and public-sector attention than what has been lavished on gentrifying neighborhoods and on areas of concentrated poverty. As with the American medical system, resources are devoted to solving acute problems rather than keeping healthy neighborhoods from falling into decline. It is far less expensive to stabilize a healthy neighborhood than to wait until it has fallen apart and then try, usually with little success, to revitalize it.

The neglect of middle neighborhoods has begun to end, albeit slowly and haltingly. Cities such as Cleveland, Philadelphia, and Des Moines have begun to look more closely at their struggling middle neighborhoods, while the national Middle Neighborhoods Initiative has been formed recently to fill this gap in the community development system.[25] The initiative supports the Middle Neighborhoods Community of Practice, a network of practitioners, researchers, and policymakers that supports research, conducts webinars, and lifts up best practices from cities across the country, including not only large central cities but also suburban communities such as Shaker Heights, Ohio, and Plano, Texas.

The widespread decline of urban middle neighborhoods highlights the fundamental challenge to the idea of neighborhood as we enter the third decade of the new millennium. Given the nature of American society and the economy today, can we create and sustain, or re-create, good neighborhoods that do not depend on their residents being disproportionately wealthy, which by definition excludes the majority of the population? The answer to that question, of course, is interwoven with many other questions about the future of the American economy and the United States as a society but is critical to any hope of restoring social health and cohesion after the multiple shocks of recent years.

12

THE PERSISTENCE OF CONCENTRATED POVERTY NEIGHBORHOODS

Jesus is memorably quoted as having said that "the poor you shall always have with you."[1] Not only have the poor always been present, but for many centuries they and their neighborhoods also made up the greater part of most cities. As urban historian Charles Duff puts it, until relatively recently "cities were squalid places with isolated bits of beauty."[2] Despite the growth of the middle class in the nineteenth century, large parts of most European and American cities remained crowded, disease-ridden areas of abject poverty, as is still true in many cities in the Global South today. As we described earlier, at the beginning of the twentieth century millions of people in American cities were still desperately poor, living in the "filthy and rotten tenements" that Jane Addams, Jacob Riis, and other reformers of the time vividly described.[3]

With the increasing prosperity of the twentieth century and the transformation of society from the 1930s through the 1960s, the number of poor people in the United States dropped sharply, from the "one-third of a nation ill-housed, ill-clad, and ill-nourished" of Franklin Roosevelt's second inaugural address in 1937 to 12 percent, or one-eighth of the nation, by 1969.[4] Impressive as that was, the distribution of poverty remained sharply unequal, with 27 percent of the Black and other nonwhite population below the poverty level, compared to only 8 percent of the white population.[5] Since then the total poverty rate has fluctuated only narrowly, rising during recessions and falling during periods of recovery. In 2019 despite ten years of economic recovery, it had dropped only slightly, to 10.5 percent. Much of this decline was attributable to the substantial drop in Black and Latinx poverty rates after the end of the Great Recession, as can be

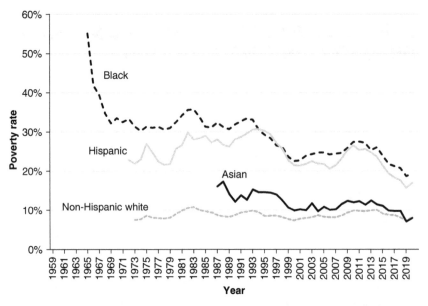

FIGURE 12.1. Poverty rate by race and ethnicity, 1959 to 2019

(Bureau of the Census, Current Population Survey)

seen in figure 12.1. Despite improvement, however, both were still more than double the white poverty rate, while the share of Black children living in poor households was just over 25 percent, compared to 8 percent in the white population. Still, there are two and a half times as many white people as Black people living below the poverty level in the United States.

Our subject, however, is less the number of people in poverty as it is their concentration. What it means to be poor is one thing, to live in a concentrated poverty area something else, and to be both poor and live in such an area yet another thing. As Paul Jargowsky writes, that last group "shoulders the 'double disadvantage' of having poverty-level income while living in a neighborhood dominated by poor families and the social problems that follow."[6] From a neighborhood perspective, the issue is that although poverty rates have changed little, poverty has become steadily more concentrated. The number of neighborhoods of concentrated poverty, along with the number of poor people living in those neighborhoods, is far greater today than in the 1970s.

While poverty has negative effects on individuals, concentrated poverty can generate spillover effects, or externalities, that negatively affect individuals and the community over and above the individual effects of poverty itself. The concentration of poverty in a neighborhood has an independent effect on outcomes, such as educational success and workforce participation, after controlling for the other factors that could influence the outcome, including individual poverty. Poor people generally experience worse life outcomes when living in an area of concentrated poverty than in an economically mixed or lower-poverty neighborhood. The ways in which the character of the neighborhood can change individual outcomes are often referred to as "neighborhood effects."[7]

There is no generally accepted standard for defining concentrated poverty areas. Different researchers use 20, 30, and even 40 percent poverty rates as cutoff points for concentrated poverty. In a review of the research on neighborhood effects, George Galster concluded that "the independent impacts of neighborhood poverty rates in encouraging negative outcomes for individuals like crime, school leaving, and duration of poverty spells appear to be nil unless the neighborhood exceeds about 20 percent poverty, whereupon the externality effects grow rapidly until the neighborhood reaches approximately 40 percent poverty; subsequent increases in the poverty population appear to have no marginal effect."[8] No absolute level of poverty in a neighborhood can be considered to be a trigger for neighborhood effects. Context matters. As we will discuss, it is one thing to live in a concentrated poverty neighborhood with an intact physical and social fabric and another thing to live in a neighborhood with a similar poverty level but with residents scattered among many vacant and abandoned properties with few social ties.

The neighborhood effects associated with concentrated poverty reflect a wide range of different causal mechanisms. Galster lists fifteen causal pathways that potentially connect a neighborhood context of concentrated poverty to individual behavioral and health outcomes.[9] Efforts of researchers to control for multiple other variables in order to isolate the effect of concentrated poverty, however, mischaracterize the process driving these effects and can inadvertently underestimate neighborhood effects. As with other neighborhood dynamics, these variables are not only affected by the poverty context but also interact with one another to produce reinforcing cycles of decline, reinforcing and exacerbating the effect of any single factor.[10]

However measured, concentrated poverty is increasing. Cortright and Mahmoudi studied the change in high-poverty census tracts in the nation's fifty-one largest metropolitan areas from 1970 to 2010.[11] Although the population of the areas they studied grew only slightly over that period, the number of people living in high-poverty census tracts more than doubled, from just under 2 million to 4.2 million, as the share of these regions' poor population living in areas of concentrated poverty went from 28 percent to 39 percent. Looking at a more recent period, Jargowsky found that after declining by 27 percent from 1990 to 2000, the number of extremely high-poverty tracts across the country increased by 76 percent, or 1,902 tracts, from 2000 to 2013.[12]

Race is deeply implicated in concentrated poverty. While there are many more poor white people than poor Black people, far more poor Black and Latinx people live in concentrated poverty areas. In 2013, 5 million poor Black and 4.3 million poor Latinx residents lived in extremely high-poverty areas compared to 3.5 million poor white residents.[13] The invidious reality of racial disparities, which affects every aspect of the conversation on concentrated poverty, is central to understanding concentrated poverty neighborhoods in America today.

The Origins and Growth of Concentrated Poverty Neighborhoods

As we noted in chapter 3, few American cities had large African American populations before World War I, and most Black residents lived in racially mixed neighborhoods although often in small segregated blocks or buildings in those neighborhoods. Large segregated Black neighborhoods such as Chicago's Bronzeville and New York's Harlem emerged with the First Great Migration in the 1910s and 1920s, often filling the spaces left by immigrant populations who were beginning to move into newer less crowded neighborhoods farther from the city center.

These areas were widely called ghettos, a term that, while contested, reflected the reality that these were not voluntary ethnic enclaves but rather segregated areas enforced by social and legal pressures imposed by the dominant white majority. They contained much grinding poverty, an inevitable result of the discrimination from which Black workers suffered. They were a world apart, however, from today's concentrated poverty areas. Stable working-class and prosperous middle-class Black families lived in the same neighborhoods as the poor, and the concentration of population and talent in these neighborhoods was a powerful impetus for robust economic activity and strong social and religious institutions. Crowded commercial streets and vibrant entertainment scenes coexisted side by side with poverty, overcrowding, and unhealthy housing conditions.[14]

The puzzle is why after World War II as opportunities for African Americans grew, segregated and increasingly disinvested areas of concentrated poverty also grew. Part of the explanation has to do with the racist system of mortgage lending, reinforced by the New Deal's creation of the Federal Housing Administration, that we discussed in chapter 4. Mortgage discrimination, however, was not an invention of the Federal Housing Administration. The typical white male banker, unconstrained by either custom or fair housing laws, did not need a federal stamp of approval to discriminate against would-be Black home buyers.

Mortgage discrimination, however, mattered less than one might think because the reality was that Black families, especially in cities, had few opportunities to become homeowners with a mortgage or otherwise. The great majority of new single-family developments were governed by racial covenants, while within the Black ghettos almost all properties were owned by absentee investors. In 1940, nationally only 15 percent of Black families were homeowners, disproportionately concentrated in the rural South. Homeownership rates for urban Black families were much lower: 8 percent in Baltimore, 7 percent in Chicago, and 6 percent in Milwaukee.

Black populations in most northern cities surged after 1940. The Second Great Migration, during and after World War II, was far larger than the first wave during and after World War I. From 1940 to 1970, the African American population of Chicago grew by over 800,000, of Detroit by over 500,000 and of Cleveland by 200,000. The influx of Black migrants led to even greater overcrowding of already densely populated segregated neighborhoods. By 1951 an estimated 140,000 people crowded into Detroit's Black Bottom neighborhood, an area probably little more than two square miles.[15] For all their vitality, these areas were pressure cookers looking for an outlet.

The urban renewal and interstate highway programs compounded matters. As we described in chapter 4, entire Black neighborhoods were swept away during the 1950s and 1960s, with devastating effects. Over half a million households, roughly half of them people of color, were officially displaced through urban renewal, a number that fails to account for the thousands who may have fallen through the program's cracks and the hundreds of thousands more displaced by the highways carved out of the hearts of American cities. With too little affordable replacement housing being built through urban renewal and nothing at all under the highway program, these families needed a place to go. That place was provided by white flight. The millions of white families who left the cities for the largely all-white suburban subdivisions or for the fast-growing Sunbelt states left both shabby immigrant neighborhoods that had seen far better days and neighborhoods of solid single-family houses built up to the 1920s and 1930s.

As Black families moved or were displaced, the Black population began to bifurcate economically and spatially. While affluent, working-class, and poor Black families had, by necessity, shared the segregated quarters to which they had previously been relegated, over the ensuing decades their paths diverged. As African American columnist Eugene Robinson wrote in 2010, "no one quite realized it at the time, but Black America was being split."[16] While prosperous African American families leapfrogged over the older and closer immigrant neighborhoods and moved into more attractive neighborhoods being vacated by the white middle class, such as Detroit's Crary–St. Mary's, poor or near-poor families either stayed in what was left of the original Black neighborhoods—many moving into hulking high-rise public housing projects—or moved into the cheaper, shabbier formerly immigrant neighborhoods nearby. Robinson sums up the change:

> Some moved out—to neighborhoods unscarred by the riots, to the suburbs . . . —and moved up, taking advantage of new opportunities. They moved up the ladder at work, purchased homes and built equity, sent their children to college, demanded and earned most of their rightful share of America's bounty. They became the Mainstream majority. Some didn't make it. They saw the row houses and apartment buildings where they lived sag from neglect; they hunkered down as big public housing projects . . . became increasingly dysfunctional and dangerous. They sent their children to low-performing schools that had already been forsaken by the brightest students and the pushiest parents. They remained while jobs left the neighborhood, as did capital, as did ambition, as did public order. They became the Abandoned.[17]

The split in the Black community has been well documented. As late as 1970, the average African American still lived in a neighborhood that was more economically mixed, with the well-to-do, middle-class, and poor living side by side, than the average white neighborhood. Only a decade later, that was no longer true. As Kendra Bischoff and Sean Reardon, two scholars who have carefully studied the spatial and economic shifts in American society, write, "segregation by income among Black families . . . grew four times as much [than among white families] between 1970 and 2009."[18]

As Joe Cortright and Dillon Mahmoudi have shown, once a neighborhood becomes an area of concentrated poverty, its likelihood of changing its condition is small. Of the 1,119 concentrated poverty census tracts in 1970 they studied, forty years later nearly three-quarters were still concentrated poverty areas. About one in five had moved slightly upward but were still above-average poverty neighborhoods, while only one in eleven had "rebounded" and become average or low poverty areas.[19] A few neighborhoods escaped the vicious cycle of increasing poverty and distress, whether through gentrification or otherwise, but mainly in cities that showed strong economic growth overall. As Cortright and Mahmoudi point out, "just three cities (New York, Chicago, and Washington) accounted for one-third of all census tracts that saw poverty rates decline from above 30 percent in 1970 to below 15 percent in 2010."[20] Conversely, in sixteen of the fifty-one metropolitan areas they studied, not one high-poverty tract escaped high poverty over that forty-year period.

The stickiness of long-term concentrated poverty neighborhoods is only one part of the challenge. Of greater concern are the many neighborhoods that were not concentrated poverty neighborhoods then but are today. These areas typically include many more persons in poverty than the long-term concentrated poverty neighborhoods, many of which have been rapidly losing population. Data from the Cleveland area bear this out. Five out of six of the poor persons living in concentrated poverty areas in 2010 were living in areas that were not concentrated poverty areas in 1970. Of those, more than half lived in areas that were low-poverty areas (under 15% poverty rate) in 1970.[21]

Most of this damage is quite recent. The number of high-poverty tracts dropped during the 1990s, only to rise dramatically since 2000. Of the sixty-five census tracts in Cleveland in which the poverty rate was over 40 percent in 2018, only twenty-six had a poverty rate of 40 percent or more in 2000. The change is powerfully visible in figure 12.2, which shows how the expansion of concentrated poverty (30% or more) in majority-Black tracts in Detroit from 2000 to 2015. While a handful of census tracts moved modestly upward, the majority of Detroit neighborhoods that were not high-poverty areas in 2000 had become so by 2015. This is the flip side of the decline of middle neighborhoods that we discussed in chapter 11. Most of the areas that went from low to high poverty in Detroit from 2000 to 2015 had been Black middle neighborhoods, home to the city's once-large Black middle class.

Many forces have driven the growth in concentrated poverty neighborhoods largely populated by people of color. Public policies, however well-intended, have exacerbated poverty concentration, beginning with the construction of the massive public housing projects of the 1950s that over the ensuing decades became increasingly populated by the poorest of the poor. Lyndon Johnson's war on poverty, while arguably helping many people to move out of poverty, did little for the neighborhoods they lived in. People who got better jobs often moved out, leaving those who did not behind.

Subsequent publicly financed low-income housing programs further compounded the problem, as the great majority of those developments were built in already high-poverty areas driven by both opposition to subsidized housing from more affluent and whiter areas, particularly in the suburbs, and an often unrealistic belief by local officials and nonprofit organizations that such developments would somehow change the neighborhoods where they were built. While they undoubtedly improved housing conditions for many families, with a handful of exceptions they rarely did anything for the neighborhood.

While concentrated poverty neighborhoods got subsidized housing and some social services, they got little else. In the meantime, the quality of life deteriorated as financially strapped cities cut back on social programs, public services,

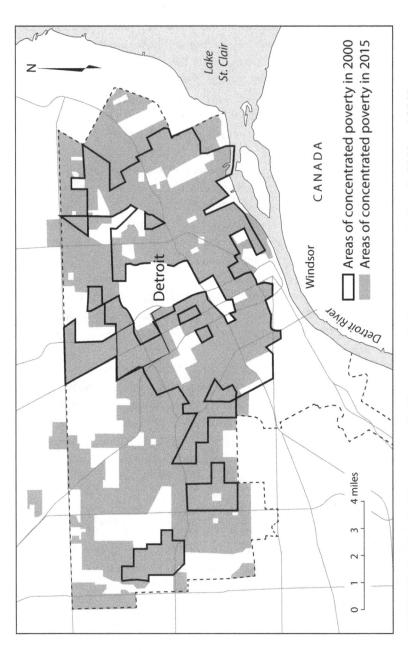

FIGURE 12.2. Majority-Black areas with 30 percent or higher poverty rate in Detroit, 2000 and 2015

(Sources: decennial census and American Community Survey data. Map by PolicyMap, adapted by Bill Nelson)

Note: Areas within black lines were high-poverty areas in 2000; gray-shaded areas were high-poverty areas in 2015 (Authors' work based on decennial census and American Community Survey data) and capital investments. Public schools in these neighborhoods declined, and as enrollments declined, schools were often closed without regard to the supportive role they played in many neighborhoods. Public safety, already uncertain, deteriorated further with the onset of the crack cocaine epidemic of the 1980s. Most of those who could do so moved out. As poverty increased and population density dropped, neighborhood stores and services disappeared. Policing in concentrated poverty areas increasingly became a matter of protecting the more prosperous parts of the city than serving these areas' residents.

These neighborhoods and the people who lived in them were mostly written off by the larger white-majority society. While Robinson's Black mainstream majority were often able to adapt to an economy in which factory jobs were replaced by jobs in eds and meds, less-skilled and less-educated workers were largely irrelevant to the new knowledge economy. As urban economies have revived, employers have recruited new workers from the suburbs and from the pool of educated young people who had begun to migrate to the cities, largely ignoring the residents of these neighborhoods. In many concentrated poverty neighborhoods, less than half of the adult population actively participates in the labor force, and of those at any given time, as many as a quarter may be without a job.

Vacancy and Abandonment

The gradual abandonment of their housing stock was part and parcel of the disinvestment of these neighborhoods. While we touched on abandonment in chapter 4, it is closely interwoven with the story of concentrated poverty. Vacancy and abandonment had not been an issue in the earlier history of American neighborhoods. From the late nineteenth century through the end of World War II, observers of low-income neighborhoods invariably noted how crowded they were, often referring to them as "teeming," "packed," or, more dismissively, "swarming." As discussed previously, at the end of World War II there were few vacant homes or apartments to be had.

By 1960, the postwar housing shortage was largely a thing of the past and in many cities was turning into an oversupply of housing. During the 1960s, property owners first began to walk away from properties they saw as worthless or unduly burdensome; by the end of the decade, people had begun to talk about "abandonment" as a serious urban issue, which it became at least briefly during the 1970s. After a flurry of activity, however, public priorities shifted, and abandonment fell off the policy radar until the late 1990s. Properties continued to be abandoned, gradually creating the landscape that is sometimes known today as

FIGURE 12.3.   Street in Northside St. Louis

(Google Earth © 2022 Google)

FIGURE 12.4.   Aerial view of blocks in Gary, Indiana

(Google Earth © 2022 Google)

the "urban prairie," as can be seen in the scenes from St. Louis, Missouri, and Gary, Indiana, shown in figures 12.3 and 12.4.

Since the 1960s, people have walked away from millions of properties in American towns and cities, cities have demolished millions of vacant buildings, and vacant, derelict properties have become a pervasive part of the urban landscape. In some cities, including Detroit and Gary, recent field surveys have found that vacant buildings and lots make up over 40 percent of the parcels in the city.[22] In a study of forty-nine Rust Belt cities, Jason Hackworth identified 262 "extreme housing loss neighborhoods," census tracts that lost more than 50 percent of their housing between 1970 and 2010.[23]

Understanding why properties are abandoned begins with economics but does not end there. Most fundamentally, it begins with the neighborhood market. If the supply of housing, storefronts, or industrial floor space exceeds the market demand for that space, some part of that space will become vacant. If supply continues to exceed demand over a long period, as is likely to be the case in any neighborhood showing sustained population decline, vacancies can become a permanent condition. If houses sit vacant for too long and are not maintained or secured, they deteriorate like the house in figure 12.3, ultimately to the point where they cannot be reused and are eventually demolished.

Population decline drives vacancy. Nearly 30,000 households in Cleveland lived in concentrated poverty Black neighborhoods in 1970, but only 11,000 remained in those same neighborhoods in 2010. Since each household occupies a housing unit, by 2010 those neighborhoods needed 19,000 fewer dwellings to house their residents than in 1970. Moreover, in 1970 those neighborhoods already had an excess supply of 4,500 empty housing units. Over the next forty years as houses were vacated, they were abandoned and, along with much of the 1970 excess supply, were ultimately demolished. The upshot was that by 2010 there were 20,500 fewer housing units in the area, leaving thousands of additional vacant lots where the houses once stood. Those lots remained vacant because there was no market demand. People were unwilling to build on these vacant lots because the cost of construction would far exceed the market value of the new buildings.

A host of public and private policies and practices exacerbated decline and abandonment, increasing the likelihood that a house, once vacated, would be abandoned. These included outright redlining by lenders and insurance companies, common in the 1950s and 1960s but less frequent in later years, as well as widespread lender reluctance to make mortgages in areas with low and declining property values. Many states' tax foreclosure laws and policies led to properties often ending up in a legal and ownership limbo and others ending up in the hands of predatory landlords likely to milk the properties and walk away after a few years.

At some point, the accumulation of vacant properties changes from being an effect of a declining neighborhood housing market to a cause, setting in motion reinforcing processes of contagious abandonment resulting in hypervacancy.[24] Based on the authors' experiences and observations, once about 20 percent or more of the neighborhood's dwellings are vacant, along with a comparable or greater number of vacant lots, the neighborhood's housing market effectively collapses. House prices decline to little more than the transaction cost, reflecting the fact that at that point, except for a few bottom-feeding speculators and odd types who relish the idea of living in an urban prairie, there are no buyers for the neighborhood's homes.

In what some people may see as a paradox, while house prices drop to near-vanishing levels, rents stay well beyond the reach of large numbers of the poor and near-poor residents of concentrated poverty areas. The reason is straightforward. For landlords to stay in business, they must collect enough rent to cover their costs, namely property taxes, insurance, maintenance costs, mortgage payments, and at least a modest profit margin or return on equity. Unlike sales prices, which can go down virtually to zero if the market is too weak, if landlords cannot collect the minimum rents they need to stay in business, they no longer have any motivation to keep renting the unit and typically walk away.

For a responsible landlord who maintains her property, conscientiously makes her property tax and mortgage payments, and is willing to accept a modest rate of return on her investment, that minimum economic rent in a typical older American city is usually somewhere—depending on property tax rates and the cost or value of the property—between $700 and $900. For a single mother working full-time at a job paying little more than the minimum wage, that rent makes up 50 percent or more of her gross earnings.[25] In Cleveland, nearly half of all renters living in concentrated poverty neighborhoods other than those living in subsidized housing spend 50 percent or more of their gross income for rent, compared to one-quarter of all renters nationally. Yet, the rent most of them pay is still barely enough to keep a conscientious landlord in business.

The unsustainable amounts for rents being spent by so many low-income households is in turn the principal trigger for the national epidemic of evictions, an epidemic concentrated in high-poverty neighborhoods. As Matthew Desmond shows in his book *Evicted*, the households most at risk of eviction and subsequent homelessness or doubling-up are single mothers with children, who are by far the poorest single demographic subgroup in American society and disproportionately live in concentrated poverty areas.[26] Constant insecurity and frequent moves triggered by eviction not only destabilize families, impair adults' chances of finding stable employment, and undermine their children's education but also erode the weak ties that are a neighborhood's lifeblood.[27]

Disinvestment by local government in schools, public safety, and other public services and infrastructure can further sap what is left of these neighborhoods' vitality. Crumbling streets, broken streetlights, trash-filled vacant lots, and boarded-up empty school buildings all send powerful signals that the neighborhood has been written off by local government and the larger society. Robinson's characterization of the people who live in these neighborhoods as the Abandoned is tragically apt.

The Effects of Concentrated Poverty

Sustained poverty is itself debilitating. Lack of enough money coupled with constant insecurity about almost every aspect of one's life turns life into a constant struggle, made worse by the fact that in American society one is constantly being reminded of how much more most other people have and how that defines one's status in society. Its effects are magnified and compounded, however, if one is both poor and lives in an area of concentrated poverty. We touched on the power of neighborhood effects in chapter 1. Here we look further at effects specific to concentrated poverty neighborhoods.

Not all racially segregated and concentrated poverty areas share all these debilitating effects. In chapter 1 we cited Eric Klinenberg's research on the effects of the 1995 Chicago heat wave, which showed that while most high-poverty Black neighborhoods had high death rates, some had among the lowest death rates.[28] Among the highest death rates was in North Lawndale, a community that lost 50 percent of its housing units between 1960 and 1990. As one local leader told Klinenberg, "North Lawndale looks like a war zone. It has been bombed out."[29] That description fits dozens of similar poor neighborhoods in older cities and towns across America.

Not only are there few stores and other places to go in North Lawndale, but many residents are also afraid to leave their homes. One resident who had lived in the North Lawndale for more than forty years told Klinenberg that drugs and gun violence had changed everything. "We used to sit outside all night and just talk and do whatever. But that's changed."[30] With lack of contact, so important for both neighboring and for the development of the networks and the successful role models that lead to opportunity, weak ties become attenuated.

Although support systems based on kinship or close friendship networks may remain intact, means of informal social control outside those networks atrophy, creating a social vacuum that parallels the physical void left by abandoned houses and vacant lots. Voids become no-man's-lands and breeding places for disorder. Higher levels of disorder and interpersonal violence, as a major Atlanta study found, are highly associated with "childhood trauma, adult trauma and PTSD," further impairing both adults' and children's ability to do more than try to survive.[31] As Charles Branas and his University of Pennsylvania colleagues found, when a local organization took over vacant lots in a low-income neighborhood, improved them, and maintained them as attractive green space, not only did the neighbors feel safer, but violent crime around those lots also declined.[32]

Physical health is closely tied to mental health and powerfully affected by neighborhood conditions. In addition to a high risk of violence and frequent lack of access to fresh food and preventive health care, many concentrated poverty neighborhoods are themselves unhealthy, sometimes because of environmental contamination from the proximity of pollution sources but more so because of the condition of the housing in which large numbers of poor people live.

Most housing in concentrated poverty neighborhoods is old; in most high-poverty areas, over half of the housing units and sometimes as much as 80–90 percent were built prior to World War II. But the problem is not simply the age of the houses. Millions of old homes across the United States provide decent, solid, and often desirable housing. The poverty of the residents in concentrated poverty areas, however, dictates that old houses receive less maintenance, fewer repairs, and less predictable replacement of worn-out systems than needed because of the limited resources of their owners or rents that are often barely enough for landlords to make ends meet, let alone upgrade their properties. As properties deteriorate, damp, mold, obsolete and poorly functioning heating and plumbing systems, and peeling paint, among other problems, create indoor pollution conditions that can trigger asthma or cause lead poisoning and other medical conditions.

Concentrated poverty neighborhoods create powerful barriers to opportunity. As William Julius Wilson has pointed out, the disappearance of the city's factory jobs and the distance between these neighborhoods and suburban job centers as well as the persistence of racial discrimination have made finding stable, well-paid employment an increasingly difficult challenge for the residents of concentrated poverty neighborhoods.[33] The weak ties that are so essential for linking to job opportunities are attenuated, and those ties that do exist are less productive. Wilson points out that Black residents of concentrated poverty neighborhoods in Chicago are less likely than residents of other neighborhoods to have at least one employed friend.[34] For those who do find suburban jobs, the low wages and the cost and time of long-distance commuting are further debilitating factors. These factors, coupled with the poor quality of the public services in most concentrated poverty neighborhoods, especially public schools, perpetuate poverty across multiple generations.

As Patrick Sharkey, who has systematically studied multigenerational poverty, has shown, growing up in an area of highly concentrated poverty drastically increases the likelihood that you will remain poor and will never leave the area. Over many generations, these factors have a powerful cumulative effect.

Children who are the product of many generations of disadvantage "show substantially worse developmental outcomes when compared to families that live in poor neighborhoods for a single generation . . . even after we account for everything else in a family that might affect children's development."[35] As Raj Chetty and his colleagues have found, holding parental income, race, and gender constant, children growing up in poor neighborhoods have significantly less economic mobility as adults than those growing up in more economically diverse areas.[36] As we noted in chapter 1, residents of many concentrated poverty areas may have average life expectancies as much as eighteen to twenty years less than the residents of more affluent neighborhoods only a few miles away.

In the final analysis, the juxtaposition of the external and internal factors makes the plight of racially segregated areas of concentrated poverty especially severe. The traumas of poverty, crime, and disorder are triggered and reinforced by widespread racial discrimination, unsafe and unhealthy housing, poor public services, punitive policing, lack of access to fresh food and preventive health care, and physical isolation. These factors are not universal, and not all concentrated poverty neighborhoods share all of them, but few such neighborhoods are unaffected by many if not most of them.

Can Concentrated Poverty Areas Become Good Neighborhoods?

Concentrated poverty areas can become good neighborhoods, but the obstacles are not only economic but also social and political. Any strategy to transform high-poverty areas suffers from the fundamental difficulty that the challenges lie simultaneously in the conditions of the neighborhood and the poverty or near-poverty of the people who live there. Those, in turn, are the product of disinvestment in the people and in the neighborhood by the larger society that denies them the opportunity to thrive. If public or nonprofit programs invest in the residents of such a neighborhood, though, enabling them to escape poverty through education, training, and better-paying employment, the evidence suggests that most of those residents would use their higher earnings to leave the neighborhood. Their lives would be better, which is no small matter, but the neighborhood would be left poorer and more depleted of population.

Along similar lines, many people have called for greater efforts to enable low-income families to move to more prosperous, opportunity-rich communities, typically in the suburbs of older cities. Over the years a variety of pilot programs, of which the federally funded Moving to Opportunity program is best known, have pursued this goal with generally positive outcomes.[37] Such programs, along with land-use initiatives such as New Jersey's Mount Laurel doctrine, which requires suburban municipalities to accommodate their fair share of the regional need for affordable low- and moderate-income housing, need to be expanded beyond their currently modest scope.[38] But even if that takes place, those initiatives are likely to affect only a small share of the poor and near-poor households currently living in high-poverty neighborhoods. Thus, programs to move poor households to more affluent areas should be seen as a complement to strategies that focus on high-poverty neighborhoods, not an alternative.

Strategies to invest in and rebuild the neighborhood physically without changing the economic conditions of the residents have little likelihood of success. In theory, it might be possible to attract an economically diverse population to some concentrated poverty areas and rebuild them as mixed-income communities in ways that would enable their existing low-income populations to remain and benefit from the change. In practice, the potential for that taking place except in rare circumstances is vanishingly small even with massive public subsidies. As we discussed earlier, outside of a handful of high-demand cities such as San Francisco and Washington, D.C., or the rare situations in which a neighborhood has unusual locational or other assets, segregated areas of concentrated poverty rarely see significant middle-class in-migration. Moreover, in those few cases in which nonprofits or others have succeeded in building strong market demand in previously concentrated poverty areas that do have those assets, their efforts are more likely to lead to gentrification and the gradual disappearance of the earlier population than to a balanced mixed-income community.

Some organizations have tried to combine physical rebuilding with helping residents escape poverty, but few such efforts have the resources to make more than modest strides in either area. An evaluation of forty-eight comprehensive community initiatives over a 20-year period concluded that individuals benefited but that "those programs did not produce population-level changes," such as reductions in poverty rates or increases in homeownership.[39] Rarely are neighborhood changes enough to prompt individuals, who can now afford to move, to stay in the community.

An unusually heavily resourced effort was mounted in Baltimore in the 1990s, when developer/philanthropist James Rouse convinced governments and foundations to invest over $130 million (nearly $250 million in 2020 dollars) for the combined physical, social, and economic revitalization of Sandtown-Winchester, a deeply distressed concentrated poverty neighborhood in Baltimore. As a 2015 *Washington Post* report described it, "The effort to revive Sandtown was massive. More than 1,000 homes were eventually renovated or built. Schools were bolstered. Education and health services were launched."[40]

Despite investing a great deal of money in a single neighborhood, the initiative failed to bring about sustained change. The *Washington Post* concluded that "visionary developer James Rouse and city officials injected more than $130 million into the community in a failed effort to transform it. Instead there are block after block of boarded-up houses and too many people with little hope."[41] It's not that there was no change. Indeed, there's some evidence that things picked up for a while. During the 1990s, household incomes picked up and unemployment dropped relative to the rest of the city. But after 2000 the gains disappeared, and the neighborhood fell back into its pre-Rouse status quo.[42]

None of this proves that high-poverty neighborhoods cannot be good neighborhoods in many respects. Indeed, many of the ethnic and religious urban neighborhoods of the late nineteenth and early twentieth centuries were good neighborhoods despite the grinding poverty of many of their residents. Even with their often horrendous housing conditions, their environments fostered community spirit and promoted opportunity and upward mobility. There were, however, at least three salient differences between those neighborhoods and most of today's neighborhoods of concentrated poverty.

First, their residents were connected by deep religious, language, and ethnic ties and shared strong indigenous institutions, such as the parish church or the Jewish landsmanschaften, to help maintain those ties. Those institutions, along with a strong sense of common identity, fostered levels of cohesion and solidarity beyond kinship networks, along with the robust network of weak ties important for neighborhood vitality. Second, while most of the residents of these neighborhoods were poor, each had its leavening of successful people—professionals, merchants, and others—who lived in the neighborhood and were well known to their neighbors. In Italian neighborhoods they were called the "prominenti" and in Jewish neighborhoods the "machers." Widely seen as role models, their intervention helped propel many a poor child on the path to opportunity.

Third, hearkening back to Klinenberg's point, these were indeed teeming neighborhoods. Every house was full of people. Some blocks on the Lower East Side, a high-density area even by the standards of the time, contained more than one thousand people per acre, six times the area's density today, and fifty to one hundred times the density of most American suburbs.[43] Its density not only enabled the neighborhood to support strong retail hubs and corridors but also promoted the constant human interaction that fosters vital neighborhood connections. All these factors, of course, were true of many Black neighborhoods in the 1930s and 1940s.

The people who lived in these neighborhoods benefited from a far more robust opportunity framework than the residents of today's concentrated poverty neighborhoods. Steady employment—although often grueling and unpleasant—was readily available for immigrants with limited English proficiency and little formal education, while a rapidly growing economy meant that as they acculturated, paths to upward mobility were widely available. Changes in the urban economy have diminished opportunities and narrowed potential paths of upward mobility. The split in the Black community described earlier deprived concentrated poverty areas of successful middle-class people who could bridge the gap between the neighborhood and the larger society. Moreover, for all the discrimination experienced by immigrants in earlier eras, it was never as pervasive and far-reaching as racial discrimination then and to a large extent even now.

Without questioning the imperative of continued investment in human opportunity, this suggests that much of the effort to revitalize concentrated poverty neighborhoods, in the sense of placing the focus on changing the economic or housing market character of those neighborhoods, is misdirected and that a different way of thinking about these neighborhoods is in order. Barring a fundamental change in the workings of the American society and economy, the evidence suggests that most concentrated poverty neighborhoods are likely to remain that way for the foreseeable future, whatever interventions are made by governments, community development corporations, or philanthropies. This does not mean, however, that those neighborhoods cannot be made far better neighborhoods.

Improving a neighborhood does not change the poverty of the people who live in it, but it can change the conditions under which they live. If their neighborhoods become safer, cleaner places and the houses they live in become safer and healthier, that can fundamentally change their quality of life. If that can be coupled with changes to the opportunity framework, such as greater job opportunities for adults and better schools for children, that will further change their lives whether they remain in the neighborhood or not. This is what happened to the South Bronx neighborhoods discussed in chapter 9. While many of those neighborhoods would still be considered concentrated poverty areas, their intact or rebuilt urban fabric, strong amenities, extensive stock of sound, affordable housing, and access to opportunity enable them to function as good neighborhoods.

Recognizing the limits of community development to change the underlying conditions of poverty suggests a radically different approach to these neighborhoods than most models being pursued in the United States. Rather than prioritizing development and efforts to draw market capital, it calls for concentrating more on public services and regulation and community building. It may also suggest new and different ways of delivering public services. One area that is particularly important, and where the challenges have become particularly apparent in recent years, is policing. Without suggesting that low-income communities can effectively police themselves, clearly today's quasi-military policing model as applied to African American neighborhoods is ineffective at ensuring the safety of the residents. Whether it is even meant to, as many commentators suggest, is another question. While beyond the scope of this book, the mere fact that the question is repeatedly raised bears reflection. Whether true community safety is possible through reform of our current urban police departments or whether new community-based institutions are needed and can be created are also complex questions for which evidence, one way or the other, is in short supply. What is clear, however, is that we need both new models and a real commitment to work with communities to make them safer places for the people who live there.

Another important area, often overlooked by neighborhood planners, is addressing the quality and stability of housing in high-poverty areas. Whatever the merits of building new affordable housing projects, the great majority of the residents of concentrated poverty areas live and will continue to live in existing privately owned housing, a mix of single-family houses, row houses, and scattered small apartment buildings, nearly all over sixty years old and often over a hundred years old. Most are absentee owned. Despite some progress, few cities are making systematic efforts to ensure that these homes and apartments meet fundamental standards of health and safety by enforcing relevant housing codes or doing what they can to help struggling poor families stay in their homes through such means as ensuring that tenants have access to lawyers when contesting eviction filings. The benefits to tenants of such a program are significant, with large numbers of evictions avoided, while the costs of such programs are largely offset by savings in other public services, including homeless shelter costs for families who have lost their homes.[44]

The single step that might have the greatest positive impact on the quality of life in high-poverty neighborhoods has on its face nothing to do with neighborhoods, namely turning the current federal Housing Choice Voucher (HCV) program—or a similar form of housing allowance—into an entitlement program analogous to the Supplemental Nutrition Assistance Program that enables low-income families to maintain food security. In contrast to the Supplemental Nutrition Assistance Program, under which anyone meeting the income qualifications receives benefits, congressional appropriations for the HCV Program, which makes up the difference between the market rent and what low-income tenants can afford without spending more than 30 percent of their income for shelter, have severely limited the program, and far more families are eligible for the benefit than can be assisted with available funds.[45] As a result, the HCV becomes a lottery in which a fortunate few gain a modicum of residential security while the great majority are left to fend for themselves in the marketplace.

The benefits of an entitlement housing allowance to low-income tenants are manifest, but the benefits to the neighborhood are just as powerful.[46] For tenants, an entitlement housing allowance dramatically reduces housing insecurity, which means they can remain in the same home longer and are far less likely to be subject to eviction and the risk of homelessness. Their family stability, the adults' ability to gain and retain stable employment, and the children's ability to benefit from education by remaining in the same school all become that much greater.

Today's constant, rapid churning in rental housing, in which low-income tenants turn over on average every two years, is unhealthy for both tenants and neighborhoods. An entitlement housing allowance will dramatically reduce that turnover, with benefits for both. By virtue of their greater stability—economic, temporal, and psychological—the family is more likely to become an active participant in neighborhood life. Since their rent will no longer consume an unconscionable share of their income, they will have greater disposable income, which is likely to benefit neighborhood merchants. Moreover, with an entitlement housing allowance in place, the fear that rigorous code enforcement could result in either untenable rent increases or landlord abandonment would largely disappear.

If community safety and decent, healthy housing are two critical prongs in the process of turning concentrated poverty areas into good neighborhoods, good schools are a third. Good neighborhood-based schools are not only a critical vehicle for mobility and opportunity for a neighborhood's children but also an important statement about the value of the neighborhood. Moreover, there is compelling albeit scattered evidence from schools around the country that it is possible to create and operate schools that do indeed take children from impoverished families in high-poverty areas and set them on the path to success.[47] Those achievements could be replicated in hundreds of concentrated poverty neighborhoods if the political will to do so existed. Instead, in older cities across the United States, hundreds of public schools in low-income neighborhoods have been closed as a result of declining enrollment, further undermining those neighborhoods' social fabric, while the ongoing warfare between public school and charter school advocates diverts attention away from the critical issue of student outcomes.

Along similar lines, the quality of public services and facilities is another critically important element. Something as seemingly simple as ensuring that all of a neighborhood's streetlights are in working order or that parks adequately maintained can improve residents' quality of life and their perception of the neighborhood. They can become building blocks of community stability and cohesion.

Implicit in all of this is that concentrated poverty neighborhoods can and should function as real communities, offering the connections and social capital needed to make them work as good neighborhoods. The level of investment and commitment by the larger society needed to accomplish this would be substantial but would be more than justified by not only the improvement to the quality of life for millions of people but also moving the United States toward becoming a more just society.

NEIGHBORHOOD CHANGE IN THE SUBURBS

In the 2020 presidential campaign Donald Trump evoked an image of American suburbs as white enclaves which he would protect from an invasion of low-income housing and crime emanating from "Democrat-run" cities. "Suburban women," he declared, "should like me more than anybody here tonight because I ended the regulation that destroyed your neighborhood. I ended the regulation that brought crime to the suburbs, and you're going to live the American dream."[1] Trump's appeal to protect suburbs from an invasion of urban ills, as many noted at the time, was not only implicitly racist but was also based on an outdated image of suburbia. Suburbs today are racially and economically diverse and many share the same problems faced by cities.

By definition, a suburb is any community within a metropolitan area located outside the central city. When we think of suburban neighborhoods, however, we conjure up a distinct image: single-family homes surrounded by lawns and occupied by middle-class families relying on cars to get to jobs and shopping, all located in separate single-use districts rather than mixed in with residential areas. We think of suburbs as green landscapes, which stress private over public spaces and encourage a privatized, individualistic lifestyle. For good or bad, the suburban lifestyle is often contrasted with the density and diversity of city life.

The increasing diversity of the suburbs has been widely documented in recent years. By 2010, 40 percent of African Americans in metropolitan areas lived in the suburbs.[2] Immigrants now often settle first in "gateway suburbs," not cities.[3] Although the percentage of poor families is higher in central cities, more poor people live in suburbs than in central cities.[4] Not only are suburbs demographically diverse, but many do not fit the physical stereotype. Many older so-called streetcar suburbs are similar in their density and mix of uses to urban neighborhoods built at the same time. Recently some postwar suburbs have created mixed-use centers, trying to make themselves more walkable in response to changing home buyer and consumer tastes.[5] Many suburban neighborhoods are grappling with concentrated poverty, disinvestment, and even vacant housing.

While the problems may be similar, the context is different, and the neighborhood issues are often more challenging in suburbs than in central cities. Their lower density and separated land uses, along with their reliance on private rather than public amenities, automobile dependency, and the limited extent of suburban institutional endowments all present challenges for community building and can make suburbs difficult environments for lower-income families moving from central cities.

The fragmentation of suburban local governments and school districts acts as a sorting machine, drawing affluent households into privileged bastions and leaving poorer households trapped in communities with fiscally strained, underperforming public institutions. Fragmented suburban institutions act like echo chambers, magnifying the feedback effects of neighborhood dynamics and creating patterns of path dependency that widen the social and economic gaps between suburban neighborhoods.

The Changing Context of Suburban Neighborhood Life

The urban middle neighborhoods we discussed in chapter 11 were re-created in the suburbs that were built around every American city after World War II. Neither rich nor poor, these postwar or inner-ring suburbs re-created the family and child-rearing–centered model of the urban middle neighborhood but with a greater emphasis on the home over the community institutions of the urban neighborhood. As Robert Beauregard writes in his book *When America Became Suburban,* "the family was to be the center of social life."[6] He adds that "the design of the typical tract house reinforced these values. . . . Mass society, U.S. style, had found its 'dream life.'"[7]

Although home and family were at the center of the new suburban neighborhoods, organized neighboring was intense. "This generation was also deeply engaged in the civic life of the community," Beauregard states, "more so than the generation before and the ones that followed. Church attendance was high, and union membership was at a twentieth-century peak. Participation in league bowling was common and neighboring was prevalent."[8] This was echoed in William

Whyte's description of the Chicago suburb of Park Forest in his classic work, *The Organization Man.* The new arrival "has plunged into a hotbed of Participation. With sixty-six adult organizations and a population turnover that makes each one of them insatiable for new members, Park Forest probably swallows up more civic energy per hundred people than any other community in the country."[9] Each of Park Forest's 105 residential "courts," containing roughly one hundred homes or apartments, became a distinct minineighborhood with its own character.

The physical setting of the new suburbs, however, was radically different from that of the typical urban neighborhood. While individual lots were small by comparison to those in twenty-first-century exurbia, they were vast by comparison to those in the urban neighborhoods that the newly minted suburbanites had left, where even detached houses were as little as six to ten feet from their neighbors. The new houses rarely had either porches or stoops and were set back from the sidewalk by a lawn, limiting the informal interaction typical of urban neighborhoods. Even more significantly, while an elementary school and a small park or playground might be nearby, stores, workplaces, and churches all required a trip by car. New generations of shopping centers filled with chain stores and surrounded by parking lots replaced the neighborhood shopping street. After the ranch houses and Cape Cods, the ubiquitous parking lot became a defining symbol of suburbia.

The distance between the houses, their design and street setback, and the auto dependency of the suburban lifestyle all meant that the number of informal encounters fostered by proximity and by the many short walks that urban neighborhoods require declined precipitously. Informal interaction was largely limited to immediate neighbors and among parents of small children. The intense level of organized interaction that Whyte dubbed "Participation" was in many respects a way for the new suburbanites to compensate for the loss of the texture of informal interactions they had previously shared.

Unlike informal interaction, which in a healthy traditional neighborhood is largely self-sustaining, formal organizational interactions require ongoing maintenance and can be exhausting and difficult to sustain over time. Fundamental changes to society and the economy meant that the high participation suburban neighborhood would be short-lived. As children grew up and left the home, their parents' child- and school-related interactions inevitably declined. Arguably the most significant factors, however, were social changes, above all the change in gender roles and the growth of female workforce participation. The stay-at-home wife and mother had been the mainstay of the participation neighborhood. As women moved into the workforce and as the number of child-rearing married couples entered a long-term decline, the intense level of neighboring that initially characterized the 1950s suburbs was no longer sustainable.

The weakness of many inner-ring suburbs to sustain themselves as good neighborhoods did not appear overnight. Although the number of children dwindled, many families remained in place for many years, carefully maintaining their houses and lawns. Churches and civic organizations remained viable, although often at levels of membership well below their heyday. But as with the Black urban middle neighborhoods of similar vintage, the original home buyers were aging out, and their children had largely moved elsewhere. Meanwhile, many of the more economically successful among the families who had initially moved into inner-ring suburbs were moving farther out to bigger houses on larger lots. In Thomas Bier's study of housing moves in the Cleveland area, he found that nearly four out of five homeowners who sold their homes in Cleveland's inner-ring suburbs during the 1980s and 1990s moved to newer suburbs farther out in the region.[10]

By the end of the century houses in these suburbs were looking far less appealing than they had in the 1950s, while the pool of well-to-do families looking for suburban homes could choose from shinier, larger, and newer alternatives. As the initial white homeowners moved away or aged out, many inner-ring suburbs began to undergo racial transition. Park Forest today is over 60 percent Black, as are many inner suburbs around Chicago, Detroit, Cleveland, and other cities with large communities of color. This reflects not only the desire of African American families for better housing and quality of life but also the continuing reality of white flight. As researcher Samuel Kye found, middle-class white suburban families tend to move away as the percentage of Black or Latinx population increases.[11]

Suburban decline is not a function of the "return to the city" or disenchantment with the suburbs generally. Three-quarters of all high-status neighborhoods are in suburbs, not central cities, a share that remained remarkably stable between 1970 and 2010.[12] The outward movement within suburbia, however, has created problems for older suburbs. A study of the one hundred largest metropolitan areas from 1970 to 2009 found that "metropolitan areas with greater levels of sprawl tended to have inner-ring suburbs with relatively lower per capita incomes," while another study found that 22 percent of all suburbs lost population from 1980 to 2010.[13]

At the same time, not all older suburbs are in trouble. Many older railroad suburbs are thriving. Built around commuter rail stations, such as those of Philadelphia's Main Line, they have distinctive historic architecture and vital mixed-use town centers. The most vulnerable suburbs are those built after World War II between 1945 and about 1960. Built to relieve the post–World War II housing shortage, they were mass-produced following methods pioneered by William Levitt in Levittowns across the Northeast (figure 13.1). Their houses are

FIGURE 13.1.   A house in Levittown, New York, unchanged from the 1950s

(Google Earth © 2022 Google)

small by today's standards and lack features such as the multiple bathrooms and central air conditioning today's buyers expect. They form a belt around every major city, as figure 13.2, which highlights areas where 50 percent or more of the houses were built between 1940 and 1969, illustrates for the Chicago area.

Where they are situated within the larger pattern of metropolitan development is also important. As Homer Hoyt noted in the 1930s, suburbs are extensions of older urban settlement patterns; once established, high-rent neighborhoods "tend to move out in that sector to the periphery of the city."[14] Suburban development corridors reflect status hierarchies established in the central city. The tony Minneapolis suburbs of Edina, Eden Prairie, and Minnetonka are in many ways extensions of the affluent Lake District neighborhoods in Minneapolis. In Chicago, an ordinary postwar ranch house in a northern suburb such as Skokie or Morton Grove, extensions of affluent white North Side city neighborhoods, sells for $300,000 to $400,000, while a similar house in a southern suburb such as Park Forest or Markham, extensions of the historic Black community on Chicago's South Side, may sell for only one-third as much. Similar patterns can be found in most metropolitan areas.

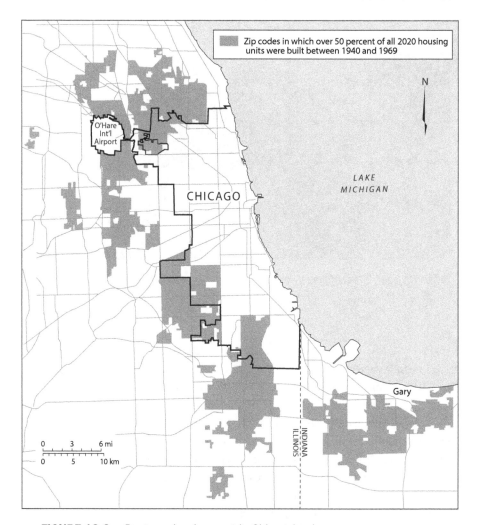

FIGURE 13.2. Postwar development in Chicagoland

(Source: PolicyMap; Map by Bill Nelson)

As with other neighborhood issues, markets matter. Studying suburban neighborhoods in the one hundred largest metropolitan areas, planner Karen Beck Pooley found that "socioeconomic changes . . . interact with local real estate market conditions in incredibly complicated and highly varied ways from one place to the next."[15] The small size and lack of architectural distinction of the homes in the first Levittown on Long Island have not doomed them to decline. The strength of the New York regional market, Levittown's proximity to Manhattan, and the lack of nearby new housing production have ensured their

FIGURE 13.3.   Reconfigured Levitt houses in Levittown, New York, today

(Google Earth © 2022 Google)

market vitality. Levittown houses initially sold in 1949 for $7,990 (roughly $93,000 in today's dollars). In January 2022, the median sales price for homes—albeit often improved and expanded—in Levittown was $575,000 (figure 13.3).[16]

In weaker market regions, where middle-income demand is modest and easily satisfied by those suburbs perceived as more desirable or farther from the urban center, an influx of low-income households can overwhelm suburban neighborhoods, as shown by increases in absentee ownership and housing vacancies. By contrast, stronger market suburbs can maintain economic diversity while accommodating rental and lower-income housing.[17] Racial change follows similar patterns. Predominantly Black suburban neighborhoods are likely to experience stagnant or declining property values in weak market metros, but in areas with stronger markets and a large Black middle class, such as Atlanta's DeKalb County and Maryland's Prince George's County, strong Black housing demand supports stable or rising suburban home values.

The decline of so many postwar inner-ring suburbs and the transformation of railroad suburbs, such as Montclair, New Jersey, into elite communities highlights an important reality. As with urban neighborhoods, suburbs are pulling apart and becoming more polarized along economic lines. Between 1980 and 2018 the percentage of the population in the nation's fifty largest metro areas living in middle-income suburbs fell from 75 percent to 56 percent while increasing in poor suburbs from 8 percent to 19 percent and in affluent suburbs from 17 percent to 25 percent (figure 13.4).[18]

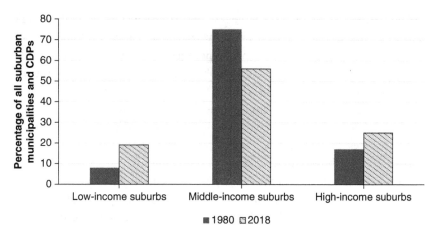

FIGURE 13.4. Distribution of suburbs by income in fifty largest metropolitan areas, 1980 and 2018

(Authors' work based on decennial census and American Community Survey data)

The economic disparities between suburbs can be huge. In the San Francisco/ Oakland metropolitan area, median per capita incomes range from $165,947 in Atherton to $20,769 across the bay in San Pablo. Median home sales prices were over $7 million in Atherton and $335,000 in San Pablo. In much lower-priced Chicagoland, relative disparities were even greater. The median sales price was nearly $1 million in wealthy Wilmette on the North Shore but only $23,000 in impoverished Harvey, south of Chicago. These disparities have a huge impact on the ability of suburbs to provide quality public services at a reasonable tax rate, a key factor in the stability of good neighborhoods.

The polarization of neighborhoods by income and, by extension, property values is a serious problem everywhere but leads to a further troubling outcome in the suburbs. While we are under no illusions about equal distribution and quality of services by neighborhood within central cities, inequality is mitigated by the fact that neighborhoods are situated within the same taxing and service providing jurisdiction. Neighborhoods such as Hough in Cleveland and Homewood in Pittsburgh would be incapable of funding even the most minimal public services and schools if they had to generate all the necessary tax revenues from within their boundaries. Moreover, the presence of robust philanthropic and nonprofit networks in many central cities acts as a redistributive mechanism, providing resources to struggling low-income communities and their residents.

Many suburban regions are divided into multiple small municipalities, with each one responsible for funding public services from its own revenues, along with whatever level of aid the state provides. The San Francisco Bay Area contains

101 municipalities, 36 of which have been incorporated since the end of World War II, as well as unincorporated areas where county government provides services. That is modest by comparison to some other metropolitan areas. Far smaller Allegheny County, which includes Pittsburgh, contains 132 cities, boroughs, and townships, the smallest of which, Haysville, has a population of seventy in 0.2 square miles. For poor municipalities, political fragmentation puts them in a situation analogous to expecting Hough or Homewood to provide their own public services. Vast disparities in municipal resources and public services are exacerbated by the thinner network of philanthropies and nonprofit organizations in suburbs compared to central cities. As we discuss in the next section, while underlying neighborhood dynamics may be driven by economic and social forces, the institutional framework within which they are embedded matters greatly.

Institutions Matter

In chapter 9 we discussed the central role of agents of change, the network of institutions and organizations that seek to intentionally revitalize neighborhoods. Although often underappreciated, the framework created by strong public as well as private institutions is a critical mainstay of the good neighborhood. The weakness of those institutions in most suburban settings combined with municipal fragmentation, overlaid on the physical and social dynamics of suburbanization, increase the risk of decline for many suburban neighborhoods.

We say "many" because it is impossible to generalize to all suburban areas. The suburbs created by and for the affluent through municipal incorporation and exclusionary land-use regulation provide a neighborhood quality of life that largely meets the needs of their residents, who can afford to pay for most of their needs through private, individual means. While the concept of neighborhood is not meaningless in such areas, it is more exiguous, something given little thought except in times of crisis, as when an affordable housing development is proposed to be built nearby. Affluent suburbs are alive and well. Our discussion focuses on the other side of the suburban coin.

It has long been recognized that the fragmentation of suburban areas into seemingly infinite numbers of small municipalities is neither a socially nor economically neutral phenomenon. In 1967, political scientist Norton Long wrote that "the suburb is the Northern way to ensure separate and unequal."[19] In 1974, sociologist Richard Hall noted that "in the context of a fragmented system of governments in the metropolis, municipal government becomes an institutional arrangement for promoting and protecting the unequal distribution of scarce resources."[20] In some cases, the motivation for splitting was both economic and racial. In a famous 1970s case, a group of St. Louis County residents incorporated as the independent municipality of Black Jack in order to obtain the zoning powers they needed to block development of a low-income housing project.[21]

Municipal fragmentation enshrines vast differences in the fiscal capacity of local governments and school districts, rarely fully compensated for by state equalization grants, in ways that perpetuate and exacerbate economic and racial segregation and disparities in conditions and opportunities. Independent of school funding, research supports the conclusion that students from low-income families do better in schools that are economically integrated compared to schools that have a high percentage of students below or near the poverty line.[22] School quality powerfully affects house prices and housing demand. White home buyers often shun racially integrated school districts, undercutting neighborhood housing values. Suburban fragmentation of school districts magnifies the feedback effects of economic and racial sorting, reinforcing downward spirals of resource-starved suburban neighborhoods.

The ability of local governments to provide the array of local public goods and services that are essential for good neighborhoods rests on their fiscal capacity, which depends in turn on a balance between expenditure need and revenue-raising capacity. While their expenditure need increases with rising poverty and aging housing stock and infrastructure, many inner-ring suburbs have limited revenue-raising capacity. Even where state laws permit local governments to raise revenues through income or sales taxes, that yields little benefit for municipalities with few industrial, office, or commercial properties. The result is that most suburbs are highly dependent on residential property taxes to pay for municipal as well as school expenditures.

These fiscal constraints undermine neighborhood vitality. Struggling inner-ring suburbs, particularly predominantly Black suburbs where property values, for reasons discussed earlier, tend to be lower than in their white counterparts, often have ruinously high property tax rates. One study found that in 2016 per capita property taxes in Chicago's middle-class Black suburbs were 73 percent higher than in middle-class white suburbs.[23] In the United States, property taxes tend to average roughly 1 percent of a home's market value; the 2021 property taxes on a house in East St. Louis, Illinois, that sold in May 2022 for $10,000 were $2,137, or 21.4 percent of value.[24] Ruinous property tax burdens drive property values down further, creating a vicious spiral while never providing enough revenues to deliver even minimally acceptable public services. Parks are dilapidated and trash-ridden, potholes proliferate, and streets lack pedestrian-scale lighting. In neighboring Missouri, where state laws limit property tax hikes, struggling suburbs in north St. Louis County have turned to traffic fines and court fees to raise municipal revenues, with devastating social consequences.[25]

Reflecting a long history of urban services, from the first settlement houses through the programs of the war on poverty, most central cities tend to have a cross section of nonprofit organizations that provide many of the benefits of the modern welfare state, such as job training, childcare, and mental health services. These services are harder to obtain in the suburbs, so poor people in suburbs have less access to needed help. In a 2017 study, policy scholar Scott Allard found that the median expenditure by nonprofit human service providers in suburban counties in 2010 was only $106 per low-income resident compared to $884 in urban counties.[26]

As with social service providers, philanthropies are disproportionately urban in their attentions. A 2007 study of community foundations in the Atlanta, Chicago, Denver, and Detroit metropolitan areas found, after examining over sixteen thousand grants, that the foundations gave $54.2 million to urban service providers compared to only $5.3 million to suburban service providers even though many more poor people lived in the suburbs than in the central city.[27]

If lower-income people face disparities by living in the suburbs, the disparities for struggling places are even greater. Few small suburban jurisdictions have the resources to plan or execute place-based programs, while strong community development corporations capable of using the decentralized tool-based system we described in chapter 5 are scarce in suburban areas.[28] Few suburbs qualify to receive direct funding under federal Community Development Block Grant and HOME grant programs; while they are eligible to share in county or state pools, those funds are far more limited than those that flow to entitlement jurisdictions.

The inequality of suburban institutions magnifies economic inequalities across neighborhoods. Encased in political boundaries, the feedback effects of neighborhood economic decline reverberate powerfully within struggling suburban municipalities, with rising tax rates and declining public services generating reinforcing cycles of neighborhood decline, while economic and racial segregation are exacerbated as more affluent households flee declining suburbs. Since its peak in 1980, Harvey's population has dropped by nearly one-third. The research is clear: all else being equal, the greater the fragmentation across municipalities and school districts, the higher the level of economic and racial segregation.[29] Other studies have found strong associations between political fragmentation and racial disparities in health and life expectancy.[30] In the next section we describe how differences in political fragmentation affect the vitality of struggling neighborhoods in two sharply contrasting governmental settings.

Comparing St. Louis and Baltimore Counties

St. Louis County, Missouri, and Baltimore County, Maryland, are good places to tease out the role of local governments. Both are large suburban counties of similar population and land area surrounding similarly struggling central cities, both of which experienced deindustrialization, substantial population losses, and the growth of African American as well as low-income populations. St. Louis County, with eighty-six separate municipalities, is highly fragmented. By contrast, Baltimore County, unusual in the United States, has no separate municipalities; all governmental functions are performed by the county. St. Louis County has twenty-three school districts; Baltimore County has only one.

Although there are many factors at work, the evidence from these two counties is consistent with the research findings that more fragmented areas have greater place inequality. A much larger share of census tracts in Baltimore County are middle-income places, while St. Louis County has larger shares of lower- and upper-income tracts. In 2019, 45,431 residents of St. Louis County lived in census tracts with over 30 percent poverty compared to 8,154 in Baltimore County, or more than five times as many.

St. Louis County is also much more racially segregated than Baltimore County. While both counties have similar Black population shares, in Baltimore County less than 7 percent, or only two out of thirty-one census-defined places, were over 80 percent Black. In contrast, nearly one-quarter, or twenty-two out of ninety-eight municipalities and census-defined places in St. Louis County were over 80 percent Black. The racial dissimilarity index measures the percentage of one group that would need to move for every tract to have the same percentage of that group as the entire county. In 2019 at the census tract level, the dissimilarity index for St. Louis County was 52.8, while for Baltimore County it was 38.7.[31] More than half of all African Americans in St. Louis County would have to move from one census tract to another to produce a fully integrated population; for Baltimore County the figure is closer to one-third.

Institutional fragmentation, we believe, played a significant role in generating higher levels of economic and racial segregation in St. Louis County compared to Baltimore County. There are two other significant differences, however, that undoubtedly also played a role. First, Baltimore County is part of the faster-growing and more affluent Baltimore—Washington, D.C., megaregion. Compared to Baltimore, the St. Louis area's lower-priced, higher-vacancy housing market makes it easier for integration-averse households to flee areas experiencing increases in Black or lower-income households. Second, in 1967 Baltimore County enacted an urban growth boundary, the Urban-Rural Demarcation Line, that since 1967 has limited peripheral sprawl, concentrating development pressures toward the center, encouraging revitalization of older suburban neighborhoods. St. Louis County has neither legal nor physical constraints to limit suburban sprawl. In short, the story on the ground strongly suggests that municipal fragmentation is a major factor in neighborhood segregation and inequality, as our case studies of St. Louis County and Baltimore County demonstrate.

Ferguson and Fragmentation

The city of Ferguson became notorious in 2014 when a white policeman shot a Black teenager Michael Brown. It is a prism that reveals how many forces, including the timing of suburban development and its location within the broader metropolitan landscape, shape neighborhood dynamics (figure 13.5).

Ferguson began as an early railroad suburb.[32] The mid-nineteenth-century railroad between St. Louis and St. Charles passed through Ferguson, allowing well-to-do downtown employees to live in a leafy suburban setting (figure 13.6). Old Ferguson was a typical railroad suburb with a mix of businesses and Victorian homes along Florissant Avenue, giving it the pedestrian quality of a small city center. By 1940, Ferguson was a small (population 5,724) but prosperous suburb. After World War II the city grew rapidly, reaching its peak population of 28,759 in 1970. New Ferguson emerged primarily to the east and north of Old Ferguson, one of many postwar suburbs in northern St. Louis County that served as a destination for white families fleeing the city of St. Louis. The new homes were generally small one-story ranch homes (figure 13.7).

By 1970 there were two distinct Fergusons, the older railroad suburb on the west side with the feel of an urban village and a new postwar area designed around separation of land uses and automobile dependency.[33] It was an entirely white community. Officials in Ferguson, which shares a border with Kinloch, one of the first Black suburbs in Missouri, built a five-foot culvert across Suburban Avenue to discourage residents of Kinloch from driving into Ferguson.[34] Until the mid-1960s Ferguson was known as a "sundown town," where the presence of Black people was only permitted during daytime hours.[35]

As African American families began moving to the suburbs in the 1960s and 1970s, St. Louis suburbs responded in one of two ways: either trying to exclude them or welcoming them and working to maintain stable integration. One St. Louis County suburb that successfully pursued an integration maintenance strategy was University City, discussed briefly in chapter 8. Although University City, which borders the campus of prestigious Washington University, benefited from "place luck," it also took action to foster racial integration, including passing a stringent point-of-sale inspection ordinance to prevent housing deterioration and banning

FIGURE 13.5.   Ferguson and its environs

(Map by Emily Blackburn)

for-sale signs to prevent blockbusting. By 1990, the Black population of University City was approaching 50 percent; since then it has slowly fallen to about 36 percent. While the majority-Black Third Ward is not without problems, it remains a viable neighborhood that has not fallen victim to reinforcing processes of decline.

Ferguson took a different path, and for a time its strategy of exclusion seemed to work.[36] During the 1960s as University City went from less than 1 percent to 20 percent Black, Ferguson remained almost totally white. Changing conditions, however, and Ferguson's location in the heart of North County meant that it was impossible for the city to indefinitely block racial change. By the 1970s the white

FIGURE 13.6. Old and new Ferguson. A gracious home in Old Ferguson.

(Photo by Todd Swanstrom)

FIGURE 13.7. A home in postwar Ferguson.

(Photo by Todd Swanstrom)

families who had initially bought the modest houses built in the 1940s and 1950s were starting to move out, while growing numbers of Black families living in the north side of St. Louis were looking for suburban housing. During the 1970s the Black population of the city of St. Louis dropped by nearly fifty thousand and from 1980 to 2019 by another sixty thousand. The proximity of suburbs such as Ferguson to centers of Black population and the higher cost of housing elsewhere in St. Louis County made North County the principal destination of Black urban out-migrants. As the pool of Black buyers grew, the pool of white buyers in North County shrank. Ferguson's Black population share went from all but zero in 1970 to 15 percent in 1980, 25 percent in 1990, 52 percent in 2000, and 67 percent by 2010. Over time as more of the small postwar houses were bought by absentee investors who then rented them out, in-migrants became increasingly lower-income often single-parent families. From 2000 to 2019, the home-ownership rate in Ferguson dropped from 66 percent to 54 percent. Since its 1970 population peak, Ferguson has lost nearly 30 percent of its population.

While Ferguson was largely zoned for single-family homes, at least in part to exclude low-income renters, fiscal pressures led the city in 1964 to annex the land occupied by Emerson Electric, a Fortune 500 company located just across the eastern border of the city. As part of the annexation, however, Ferguson also acquired land that had been zoned multifamily by the county. Five large apartment complexes were constructed on this land, including Canfield Green, Park Ridge, and Northwinds, where Michael Brown lived with his grandmother at the time he was shot. At the time these apartment complexes were not considered a problem—if anything, the opposite. Built in 1970, the 415-unit Canfield Green complex, for example, was described in a 1978 advertisement as "deluxe" housing "tucked away among single-family homes" featuring a swimming pool, a tennis court, and a clubhouse.[37]

Over time, however, the residents of these apartment complexes became poorer, and conditions deteriorated. The owners took advantage of the Low-Income Housing Tax Credit program to refurbish the units, from which point the complexes were limited to low-income families earning less than 60 percent of the area median income. While the physical condition of the apartment complexes was much improved, the new income restrictions turned the area, with well over one thousand apartment units, into an increasingly distressed area of concentrated poverty. This cluster of concentrated poverty was hidden from the rest of the community, with only one road leading into it from West Florissant Avenue, a grim, barren five-lane highway largely lacking sidewalks and lined with fast-food outlets, liquor stores, and check-cashing establishments (figure 13.8).[38] Michael Brown and his companion had crossed this road and were walking back along Canfield Drive when Brown was shot.

FIGURE 13.8.   West Florissant Avenue near Canfield Drive in Ferguson

(Google Earth © 2022 Google)

During the 1990s as the apartments along Canfield Drive were becoming increasingly problem-ridden and isolated, the City of Ferguson was working hard to revitalize the heart of historic Old Ferguson along South Florissant Road, installing new streetlights and sidewalks as well as a gazebo and a clock tower. A special district was formed supported by assessments on property owners, buildings were refurbished, and a handful of new stores and restaurants opened, including a wine bar and microbrewery. While the revitalization of Old Ferguson was a modest success, the city's overall fiscal condition was gradually deteriorating.

The median house price in Ferguson, where most of the recent home purchase loans were high-cost or subprime loans, was only $75,000 even at the peak of the housing bubble but plummeted as the foreclosure epidemic hit the city hard. When the bubble burst, foreclosures exploded. Between 2006 and 2013, 2,402 distressed sales occurred in Ferguson.[39] Formerly owner-occupied homes were bought by absentee investors and rented out, further destabilizing many neighborhoods. The homeownership rate in Ferguson dropped while the poverty rate nearly doubled, rising from 12 percent to 23 percent. By 2017 the median sales price for a home was $29,820. That year, only ninety-eight homes changed hands in a city with over seven thousand single-family homes, a sure sign of a weak housing market.

Ferguson was in a fiscal bind. With existing tax revenues making it impossible to maintain adequate municipal services and with tax increases capped by Missouri state law, Ferguson, along with many other North County municipalities, took the path of raising revenue by ramping up traffic fines and court fees. Predictably, law enforcement was soon subordinated to the goal of raising money; by 2013, 20 percent of the city's general fund revenue came from traffic fines and court fees. With fifty white police officers of the fifty-four total in a city that was two-thirds Black, ticket writing was pursued in a racist fashion with devastating effects on low-income African Americans. After Michael Brown's shooting the US Department of Justice conducted a study of policing in Ferguson, which concluded that "many officers appear to see some residents, especially those who live in Ferguson's predominantly African-American neighborhoods, less as constituents to be protected than as potential offenders and sources of revenue."[40] The protests following Michael Brown's shooting and the violence that followed were a disaster for Ferguson and in particular for the Canfield Drive area. Based on a visual inspection in 2021, most of the units in the 438-unit apartment complex where Brown had lived were boarded up and vacant. Stigmatized by the shooting and plagued by crime, many people simply refused to live in the area, while many businesses along West Florissant Avenue, where most of the property damage from the protests was concentrated, remained empty.

Although the shooting of Michael Brown put the national spotlight on Ferguson, it is less an outlier than an exemplar of contemporary struggling suburbia. The racism that drove the city's leaders to try to exclude Black residents and to retain white political control long after Black residents had become a majority is not unusual in American suburbs.[41] Racism is simply an incremental layer on top of already powerful structural issues, beginning with the political fragmentation that undermines the ability of a small, poorly resourced municipality to cope with complex challenges. Adding to the difficulty, an indifferent county government has provided little help, and the state has imposed rigid fiscal controls on cities such as Ferguson without providing the means to deliver adequate services. Ferguson was not alone in turning to traffic fines and fees as a way out of its fiscal bind or in letting that process turn into a pernicious hunt for money at all costs.[42]

Ferguson is the product of three distinct legacies, all of which contributed to its difficulties: First, the legacy of the small, aging postwar houses and their lack of market appeal in more recent decades; second, the legacy of suburban zoning, which created such dysfunctional environments as the concentration of poverty on Canfield Drive; and third, the creation of barren pedestrian-unfriendly environments, such as West Florissant Avenue, fostering an automobile-dependent setting adverse to low-income families. To this must be added the legacy of subprime lending and the ensuing foreclosure crisis.

While Ferguson's efforts through the 1960s to remain a segregated white community can be seen as both racist and foolhardy and while it would be tempting to suggest that had the Ferguson behaved more like University City things would be fundamentally different today, that is unlikely. Ferguson lacked the assets that made it possible for University City to succeed. Ferguson's proximity to the University of Missouri–St. Louis, a commuter school separated from the city by Interstate 70, is a far cry from the close spatial and economic relationship between University City and Washington University. University City, largely built up before World War II, has a larger share of architecturally distinctive prewar homes that continue to draw middle-class buyers. Even Ferguson's self-proclaimed historic downtown is little more than a handful of undistinguished buildings scattered across barely two city blocks. Ferguson made many mistakes, but its spatial context and the political fragmentation of St. Louis County meant that it was always going to face fierce headwinds in trying to build stable, integrated neighborhoods.

Baltimore County and Dundalk

Baltimore County, which all but surrounds Baltimore City (figure 13.9), shares many of St. Louis County's challenges, including the pressures of demographic, economic, and social changes beyond its control. Its inner suburbs are characterized by the same modest postwar housing. As the county's Strategic Plan 2020 put it, there are "pockets of housing that did not age gracefully: many are obsolete by current market standards."[43] What sets Baltimore County apart from St. Louis County as well as most other metropolitan counties is that it is entirely governed by a single entity, the Baltimore County government. There are no incorporated municipalities within the county's 682 square miles. County government manages all municipal and school functions for its 854,535 (2020) residents. If it were a city, it would be the eleventh-largest city in the United States.

Baltimore County controls all land use within the county. In 1967 at the height of the county's population boom, Baltimore County adopted an Urban-Rural Demarcation Line, which restricts extension of public infrastructure in roughly two-thirds of the county's land area and has led to 90 percent of the county's development being concentrated in the remaining one-third. Moreover, the county's efforts have been supported by the State of Maryland, which since the 1997 Smart Growth Areas Act has targeted state funding to areas with existing public infrastructure. As the county's inner-ring suburbs were suffering from rapid decline in the 1990s, Baltimore County enacted, in the words of researcher Thomas Vicino, "one of the most comprehensive local approaches in the nation to confronting suburban decline."[44] How did this institutional and policy environment shape neighborhood change in Baltimore County?

Most suburban development in the county lies along three corridors radiating out of the central city and reflecting the character of the adjacent central city areas.

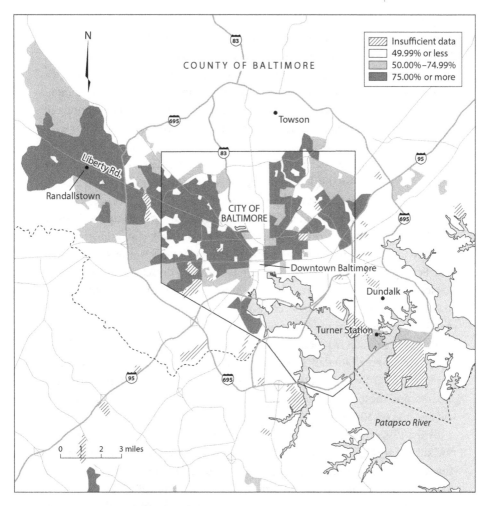

FIGURE 13.9.   Black population distribution in Baltimore County, 2019

(Source: PolicyMap; adapted by Bill Nelson)

The northern suburbs, such as the county seat of Towson, tend to be largely white and upper income, extensions of Baltimore City's most expensive upscale older neighborhoods. The eastern corridor is predominantly white and working class, while the western corridor is heavily African American, largely following a path along Liberty Road extending from the African American neighborhoods of West Baltimore (figure 13.9). Looking at the census tracts bordering Liberty Road from the city border to the Urban-Rural Demarcation Line, Gregory Smithsimon found that between 1970 and 2010 the percentage of African Americans along Liberty Road increased from 5 percent to 83 percent.[45] Some of these communities are struggling, but for the most part they have avoided the rapid racial tipping and economic decline of the suburbs of North St. Louis County. Randallstown, a predominantly Black suburb, has maintained itself as a stable middle-income neighborhood, with its per capita income remaining steady since 2009 at roughly 92 percent of the regional average. The racially changing suburbs of Baltimore County, Smithsimon concludes, "have been remarkably successful at altering the traditional story of racial transition . . . that often results in a decrease of property values and median household incomes."[46] Racial change has taken place slowly over a forty-year period and has in most cases been accompanied by social and economic stability. Roughly half of the majority-Black census tracts along Liberty Road have median household incomes above the county average.

By contrast, the largely white working-class suburbs of east Baltimore County have faced the greatest threat of suburban decline. Dundalk is an industrial suburb founded in 1917 by the Bethlehem Steel Company for workers in its Sparrows Point plant. Made up mostly of modest one-story detached homes and row houses, it grew steadily through the 1960s, reaching a peak population of 85,377 in 1970. For its first thirty years restrictive covenants forbade sales to Black steelworkers, who were only allowed to live in Turner Station, a separate area immediately south of Dundalk proper. Beginning in the 1970s as industrial jobs began to disappear, Dundalk's modest houses became less appealing in the marketplace. Upwardly mobile households moved to newer homes elsewhere in the suburbs, and the area fell into a steep decline.[47] By 2000, Dundalk's population had fallen to 62,306, a drop of 27 percent.

By the 1990s, Baltimore County officials saw neighborhood decline as a significant countywide concern. In 1995, the county created the Office of Community Conservation and launched its Renaissance Development Initiative to revitalize aging suburban communities. Between 1995 and 2005 the county invested about $1 billion in declining neighborhoods, effectively redirecting resources from affluent parts of the county to struggling areas.[48] Dundalk was one of the neighborhoods targeted for funding. The county fostered the formation of the Dundalk Renaissance Corporation, a community development corporation that now has five full-time staff and an annual budget of about $1 million. From 2002 to 2007, the county invested some $70 million in housing rehabilitation, demolition of substandard housing, and other improvements in Dundalk.[49]

Like the two Fergusons, though, there are two Dundalks. From Turner Station's origins as a squatter settlement, by midcentury it had become a vital tight-knit African American community characterized by solid middle-class values and strong collective efficacy.[50] Solidly and prosperously working class thanks to jobs at the steel mill, it had its own school and movie theater, and a two thousand-seat ballpark. In many respects, Turner Station was a Bronzeville or

Black Bottom in miniature. With the end of Jim Crow, though, the neighborhood school closed, and more prosperous families began to move out. As the industrial jobs that sustained Turner Station began to disappear, the steelworkers' children sought opportunities elsewhere, and the neighborhood declined. Between 1970 and 2000, its population fell from 4,958 to 3,301. Turner Station was replicating the fate of hundreds of once-solid Black neighborhoods across the country.

Beginning in the 2000s, however, Turner Station benefited from the Baltimore County revitalization initiative. The Dundalk Renaissance Corporation chose Turner Station as one of its five target areas, making the area eligible for a variety of assistance programs. The county's Community Conservation Plan was created with strong community input, and a neighborhood organization, called the Turner Station Conservation Teams, was formed to implement the plan. The county built the Sollers Point Multi-Purpose Center, with an auditorium, meeting spaces for community events, a library, and the Turner Station Historical Center, and spent $25 million in federal funds to upgrade Lyon Homes, which had been built as war-worker housing in 1942. In 2011, the Henrietta Lacks Legacy Group was established to honor the memory of Turner Station's most famous resident,[51] supporting community activities and increased educational opportunities for neighborhood youths.

The investments in rebuilding Turner Station have had an effect. Population decline has slowed since 2000, while household incomes have kept pace with inflation over that period, unusual for older African American neighborhoods. The neighborhood has become somewhat more racially diverse, with the Black population down to 68 percent from 82 percent in 2000.[52] The cohesive working-class community of the mid-twentieth century, though, is long gone, and the area struggles with economic and social as well as environmental challenges. That said, Baltimore County's intervention and the energy of the community have in many respects stabilized the neighborhood, albeit at a low and still challenged level. While perhaps not a success story, it is a far better outcome than that of the many Black minicities and neighborhoods in north St. Louis County that are desperately struggling for survival.

The unified governance of Baltimore County, its growth boundary, and its significant investment in revitalizing inner-ring suburbs such as Dundalk and Turner Station have helped stabilize the county's neighborhoods. Racial transition in the county has been more gradual and has led to less concentrated poverty and segregation than the parallel racial transition in St. Louis's suburbs. This is not to suggest that Baltimore County lacks serious challenges of both poverty and racial inequity, including issues of policing and public education, where rapid racial transition and the growing numbers of students from poor families increased since 2000. The unified public institutions of Baltimore County, however, mean that affluent families cannot secede from the larger community and form their own enclaves. In addition, the financial, institutional, and organizational resources of a relatively affluent large and diverse political entity are available to all its residents, thus increasing the likelihood that the institutional network critical for good neighborhoods is widely available. In both white Dundalk and Black Turner Station, the county actively redirected resources toward stabilization and revitalization. Such an environment makes maintaining good neighborhoods easier than in the fragmented setting of St. Louis County. Good neighborhoods, however, we must acknowledge, only address structural racism and rising economic inequality at the margins.

Suburbs and Neighborhoods

Suburbs are neighborhoods too. And with most of America's population living in suburbs or thinking of their environments as suburban, suburbs matter greatly in the picture and prospects for the twenty-first-century neighborhood.[53] As we have stressed, however, suburbs vary as much as cities even within a single county, from the struggling streets of Turner Station to the horsey country in north Baltimore County. Still, a few tentative generalizations are in order.

Suburbs are, after all, suburban. Although the suburban matrix includes some higher-density communities, such as the nineteenth-century railroad suburbs, they are defined by lower population density, consistent separation of land uses, and settlement patterns that depend on access to the automobile for their economic and social functioning. To the extent, then, that the concept of neighborhood is dependent on face-to-face interaction and on the weak ties associated with informal and unplanned social interactions, one can reasonably argue that suburbanization itself strains the vitality of neighborhoods and that suburban sprawl at progressively lower and lower densities all but inevitably leads to fewer weak ties and more vulnerable neighborhoods.[54]

On the other hand, most suburbs are clearly viable somethings. Exurban communities of McMansions on two-, three-, or five-acre lots are not struggling, nor are exclusive inner suburbs such as Scarsdale in Westchester County north of New York City, where the median income is $250,000 and the least expensive house for sale early in 2021, on the border with significantly less tony New Rochelle, was listed at $1.4 million. Are they neighborhoods? While leaving that admittedly subjective question open, we suggest that in many respects they are less neighborhoods than communities of interest. They exist because they meet the needs of people who have a common interest in buying certain public or private goods such as open space, excellent schools, and public safety for themselves and have the means to pay for those goods or simply want to live among people of similarly high economic status. That may be unfair. Scarsdale, at least, thinks of itself as a neighborhood-oriented community, with clearly defined neighborhoods and neighborhood associations that organize events and advocate on behalf of neighborhood interests for such things as pedestrian crossings and playgrounds.[55] Scarsdale, however, is a railroad suburb, with a small but vital town center that may play a role in fostering community identity.

Neighborhoods play a less significant role in the lives of the affluent, especially the well-educated affluent with their geographically dispersed social networks. As one moves down the economic ladder, however, the role of neighborhoods becomes progressively more important. This is where the inherent qualities of the American suburb become increasingly problematic. A low-income Black resident in a suburban single-family subdivision or worse renting an apartment in a project tucked away such as Canfield Green without a car (or at best one car per family) in a place where a car is needed for access to jobs, shopping, and community connections may desperately need neighborhood ties but be unable to find them. The vitality of the postwar subdivisions described by Whyte and Beauregard was the product of intense organizational activity, which was in turn heavily dependent on a long-gone generation of stay-at-home wives and mothers.[56] It could not last and cannot be resuscitated in those neighborhoods today.

The problems of struggling neighborhoods and their residents are greatly exacerbated by the twofold patterns of governmental fragmentation and the absence of what might be called a communitarian safety net in the form of foundations, social service organizations, community development corporations, and the like. Governmental fragmentation drives an inequitable distribution of public goods and resources, allowing the wealthy residents of towns such as Atherton and Scarsdale to claim a disproportionate share and forcing the residents of towns such as Ferguson and Park Forest to do with less. Suburban tax revenues and services are a zero-sum proposition. Municipalities such as Park Forest find themselves in a vicious cycle, a feedback system of declining homeownership rates and home values along with rising vacancy, poverty, and tax rates. In the absence of a concerted effort at redistribution from the state or federal government, their opportunity space for building good neighborhoods is tightly constricted.

While recognizing the role that racism plays in suburban inequities and the difficult challenges this raises, it remains that this is an area where, far more than in other settings, public policy can play a meaningful role in redressing imbalances and fostering good neighborhoods. We would not argue that the people of Baltimore County are necessarily any less racist than those of St. Louis County, but it is clear that the institutional structure of Baltimore County has furthered an environment of significantly greater neighborhood-level equity along lines of race and economic class than in St. Louis County. This is a function not only of a unitary system of service delivery across racially and economically diverse neighborhoods but also of the capacity of a large government to engage in intentional activities to redistribute resources and stabilize or revive struggling neighborhoods.

In many respects the proposition———that the larger the governmental jurisdiction the healthier the neighborhoods———is ironic in that a longstanding American tradition prizes governments that are small and, at least nominally, close to the people. That tradition has value, but in much of today's suburbia it has become a vehicle for racial and economic segregation and for the hoarding of public resources, with pernicious effects for those on the wrong side of the metaphorical tracks.

THE THEORY AND PRACTICE OF NEIGHBORHOOD CHANGE

Neighborhoods are constantly changing——economically, socially, demographically, and physically. Neighborhood stability is largely an illusion. In recent decades, however, neighborhood change has become in many ways more challenging than ever. While neighborhood decline in the 1960s and 1970s was part and parcel of a larger process of urban decline, since the millennium neighborhood decline has been spreading even in the face of the economic revival of many American cities, accentuating spatial inequality. In this process of decline, the neighborhoods we have dubbed "good neighborhoods" are both particularly important and particularly under threat.

A proper understanding of neighborhood change is essential to address the threat to good neighborhoods. Unfortunately, much writing about neighborhoods not only fosters a poor understanding of the dynamics of change but also provides little or no guidance for practitioners. It often fosters the illusion that neighborhoods can be frozen in time or that neighborhood change is a zero-sum chronicle of invasion and succession, with predetermined plot lines, attributing too much significance to isolated variables, on the one hand, or large structural forces, on the other. The effect is either excessive pessimism in the face of structural forces or excessive optimism about the efficacy of isolated interventions.

In this book we have made the case for a different approach. First, to understand neighborhoods, we must grasp that they are always changing. And we must reconcile the idea of the good neighborhood, which arguably implies stability and reliability, with the reality of change. Instead of understanding neighborhoods as mechanical objects that can be assembled piece by piece from separate parts, we must comprehend neighborhoods holistically, as dynamic systems with powerful internal feedback systems. Neighborhood change reflects the impacts of three separate systems: economic, social, and governmental/institutional. While the triggers of change are usually forces that originate outside the neighborhood, such as migration and economic shocks, their impact is mediated by the perceptions of those acting within or on the neighborhood, such as residents, public officials, and bankers. Those perceptions determine the actions people take, which in turn drive the trajectory of neighborhood change. All of these factors are constantly subject to powerful feedback loops, which are in turn magnified by the local context, including the governmental and institutional environment.

In this conclusion, we summarize our understanding of the good neighborhood as well as why good neighborhoods matter and how they are threatened. We then turn to the central question: If, indeed, neighborhoods are important and yet under serious threat, what can be done? Can good neighborhoods be nurtured and preserved in the twenty-first-century city?

Why Good Neighborhoods Matter

At the beginning of this book, we offered a definition of the good neighborhood that, while unquantifiable and often difficult to apply in practice, is, we believe, clear and compelling. Good neighborhoods are places that meet our basic needs as individuals and as social beings. Those needs include safety, a decent quality of life, access to good public goods and services, and a modicum of community identity and commitment. They are places where one can aspire to a good life for one's children. Good neighborhoods do not need to meet an ideal standard, but they do need to be good enough to meet people's needs. As American society has become more divided and polarized, good neighborhoods have become increasingly important. Good neighborhoods nurture weak ties that link people across social divides, nurturing the bridging social capital that helps to reconcile the tension between individualism and community in American life. They help us to get along at the same time that they help us to get ahead.

It is important to understand what types of places we are (and are not) talking about. Good neighborhoods are places where people live in sufficient proximity to one another that residents encounter each other during their daily routines. This includes most suburban as well as urban communities, but we hesitate to call the very low-density exuburban areas—where all needs outside the home are accessed through the automobile—good neighborhoods. They may be good places that meet the needs of their residents, as they perceive them, but

they function differently than traditional neighborhoods, particularly with respect to the sorts of encounters that build weak ties. In many respects, they are
not so much neighborhoods as communities of interest where people choose
whom they will interact with. We are not physical determinists and offer no rules
for density or mixed land uses that enable a place to be considered a neighborhood. What matters is not physical configuration but instead whether opportunities exist for serendipitous encounters that build neighborly relations.

We want to be clear that we are not pining for a golden age of neighborhood
closeness and stability. Whatever may have been the dynamics of American
neighborhoods twenty, fifty, or a hundred years ago, that was then and this is
now. The ethnically and racially homogenous neighborhood of the first half of
the twentieth century, with its intense interactions and intimacy, is largely an
artifact of the past. Neighborly relations then were more all-encompassing and
more intimate. They were also more gendered and racialized. The United States
today is a different country with different norms and neighborhoods that serve
different social functions. Neighborhoods no longer occupy the central position
in people's lives that they once did.

The demise of the traditional ethnic neighborhood was anticipated even when
it was seemingly alive and well. In an influential 1938 essay, sociologist Louis
Wirth predicted that urban life would gradually erode the sentimental ties that he
associated with folk traditions. In the city of the future, he expected human relations to become more "impersonal, superficial, transitory, and segmental" and
neighborhoods, as traditionally understood, to disappear.[1] Wirth overstated his
case. But he was right that relationships rooted in neighborhood ties would become more superficial and transitory. While people are less mobile—in the sense
of how often they move—than they were during the decades immediately following World War II, they are also less psychologically tied to place. Kinship and
friendship networks are more geographically dispersed and are increasingly
linked not through direct personal contacts but instead through virtual relationships and social media. Widespread anecdotal evidence suggests that the
COVID-19 pandemic and the increased use of Zoom and similar technologies to
stay in contact with far-flung friends and family may have enhanced long-distance
relationships. As increased digital connectivity means that more relationships no
longer require proximity, neighborly relations inevitably become more marginal.

They may be more marginal, but neighborhood ties are as important as ever.
While Granovetter dismisses as "absent" ties such ties as the "'nodding' relationship between people living on the same street, or the 'tie' to the vendor from
whom one customarily buys a morning newspaper," we disagree.[2] These diffuse
neighborhood contacts are valuable. Casual encounters foster a degree of familiarity that enhances the experience of sharing a neighborhood space, facilitating

a degree of tolerance and peaceful coexistence even between people who have little else in common.[3] The "being together of strangers," as political scientist Iris Marion Young put it, is a valuable aspect of life in city neighborhoods.[4]

While neighborly relations today are less intense in many ways, ironically the lower intensity of the ties that good neighborhoods nurture are precisely what makes them so valuable in bridging the economic, racial, and religious divides that plague American society. In contrast to people's strong ties, which are usually closed to those outside a limited circle of kinship or friendship, the weak ties nurtured in good neighborhoods establish links across social, economic, and racial differences. While not intimate, these links enable us to share space and participate in shared projects with people who are different from us.

In short, although many Americans today see neighborhoods as playing only a marginal role in their lives, they remain important. Good neighborhoods not only benefit their residents but also benefit society as a whole. Good neighborhoods should be understood as a public good, something all people have a right to have, not something left to the vagaries of the private market. Ensuring an adequate supply of good neighborhoods should be a public responsibility. There are sound reasons to believe, however, that fewer good neighborhoods exist today than fifty or even twenty years ago, and many that do survive are under stress. The fact that good neighborhoods confer broad benefits on society makes it all the more troubling that in recent decades they seem to have increasingly become a luxury good that can only be purchased at great expense.

The Threat to Good Neighborhoods

In making his case for why some things should not be bought and sold, Harvard philosopher Michael Sandel discusses what he calls the "skyboxification" of American life, the construction of exclusive skyboxes for the wealthy high above the ordinary fans in the stands and, by extension, the tendency for those with the money to pay for luxury goods that separate them from those with fewer resources.[5] Skyboxification exemplifies a central threat to American neighborhoods. Affluent households are withdrawing from traditional neighborhoods, insulating themselves in increasingly exclusive communities. As they isolate themselves from others, the poor become increasingly trapped in areas of concentrated multigenerational poverty, the supply of good neighborhoods in the middle shrinks, and competition for the remaining supply drives up the cost of housing for middle-class families.

Up to a point, neighborhoods can be seen as commodities. Access to them is in large part determined by the market, and the choice of a neighborhood usually has an economic dimension. Skyboxification, however, accentuates their commodification, upsetting the balance between individual and communitarian motives that is the essence of a good neighborhood. In good neighborhoods, loyalty to place takes some of the edge off peculiarly pecuniary considerations. As pecuniary motivations come to dominate, the idea of a neighborhood as a shared public good that ties people together gradually unravels.

The commodification of neighborhoods is but one of a series of interwoven trends under way for the past fifty years that reduce the number of people able to enjoy the benefits of a good neighborhood. At one level, neighborhoods have been victims of large-scale economic and social forces beyond their control, most importantly the shrinkage of the middle class. The effect on neighborhoods of the hollowing out of the middle class has been exacerbated by increased economic sorting of households into separate neighborhoods. While the rise of single-person and nontraditional households has led to some new neighborhood formations, such as the millennial neighborhoods that have emerged in or near the downtowns of major cities, the decline in child-raising families has undermined the traditional single-family neighborhoods that make up the greater part of those cities, along with their postwar inner suburbs.

The economic polarization of America has been accompanied by growing social and cultural fragmentation. In Putnam and Garret's phrase, the United States has moved from a "we" to an "I" society, and the social and political fault lines in American society have become increasingly pronounced.[6] In a society dominated by increasingly narrow definitions of the community to which one belongs, which today may be an online or even imaginary community rather than a physical one, the meaning of neighborhood has diminished. And the physical neighborhood to which one belongs is increasingly stratified by not only income but also education, lifestyle preferences, and political affiliation.

In many ways, good neighborhoods have also been collateral damage in the over forty-year-long attack on government that began with Ronald Reagan's election in 1980. The significance of public goods to the vitality of neighborhoods has never been fully acknowledged. The good neighborhood rests on a substructure of public institutions and well-functioning public services, such as public schools, parks, and transit. The informal social controls of the urban neighborhood, depicted by Ehrenhalt and others, did not exist in a vacuum but were supported by that substructure.[7]

The weakening of the public sector and the privatization of American life are central to the story of the decline of good neighborhoods. In a society that devalues public goods and valorizes low taxes and a privatized lifestyle, economic sorting accentuates the decline of the public sphere. Those with resources seek out low-tax jurisdictions at the suburban fringe where they can pursue a privatized lifestyle and do not have to bear the burden, as it were, of paying taxes to support the public services needed by less economically self-sufficient households. Moreover, the political jurisdictions in which a growing share of the less affluent live find themselves with increasing demands for services but less ability to pay for them and with little assistance from the state or federal government. And while the affluent may be willing to pay for the private goods that substitute for what might be public goods elsewhere, their choices reduce the resource base for the public goods available to others.

One element that can never be left out of the American story of neighborhood decline is race. Following our conviction that neighborhood change is always about race but never only about race, it is important to understand how neighborhood racial dynamics have played out against the backdrop of privatization and the decline of public goods. Racial dynamics have often been perceived as a zero-sum proposition in which gains by African Americans lead inevitably to losses by whites. Heather McGhee offers a powerful illustration of this in the story of public swimming pools in American cities. Through the middle of the twentieth century, cities across the United States built grand resort-like public pools as a recreational amenity for their residents (figure 1). In some cities more modest pools were built for Black residents, while in others no facilities were provided for them.

The decision by St. Louis's public welfare director to open the city's pools to Black residents in 1949 led to violent attacks on Black people. According to a newspaper account the next day, "approximately 400 policemen and detectives were called out to restore order early last night as crowds of white youths attacked Negroes in Fairgrounds Park and in streets near the park."[8] The following day the mayor rescinded the decision, closing some pools and resegregating others.

When the Oak Park pool in Montgomery, Alabama, was integrated in 1959, the city council decided to close it down rather than let Blacks and whites share it. "Uncomprehending white children," McGhee writes, "cried as the city contractors poured cement into the pool, paved it over, and seeded it with grass that was green by the time summer came along again. To defy segregation, Montgomery would go on to close every single public park and padlock the doors of the community center. It even sold off the animals in the zoo. The entire park system closed for over a decade."[9] Across the country private swimming clubs and pools took the place of public pools. In 1950 there were only about 2,500 private in-ground swimming pools in the United States; by 2009 there were 5.2 million private pools.[10] The privatization of swimming pools is an apt metaphor for the way racism drained shared public resources from American cities.[11]

The belief that neighborhood racial change is a zero-sum proposition has played a significant role in the decline of many neighborhoods. In some respects

FIGURE 14.1. The segregated Mullanphy Pool in St. Louis in 1914

(Photograph courtesy of Missouri Historical Society)

that thinking is rooted in the invasion-succession model of neighborhood change going back to the Chicago School of Human Ecology. In contrast to seeing the neighborhood as a place shared by diverse populations linked by weak ties, the invasion-succession model frames neighborhood change as a kind of war of "us versus them," whether couched in racial, ethnic, economic, or cultural terms. The implicit premise is that inevitably one side, typically the invaders, wins, taking over the neighborhood and driving out longtime residents, in a contemporary parallel to the popular but misleading story of how modern humans displaced the Neanderthals. The same thinking and much the same presumption of inevitability color much of the thinking about gentrification today.

We are not naive enough to believe that neighborhood change is devoid of conflicts. There is an important difference, however, between seeing change as conflictual and seeing it as zero-sum. Neighborhood change is not inherently a zero-sum game, and neighborhood outcomes are not predetermined. As we discussed earlier, the widely accepted tipping point theory, which holds that if a neighborhood's Black population exceeds some modest level the neighborhood will inevitably become entirely Black, embodies fundamental demographic and economic fallacies. Similar presumptions applied to gentrification are equally fallacious. The many neighborhood pathways we have explored throughout this book show that a wide variety of outcomes are possible. Neighborhoods and their allies cannot choose the exogenous forces that affect them, but they retain considerable agency in how they respond to them. The ability to understand both the scope and the limitations of that agency, in addition to the nature of the processes by which it can be expressed, lies at the heart of the ability to craft local initiatives capable of stabilizing or reviving struggling neighborhoods and replacing zero-sum with positive-sum neighborhood change.

Can This Neighborhood Be Saved?[12]

Many of the forces that threaten strong neighborhoods are rooted in large-scale demographic, economic and technological trends over which local practitioners and often even national policymakers have little control. Yet, those trends are not the whole story. The fact that many European countries are part of the same global economy and share similar demographic and technological trends but have experienced far less decline in their traditional urban neighborhoods suggests that other factors play significant roles. Political institutions and public policies are an important part of that story.

American political institutions and public policies have promoted the outward movement of population that continues to drain the vitality of urban and inner-ring suburban neighborhoods. Racial exclusion during the early years of suburban expansion and exclusionary zoning since then, coupled with the American pattern of fragmented municipal government and public education, have exacerbated economic and racial segregation. Neighborhood inequality and neighborhood decline are baked into our state and local governance framework.

Many federal policies have created perverse incentives that, while not intentionally aimed at neighborhoods, have the effect of undermining good neighborhoods for ordinary Americans while subsidizing places for economically privileged households. What might be called "stealth" neighborhood policies, including federal sewer and water grants, the federal income tax deduction of mortgage interest and property taxes, and policies favoring road construction over public transit, have promoted the movement of population out of older urban neighborhoods and new construction over rehabilitation of older structures.[13] While the implicit bias in federal programs is less today than it was in the 1950s and 1960s, it is still present.

Although the federal government has few tools to directly address suburban exclusion and political fragmentation, any federal initiatives that would redress the underlying inequality of resources at both the individual and governmental levels would help preserve and strengthen good neighborhoods.[14] Converting the current program of housing vouchers into a housing allowance entitlement so that every eligible household could live in decent housing at an affordable rent would not only transform the lives of millions of struggling households but also, by reducing evictions and involuntary mobility, help stabilize poor neighborhoods.

Demand-side subsidies, however, do not directly address the central issue in this book: the inadequate supply of good places for people to live in. To foster good places, the United States has evolved a complex and distinctive community development system. Emerging during the urban crisis era and growing out of a variety of influences, including neighborhood organizing against urban renewal and highway construction, over time its evolution has reflected many of the same privatization trends that have undermined local public services. Community development corporations (CDCs) have become more professionalized, resulting in often impressive real estate development activity achieved at the cost of community building, neighborhood organizing, and advocacy. Tax credits have largely replaced direct public spending, fostering a development culture powerfully influenced by investor preferences and culminating in the problematic and irresponsible 2018 Opportunity Zone tax credit program.

The shift to what we call network governance, the decentralized and complex system of collaboration among public, private, and nonprofit actors, may have been a necessary political compromise in the context of the rise to power of free market political forces beginning in the 1980s, but it is not well designed to address unequal neighborhood outcomes. Despite the creation of an elaborate support system made up of national and local intermediaries, foundations, and trade organizations, the results are uneven. Cities and neighborhoods with well-connected, professionally run CDCs capable of fully utilizing the tools offered by the system of network governance see visible results, including tangible projects and sometimes overall neighborhood improvement. Many other communities are left out in the cold.[15]

Despite these limitations, community development practitioners are doing valuable work, grappling with the tensions that have bedeviled the movement since its inception. The central, arguably permanent, tension in community development is between helping people and helping places. If people move out of poverty they may move out of the neighborhood, leaving behind a poorer place. Conversely, initiatives that improve the place but lead to rising rents and house prices may force longtime residents out of the neighborhood, undermining community. CDCs and others can and do try to manage this tension, but it never fully disappears. The people-place tension reflects the larger societal tension between individualism and community, a tension that good neighborhoods help to bridge by furthering individual achievement while at the same time nurturing commitment to community.

A fundamental premise of neighborhood change, which all would-be community developers should acknowledge, is that change is unavoidable but no one direction of change is inevitable. Not only is it pointless to try to re-create a neighborhood as it was twenty or fifty years ago, it is equally pointless to expect it to remain the same ten years from now or perhaps even next year. With the possible exception of the most distressed areas and the most solidly prosperous areas, neighborhoods are constantly changing. That said, no neighborhood is subject to one particular form of change. This belief is at the heart of much of the conflict and misunderstanding in the neighborhood change discourse, from the neighborhood life cycle and tipping point theorists of the 1960s and 1970s to the more recent adherents of Neil Smith's rent gap theory of gentrification. Assumptions that a modest percentage of Black in-movers inevitably leads to an all-Black neighborhood and that a rent gap inevitably leads to gentrification are both demonstrably false. Neighborhood change is driven by complex feedback systems. Any theory that claims to predict neighborhood outcomes along linear paths of causation is of dubious value.

An unvoiced premise, while clearly fallacious, underpins these theories, namely that the potential demand from what might be called the "trigger population" is effectively infinite. Tipping point theory implicitly assumes that there is an infinite number of Black households trying to move into white neighborhoods. While it may have seemed that way to some panic-stricken observers in the 1960s, it is clearly not true. Once we acknowledge that the number of white in-movers into white neighborhoods substantially outnumbers Black in-movers, we recognize that tipping point theory cannot be generally true, a conclusion substantiated by decades of data. The same point is relevant to gentrification. For all potentially gentrifiable neighborhoods to actually gentrify, the supply of affluent, well-educated millennials would have to be if not literally infinite at least vastly larger than it actually is. As a result, outside of a handful of magnet cities such as Seattle, the number of neighborhoods that actually gentrify is far smaller than the number that theoretically could. Yet, the fear of gentrification is pervasive.

The truism that no category of demand for homes and neighborhoods is unlimited has another more troubling implication, which directly affects the possibility of reviving many struggling neighborhoods. As we discussed in chapter 7, the demographic character of the United States has changed markedly since most urban and inner-ring suburban neighborhoods were built. Household formation has slowed down, while the traditional child-rearing nuclear family that formed the core market for these neighborhoods is a diminishing part of the national household pool. For a neighborhood whose raison d'être was, in the old marketing phrase, "a good place to raise a family" and where the aggregate number of households raising families is no longer sufficient to replace those who have already raised children and are ready to move out, this is bad news. And so long as developers continue to build at the suburban edge and siphon off demand, the brunt of declining household formation will fall on older neighborhoods in central cities and inner-ring suburbs.

Restoring Good Neighborhoods: What Can Be Done?

The limited demand for traditional urban neighborhoods is not an argument for inaction. It is an argument, however, for caution and managing expectations and, even more so, for exploring whether there are alternative ways to understand the relationship between market demand and good neighborhoods. While the driving issue in gentrifying neighborhoods can be characterized as managing the market, in neighborhoods of concentrated poverty it is one of doing without the market, while in middle neighborhoods it is a matter of building the market. The contextual patterns associated with each of these three neighborhood strategy frameworks make it possible to produce a middle-level theory of neighborhood change, which in turn can enable practitioners working in similar, if not identical, contexts to learn from one another.

Managing the Market in Gentrifying Neighborhoods

The term "gentrification" is commonly applied to what might otherwise be called economically ascending neighborhoods, that is, neighborhoods experiencing an in-migration of more affluent households, raising household incomes and, by extension, home prices. As we discussed in chapter 10, the term has taken on a life of its own and become fraught with negative associations. Gentrification, in the context of neighborhood change, is a phenomenon rooted in the restructuring of urban economies and the changing preferences of young educated workers for urban living. Assuming that it is not reversed as a result of possible changes in the work world following the COVID-19 pandemic, an outcome we consider unlikely, gentrification will not disappear.

Given a certain level of demand on the part of affluent young urban in-migrants, their rising demand must go somewhere. Ironically, much of the opposition to gentrification focuses on blocking construction of new housing, although there is compelling evidence that increasing supply can help moderate increases in housing costs.[16] Moreover, many opponents appear to forget the basic point that neighborhoods are always changing. Assuming that the residents of neighborhood X are successful in preventing affluent young people from moving into their neighborhood, the results will be twofold: they will move somewhere else, with unknown effects, and neighborhood X will not remain the same and will change anyway, quite possibly in ways neither anticipated nor desired by its residents.

Gentrification, as we have stated, is simply one form of neighborhood change, following the model of feedback systems linking perceptions and behavior. As such, it can be managed. New housing can be built to channel demand, and affordable housing can be developed to provide long-term accommodation for lower-income households that might otherwise be displaced. Indeed, the market strength represented by gentrification can be harnessed to create affordable housing either through inclusionary zoning or with less negative effect on the market through neighborhood-level tax increment financing schemes that channel the additional tax revenues flowing from the increase in the market values into affordable housing. Such a scheme in Portland, Oregon, supported the construction of 2,200 affordable units in and around that city's gentrifying Pearl District.[17] Potential harms from rising property values can also be managed. Cook County, Illinois, and Philadelphia have adopted property tax measures that protect lower-income homeowners from being burdened by the higher taxes that might otherwise result from housing market appreciation in gentrifying areas.

Any effective strategy to manage gentrification requires the active engagement of the local government, but the political will needed to drive that engagement is not always present. In cities where gentrification is a widespread rather than isolated phenomenon, advocates' energies would be more productively employed in fighting for local government measures to manage gentrification than in trying to prevent it from taking place. In other cities, of which there are probably many more, practitioners should recognize that, as we have noted earlier, we do not live in an age of gentrification; we live in an age of simultaneous urban revival and urban decline. The greater threat to good neighborhoods comes not from reinvestment and repopulation but from disinvestment and depopulation.

We are not saying that there are no conflicts between newcomers and old-timers in gentrifying neighborhoods. Such conflicts are not a function of gentrification per se but are common to all forms of demographic, social, and economic neighborhood change. Moreover, the sense of cultural or social displacement that change triggers is real and needs to be addressed. While the gentrification discourse muddles our understanding of neighborhood change, the anxieties that it taps into are real and based on lived experience. As we suggest in chapter 10, gentrification is as much, if not more so, about power than it is about the specifics of neighborhood change. For good reason, residents of low-income neighborhoods feel that they are largely powerless to shape the future of their neighborhoods. Not long ago in the days of urban renewal and highway building, the coercive power of the state was used to displace hundreds of thousands of African American families. Based on both lived experience and the discourse that surrounds them today, they have good reason to doubt that any change will result in a socially and economically mixed neighborhood with a place for them.

As Andrew Volmert and his colleagues at the FrameWorks Institute, who have studied the neighborhood change discourse, write, "The idea of encouraging socioeconomically mixed neighborhoods is largely absent from public thinking: It is a 'cognitive hole' which, empty of a robust concept, is filled in with miscellaneous detritus of discourse," adding that "in the public definition of gentrification, affluent people are the 'winners' and low-income people are the 'losers.'"[18] It is crucial to move the gentrification discourse away from an inside-out version of the Chicago School's invasion-succession model looming over a city's neighborhoods. Such a discourse polarizes and paralyzes policy deliberations. While it is essential to frame the conversation about mixed-income neighborhoods so they are perceived as both desirable and possible and not only a matter of winners and losers, it is also important to remember that actually creating successful mixed-income neighborhoods is a far more complicated process requiring both political will and broad-based commitment. It also necessitates engaging with the residents of lower-income communities and ensuring that they have a strong say in the future of heir neighborhood.

Low-Income Neighborhoods: Succeeding Despite the Market

The rigid gentrification discourse has often made the work of local officials, CDCs, and others to improve concentrated poverty neighborhoods more difficult, with some arguing that any improvement to such neighborhoods—from new housing to community gardens and the removal of environmental nuisances—is a harbinger of gentrification.[19] That stance, while it might have some basis in isolated cases, is more often badly misplaced. Moreover, it offers no alternative way to approach the well-documented negative effects of living or growing up in concentrated poverty neighborhoods and the equally well-documented reality that the number of people living in such areas has increased significantly over the past decades. Under those circumstances, undermining people's efforts to create a better quality of life for themselves on such questionable grounds is far from harmless.

Creating a better quality of life does not necessarily mean creating a mixed-income neighborhood. In many cases, that goal may be out of reach. If the pool of middle-income families is not even large enough to replace the turnover in struggling middle neighborhoods, as is often the case, it is hard to make a credible case that enough such families can be found to turn concentrated poverty neighborhoods into mixed-income ones. And while some concentrated poverty neighborhoods may gentrify in hot market cities such as Seattle, that outcome is remote for most such neighborhoods elsewhere. This brings us to the question posed earlier: Is it possible to create good neighborhoods without building strong market demand?

We believe, first, that the answer is a qualified yes and, second, that whatever the risks and uncertainties, creating good neighborhoods is too important not to be pursued. Some would argue that it makes more sense to help the residents move to high-opportunity areas rather than attempt the difficult, if not impossible, effort to revitalize concentrated poverty neighborhoods. The problem with this line of thinking is that high-poverty neighborhoods do not go away; they are the housing of last resort for people at the bottom of the economic order. The likelihood that enough affordable housing will be available in high-opportunity areas in the foreseeable future to make a significant dent in the population of concentrated poverty neighborhoods is remote in the extreme. To abandon those neighborhoods, as the triage model of policymaking would suggest, is immoral. Moreover, smart interventions can make a difference even when market conditions remain unchanged. Improving a neighborhood does not change the poverty of the people who live there, but it can meaningfully alter the conditions under which they live. That in turn is likely to have a significant effect on their life chances and those of their children. As George Galster concluded, while "good neighborhoods alone will be *insufficient* to ending poverty and inequality, I hasten to add that they are necessary."[20]

Turning a concentrated poverty neighborhood into a good neighborhood requires a three-pronged strategy that can be justified on both moral grounds and the public benefits to society. First, it requires a decent level of public safety. The pattern of militarized overpolicing of low-income minority neighborhoods needs to change. Respectful policing, coordinated with mental health professionals, other social service providers, and neighborhood organizations, can improve safety in poor neighborhoods. Second, decent housing and the removal of environmentally noxious uses are essential. The tools needed to ensure that low-income families can live securely in environments that are not hazardous to their health and safety are well known and well understood. They include effective code enforcement, adequate funds for home repairs, an entitlement housing allowance, and the removal of environmental pollutants as well as remediation of contaminated brownfield sites. Moreover, the social benefits of such investments are equally widely recognized, whether it is reduced energy consumption or fewer hospital admissions through improved indoor air quality.[21] Finally, we need to invest in good schools in poor neighborhoods beginning with early childhood education, which itself has shown to have a significant social return on investment. Nobel Laureate James Heckman writes that "the rate of return for investment in quality early education for disadvantaged children is 7 to 10 percent per annum through better outcomes in education, health, sociability, economic productivity and reduced crime."[22]

All of these changes are feasible whatever the level of market demand a neighborhood commands. Low-income neighborhoods that have safe streets, decent housing, and good schools can nurture the kinds of weak ties that support neighborhood organizing efforts to build stronger social cohesion and collective efficacy. The realities of their physical setting dictates that such neighborhoods will not be manicured or elegant places. But they can be decent places to live that do not foster trauma or consign their residents to multigenerational poverty.

Building the Market in Middle Neighborhoods

In between gentrification and concentrated poverty lie middle neighborhoods. Despite the erosion of the middle class and the rise of economic sorting, they are home to 25–40 percent of the residents of most older cities and a larger share of the inner-ring suburban population. Middle neighborhoods fall into a blind spot, receiving far less attention from scholars, media, or policymakers than gentrifying neighborhoods and areas of concentrated poverty. Many federal policies are means-tested, restricting eligibility to either lower-income individuals or low-income communities. People appear to have assumed that middle neighborhoods will take care of themselves and have only belatedly begun to realize that these neighborhoods, particularly those predominantly populated by Black households, are in crisis today, threatening not only their survival as good neighborhoods but also the survival of the urban middle class as a counterweight to the polarization of American cities into rich and poor.

In chapter 11 we described both the importance of middle neighborhoods and the extent to which they are threatened. While we believe that middle neighborhoods generally are worth saving, we suggest that policymakers and practitioners need to focus particularly on Black middle neighborhoods, which are disproportionately at risk of decline compared to their largely white and racially mixed counterparts. Black middle neighborhoods were hammered by the foreclosure crisis and the Great Recession and are now suffering from the collapse of home buyer demand since then, triggered by the increasing suburbanization of Black home buyers over the past decade. Widespread, albeit anecdotal, reports suggest that many of those home buyers would move into older Black middle neighborhoods if those neighborhoods met their needs for reasonably safe communities with good schools and homes in move-in condition or requiring only modest repairs.

Middle neighborhoods are places where historically most middle-class households, broadly defined, have made their homes. The future of these neighborhoods, particularly Black middle neighborhoods, will depend on their ability to capture enough middle-class demand to replace aging homeowners and sustain high levels of homeownership. Much of that depends on the public sector providing these neighborhoods with the public goods they need: good schools, effective policing, and a well-maintained public realm of streets, sidewalks, and public open spaces. Beyond supportive public policies, it is equally a matter of building confidence not only that the neighborhood is a good neighborhood but also that it is likely to remain a good neighborhood rather than one on an inevitable downward trajectory.[23]

Sustaining homeownership is an important part of sustaining middle neighborhoods. Providing greater access to mortgages for Black home buyers is valuable, but it is important to recognize that the continued homeownership gap between Black and white households is as much if not more a function of the greater instability of Black homeownership tenure than a shortfall in the number of Black home buyers. Shorter homeownership spells reflect not only many households' economic instability and susceptibility to economic shocks but also the effects of more expensive mortgages, disproportionately higher property taxes, and frequently higher insurance costs. Efforts to increase mortgage access need to be paralleled by greater efforts to foster stable homeownership and reduce the risk that once becoming homeowners, families will lose their homes. As Donald Haurin and Stuart Rosenthal point out, "policies that lengthen existing ownership spells will also raise the ownership rate, even if the rate of attaining first-time . . . ownership is not affected."[24]

The survival of Black middle neighborhood as good neighborhoods is subject to the same demand constraints that we discussed earlier. The emergence of large numbers of Black middle neighborhoods in the 1960s and 1970s coincided with a unique period in history characterized by large-scale family formation and massive pent-up homeownership demand and accumulated savings by Black households previously barred from most homeownership opportunities. From 1960 to 1980 the number of Black homeowners in the United States more than doubled, with much if not most of that increase taking place in emerging Black middle neighborhoods. Today the pool of Black home buyers, even if it can be expanded to some extent, is smaller, while the alternatives available to them are far greater.

Thus, as long as the racialized nature of the home-buying market means that white buyers will rarely buy homes in Black neighborhoods, making those neighborhoods dependent on the smaller pool of Black buyers, many Black middle neighborhoods may be unable to generate enough demand to sustain or regain an adequate number of homeowners. What this suggests is a concerted strategy to encourage more non-Black households to buy in Black neighborhoods. Given the pervasive nature of racialized behavior, however, such an approach would be difficult to implement and might well provoke considerable opposition from some Black residents who would see such a strategy as tantamount to gentrification.

In the final analysis, the key to the survival of middle neighborhoods may be less dependent on concrete strategies and physical improvements than on building confidence in the neighborhood and its future. If residents have confidence in their neighborhood, landlords as well as homeowners, even those of modest means, will invest in their properties. Homeowners and perhaps some renters will become more engaged with their neighborhood, building community social capital. Without such confidence, property owners will invest progressively less in their properties and engage less with the community, withdrawing into the defensive private sphere of family and friends or leaving the neighborhood entirely. This is indeed what has been taking place in many middle neighborhoods over the past two decades. More than anything else, the central task of revival, to paraphrase Michael Schubert, is to build not just new structures but also a new neighborhood narrative, creating an environment in which people believe in the neighborhood and replace a vicious cycle of decline with a virtuous circle of renewal.[25]

Ultimately, neighborhood and community are a function of the meaning that people give them. Each individual action we take as part of a community reflects the meaning we give it, and even the most modest action, from helping a neighbor push her car out of a snowdrift to taking a plot in a community garden, helps build community. The number of different factors that can influence a neighborhood's trajectory, from the regional economy to whether the streetlights work, are innumerable, and they all matter. Yet in the final analysis, their effect is mediated through the perceptions of those who live in, work in, and otherwise influence the course of the neighborhood by their behavior. And through those perceptions we define our environment and give it meaning.

Notes

INTRODUCTION

1. For good historical background on Roosevelt and the New Deal program of re-settlement communities, see Paul K. Conkin, *Tomorrow a New World: The New Deal Community Program* (Ithaca, NY: Cornell University Press, 1959).

2. Perdita Buchan, *Utopia New Jersey: Travels in the Nearest Eden* (New Brunswick, NJ: Rivergate Books, 2003), 197.

3. *Oxford English Dictionary*, https://oed-com.ezproxy.umsl.edu/view/Entry/125931 ?redirectedFrom=neighborhood+#eid.

4. Emily Talen, *Neighborhood* (New York: Oxford University Press, 2019), 11.

5. Bert J. Lott, *The Neighborhoods of Augustan Rome* (Cambridge: Cambridge University Press, 2003).

6. In the parable, each blind man grasps a different part of the elephant. The one feeling the trunk says it is a snake, the one grasping a leg says it is a tree, and so on. Only by putting the different parts together does one realize, of course, that it is an elephant.

7. Talen, *Neighborhood*, 4, 247–54. We feel, however, that what she defines as "everyday" is actually deeply and, in the context of twenty-first-century society, unrealistically aspirational.

8. We thank Karen Black for alerting us to this point.

9. George Knight, quoted in "A Knight to Remember," *NeighborWorks Journal* 18, nos. 3–4 (2000): 27.

10. See Mark S. Granovetter, "The Strength of Weak Ties," *American Journal of Sociology* 78, no. 6 (1973): 1360–80. Reflecting its influence, according to Google Scholar (accessed November 9, 2022), this article has been cited more than sixty-seven thousand times.

11. Robert D. Putnam with Shaylyn Romney Garrett, *The Upswing: How America Came Together a Century Ago and How We Can Do It Again* (New York: Simon & Schuster, 2020), 12.

12. Bill Bishop, *The Big Sort: Why the Clustering of Like-Minded America Is Tearing Us Apart* (New York: Houghton Mifflin Harcourt, 2009).

13. The term is of fairly recent coinage and was first explored in depth in Paul Brophy, ed., *On the Edge: America's Middle Neighborhoods* (New York: American Assembly, 2016). Brophy, a veteran and widely respected figure in the field of community development, deserves recognition for originating and disseminating the idea.

14. Henry S. Webber, "Local Public Policy and Middle Neighborhoods," in *On the Edge: America's Middle Neighborhoods*, 165.

15. Jacob R. Brown and Ryan D. Enos, "The Measurement of Partisan Sorting for 180 Million Voters," *Nature Human Behavior* 5, no. 8 (2021): 998–1008, 1005.

16. Joe Cortright, "Less in Common," City Observatory, June 2015, http://cityobservatory .org/wp-content/uploads/2015/06/CityObservatory_Less_In_Common.pdf.

1. WHY GOOD NEIGHBORHOODS?

1. Suzanne Keller, *The Urban Neighborhood: A Sociological Perspective* (New York: Random House, 1968), 29.

2. An influencial source on the tension between ethnic/racial diversity and social capital and civic involvement is Robert Putnam, "*E Pluribus Unum*: Diversity and Community in the Twenty-First Century," *Scandinavian Political Studies* 30, no. 2 (2007): 137–74.

3. J. Eric Oliver, *The Paradoxes of Integration: Race, Neighborhood, and Civic Life in Multiethnic America* (Chicago: University of Chicago Press, 2010).

4. William H. Whyte, *The Organization Man* (New York: Simon & Schuster, 1956), 314.

5. Jane Jacobs, *The Death and Life of Great American Cities* (New York: Random House, 1961), 77–78. Putnam describes Jacobs as "one of the inventors" of the term "social capital." Robert Putnam, *Bowling Alone: The Collapse and Revival of American Community* (New York: Simon & Schuster, 2000), 308.

6. Robert D. Putnam and Shaylyn Romney Garrett, *The Upswing: How America Came Together a Century Ago and How We Can Do It Again* (New York: Simon & Schuster, 2020), 158.

7. Alexis de Tocqueville, *Democracy in America—Volume 2*, ed. Eduardo Nolla, trans. James T. Schleifer (Indianapolis: Liberty Fund, 2012 [1835]), chap. 8.

8. Nancy L. Rosenblum, *Good Neighbors: The Democracy of Everyday Life in America* (Princeton, NJ: Princeton University Press, 2016).

9. Robert J. Sampson, *Great American City: Chicago and the Enduring Neighborhood Effect* (Chicago: University of Chicago Press, 2012).

10. Rosenblum, *Good Neighbors*, 2.

11. The seminal essay on weak ties is Mark S. Granovetter, "The Strength of Weak Ties," *Social Networks* 78, no. 6 (1977): 1360–80.

12. Robert D. Putnam, "Social Capital Primer," n.d., http://robertdputnam.com /bowling-alone/social-capital-primer/ (brackets in the original).

13. Collective efficacy can also be an important concept for understanding behavior in institutions such as schools and workplaces.

14. See, among others, Robert J. Sampson, Stephen W. Raudenbush, and Felton Earls, "Neighborhoods and Violent Crime: A Multilevel Study of Collective Efficacy," *Science* 277, no. 5328 (1997): 918–24; and Jeffrey D. Morenoff, Robert J. Sampson, and Stephen W. Raudenbush, "Neighborhood Inequality, Collective Efficacy, and the Spatial Dynamics of Urban Violence," *Criminology* 39, no. 3 (2001): 517–58. From the publication of that 1997 essay to the present thousands of scholarly papers have been published on the theme of collective efficacy.

15. Putnam (*Bowling Alone*, 446) traces the origin of the distinction between "bridging" and "bonding" social capital to Ross Gittell and Avis Vidal, *Community Organizing: Building Social Capital as a Development Strategy* (Thousand Oaks, CA: Sage, 1998).

16. Herbert J. Gans, *The Urban Villagers: Group and Class in the Life of Italian-Americans* (New York: Free Press, 1962).

17. Granovetter, "The Strength of Weak Ties," 1373–76.

18. See, for example, Timothy J. Haney, "'Broken Windows' and Self-Esteem: Subjective Understandings of Neighborhood Poverty and Disorder," *Social Science Research* 36, no. 3 (2007): 968–94.

19. de Tocqueville, *Democracy in America*, 55.

20. See especially Raj Chetty et al., "The Opportunity Atlas: Mapping the Childhood Roots of Social Mobility," National Bureau of Economic Research, Working Paper 25147, 2018. The Equality of Opportunity Project has developed an interactive website that enables you to see how different neighborhoods affect the chance of escaping from poverty: "The Opportunity Atlas," https://www.opportunityatlas.org/.

21. For a synthesis of the research on how place impacts economic success, see Peter Dreier, John Mollenkopf, and Todd Swanstrom, *Place Matters: Metropolitics for the Twenty-First Century*, 3rd ed. (Lawrence: University Press of Kansas, 2014), 62–67. For a

synthesis of how neighborhood conditions affect children, see Robert Putnam, *Our Kids: The American Dream in Crisis* (New York: Simon & Schuster, 2015), chap. 6.

22. The Robert Wood Johnson Foundation has created an interactive website where one can compare life expectancy for individual census tracts with the county, state, and nation. "Life Expectancy: Could Where You Live Influence *How Long You Live*?," Robert Wood Johnson Foundation, n.d., https://www.rwjf.org/en/library/interactives/where youliveaffectshowlongyoulive.html.

23. Nancy E. Adler and Katherine Newman, "Socioeconomic Disparities in Health: Pathways and Policies," *Health Affairs* 21, no. 2 (2002): 60–76.

24. Mark Gapen et al., "Perceived Neighborhood Disorder, Community Cohesion, and PTSD Symptoms among Low-Income African Americans in an Urban Health Setting," *American Journal of Orthopsychiatry* 81, no. 1 (2011): 31.

25. Patrick Sharkey, *Uneasy Peace, The Great Crime Decline, the Renewal of City Life, and the Next War on Violence* (New York: Norton, 2018), 86–87.

26. Eric Klinenberg, *Heat Wave: A Social Autopsy of Disaster in Chicago* (Chicago: University of Chicago Press, 2002), 85, 126.

27. Annie E. Casey Foundation, "Children Living in High-Poverty, Low-Opportunity Neighborhoods," September 24, 2019, https://www.aecf.org/resources/children-living -in-high-poverty-low-opportunity-neighborhoods/. Concentrated poverty is defined here as census tracts with 30 percent or higher poverty rates.

28. Robert Sampson (*Great American City*, chap. 10) stresses the importance of the broader spatial context or a "neighborhood's neighbors."

29. It is actually a *series* of economic decisions rather than a single decision, as it is often characterized, because relatively few families who buy a home buy just one and instead buy two or more, often interrupted by spells of renting, during their lifetimes.

30. See, e.g., Allison Wainer and Jeffrey Zabel, "Homeownership and Wealth Accumulation for Low-Income Households," *Journal of Housing Economics* 47 (2020): 101624; Alan Mallach, "Building Sustainable Ownership: Rethinking Public Policy toward Lower-Income Homeownership," Discussion paper, Federal Reserve Bank of Philadelphia, 2011.

31. As reported in Valerie Wilson, "Racial Disparities in Income and Poverty Remain Largely Unchanged amid Strong Income Growth in 2019," Working Economics Blog, Economic Policy Institute, September 16, 2020, https://www.epi.org/blog/racial -disparities-in-income-and-poverty-remain-largely-unchanged-amid-strong-income -growth-in-2019/; and Emily Moss et al., "The Black-White Wealth Gap Left Black Households More Vulnerable," The Brookings Institution, December 8, 2020, https:// www.brookings.edu/blog/up-front/2020/12/08/the-black-white-wealth-gap-left-black -households-more-vulnerable/.

32. Dan Immergluck, Stephanie Earl, and Allison Powell, "Black Homebuying after the Crisis: Appreciation Patterns in Fifteen Large Metropolitan Areas," *City & Community* 18, no. 3 (2019): 983–1002.

33. For a summary of seven studies that examine the search method for finding jobs, see Katherine M. O'Regan, "The Effect of Social Networks and Concentrated Poverty on Black and Hispanic Youth Unemployment," *Annals of Regional Science* 27, no. 4 (1993): 329.

34. Granovetter, "The Strength of Weak Ties."

35. Ray Suarez, *The Old Neighborhood: What We Lost in the Great Suburban Migration* (New York: Free Press, 1999), 2, 19 and 12.

36. Maxwell King, *The Good Neighbor: The Life and Work of Fred Rogers* (New York: Abrams, 2018), 12.

37. Sean F. Reardon and Kendra Bischoff, "Growth in the Residential Segregation of Families by Income, 1970–2009," US 2010 Project, November 2011, https://s4.ad.brown .edu/projects/diversity/Data/Report/report111111.pdf.

38. Joseph Cortright and Dillon Mahmoudi, "Lost in Place: Why the Persistence and Spread of Concentrated Poverty—Not Gentrification—Is Our Biggest Urban Challenge," City Observatory, December 9, 2014.

39. Patrick Sharkey, *Stuck in Place: Urban Neighborhoods and the End of Progress toward Racial Equality* (Chicago: University of Chicago Press, 2013), 16.

40. Putnam and Garrett, *The Upswing*, 128. See also Putnam, *Bowling Alone*, 42.

41. Cortright, "Less in Common," City Observatory, September 6, 2015, https://cityobservatory.org/less-in-common/.

42. Neil Caren, "Big City, Big Turnout? Electoral Participation in American Cities," *Journal of Urban Affairs* 29, no. 1 (2007): 42. See also Sidney Verba, Kay Lehman Schlozman, and Henry E. Brady, *Voice and Equality: Civic Voluntarism and American Life* (Cambridge, MA: Harvard University Press, 1995), 72.

43. "Who Votes for Mayors?," http://www.whovotesformayor.org/, n.d. Notably, in every city the median age of actual voters was higher, usually much higher, than the median age of eligible voters.

44. Putnam, *Bowling Alone*, 35.

45. Putnam, 283.

46. For a review of the literature on internet use and social capital that supports a generally positive relationship, see Barbara Barbosa Neves, "Social Capital and Internet Use: The Irrelevant, the Bad, and the Good," *Sociology Compass* 7, no. 8 (2013): 599–611. See also Keith Hampton and Barry Wellman, "Neighboring in Netville: How the Internet Supports Community and Social Capital in a Wired Suburb," *City and Community* 2 no. 3 (2003): 277–311.

47. The classic work on "third places" is Ray Oldenburg, *The Great Good Place: Cafés, Coffee Shops, Bookstores, Bars, Hair Salons, and Other Hangouts at the Heart of a Community* (Boston: Da Capo, 1989).

48. Analysis by authors using 1960 US Census Bureau and 2019 5-Year American Community Survey data.

49. James A. Sweet and Larry L. Bumpass, *American Families and Households* (New York: Russell Sage Foundation, 1987), table 9.2; US Census Bureau, 2000 and 2010 decennial censuses; 2017 American Community Survey, all as reported in Alicia Vanorman and Linda R. Jacobsen, *U.S. Household Composition Shifts as the Population Grows Older: More Young Adults Live with Parents*, Population Reference Bureau, February 12, 2020.

50. As reported in Vanorman and Jacobsen, *U.S. Household Composition Shifts*.

51. Alan Ehrenhalt, *The Great Inversion and the Future of the American City* (New York: Vintage Books, 2012), 97.

52. Based on Current Population Survey data, as reported in Bureau of Labor Statistics, "Employment Characteristics of Families—2019," News release, April 20, 2022, US Department of Labor, https://www.bls.gov/news.release/pdf/famee.pdf.

53. Elizabeth Warren and Amelia Tyagi, *The Two-Income Trap: Why Middle-Class Parents Are Going Broke* (New York: Basic Books, 2003), 28.

54. Robert B. Reich, *The Work of Nations* (New York: Knopf, 1991).

55. There is a significant amount of literature on this point. See especially Justin P. Steil, Len Albright, Jacob S. Rugh, and Douglas S. Massey, "The Social Structure of Mortgage Discrimination," *Housing Studies* 33, no. 5 (2018): 759–76.

56. US Census and Home Mortgage Disclosure Act data (authors' files).

57. Alec MacGillis, "Amazon and the Breaking of Baltimore," *New York Times*, March 9, 2021.

58. Zillow, listing for 910 Savannah Street SE, https://www.zillow.com/homedetails/910-Savannah-St-SE-Washington-DC-20032/527250_zpid/.

59. Analysis by authors of Zillow House Value Index by metropolitan area for June 30, 2011, https://www.zillow.com/research/data/.

2. A DYNAMIC SYSTEMS APPROACH TO UNDERSTANDING NEIGHBORHOOD CHANGE

1. Bill Turque, "Are Cities Obsolete?" *Newsweek*, September 9, 1991.

2. Zachary Karabell, "The Golden Age of American Cities—And What's Really Behind It," *The Atlantic*, October 25, 2013.

3. Alan Ehrenhalt, *The Great Inversion and the Future of the American City* (New York: Knopf, 2012), 7.

4. Edward Luce, "The Future of the American City," *Financial Times*, June 7, 2013.

5. See Christoper Leinberger, "The Next Slum?," *The Atlantic*, March 2008, https://www.theatlantic.com/magazine/archive/2008/03/the-next-slum/306653/.

6. Our approach has many similarities to assemblage and complexity theory in geography. For an introduction to these theories and their application to neighborhood change in Leipzig, Germany, see Katrin Grossmann and Annegret Haase, "Neighborhood Change beyond Clear Storylines: What Can Assemblage and Complexity Theories Contribute to Understandings of Seemingly Paradoxical Neighborhood Development," *Urban Geography* 37, no. 5 (2016): 727–47.

7. William Faulkner, "Requiem for a Nun," in *Faulkner, Novels: 1942–1954*, ed. Joseph Bloom and Noel Park (New York: Library of America, 1994), 535.

8. Louis Wirth, "Urbanism as a Way of Life," *American Journal of Sociology* 44, no. 1 (1938): 1–24.

9. We agree with Kenneth Temkin and William Rohe, "Neighborhood Change and Urban Policy," *Journal of Planning Education and Research* 15, no. 3 (1996): 159–70, who call housing filtering a "reformulation of the invasion/succession approach" (160).

10. Robert W. Park, "The City as a Social Laboratory," in *Chicago: An Experiment in Social Research*, ed. T. V. Smith and Leonard D. White, 1–19 (New York: Greenwood, 1929).

11. Roderick D. McKenzie, "The Ecological Approach to the Study of the Human Community," in *The City*, ed. Robert E. Park and Ernest W. Burgess (Chicago: University of Chicago Press, 1925), 73.

12. Robert E. Park, "The City: Suggestions for the Investigation of Human Behavior in the Urban Environment," in *The City*, 54–56.

13. Park, "The City as a Social Laboratory," 14.

14. Park, 14.

15. Homer Hoyt, *The Structure and Growth of Residential Neighborhoods in American Cities* (Washington, DC: Federal Housing Administration, 1939), 116.

16. Frederick Babcock, *The Valuation of Real Estate* (New York: McGraw Hill, 1932), 75 (our emphasis).

17. Edgar M. Hoover and Raymond Vernon, *Anatomy of a Metropolis* (Cambridge, MA: Harvard University Press, 1959).

18. Real Estate Research Corporation, *The Dynamics of Neighborhood Change* (Washington, DC: US Department of Housing and Urban Development, 1975).

19. John T. Metzger, "Planned Abandonment: The Neighborhood Life-Cycle Theory and National Urban Policy," *Housing Policy Debate* 11, no. 1 (2000): 7–40.

20. Jane Jacobs, *The Death and Life of Great American Cities* (New York: Random House, 1961), 25, 264. In the latter part of the passage, Jacobs is quoting Dr. Warren Weaver from the 1958 Annual Report of the Rockefeller Foundation.

21. Jacobs, 171.

22. William F. Whyte, *Street Corner Society* (Chicago: University of Chicago Press, 1943); Herbert Gans, *The Urban Villagers: Group and Class in the Life of Italian-Americans* (New York: Free Press, 1962).

23. Andreis Skaburskis, "Filtering, City Change and the Supply of Low-Priced Housing in Canada," *Urban Studies* 43, no. 3 (2006): 533–58; C. Tsuriel Somerville and Cynthia Holmes. "Dynamics of the Affordable Housing Stock: Microdata Analysis of Filtering," *Journal of Housing Research* (2001): 115–40.

24. Rolf Goetze, *Understanding Neighborhood Change: The Role of Expectations in Urban Revitalization* (Cambridge, MA: Ballinger. 1979).

25. Roger S. Ahlbrandt Jr. and Paul C. Brophy, *Neighborhood Revitalization* (Lexington, MA: Lexington Books, 1975).

26. Temkin and Rohe, "Neighborhood Change and Urban Policy."

27. Whitney Airgood-Obrycki, "Are the Suburbs Losing Status?," Joint Center for Housing Studies of Harvard, February 4, 2019, https://www.jchs.harvard.edu/blog/are-the-suburbs-losing-status.

28. This is true of Manhattan but not of New York City as a whole.

29. Elizabeth Kneebone and Alan Berube, *Confronting Suburban Poverty in America* (Washington, DC: Brookings Institution Press, 2014).

30. There are a few examples of (somewhat) controlled experiments in housing policy. In the 1970s the federal government applied housing vouchers to different metropolitan areas to study their effects, and later the Moving to Opportunity demonstration program assigned households in a quasi-random manner to housing mobility programs and studied their effects. In neither case, however, were neighborhoods the focus of the experiment.

31. The strength of the association is measured in terms of statistical significance; for example, a statistical test may show that it is significant at the .05 level, meaning there is only a 5 percent likelihood that the association is due to chance or that a particular variable is responsible for X percent of the variation in another variable.

32. Angus Deaton, "Instruments of Development: Randomization in the Tropics, and the Search for the Elusive Keys for Economic Development," London: The Keynes Lecture, British Academy, October 9, 2008; quoted in Robert J. Sampson, *Great American City: Chicago and the Enduring Neighborhood Effect* (Chicago: University of Chicago Press, 2012), 378.

33. Sampson, *Great American City*, esp. 378–80.

34. Sampson, 379 (our emphasis).

35. Lin Cui and Randall Walsh, "Foreclosure, Vacancy and Crime," *Journal of Urban Economics* 87 (2015): 72–84.

36. For an introduction to systems dynamics modeling for the social sciences, see George P. Richardson, *Feedback Thought in Social Science and Systems Theory* (Philadelphia: University of Pennsylvania Press, 1999).

37. Chicago School scholars had a similarly sanguine attitude toward the most distressed areas, arguing that they performed a valuable function by accommodating those at the bottom of the labor market. Adverse neighborhood conditions motivate those households, as they move up in the labor market, to move out and assimilate into American society. Efforts to improve conditions in those areas would then create a kind of moral hazard, encouraging people to stay in areas that were ultimately dysfunctional. For an early critique of human ecology's reliance on the individualistic model of classical economics, see William Form, "The Place of Social Structure in the Determination of Land Use: Some Implications for a Theory of Urban Ecology," *Social Forces* 32, no. 4 (1954): 317–23.

38. George C. Galster, Roberto G. Quercia, and Alvaro Cortes, "Identifying Neighborhood Thresholds: An Empirical Exploration," *Housing Policy Debate* 11, no. 3 (2000): 701–32.

39. George Galster, *Making Our Neighborhood, Making Ourselves* (Chicago: University of Chicago Press, 2019).

40. George C. Galster, *Homeowners and Neighborhood Reinvestment* (Durham, NC: Duke University Press, 1987).

41. Michael Schubert, "Through a Glass Darkly: Trying to Make Sense of Neighborhood Revitalization," paper prepared for the Workshop on Neighborhood Change in Legacy Cities sponsored by the Center for Community Progress and the Lincoln Institute of Land Policy, 2016, 1.

42. For a discussion of the role of state government in driving or thwarting urban revitalization, see Alan Mallach, *From State Capitols to City Halls: Smarter State Policies for Stronger Cities* (Cambridge, MA: Lincoln Institute of Land Policy, 2022).

43. Robert K. Merton, "On Sociological Theories of the Middle Range," in *Social Theory and Social Structure* (New York: Free Press, 1968), 39.

3. THE RISE OF THE AMERICAN URBAN NEIGHBORHOOD, 1860–1950

1. Benjamin Looker, *A Nation of Neighborhoods: Imagining Cities, Communities and Democracy in Postwar America* (Chicago: University of Chicago Press, 2015).

2. Lance Freeman, *A Haven and a Hell: The Ghetto in Black America* (New York: Columbia University Press, 2019).

3. Patricia Mooney-Melvin, "Changing Contexts: Neighborhood Definition and Urban Organization," *American Quarterly* 37, no. 3 (1985): 357–67. One dissenter making a claim for the importance of neighborhoods in eighteenth-century America is Carl Abbott, whose research focused on New York City, arguably then as now an outlier on the American urban scene. See Carl Abbott, "The Neighborhoods of New York, 1760–1775," *New York History,* 55, no. 1 (1974): 35–54.

4. Charles Duff, *The North Atlantic Cities* (Liverpool: Bluecoat, 2019), 131.

5. By comparison, Manchester's population grew by six thousand per year from 1801 to 1851, a growth rate seen as explosive at the time.

6. The US West then being Ohio, Michigan, and other states east of and along the Mississippi River.

7. Harvey W. Zorbaugh, *The Gold Coast and the Slum: A Sociological Study of Chicago's Near North Side* (Chicago: University of Chicago Press, 1929), 38.

8. See Robert M. Fogelson, *Downtown: Its Rise and Fall, 1880–1950* (New Haven, CT: Yale University Press, 2001), 18–22.

9. "History," Llewellyn Park, n.d., http://llewellynpark.com/Page/13266~93841/History.

10. Jacob Riis, *How the Other Half Lives* (New York: Scribner, 1890), 21–22.

11. Oliver Zunz, *Detroit's Ethnic Neighborhoods at the End of the Nineteenth Century,* revised ed. (Ann Arbor: Center for Research on Social Organization, University of Michigan, 1978), 4.

12. Zorbaugh, *The Gold Coast and the Slum,* 4.

13. Zorbaugh, 34.

14. Riis, *How the Other Half Lives,* 64–65.

15. Anne Sinclair Holbrook, "Map Notes and Comments," in "Residents of Hull-House," *Hull-House Maps and Papers* (New York: Thomas Y. Crowell, 1895), 5.

16. Riis, *How the Other Half Lives,* 105.

17. Peter Krass, *Carnegie* (Hoboken, NJ: Wiley, 2002), quoted in "Andrew Carnegie: Pittsburgh Pirate" (book review), *The Economist,* January 30, 2003.

18. Riis, *How the Other Half Lives,* 125.

19. Florence Kelley, "The Sweating System" in *Hull-House Maps and Papers,* 38.

20. Kay Hymowitz, "Review of *City of Dreams: The 400-Year Epic History of Immigrant New York,* by Tyler Anbinder," *New York Times,* November 1, 2016.

21. Steve Chicon, "Buffalo in the '20s: The Polish Colony 'Out Broadway,'" *Buffalo News*, January 2, 2017.

22. Alzada P. Comstock, "Chicago Housing Conditions, VI: The Problem of the Negro." *American Journal of Sociology* 18 (1912): 241–57, cited in John R. Logan, Weiwei Zhang, and M. D. Chunyu, "Emergent Ghettos: Black Neighborhoods in New York and Chicago, 1880–1940," *American Journal of Sociology* 120, no. 4 (2015): 1055–94 (our emphasis).

23. "Baltimore Tries Drastic Plan of Race Segregation," *New York Times Sunday Magazine*, December 25, 1910.

24. Although the First Great Migration is generally described as taking place from 1910 to 1940, nearly all of the migration took place before the Great Depression. See Charles Hirschman and Elizabeth Mogford, "Immigration and the American Industrial Revolution from 1880 to 1920," *Social Science Research* 38, no. 4 (2009): 897–920.

25. St. Clair Drake and Horace A. Cayton, *Black Metropolis: A Study of Negro Life in a Northern City* (New York: Harcourt, Brace, 1945), 62.

26. Drake and Cayton, *Black Metropolis*, 17.

27. *Buchanan v. Warley* (245 U.S. 60).

28. Drake and Cayton, *Black Metropolis*, 82.

29. *Detroit Free Press*, June 3, 1917, quoted in Beth Tomkin Bates, *The Making of Black Detroit in the Age of Henry Ford* (Chapel Hill: University of North Carolina Press, 2012), 97.

30. During the 1920s, the nation's housing stock grew at a rate more than double that of the recent 2001–2005 housing bubble. Between 1923 and 1927 there were 4.36 million housing starts, representing an increase of 16.5 percent in the 1920 housing stock. By comparison, there were 9.18 million starts between 2001 and 2005, the peak years of the early twenty-first-century boom, representing an increase of 7.8 percent in the 2000 housing stock.

31. "When Chicago Buildings Were Built," *Chicago Tribune*, September 5, 2014, http://www.chicagotribune.com/news/chi-when-chicago-buildings-were-built-20140905 -htmlstory.html.

32. This is in dispute among urban historians. Based on the percentage of foreign-born residents, some scholars have argued that there was a significant increase in spatial integration of ethnic communities during this period. Eriksson and Ward, however, make the point, which we find compelling, that the reported fall in segregation is somewhat misleading. Immigrants lived near native-born people, but the latter were often the children of immigrants from the same source country. If researchers measure segregation from the third-plus generation (i.e., US-born to US-born parents), then the level of segregation was higher. Katherine Eriksson and Zachary A. Ward, "The Ethnic Segregation of Immigrants in the United States from 1850 to 1940," Working paper 24764, National Bureau of Economic Research, June 2018.

33. Beth S. Wenger, *New York Jews and the Great Depression* (Syracuse, NY: Syracuse University Press, 1999), 203.

34. Looker, *Nation of Neighborhoods*, 23.

35. Jack Smith "Give Me Shelter: L.A.'s Post-WWII Housing Shortage Foreshadowed the Crisis of the 1980s," *Los Angeles Times*, September 17, 1989, https://www.latimes .com/archives/la-xpm-1989-09-17-tm-78-story.html.

36. Becky Nicolaides and Andrew Wiese. "Suburbanization in the United States after 1945," American History, Oxford Research Encyclopedias, April 26, 2017, http:// oxfordre.com/americanhistory/view/10.1093/acrefore/9780199329175.001.0001 /acrefore-9780199329175-e-64.

37. Ray Suarez, *The Old Neighborhood: What We Lost in the Great Suburban Migration 1966–1999* (New York: Free Press, 1999), 3.

4. THE AMERICAN URBAN NEIGHBORHOOD UNDER SIEGE, 1950–1990

1. Ray Suarez, *The Old Neighborhood: What We Lost in the Great Suburban Migration, 1966–1999* (New York: Free Press, 1999), 4.

2. Leah Boustan, "The Culprits behind White Flight," *New York Times*, May 15, 2017, https://www.nytimes.com/2017/05/15/opinion/white-flight.html.

3. One factor affecting the magnitude of each city's urban exodus was whether there was still room to build new houses inside the city limits. Many cities, including Chicago, Philadelphia, and Detroit, still had vacant land within their boundaries. Thousands of new homes, mostly the row houses Philadelphians knew well, were built in the 1950s in the part of Philadelphia known as the Far Northeast. Many white families who might otherwise have bought in the surrounding suburbs moved there.

4. William H. Whyte, *The Organization Man* (New York: Simon & Schuster, 1956), 331.

5. Alan Ehrenhalt, *The Lost City: The Forgotten Virtues of Community in America* (New York: Basic Books, 1996), 214.

6. Our account draws from Kenneth T. Jackson, *Crabgrass Frontier: The Suburbanization of the United States* (New York: Oxford University Press, 1985), chap. 11.

7. Homer Hoyt, "The Future Trend of Land Values," *Appraisal Journal* 12, no. 2 (1944): 121–26.

8. Homer Hoyt, *The Structure and Growth of Residential Neighborhoods in American Cities* (Washington, DC: US Government Printing Office, 1939), 62.

9. Jackson, *Crabgrass Frontier*, 213.

10. Jackson, 215.

11. For an insightful synthesis of how the changes of the era were perceived and presented, see Robert A. Beauregard, *Voices of Decline: The Postwar Fate of US Cities* (Cambridge, MA: Blackwell, 1993), esp. 109–31.

12. Beauregard, 94.

13. Joseph D. McGoldrick, "The Superblock Instead of Slums," *New York Times Magazine* (November 19, 1944), 54. See also Alan Mallach, *The Divided City: Poverty and Prosperity in Urban America* (Washington, DC: Island Press, 2018), 81.

14. Wendell E. Pritchett, *Robert Clifton Weaver and the American City: The Life and Times of an Urban Reformer* (Chicago: University of Chicago Press, 2008), 250–51.

15. Steve Conn, *Americans against the City: Anti-Urbanism in the Twentieth Century* (New York: Oxford University Press, 2014), 159.

16. Anthony Downs, *Urban Problems and Prospects* (Chicago: Markham, 1970), 204–5.

17. Interview on WNDT-TV, New York City, May 28, 1963, cited in W. B. Dickinson Jr., "Urban Renewal under Fire," *Editorial Research Reports*, Vol. 2 (Washington, DC: CQ Press, 1963).

18. Martin Anderson, *The Federal Bulldozer: A Critical Analysis of Urban Renewal, 1949–1962* (Cambridge, MA: MIT Press, 1964), 65 (citing federal statistics). The statistics that were published by the federal Urban Renewal Agency conflated Black and Puerto Rican households into a single "non-white" category. Outside a handful of cities, most notably New York City, however, the great majority of these households were African American.

19. Anderson, *The Federal Bulldozer*, 53 estimates that as of the end of 1962, 427,000 families were impacted by urban renewal, including 260,000 living in approved urban renewal areas (counted by the federal government), and another 167,000 in areas that were in the planning stages as of 1962. Since relatively few new urban renewal projects went into planning after 1962 until the program's demise in 1974, 500,000 families would appear to be a reasonable outside estimate.

20. "Urban Renewal Project Characteristics, June 30, 1966" (Washington, DC: US Department of Housing & Urban Development), 28–29; from University of Richmond, Digital Scholarship Lab, "Renewing Inequality: Urban Renewal, Family Displacements, and Race 1950–1966," https://dsl.richmond.edu/panorama/renewal/#view=0/0/1&viz =cartogram.

21. For a vivid first-person account of what life was like in Mill Creek Valley before urban renewal, see Vivian Gibson, *The Last Children of Mill Creek* (Lakewood, OH: Belt Publishing, 2020).

22. The recent construction of Citypark, a state-of-the-art major league soccer stadium, has added some vitality to the area.

23. John Williamson, *Federal Aid to Roads and Highways since the 18th Century: A Legislative History* (Washington, DC: Congressional Research Service, 2012), 12.

24. Katherine M. Johnson, "Captain Blake versus the Highwaymen: Or, How San Francisco Won the Freeway Revolt," *Journal of Planning History* 8, no. 1 (2009): 60.

25. Similarly, with equally devastating effect on many cities' fabric and quality of life, urban parks and waterfronts also became "targets of opportunity" for highway construction.

26. Johnson, "Captain Blake," 74.

27. A survey conducted by the federal Department of Transportation in 1967 and 1968 identified 123 separate freeway revolts. Raymond A. Mohl, "The Interstates and the Cities: Highways, Housing and the Freeway Revolt" (Washington, DC: Poverty & Race Research Action Council, 2002), https://www.prrac.org/pdf/mohl.pdf.

28. Robert Fisher, *Let the People Decide: Neighborhood Organizing in America*, updated ed. (New York: Twayne, 1994), 99.

29. Quoted in "History," Bedford Stuyvesant Restoration Corporation, n.d., https:// restorationplaza.org/history/.

30. Sara E. Stoutland, "Community Development Corporations: Mission, Strategy and Accomplishments," in *Urban Problems and Community Development*, ed. Ronald F. Ferguson and William T. Dickens (Washington, DC: Brookings Institution Press, 1999), 198.

31. See Benjamin Looker, *A Nation of Neighborhoods: Imagining Cities, Communities and Democracy in Postwar America* (Chicago: University of Chicago Press, 2015), 259–89.

32. National Commission on Neighborhoods, *People Building Neighborhoods: Final Report to the President and the Congress of the United States* (Washington, DC: US Government Printing Office, 1979), vii.

33. Looker, *A Nation of Neighborhoods*, 332.

34. Leah Platt Boustan, "Was Postwar Suburbanization 'White Flight'? Evidence from the Black Migration," *Quarterly Journal of Economics* 125, no. 1 (2010): 417.

35. See Ann B. Shlay and Gordon Whitman, "Research for Democracy: Linking Community Organizing and Research to Leverage Blight Policy," *City & Community* 5, no. 2 (2006): 162; and Econsult Corporation, Penn Institute for Urban Research, and May 8 Consulting, *Vacant Land Management in Philadelphia: The Costs of the Current System and the Need for Reform*, report prepared for Philadelphia Redevelopment Authority and Philadelphia Association of Community Development Corporations, 2010.

36. Charles C. Branas, David Rubin, and Wensheng Guo, "Vacant Properties and Violence in Neighborhoods," *ISRN Public Health* (2012): 1–23.

37. Erwin de Leon and Joseph Schilling, *Urban Blight and Public Health: Addressing the Impact of Substandard Housing, Abandoned Buildings, and Vacant Lots* (Washington, DC: Urban Institute, 2017), 11.

38. de Leon and Schilling, 12.

39. Philip Brownstein speech, October 23, 1967, quoted in Sarah Rachel Siegel, "'By the People Most Affected': Model Cities, Citizen Control, and the Broken Promises of Urban Renewal" (PhD diss., Washington University in St. Louis, 2019), 58–59.

40. John McClaughry, "The Troubled Dream: The Life and Times of Section 235 of the National Housing Act," *Loyola University Law Journal* 6 (1975): 1.

41. Steven Arthur Waldhorn and Judith Lynch Waldhorn, "Model Cities: Liberal Myths and Federal Interventionist Programs," *Urban Law Annual* (1972): 48.

42. Susanne Schindler, "Model Cities Redux," Urban Omnibus, October 26, 2016, https://urbanomnibus.net/2016/10/model-cities-redux/.

43. Office of Community Development, Evaluation Division, *The Model Cities Program: A Comparative Analysis of City Response Patterns and Their Relation to Future Urban Policy* (Washington, DC: US Department of Housing and Urban Development, 1973), 80.

44. Jody H. Schechter, "An Empirical Evaluation of the Model Cities Program" (BA thesis, University of Michigan, 2011).

45. The earliest work found in a Google search of over 100 works with the words "neighborhood dynamics" in the title was from 1974. Of 107 works searched, nearly two-thirds appeared after 2000.

46. Neal M. Cohen, "The Reagan Administration's Urban Policy." *Town Planning Review* 54, no. 3 (1983): 304.

47. Beauregard, *Voices of Decline*, 247.

48. Paul E. Peterson, *City Limits* (Chicago: University of Chicago Press, 1981), 20 and 30.

49. Patrick Sharkey, *Uneasy Peace: The Great Crime Decline, the Renewal of City Life, and the Next War on Violence* (New York: Norton, 2018), 15.

50. Ta-Nehisi Coates, *A Father, Two Sons and an Unlikely Road to Manhood* (New York: Random House, 2008), quoted in Sharkey, *Uneasy Peace*, 18.

51. Sharkey, *Uneasy Peace*, 20.

52. As we write, violent crime is increasing across major American cities, though for the most part crime rates are still below where they were at their peak in the 1990s. It remains to be seen whether this increase in crime is a temporary result of COVID-19 and its attendant economic damage or whether it reflects a longer-term change.

53. Assessments of the number of CDCs that exist vary widely depending on the source and the definition used. The number cited in text, from Stoutland ("Community Development Corporations," 198, excludes nonurban organizations as well as those that are not explicitly neighborhood-based. A more universal definition, used in a survey by the now-defunct National Congress for Community Economic Development, came up with a number more than three times as great. Many of these organizations were exiguous in the extreme.

54. The tools-based approach to public policies used in this chapter is based on Lester M. Salamon, ed., *The Tools of Government: A Guide to the New Governance* (New York: Oxford University Press, 2002).

55. Enterprise Community Partners, "How It All Started," https://www.enterprise community.org/about/founding-story#:~:text=Jim%20and%20Patty%20Rouse%2C %20inspired,up%20and%20out%20of%20poverty.

56. Robert Kuttner, "Ethnic Renewal," *New York Times*, May 9, 1976.

57. The US Department of Housing and Urban Development maintains a national data base on LIHTC projects: "Low-Income Housing Tax Credit (LIHTC)," https:// www.huduser.gov/portal/datasets/lihtc.html.

58. While this is the statutory minimum, in practice most credits are awarded subject to commitments for much longer periods of low-income occupancy, generally at least thirty years and often much longer.

59. Chester Hartman, "Debating the Low-Income Housing Tax Credit: Feeding the Sparrows by Feeding the Horses," *Shelterforce*, January–February 1992, 12.

60. Jesse Drucker and Eric Lipton, "How a Trump Tax Break to Help Poor Communities Became a Windfall for the Rich," *New York Times*, August 31, 2019.

61. Dees Stribling, "A Yacht Club, Michael Milken and Tesla: Meet 10 of the Nation's Swankiest Opportunity Zones," Bisnow, August 24, 2020, https://www.bisnow.com/national/news/opportunity-zones/10-upscale-opportunity-zones-105712.

62. Center for Community Change, *Opening the Door to Homes for All: The 2016 Housing Trust Fund Report* (Washington, DC: Center for Community Change, 2016), 3, 6, and 17.

63. David Erickson, *The Housing Policy Revolution: Networks and Neighborhoods* (Washington, DC: Urban Institute Press, 2009), 172–73.

64. Erickson, 127.

65. On flexible specialization, see Michael J. Piore and Charles F. Sabel, *The New Industrial Divide: Possibilities for Prosperity* (New York: Basic Books, 1984).

66. An early analysis of the importance of network governance in community development systems is Langley C. Keyes et al., "Networks and Nonprofits: Opportunities and Challenges in an Era of Federal Devolution," *Housing Policy Debate* 7, no. 2 (1996): 201–29. Our treatment also draws on Erickson, *The Housing Policy Revolution*.

5. THE POLARIZATION OF THE AMERICAN NEIGHBORHOOD, 1990–2020

1. For a more extensive treatment of the material discussed in the first part of this chapter, see Alan Mallach, *The Divided City: Poverty and Prosperity in Urban America* (Washington, DC: Island Press, 2018), particularly chaps. 2 and 3.

2. The earliest use of this term that we have been able to discover is in Elizabeth Chang et al., "The March of the Millennials: As Young People Flood into the City, the Only Constant Is Change," *Washington Post*, October 18, 2013, https://www.washingtonpost.com/sf/style/2013/10/18/march-of-the-millennials/.

3. Thomas E. Bier, *Housing Dynamics in Northeast Ohio: Setting the Stage for Resurgence* (Cleveland, OH: MSL Academic Endeavors eBooks, 2017), 28, http://engagedscholarship.csuohio.edu/msl_ae_ebooks/4.

4. William H. Whyte, *The Organization Man* (New York: Simon & Schuster, 1956), esp. pages 310–29. For a more detailed description of conditions in Park Forest today, see Mallach, *The Divided City*, 162–65.

5. John Ostenburg, "Confronting Suburban Poverty in Park Forest, Illinois," ConfrontingSuburbanPoverty,blogpost,February5,2014,http://confrontingsuburbanpoverty.org/2014/02confronting-suburbaqn-poverty-in-park-forest-illinois/ (site discontinued).

6. Wava G. Haney and Eric S. Knowles, "Perception of Neighborhoods by City and Suburban Residents," *Human Ecology* 6, no. 2 (1978): 201–14.

7. Jeanne R. Lowe, *Cities in a Race with Time* (New York: Random House, 1967).

8. See "Neighborhoods: Highlighted Programs & Upcoming Events," Garland, Texas, https://www.garlandtx.gov/2107/Neighborhoods.

9. "American Neighborhood Change," University of Minnesota, n.d., https://www.law.umn.edu/institute-metropolitan-opportunity/gentrification.

10. Joe Cortright, "Lost in Place," City Observatory, September 12, 2014, http://cityobservatory.org/lost-in-place/ (our emphasis).

11. Defined here as those with a median household income between 80 percent and 120 percent of the citywide median.

12. A thoughtful summary of the problems of the subprime market, written as the crisis was unfolding, is Randall Dodd and Paul Mills, "Outbreak: U.S. Subprime Conta-

gion," *Finance and Development* 45, no. 2 (June 2008), https://www.imf.org/external
/pubs/ft/fandd/2008/06/dodd.htm#author.

13. Richard Greenberg and Chris Hansen, "If You Had a Pulse, We Gave You a
Loan," NBC News, March 22, 2009, https://www.nbcnews.com/id/wbna29827248.

14. Alan Mallach, "Lessons from Las Vegas: Housing Markets, Neighborhoods, and
Distressed Single-Family Property Investors," *Housing Policy Debate* 24, no. 4 (2014):
769–801.

15. The Reinvestment Fund, *NIC Reports Nationwide Summary*, Department of
Housing and Urban Development. March 21, 2014, https://www.hudexchange.info
/resources/documents/NICReportsNationwideSummary.pdf.

This study, which compared areas that had received concentrated Neighborhood
Stabilization Program investment with control areas in the same city or county, found
that the outcomes of the subject areas compared to the controls were not different from
would be expected in a random draw. A more ambitious study funded by HUD also
found no statistically significant relationship between Neighborhood Stabilization Program investment and neighborhood outcomes. Jonathan Spader et al., *The Evaluation
of the Neighborhood Stabilization Program*, HUD User, 2015, https://www.huduser.gov
/publications/pdf/neighborhood_stabilization.pdf.

16. The data is not for these neighborhoods, which have imprecise boundaries, as a
whole, but in each case are for a single census tract in each neighborhood, as follows:
Lincoln Park (Tract 713), Wicker Park (Tract 2415), Chatham (Tract 4402.02), and
South Shore (Tract 4304).

17. Among the many studies documenting these patterns, see Gregory D. Squires,
Derek S. Hyra, and Robert N. Renner, "Metropolitan Segregation and the Subprime
Lending Crisis," *Housing Policy Debate* 23, no. 1 (2013): 117–98; and Jacob W. Faber,
"Racial Dynamics of Subprime Mortgage Lending at the Peak," *Housing Policy Debate*
23, no. 2 (2013): 328–49.

18. Quoted in Michael Powell, "Banks Accused of Pushing Mortgage Deals on
Blacks," *New York Times*, June 6, 2009, https://www.nytimes.com/2009/06/07/us/07balti
more.html.

19. Alan Mallach, "Over the Edge: Trajectories of African-American Middle Neighborhoods in St. Louis since 2000," *Journal of Urban Affairs* 42, no. 7 (2020): 1063–85.

20. US Bureau of the Census, "Week 19 Household Pulse Survey: November 11–23,
2020," https://www.census.gov/data/tables/2020/demo/hhp/hhp19.html, Housing Table 1B.
This includes only those tenants who reported and who pay cash rent.

21. US Bureau of the Census, Housing Table 1A.

22. Leland D. Cran et al., "Business Exit during the COVID-19 Pandemic: Non-
Traditional Measures in Historical Context," Federal Reserve Board, 2021, https://www
.federalreserve.gov/econres/feds/files/2020089r1pap.pdf.

23. Nicholas Nissim Taleb, *The Black Swan: The Impact of the Highly Improbable*
(New York, Random House, 2007).

24. See Sean F. Reardon and Kendra Bischoff, "Income Inequality and Income Segregation," *American Journal of Sociology* 116, no. 4 (2011): 1092–153; and Kendra
Bischoff and Sean F. Reardon, "Residential Segregation by Income, 1970–2009," in *Diversity and Disparities: America Enters a New Century*, ed. John Logan, 208–34 (New
York: Russell Sage, 2014).

6. NEIGHBORHOODS AS MARKETS

1. "Market (Economics)," Wikipedia, https://en.wikipedia.org/wiki/Market
_(economics).

2. Zillow.com, accessed January 5, 2020.

3. The other major government-insured mortgage program is through the Veterans Administration. These loans were a major part of the mortgage market during the years following World War II but are far fewer today.

4. Continued racial steering on Long Island, New York, was documented in an investigation by *Newsday*, the regional newspaper. See Ann Choi, Bill Dedman, Keith Herbert, and Olivia Winslow, "Long Island Divided," *Newsday,* November 17, 2019.

5. Andre M. Perry, Jonathan Rothwell, and David Harshbarger, *The Devaluation of Assets in Black Neighborhoods: The Case of Residential Property* (Washington, DC: Brookings Institution, 2018). See also Junia Howell and Elizabeth Korver-Glenn, "The Increasing Effect of Neighborhood Racial Composition on Housing Values, 1980–2015," *Social Problems* 68, no. 4 (2021): 1051–71.

6. We put the word "true" in quotation mark to reflect the fact that in contrast to the widely held notion that every property has a precise true market value, the process by which market value is determined is highly subjective and value-laden, particularly with respect to properties and neighborhoods that vary from standard suburban models.

7. Nathaniel Baum-Snow, "Did Highways Cause Suburbanization?," *Quarterly Journal of Economics* 122, no. 2 (2007): 775–805. In many respects, the mass suburbanization of the 1950s and 1960s was the continuation of patterns that originated in the 1920s, which were interrupted by the Great Depression and World War II, only to resume with greater intensity after the war. See Kenneth Jackson, *Crabgrass Frontier: The Suburbanization of the United States* (New York: Oxford University Press, 1985), and, in particular, Robert A. Beauregard, "Federal Policy and Postwar Urban Decline: A Case of Government Complicity?," *Housing Policy Debate* 12, no. 1 (2001): 129–51.

8. An excellent overview of the political, economic, and social dynamics of this period is Robert Beauregard, *When America Became Suburban* (Minneapolis: University of Minnesota Press, 2006). While the full history of the urban renewal program remains to be written, Jon C. Teaford, "Urban Renewal and Its Aftermath," *Housing Policy Debate*, 11, no. 2 (2000): 443–65, is an excellent summary. A good summary of the role of the FHA appears in Jackson, *Crabgrass Frontier*, 203–18. See also Richard Rothstein, *The Color of Law: A Forgotten History of How Our Government Segregated America* (New York: Norton, 2017); and Alan Mallach, *The Divided City: Poverty and Prosperity in Urban America* (Washington, DC: Island Press, 2018).

9. While Black home buyers express racial preferences as well, their willingness to move into mixed and predominantly white neighborhoods is significantly greater than the converse.

10. For further information, see "Segment Details," Claritas, n.d., https://claritas360 .claritas.com/mybestsegments/#segDetails.

11. For a discussion of these factors, see Bill Bishop, *The Big Sort: Why the Clustering of Like-Minded America Is Tearing Us Apart* (Boston: Houghton Mifflin Harcourt, 2008).

12. The estimate of a median tenure of twenty-one months for renters is based on our analysis of the 2019 American Community Survey, which found that 59 percent of all renters in Indianapolis had moved to their present units from the beginning of 2017 through April 2019, so the median tenure is well under two years.

13. This thesis was first proposed in Andrew J. Oswald, *A Conjecture on the Explanation for High Unemployment in the Industrialized Nations: Part I* (Warwick Economic Research Papers, No. 475, 1996), and has been the subject of an extensive literature in both support of and opposition to what has come to be known as the Oswald hypothesis.

14. Being accepted by a landlord, while not extensively addressed in the literature, may be a significant and growing constraint on choice, particularly among tenants with prior problems of rent paying and eviction or threatened eviction. The use of credit reports, eviction filing records (even if the filing did not lead to eviction), and similar in-

formation for tenant selection appears to be increasing. See Kristin Ginger, "Eviction Filings Hurt Tenants, Even If They Win," *Shelterforce,* July 30, 2018, https://shelterforce .org/2018/07/30/eviction-filings-hurt-tenants-even-if-they-win/.

15. The literature itself, while far too extensive to list here, has been summarized by a number of authors. See William Rohe and Mark Lindblad, *Re-examining the Social Benefits of Homeownership after the Housing Crisis* (Working paper, Harvard Joint Center for Housing Studies, 2013); Alan Mallach, *What Drives Neighborhood Trajectories in Legacy Cities?* (Working paper, Lincoln Institute of Land Policy, 2015); and Lawrence Yun and Nadia Evangelou, *Social Benefits of Homeownership and Stable Housing,* National Association of Realtors, December 2016, https://www.gmar.com/data/resources _files/Social%20Benefits%20of%20Homeownership%20%20Stable%20Housing.pdf.

16. There is evidence that a decline in homeownership in a neighborhood, however, can trigger declines in property values. See Chengri Ding and Gerrit-Jan Knapp, "Property Values in Inner-City Neighborhoods: The Effects of Homeownership, Housing Investment and Economic Development," *Housing Policy Debate* 13, no. 4 (2003): 701–27.

17. Children and Nature Network, https://research.childrenandnature.org/research /neighborhood-amenities-such-as-parks-play-a-role-in-the-physical-activity-levels-of -children-with-special-health-care-needs/, citing Ruopeng An, Yan Yang, and Kaigang Li, "Residential Neighborhood Amenities and Physical Activity among U.S. Children with Special Health Care Needs," *Maternal and Child Health* 21, no. 5 (2017): 1026–36.

18. Andrea L. Rosso et al., "Neighborhood Amenities and Mobility in Older Adults," *American Journal of Epidemiology* 178, no. 5 (2013): 761–69.

19. "12 Things That Make a Neighborhood Truly Great," *Forbes,* November 29, 2014, https://www.forbes.com/sites/trulia/2014/11/29/12-things-that-make-a-neighborhood -truly-great/#1c0f6b5435f6.

20. The role of assets in community development is closely associated with John Kretzmann and John McKnight and their book *Building Communities from the Inside Out: A Path toward Finding and Mobilizing a Community's Assets* (Chicago: ACTA Publications, 1993).

21. Daniel Kahneman and Amos Tversky, "Prospect Theory: An Analysis of Decision under Risk," *Econometrica* 47, no. 2 (1979): 263–91.

22. Surprisingly, although there has been a fair amount of scholarly research on the role that risk plays in the purchase of consumer goods and investment decision making, we are unaware of any formal research on risk assessment in home-buying decisions.

23. National Association of Realtors Research Staff, *2019 Homebuyers and Sellers Generational Trends Report* (Washington, DC: National Association of Realtors, 2019). Since the data in the report did not distinguish between ages of children under eighteen, we interpolated based on the national distribution of households by age of children in the 2017 American Community Survey.

24. There is a moderately extensive body of economics literature on this theme. See, for example, Kathy J. Hayes and Lori L. Taylor, "Neighborhood School Characteristics: What Signals Quality to Homebuyers?," *Economic Review-Federal Reserve Bank of Dallas* (1996): 2–9.

25. A major work on the subject was published almost forty years ago: Richard P. Taub, D. Garth Taylor, and Jan D. Dunham, *Paths of Neighborhood Change* (Chicago: University of Chicago Press, 1984).

26. See Wesley Skogan, *Disorder and Decline: Crime and the Spiral of Decay in American Neighborhoods* (Berkeley: University of California Press, 1990); and Jackelyn Hwang and Robert J. Sampson, "Divergent Pathways of Gentrification: Racial Inequality and the Social Order of Renewal in Chicago Neighborhoods," *American Sociological Review* 79, no. 4 (2014): 726–51.

27. See Lincoln Quillian and Devah Pager, "Black Neighbors, Higher Crime? The Role of Racial Stereotypes in Evaluations of Neighborhood Crime," *American Journal of Sociology* 107, no. 3 (2001): 717–67; Rebecca Wickes, John R. Hipp, Renee Zahnow, and Lorraine Mazerolle, "'Seeing' Minorities and Perceptions of Disorder: Explicating the Mediating and Moderating Mechanisms of Social Cohesion," *Criminology* 51, no. 3 (2013): 519–60; and Robert J. Sampson, *Great American City: Chicago and the Enduring Neighborhood Effect* (Chicago: University of Chicago Press, 2012), chap. 6.

28. Maria Krysan, Reynolds Farley, and Mick P. Couper, "In the Eye of the Beholder: Racial Beliefs and Residential Segregation," *Du Bois Review: Social Science Research on Race* 5, no. 1 (2008): 5–26.

29. See Maria Krysan, "Does Race Matter in the Search for Housing? An Exploratory Study of Search Strategies, Experiences, and Locations," *Social Science Research* 37, no. 2 (2008): 581–603; and Maria Krysan and Kyle Crowder, *Cycle of Segregation: Social Processes and Residential Stratification* (New York: Russell Sage Foundation, 2017).

30. These trends are documented and analyzed in Alan Mallach and Austin Harrison, "Leaving the Old Neighborhood: Shifting Spatial Patterns of Black Homebuyers and Their Implications for Black Urban Middle Neighborhoods in Legacy Cities," *Housing Policy Debate* 31, no. 6 (2021): 891–923.

31. Jane Jacobs, *The Death and Life of Great American Cities* (New York: Random House, 1961), 146.

32. Rachel A. Woldoff, *White Flight/Black Flight* (Ithaca, NY: Cornell University Press, 2011).

33. According to a 2013 study by the National Association of Realtors and Google, 90 percent of home buyers searched online at some point during their search process. National Association of Realtors and Google, "The Digital House Hunt: Consumer and Market Trends in Real Estate," National Association of Realtors, 2013, https://www.nar.realtor/sites/default/files/documents/Study-Digital-House-Hunt-2013-01_1.pdf. The study did not address the extent to which buyers used online searches to obtain neighborhood (as distinct from house) information. While we argue that the underlying dynamics of the search process have not been fully studied, there has been some recent research specifically on the use of the internet in home searches. See Krysan, "Does Race Matter in the Search for Housing?"

34. Krysan, "Does Race Matter in the Search for Housing?," 18.

35. Live Baltimore, https://livebaltimore.com/.

36. The Live Baltimore website provides links to twenty-two separate programs through which prospective buyers may be able to obtain assistance with down payments and closing costs. "Down Payment & Closing Costs," Live Baltimore, n.d., https://livebaltimore.com/buy/affording-a-home/down-payment-closing-costs/.

37. The insights of Robert Shiller may be relevant to neighborhood change. See Robert Shiller, *Narrative Economics: How Stories Go Viral and Drive Major Economic Events* (Princeton, NJ: Princeton University Press, 2019).

38. A major confounding factor is the variation in the attributes (size, condition, other features) of the housing stock from one neighborhood to another, which may account for some part of the variation. Moreover, the smaller the neighborhood is, there are fewer sales that are likely to take place, which means the likelihood that the houses sold in any given year that are unrepresentative will increase. Despite these concerns, we have found that sales price patterns and variations tend to be highly consistent both geographically and over time.

39. The research on the deleterious effects of vacant properties on neighborhood conditions, particularly the value of adjacent properties and the effect on criminal ac-

tivity and the perception of safety, is extensive. For a summary of salient research, see Alan Mallach, *What Drives Neighborhood Trajectories in Legacy Cities?*

40. An exception to this rule is in rapidly appreciating markets, where the owner expects the property to be worth substantially more within a short period, typically no more than two or three years. As a result, the owner may operate it at a loss or even keep it vacant for the duration. Those markets, of course, are rare, particularly in distressed urban neighborhoods.

41. For a detailed discussion of this and other variations of landlord business models, see Alan Mallach, "Lessons from Las Vegas: Housing Markets, Neighborhoods, and Distressed Single-Family Property Investors," *Housing Policy Debate* 24, no. 4 (2014): 769–801.

42. Depending on state law, the accuracy of sales volume data may vary, since it is based on sales that are recorded and thus become matters of public record. Not all states, however, require buyers to record their purchases. While lenders and title insurers will typically require recordation and lawyers and real estate professionals encourage it, in some communities, such as immigrant enclaves, many cash transactions take place that may not be recorded.

43. See, for example, Maria Piazzesi and Martin Schneider, "Housing and Macroeconomics," in *Handbook of Macroeconomics, Part 2*, ed. Charles I. Jones, John B. Taylor, and Harald Uhlig, 1547–640 (Amsterdam: Elsevier, 2016); and Frank J. Fabozzi, *The Handbook of Mortgage-Backed Securities* (New York: McGraw-Hill, 2005).

44. Data aggregated by the Mortgage Bankers Association and published in Brena Swanson, "This MBA Chart Shows Existing Home Turnover. But, What Does It Mean?," *Housing Wire*, June 26, 2015, https://www.housingwire.com/articles/34324-this-mba-chart-shows-existing-home-turnover/.

45. Sales volumes significantly in excess of the replacement range are likely to be the product of either significant new housing inventory coming on the market or, if that is not the case, speculative activity and flipping.

46. This method is not 100 percent accurate, since for various reasons some investors have the tax bill sent directly to the property. It can be made more accurate by a second scan of properties where the two addresses are the same to eliminate owner names that are not normal human being names, such as "Flip-that-property LLC" and "Make Omaha Great Again Real Estate Co."

47. Some states that provide homestead exemptions on property taxes to owner occupants require a declaration that the house will be the buyer's primary residence, which is recorded with the deed. Where available, that can be considered a reasonably accurate measure.

7. NEIGHBORHOODS IN AN ERA OF DEMOGRAPHIC CHANGE AND ECONOMIC RESTRUCTURING

1. Alan Ehrenhalt, *The Great Inversion and the Future of the American City* (New York: Vintage Books, 2012), 97–98.

2. See especially Ali Modarres and Joel Kotkin, "The Childless City," *City Journal*, Summer 2013.

3. See Alan Mallach and Austin Harrison, "Leaving the Old Neighborhood: Shifting Spatial Decisions by Black Home Buyers and Their Implications for Black Urban Middle Neighborhoods in Legacy Cities," *Housing Policy Debate* 31, no. 6 (2021): 891–923.

4. Elizabeth Chang, Neely Tucker, Jessica Goldstein, Clinton Yates, and Marcia Davis, "March of the Millennials: As Young People Flood into the City, the Only Constant Is Change," *Washington Post*, October 18, 2013.

5. Terry Nichols Clark, *The City as an Entertainment Machine* (Lanham, MD: Lexington Press, 2011), 2.

6. National Association of Area Agencies for the Aging et al., *The Maturing of America: Communities Moving Forward for an Aging Population*, USAging, June 2011, https://www.usaging.org/files/Maturing_of_Ameria_ll.pdf.

7. Nate Silver, *The Signal and the Noise. Why So Many Predictions Fail—But Some Don't* (New York: The Penguin Press, 2012).

8. Data from "U.S. Immigrant Population and Share over Time, 1850–Present," Migration Policy Institute, n.d., https://www.migrationpolicy.org/programs/data-hub/charts/immigrant-population-over-time.

9. Bureau of the Census, *Statistical Abstract of the United States, 1961* (Washington, DC: U.S. Government Printing Office, 1961), Table 112, Annual Quotas Allotted and Quota Immigrants, by Quota Area, 1936 to 1960, 92.

10. Sean F. Reardon and Kendra Bischoff, "Residential Segregation by Income, 1970–2009," in John Logan, ed. *Diversity and Disparity: America Enters a New Century* (New York: Russell Sage Foundation, 2015), 208–34.

11. Sebastian John, "Edison, New Jersey: An Indian-American Town," *Span*, January–February 2008, https://issuu.com/spanmagazine/docs/200801-02-combined.

12. Kate King, "'Little India' Thrives in Central New Jersey," *Wall Street Journal*, September 25, 2017, https://www.wsj.com/articles/little-india-thrives-in-central-new-jersey-1506340801.

13. Robert Sampson, "Immigration and the New Social Transformation of the American City," in *Immigration and Metropolitan Revitalization in the United States*, ed. Dominic Vitiello and Thomas J. Sugrue, (Philadelphia: University of Pennsylvania Press, 2017), 11–24.

14. This was the consensus of a focus group of Bangladeshi homeowners in Banglatown with whom one of the authors met in Hamtramck on December 16, 2019.

15. Salena Zito, "The Day That Destroyed the Working Class and Sowed Seeds of Trump," *New York Post*, September 16, 2017, https://nypost.com/2017/09/16/the-day-that-destroyed-the-working-class-and-sowed-the-seeds-for-trump/.

16. "Table 3. Union Affiliation of Employed Wage and Salary Workers by Occupation and Industry, 2020–2021 Annual Averages," Bureau of Labor Statistics, https://www.bls.gov/news.release/union2.t03.htm.

17. Robert D. Putnam and Shaylyn Romney Garrett, *The Upswing: How America Came Together a Century Ago and How We Can Do It Again* (New York: Simon & Schuster, 2020), 145.

18. Reardon and Bischoff, "Residential Segregation by Income."

19. High school graduates include individuals who received equivalency certificates (GEDs).

20. While an associate degree offers some financial advantage over a high school diploma, the wage premium is much less than 50 percent of the BA premium.

21. Alison Aughinbaugh, Omar Robles, and Hughette Sun, "Marriage and Divorce: Patterns by Gender, Race and Educational Attainment," *Monthly Labor Review* 136 (2013): 1.

22. Claire Cain Miller, "How Did Marriage Become a Mark of Privilege?," *New York Times*, September 25, 2017, https://www.nytimes.com/2017/09/25/upshot/how-did-marriage-become-a-mark-of-privilege.html.

23. J. S. Schiller, J. W. Lucas, B. W. Ward, and J. A. Peregoy, *Summary Health Statistics for United States Adults: National Health Interview Survey 2010*, Centers for Disease Control and Prevention, 2012, https://www.cdc.gov/nchs/data/series/sr_10/sr10_252.pdf.

24. See Bill Bishop, *The Big Sort: Why the Clustering of Like-Minded America Is Tearing Us Apart* (Boston: Mariner Books, 2009).

25. "A Wider Ideological Gap between More and Less Educated Adults," Pew Research Center, April 26, 2016, https://www.people-press.org/2016/04/26/a-wider-ideological-gap-between-more-and-less-educated-adults/.

26. Michael Dimock et al., *Political Polarization in the American Public: How Increasing Ideological Uniformity and Partisan Antipathy Affect Politics, Compromise and Everyday Life* (Washington, DC: Pew Research Center, 2014).

27. Putnam and Garrett, *The Upswing*, 96.

28. Putnam and Garrett, 12.

29. See Christopher Lasch, *The Culture of Narcissism: American Life in an Age of Diminishing Expectations* (New York: Norton, 1979); and Richard Sennett, *The Fall of Public Man* (New York: Vintage Books, 1978).

30. Sennett, *The Fall of Public Man*, 263.

31. Sennett, 264.

32. Sennett would argue that the focus was on the self as reflected or developed through intimate relationships rather than on the self per se.

33. Putnam and Garrett, *The Upswing*, 191.

34. Sennett, *The Fall of Public Man*, 265–66.

35. See Mallach and Harrison, "Leaving the Old Neighborhood"; Maria Krysan, "Does Race Matter in the Search for Housing? An Exploratory Study of Search Strategies, Experiences, and Locations," *Social Science Research* 37, no. 2 (2008): 581–603; and Maria Krysan and Kyle Crowder, *Cycle of Segregation: Social Processes and Residential Stratification* (New York: Russell Sage Foundation, 2017).

36. Putnam and Garrett, *The Upswing*, 244.

8. THE CONTINUING YET CHANGING SIGNIFICANCE OF RACE

1. Isabel Wilkerson, "America's Enduring Caste System," *New York Times Sunday Magazine*, July 1, 2020.

2. See Elijah Anderson, *Black in White Space: The Enduring Impact of Color in Everyday Life* (Chicago: University of Chicago Press, 2022); and Sheryll Cashin, *White Space, Black Hood: Opportunity Hoarding and Segregation in the Age of Inequality* (Boston: Beacon, 2021).

3. Anderson, *Black in White Space*, 27.

4. Courtney Bonam, Caitlyn Yantis, and Valerie Jones Taylor, "Invisible Middle-Class Black Space: Asymmetrical Person and Space Stereotyping at the Race-Class Nexus," *Group Processes & Intergroup Relations* 23, no. 1 (2020): 24–47.

5. "Baltimore Tries Drastic Plan of Race Segregation," *New York Times Sunday Magazine*, December 25, 1910.

6. *Buchanan v. Warley*, 245 U.S. 60 (1917). For a detailed discussion of the short history of racial zoning and the background of the *Buchanan* decision, see Roger L. Rice, "Residential Segregation by Law, 1910–1917," *Journal of Southern History* 34, no. 2 (1968): 179–99.

7. "How Covenants Changed Minneapolis," Mapping Prejudice, University of Minnesota Libraries, https://mappingprejudice.umn.edu/. The area shown on the map is one of Minneapolis's most expensive neighborhoods today. Houses on Lake of the Isles sell for well over one million dollars. The neighborhood's Black population share is only slightly over 1 percent.

8. Catherine Silva, "Racial Restrictive Covenants History: Enforcing Neighborhood Segregation in Seattle," Seattle Civil Rights & Labor History, University of Washington, n.d., https://depts.washington.edu/civilr/covenants_report.htm.

9. *Corrigan v. Buckley*, 271 US 323 (1926).

10. *Shelley v. Kraemer*, 334 US 1 (1948).

11. US Commission on Civil Rights, *Understanding Fair Housing*, Clearinghouse Publication 42 (1973), 4. The report does not provide a citation for the article that was the source of this statistic. Colin Gordon argues that private actors led the way in segregating America's neighborhoods, with governments following their lead. "Who Segregated America?" *Dissent*, June 29, 2022.

12. Edward Glaeser and Jacob Vigdor, "The End of the Segregated Century: Racial Separation in America's Neighborhoods, 1890–2010," Manhattan Institute for Policy Research 2012, https://www.manhattan-institute.org/html/end-segregated-century-racial -separation-americas-neighborhoods-1890-2010-5848.html; John Logan and Brian J. Stults, *The Persistence of Segregation in the Metropolis: New Findings from the 2010 Census*, US 2010 Project (2013), 160–68.

13. See Morton Grodzins, *The Metropolitan Area as a Racial Problem* (Pittsburgh, PA: University of Pittsburgh Press, 1958); and Thomas C. Schelling, "Dynamic Models of Segregation," *Journal of Mathematical Sociology* 1 (1971): 143–86.

14. Walter Johnson depicts St. Louis as incorrigibly racist in *The Broken Heart of America: St. Louis and the Violent History of the United States* (New York: Basic Books, 2020).

15. See Mary Pattillo, "Black Middle-Class Neighborhoods," *Annual Review of Sociology* 31 (2005): 305–29.

16. There are also a small but not insignificant number of affluent majority-Black neighborhoods in the United States, most notably in Prince George's County, Maryland, and in an area straddling the Queens–Nassau County boundary in New York.

17. Mary Pattillo, *Black Picket Fences: Privilege and Peril among the Black Middle Class* (Chicago: University of Chicago Press, 1999).

18. Pattillo, *Black Picket Fences*, 34.

19. William Lee, "A Crumbling, Dangerous South Side Creates Exodus of Black Chicagoans," *Chicago Tribune*, March 18, 2016.

20. Michelle Obama, *Becoming* (New York: Crown, 2018), 5.

21. Obama, *Becoming*, 21.

22. National Commission on Neighborhoods, *People, Building Neighborhoods: Final Report to the President and the Congress of the United States* (Washington, DC: US Government Printing Office, 1979), 339–40, cites nine studies published between 1952 and 1976 documenting this point. According to Anthony Downs, "property values fall *before* blacks enter the neighborhood but rise *after* they begin entering in large numbers, especially if they are buying their own homes." Anthony Downs, *Neighborhoods and Urban Development* (Washington, DC: Brookings Institution, 1981), 94. In his detailed study of Detroit, Thomas Sugrue, *The Origins of the Urban Crisis* (Princeton, NJ: Princeton University Press, 2012) 199, reports that Blacks living in the areas undergoing racial transition (0–10% Black) had higher incomes than Blacks living in areas that were 11–49 percent Black. Blacks living in majority-Black neighborhoods had the lowest average incomes.

23. Charles L. Leven et al., *Neighborhood Change: Lessons in the Dynamics of Urban Decay* (New York: Praeger, 1976), 137.

24. Patillo, *Black Picket Fences*, 205.

25. Patillo, 203.

26. Mary Pattillo, "The Problem of Integration," in *The Dream Revisited: Contemporary Debates about Housing, Segregation, and Opportunity*, ed. Ingrid Gould Ellen and Justin Peter Steil (New York: Columbia University Press, 2019), 29–32.

27. Homer Hoyt, *The Structure and Growth of Residential Neighborhoods in American Cities* (Washington, DC: Federal Housing Administration, 1939), 54, quoted in

Lance Freeman, *A Haven and a Hell: The Black Ghetto in America* (New York: Columbia University Press, 2019), 78.

28. See Morton Grodzins, *The Metropolitan Area as a Racial Problem* (Pittsburgh, PA: University of Pittsburgh Press, 1958); and Thomas C. Schelling, "Dynamic Models of Segregation," *Journal of Mathematical Sociology* 1 (1971): 143–86.

29. Quoted in Marion K. Sanders, *The Professional Radical: Conversations with Saul Alinsky* (New York: Harper and Row, 1970), 86.

30. Ingrid Gould Ellen, *Sharing America's Neighborhoods: The Prospects for Stable Racial Integration* (Cambridge, MA: Harvard University Press, 2000), 21, 24.

31. Kwan Ok Lee, "Temporal Dynamics of Racial Segregation in the United States: An Analysis of Household Residential Mobility," *Journal of Urban Affairs* 39, no. 1 (2016): 40–67. Lee defines Black-white neighborhoods as census tracts that are between 10 percent and 50 percent non-Hispanic Black and less than 10 percent Hispanic or non-Hispanic Asian.

32. William Easterly, "The Racial Tipping Point in American Neighborhoods: Unstable Equilibrium or Urban Legend," Department of Economics, New York University, June 2003, https://users.nber.org/~confer/2003/si2003/papers/efbdg/easterly.pdf. A revised version of this paper, which, however, does not include the quoted language, appeared as William Easterly, "Empirics of Strategic Interdependence: The Case of the Racial Tipping Point," *BE Journal of Macroeconomics* 9, no. 1 (2009): Article 25.

33. Maria Krysan and Kyle Crowder, *Cycle of Segregation: Social Processes and Residential Stratification* (New York: Russell Sage Foundation, 2017).

34. Krysan and Crowder, *Cycle of Segregation*, 6.

35. Krysan and Crowder, 124.

36. Douglas S. Massey and Nancy A. Denton, *American Apartheid: Segregation and the Making of the Underclass* (Cambridge, MA: Harvard University Press, 1993), 77.

37. Ellen, *Sharing America's Neighborhoods*, 84–85.

38. Richard P. Traub, D. Garth Taylor, and Jan D. Dunham, *Paths of Neighborhood Change: Race and Crime in Urban America* (Chicago: University of Chicago Press, 1984), 186.

39. Ellen, *Sharing America's Neighborhoods*, 165.

40. Juliet Saltman, *A Fragile Movement: The Struggle for Neighborhood Stabilization* (New York: Greenwood, 1990).

41. Rodney A. Smolla, "Integration Maintenance: The Unconstitutionality of Benign Programs That Discourage Black Entry to Prevent White Flight," *Duke Law Journal* 30, no. 6 (1981): 891–939.

42. For discussion of the legality of local integration maintenance policies, see W. Dennis Keating, *The Suburban Racial Dilemma: Housing and Neighborhoods* (Philadelphia: Temple University Press, 1994), chap. 12; and Ellen, *Sharing America's Neighborhoods*, 165–69.

43. Saltman, *A Fragile Movement*, 25.

44. The results of this research are summarized in Philip Nyden, Michael Maly, and John Lukehart, "The Emergence of Stable Racially and Ethnically Diverse Urban Communities: A Case Study of Nine U.S. Cities," *Housing Policy Debate* 8, no. 2 (1997): 491–534.

45. Our account relies heavily on Barbara Ferman, Theresa Singleton, and Don DeMarco, "West Mount Airy, Philadelphia," *Cityscape* 4, no. 2 (1998): 29–59.

46. Zillow Data, neighborhood Zillow Home Value Index through May 31, 2021.

47. Ferman, Singleton, and DeMarco, "West Mount Airy, Philadelphia," 42.

48. Our account relies heavily on Michael Kirby, "Vollintine-Evergreen, Memphis," *Cityscape* 4, no. 2 (1998): 61–87.

49. Stokely Carmichael, "What We Want," *New York Review of Books*, September 22, 1966, quoted in Edward Goetz, *The One-Way Street of Integration: Fair Housing and the Pursuit of Racial Justice in American Cities* (Ithaca, NY: Cornell University Press, 2018), vii.

50. Derek Hyra, *Race, Class, and Politics in the Cappuccino City* (Chicago: University of Chicago Press, 2017).

51. Jennifer Hochschild, Vesla Weaver, and Traci Burch, *Creating a New Racial Order: How Immigration, Multiracialism, Genomics, and the Young Can Remake Race in America* (Princeton, NJ: Princeton University Press, 2012), 115.

52. A national study found that in 2010 whites under the age of forty-four were much more likely to live on minority-majority blocks than whites over the age of sixty. Daniel T. Lichter, Domenico Parisi, and Michael C. Taquino, "Together but Apart: Do Whites Live in Racially Diverse Cities and Neighborhoods?," *Population and Development Review* 43, no. 2 (2017): 245.

53. Wenquan Zhang and John Logan, "Global Neighborhoods: Beyond the Multiethnic Metropolis," *Demography* 33, no. 6 (2016): 1933.

54. Zhang and Logan, "Global Neighborhoods," 1951.

55. The buffering hypothesis was first proposed by William Frey and Reynolds Farley, "Latino, Asian, and Black Segregation in U. S. Metropolitan Areas: Are Multi-Ethnic Metros Different?," *Demography* 33 (1996): 35–50.

56. Alan Mallach and Austin Harrison, "Leaving the Old Neighborhood: Shifting Spatial Decisions by Black Home Buyers and Their Implications for Black Urban Middle Neighborhoods in Legacy Cities," *Housing Policy Debate* 31, no. 6 (2021), 891–923.

57. For an exploration of these issues through a case study of Philadelphia, see Meg Bloomfied Cucchiara, *Marketing Schools, Marketing Cities: Who Wins and Loses When Schools become Urban Amenities* (Chicago: University of Chicago Press, 2013).

58. Robert Putnam, "E Pluribus Unum: Diversity and Community in the Twenty-First Century: The 2006 Johan Skytte Prize Lecture," *Scandinavian Political Studies* 30, no. 2 (2007): 137–74.

59. Hyra, *Race, Class, and Politics.*

60. Michael T. Maly, *Beyond Segregation: Multiracial and Multiethnic Neighborhoods in the United States* (Philadelphia: Temple University Press, 2005), 226.

9. AGENTS OF NEIGHBORHOOD CHANGE

1. States vary widely in the extent to which local governments can act to address health and safety concerns through local ordinances without explicit state authority, a complex subject that is beyond the scope of this book. For a closer look at the role of state government in limiting the scope of local action, see Gerald E. Frug and David J. Barron, *City Bound: How States Stifle Urban Innovation* (Ithaca, NY: Cornell University Press, 2008); and Alan Mallach, *From State Capitols to City Halls: Smarter State Policies for Stronger Cities* (Cambridge, MA: Lincoln Institute of Land Policy, 2022).

2. J. C. Reindl, "Why Detroit's Lights Went Out," *Detroit Free Press*, November 17, 2013, https://www.usatoday.com/story/news/nation/2013/11/17/detroit-finances-dark-streetlights/3622205/.

3. Evgenia Gorina and Craig Maher, *Measuring and Modeling Determinants of Fiscal Stress in US Municipalities*, Mercatus Center Working Paper, Mercatus Center, George Washington University, November 2016.

4. Between 2010 and 2020, per capita spending by local public health departments fell by 18 percent. Lauren Weber et al., "Hollowed-Out Public Health System Faces More Cuts amid Virus," *Kaiser Health News*, July 1, 2020.

5. Dennis R. Judd and Annika M. Hinze, *City Politics: The Political Economy of Urban America*, 10th ed. (New York: Routledge, 2019), 462.

6. Paul E. Peterson, *City Limits* (Chicago: University of Chicago Press, 1981).

7. Peterson, *City Limits*, 23.

8. The literature on sports stadium subsidies is voluminous. Two general sources are Roger G. Noll and Andrew Zimbalist, eds., *Sports, Jobs, and Taxes: The Economic Impact of Sports Teams and Stadiums* (Washington, DC: Brookings Institution Press, 1997); and Mark S. Rosentraub, *Major League Losers: The Real Cost of Sports and Who's Paying for It*, revised ed. (New York: Basic Books, 1999).

9. Peterson, *City Limits*, ch. 3.

10. Richard Schragger, *City Power: Urban Governance in a Global Age* (New York: Oxford University Press, 2016), 13–14.

11. Alan Mallach, *The Divided City: Poverty and Prosperity in Urban America* (Washington, DC: Island Press, 2018), 102.

12. Clarence N. Stone and Robert P. Stoker, *Urban Neighborhoods in a New Era: Revitalization Politics in a Postindustrial Era* (Chicago: University of Chicago Press 2015), 2, 21.

13. Howard Husock, "Don't Let CDCs Fool You," *City Journal*, Summer 2001.

14. Nicholas Lemann, "The Myth of Community Development," *New York Times*, January 9, 1994.

15. John F. Kain and Joseph J. Persky, "Alternatives to the Gilded Ghetto," *Public Interest* 14 (1969): 74–87.

16. Myron Orfield et al., "High Costs and Segregation in Subsidized Housing Policy," *Housing Policy Debate* 25 no. 3 (2015): 574–607. In a contentious rejoinder, Edward Goetz defends the CDC approach. See Edward Goetz, "Poverty-Pimping CDCs: The Search for Dispersal's Next Bogeyman," *Housing Policy Debate* 25, no. 3 (2015): 608–18.

17. Randy Stoecker, "The CDC Model of Urban Redevelopment: A Critique and an Alternative," *Journal of Urban Affairs* 19, no. 1 (1997): 9.

18. George Galster et al., *The Impact of Community Development Corporations on Urban Neighborhoods* (Washington, DC: Urban Institute, 2005), 3. While many important aspects of neighborhoods are indeed capitalized into market values, many are not, including community connections, civic engagement, and emotional attachments to place.

19. Galster et al., *The Impact of Community Development Corporations*, 2.

20. Denver County, Colorado, Census Tract 24.03.

21. Galster et al., *The Impact of Community Development Corporations*, 50.

22. Galster et al., 47.

23. While quality of life improvement, from the standpoint of economic theory, should strengthen the market, there are many reasons why that would not necessarily take place in a city that continues to lose population, where housing supply significantly exceeds demand and racial and other barriers impede the flow of information.

24. Anne C. Kubisch et al., *Voices from the Field: Lesson and Challenges from Two Decades of Community Change Efforts* (Washington, DC: Aspen Institute, 2010). See also Meir Rinde, "Did the Comprehensive Community Initiatives of the 1990s, Early 2000s Bring about Change?," *Shelterforce*, March 15, 2021.

25. Xavier De Souza Briggs and Elizabeth J. Mueller (with Mercer L. Sullivan), *From Neighborhood to Community: Evidence on the Social Effects of Community Development* (New York: Community Development Research Center, New School for Social Research, 1997).

26. Briggs and Mueller, *From Neighborhood to Community*, 7.

27. Patrick Sharkey, Gerard Torrats-Espinosa, and Delaram Takyar, "Community and the Crime Decline: The Causal Effect of Local Nonprofit on Violent Crime," *American Sociological Review* 82, no. 6 (2017): 1214–40.

28. Our account of the South Bronx draws from Paul S. Grogan and Tony Proscio, *Comeback Cities: A Blueprint for Urban Neighborhood Revival* (Boulder, CO: Westview, 2000); and Robert Worth, "Guess Who Saved the South Bronx?," *Washington Monthly*, April 1, 1999.

29. Furman Center for Real Estate and Urban Policy, *Housing Policy in New York City: A Brief History* (New York: Furman Center for Real Estate and Urban Policy, n.d.).

30. Furman Center, *Housing Policy in New York City*, 6–7.

31. Hunts Point–Longwood includes the following census tracts: Tracts 83, 85, 87, 89, 93, 115.02, 117, 119, 121.02, 127.01, 129.01, 131, and 159.

32. Uniform Crime Report data as reported in City of New York Police Department, "CompStat," https://www1.nyc.gov/assets/nypd/downloads/pdf/crime_statistics/cs-en-us-041pct.pdf. The data is from the 41st precinct, which serves Hunts Point and Longwood.

33. The total does not include 3,277 otherwise unsubsidized units that received tax exemptions, helping to keep rents down. To include these would lead to significant double counting, since many projects receive tax exemptions in addition to other subsidies.

34. Data is from NYU Furman Center, "Hunts Point/Longwood (Bx02)," https://furmancenter.org/neighborhoods/view/hunts-point-longwood.

35. National Alliance of Community Economic Development Associations, *Rising Above: Community Economic Development in a Changing Landscape* (Washington, DC: National Alliance of Community Economic Development Associations, 2010), 7.

36. Alexander Von Hoffman, *House by House, Block by Block: The Rebirth of America's Urban Neighborhoods* (New York: Oxford University Press, 2003), 62.

37. Orfield et al., "High Costs and Segregation."

38. Mark McDermott tells the story of the evolution of Cleveland's robust system of network governance in "The Evolution of the Community Development Industry: A Practitioner's Perspective," in *Equity Planning Now,* ed. Norman Krumholz and Kathryn Wertheim Hexter, (Ithaca, NY: Cornell University Press, 2018), 44–59.

39. "About 3CDC," Cincinnati Center City Development Corporation, https://www.3cdc.org/about-3cdc/.

40. See, e.g., Brianne Brenneman, "Gentrification Disguised as Urban Revitalization," *Agora*, February 21, 2018, https://agorajournal.squarespace.com/blog/2018/2/12/gentrification-disguised-as-urban-revitalization.

41. Henry S. Webber and Mikael Karlstrom, *Why Community Investment Is Good for Nonprofit Anchor Institutions: Understanding Costs, Benefits, and the Range of Strategic Options* (Chicago: Chapin Hall at the University of Chicago, 2009), 4.

42. US Census Bureau, LEHD Origin-Destination Employment Statistics (2002–2019) (Washington, DC: U.S. Census Bureau, Longitudinal-Employer Household Dynamics Program, 2021), accessed on January 17, 2021 at https://onthemap.ces.census.gov.

43. John L. Puckett, "Federal- and State-Funded Urban Renewal at the University of Pennsylvania," West Philadelphia Collaborative History, https://collaborativehistory.gse.upenn.edu/stories/federal-and-state-funded-urban-renewal-university-pennsylvania. By 1964, 120 colleges and universities and 75 hospitals had taken advantage of Section 112.

44. Judith Rodin, *The University & Urban Revival: Out of the Ivory Tower and into the Streets* (Philadelphia: University of Pennsylvania Press, 2007), 37.

45. Peter Marcuse and Cuz Potter, "Columbia University's Heights: An Ivory Tower and Its Communities," in *The University as Urban Developer: Case Studies and Analysis,* ed. David C. Perry and Wim Wiewel (Armonk, NY: M. E. Sharpe, 2005), 49.

46. David C. Perry, Wim Wiewel, and Carrie Menendez, "The University's Role in Urban Development: From Enclave to Anchor Institution," *Land Lines*, Lincoln Institute of Land Policy, July 2009.

47. See J. Brian Charles, "For College Towns, Having a World-Famous University Is a Mixed Blessing," *Governing*, October 2018; and "University Will Pay More to New Haven," *Yale Alumni Magazine*, January/February 2022.

48. Chapter 17, Public Laws of 2021, signed into law February 22, 2021.

49. Rodin, *The University & Urban Revival*, 134.

50. Rita Axelroth Hodges and Steve Dubb, *The Road Half Travelled* (East Lansing: Michigan State University Press, 2012), 65.

51. Our analysis builds on Meagan Ehlenz, "Neighborhood Revitalization and the Anchor Institution: Assessing the Impact of the University of Pennsylvania's West Philadelphia Initiatives on University City," *Urban Affairs Review* 52, no. 5 (2016): 714–50. Ehlenz's data analysis ends in 2010; we have supplemented her analysis with 2015–2019 American Community Survey data.

52. Kevin Gillen and Susan Wachter, *Neighborhood Value Updated: West Philadelphia Price Indexes* (Philadelphia: University of Pennsylvania Institute for Urban Research, 2011).

53. Samantha Melamed, "The Penn Alexander Effect: Is There Any Room Left for Low-Income Residents in University City?," *Philadelphia Inquirer*, November 1, 2018, https://www.inquirer.com/philly/news/penn-alexander-university-city-west-philly-low -income-affordable-housing-20181101.html.

54. One question is whether these figures reflect a large number of students, who often report low incomes but usually are not, in fact, poor. Students, however, compose less than 15 percent of University City's population. See Ehlenz, "Neighborhood Revitalization and the Anchor Institution," 734.

55. The census tracts we used to track trends in the West Philadelphia area outside of University City were 65, 72, 73, 80, 81.01, 81.02, 82, 83.01, 83.02, 84, 85, 93, 94, 95, 96, 98.01, 98.02, 100, 101, 104, 105, 106, 107, 108, 109, 110, 111, 112, 113, 114, 115, 117, 118, 119, 120, 121, 122.01, 122.03, 122.04, 375, 9800, and 9808.

56. Rodin, *The University & Urban Revival*, 57.

57. Carolyn T. Adams, *From the Outside In: Suburban Elites, Third-Sector Organizations, and the Reshaping of Philadelphia* (Ithaca, NY: Cornell University Press, 2014), 154.

58. Sabina Dietrick and Tracy Soska, "The University of Pittsburgh and the Oakland Neighborhood: From Conflict to Cooperation, or How the 800-Pound Gorilla Learned to Sit with—and Not on—Its Neighbors," in *The University as Urban Developer: Case Studies and Analysis,* ed. David Perry and Wim Wiewel (Armonk, NY: M. E. Sharpe, 2005), 25–44.

59. McCormack Baron Salazar, https://www.mccormackbaron.com/ (our emphasis).

60. Estimate from Sandra Moore in Rachel Bratt, *Affordable Rental Housing Development in the For-Profit Sector: A Case Study of McCormack Baron Salazar* (Cambridge, MA: Harvard Joint Center for Housing Studies, Working Paper, March 2016), 47–48.

61. Cheryl Lovett, former executive director, St. Louis Housing Authority, quoted in Bratt, *Affordable Rental Housing Development in the For-Profit Sector*, 48.

10. DECONSTRUCTING GENTRIFICATION

1. Ruth Glass, *London: Aspects of Change* (London: MacGibbon & Kee, 1964), xiii.

2. See Andrew J. Dufton, "The Architectural and Social Dynamics of Gentrification in Roman North Africa," *American Journal of Archaeology* 123, no. 2 (2019): 263–90; Helen Parkins and Christopher Smith, eds., *Trade, Traders, and the Ancient City* (London: Routledge, 1998); and Friedrich Engels, *The Housing Question* (Moscow: Cooperative Publishing Society of Foreign Workers, 1995), https://www.hlrn.org/img /documents/Engels%20The%20Housing%20Question.pdf.

3. Jane Jacobs, *The Death and Life of Great American Cities* (New York: Random House, 1961), 270–90.

4. The phrase "back to the city" implies that the typical gentrifier was moving back to the city from its suburbs and is thus very misleading. As research at the time showed, the great majority of gentrifiers moved from other neighborhoods in the same central city or from other metropolitan areas entirely. See, for example, R. T. LeGates and Chester W. Hartman, "The Anatomy of Displacement in the United States," in *Gentrification of the City*, ed. Neil Smith and Peter Williams (Boston: Allen & Unwin, 1986), 178–203.

5. Susanna McBee, "HUD Finds Little Displacement of Poor in Inner-City Revivals," *Washington Post*, February 14, 1979, https://www.washingtonpost.com/archive/politics /1979/02/14/hud-finds-little-displacement-of-poor-in-inner-city-revivals/1d7e5185 -1812-4e2c-b119-47423ed7425c/.

6. Brian J. L. Berry, "Islands of Renewal in Seas of Decay," in *The New Urban Reality*, ed. Paul E. Peterson (Washington, DC: Brookings Institution Press, 1985), 69–96.

7. Nadia Khomami and Josh Halliday, "Shoreditch Cereal Killer Cafe Targeted in Anti-Gentrification Protests," *The Guardian*, September 27, 2015.

8. https://zmenu.com/cereal-killer-cafe-london-online-menu/.

9. It is worth noting that given Glass's reference to the large Victorian homes that had been subdivided, the "working-class occupiers" being displaced by gentrification were not the original occupiers of the neighborhood but rather products of a prior but downward neighborhood change.

10. Neil Smith, "Gentrification and Uneven Development," *Economic Geography* 58 (1982): 139n1.

11. Mark Davidson and Loretta Lees. "New-Build 'Gentrification' and London's Riverside Renaissance," *Environment and Planning A* 37, no. 7 (2005): 1165–90.

12. Markus Moos, "From Gentrification to Youthification? The Increasing Importance of Young Age in Delineating High-Density Living," *Urban Studies* 53, no. 14 (2016): 2903–20. We disagree with Moos that "youthification" should be distinguished from gentrification. Moos's youthification is not a separate phenomenon but instead is a central element of the most representative form of gentrification and should not be treated separately.

13. See, generally, Patrick Sharkey, *Uneasy Peace: The Great Crime Decline, the Renewal of City Life, and the Next War on Violence* (New York: Norton, 2018).

14. See Terry Nichols Clark, ed., *The City as an Entertainment Machine* (Lanham, MD: Lexington Books, 2011); and Michael Sorkin, ed., *Variations on a Theme Park: The New American City and the End of Public Space* (New York: Hill & Wang, 2011).

15. See Clark, *The City as an Entertainment Machine*.

16. Yongsung Lee, Bumsoo Lee, and Md Tanvir Hossain Shubho, "Urban Revival by Millennials? Intraurban Net Migration Patterns of Young Adults, 1980–2010," *Journal of Regional Science* 59, no. 3 (2019): 538–66.

17. Neil Smith. "Toward a Theory of Gentrification: A Back to the City Movement by Capital, Not People," *Journal of the American Planning Association* 45, no. 4 (1979): 538–48.

18. Stage models of gentrification in which risk-oblivious "pioneers" start the process, only later giving way later to risk-averse large-scale developers and investors, have been around for a long time. See Phillip L. Clay, *Neighborhood Renewal* (Lexington, MA: Lexington Books, 1979); and Dennis E. Gale, "Middle Class Resettlement in Older Urban Neighborhoods," *Journal of the American Planning Association* 45, no. 3 (1979): 293–304.

19. Smith, "Toward a Theory of Gentrification," 545 (our emphasis). Many years later Smith half-heartedly recanted, writing in the early 1990s that "the original 1979 article was deliberately aimed at the near total domination of the gentrification discourse by neo-classical approaches which privileged demand as the dynamo of urban change."

Neil Smith, "Blind Man's Bluff, or Hamnett's Philosophical Individualism in Search of Gentrification," *Transactions of the Institute of British Geographers* 17, no. 1 (1992): 110–15. Smith, most probably disingenuously, claimed even more years later in a 2010 personal reflection that "I did not guess at the time that anyone would take the paper too seriously." Commentary in Loretta Lees, Tom Slater, and Elvin Wyly, eds. *The Gentrification Reader* (London: Routledge, 2010), 97. Despite these statements, however, Smith never materially changed his position to accept any of the points raised in the numerous papers challenging his thesis.

20. Robert Beauregard, "The Chaos and Complexity of Gentrification," in *Gentrification of the City*, ed. Neil Smith and Peter Williams (Boston: Allen & Unwin, 1986), 39.

21. See especially Chris Hamnett, "The Blind Men and the Elephant: The Explanation of Gentrification," *Transactions of the Institute of British Geographers* (1991): 173–89; Steven C. Bourassa, "The Rent Gap Debunked," *Urban Studies* 30, no. 10 (1993): 1731–44; and David Ley, "Reply: The Rent Gap Revisited," *Annals of the Association of American Geographers* 77, no. 3 (1987): 465–68.

22. Veronica Guerrieri, Daniel Hartley, and Erik Hurst, "Endogenous Gentrification and Housing Price Dynamics," *Journal of Public Economics* 100 (2013): 45–60; and Ken Steif, Michael Fichman, and Simon Kassel, "Predicting Gentrification Using Longitudinal Census Data," Urban Spatial Analysis, 2016, https://urbanspatialanalysis.com /portfolio/predicting-gentrification-using-longitudinal-census-data/.

23. C. J. Quartlbaum, "Grieving the Gentrification of Food," *Christ and Pop Culture Magazine* 6, no. 3 (2018), https://christandpopculture.com/grieving-the-gentrification -of-food/ (our emphasis).

24. For Chicago, see Jackelyn Hwang and Robert J. Sampson, "Divergent Pathways of Gentrification: Racial Inequality and the Social Order of Renewal in Chicago Neighborhoods," *American Sociological Review* 79, no. 4 (2014): 726–51. For New York and Chicago, see Jeffrey M. Timberlake and Elaina Johns-Wolfe, "Neighborhood Ethno-Racial Composition and Gentrification in Chicago and New York, 1980 to 2010," *Urban Affairs Review* 53, no. 2 (2017): 236–72. For St. Louis, see Todd Swanstrom, Henry S. Webber, and Molly W. Metzger, "Rebound Neighborhoods in Older Industrial Cities: The Case of St. Louis," in *Economic Mobility: Research & Ideas on Strengthening Families, Communities and the Economy*, ed. Alexandra Brown et al. (St. Louis: Federal Reserve Bank of St. Louis and Board of Governors of the Federal Reserve System, 2016), 325–52. For Philadelphia, see Aaron Moselle and Annette John-Hall, "The Surprising Truth behind the Racial Dynamics of Gentrification in Philly," WHYY, March 13, 2018, https://whyy.org /articles/surprising-truth-behind-racial-dynamics-gentrification-philly/. For St. Louis and Baltimore, see Alan Mallach and Karen Beck Pooley, "What Drives Neighborhood Revival? Qualitative Research Findings from Baltimore and St. Louis," Working paper WP18AM12018, Lincoln Center of Land Policy, 2018. For Baltimore, see Alan Mallach, *Drilling Down in Baltimore's Neighborhoods: Changes in Racial/Ethnic composition and Income from 2000 to 2017* (Baltimore: Abell Foundation, 2020).

25. Mallach, *Drilling Down in Baltimore's Neighborhoods*, 14.

26. Timberlake and Johns-Wolfe, "Neighborhood Ethno-Racial Composition."

27. Mindy Thompson Fullilove, *Root Shock: How Tearing Up City Neighborhoods Hurts America and What We Can Do about It* (New York: One World/Ballantine Books, 2004), 224.

28. This was the method used to measure displacement in a highly publicized but badly flawed gentrification study conducted by the National Community Reinvestment Coalition. Jason Richardson, Bruce Mitchell, and Juan Franco, *Shifting Neighborhoods: Gentrification and Cultural Displacement in American Cities* (Washington DC: National Community Reinvestment Coalition, 2019), https://ncrc.org/gentrification/.

29. George Grier and Eunice Greer, "Urban Displacement: A Reconnaissance," in *Back to the City: Issues in Neighborhood Renovation,* ed. Shirley Bradley Laska and Daphne Spain (New York: Pergamon Press, 1980), 256. This piece was previously published separately as a report commissioned for the US Department of Housing and Development.

30. Even in New York City, some research suggests that gentrification typically does not lead to displacement. See Kacie Dragan, Ingrid Ellen, and Sherry A. Glied, "Does Gentrification Displace Poor Children? New Evidence from New York City Medicaid Data." Working paper 25809, National Bureau of Economic Research, May 2019, https://www.nber.org/system/files/working_papers/w25809/w25809.pdf. For earlier evidence, see Lance Freeman and Frank Braconi, "Gentrification and Displacement: New York City in the 1990s," *Journal of the American Planning Association* 70, no. 1 (2004): 39–52; and Lance Freeman, "Displacement or Succession? Residential Mobility in Gentrifying Neighborhoods," *Urban Affairs Review* 40, no. 4 (2005): 463–91.

31. For a checklist of action steps that can be taken to minimize displacement, see Alan Mallach, *Managing Neighborhood Change* (Montclair, NJ: National Housing Institute, 2008).

32. This can be easily shown with a simple arithmetical model. If one takes a hypothetical universe of one hundred rental units that are all occupied by Black tenants in Year 1, at which time the pool of potential renters is also 100 percent Black, and assume that (1) 25 percent of the rental units turn over each year, (2) each subsequent year one white household is added to the pool of twenty-five potential tenants, and (3) white and Black households have equal opportunities to rent available units—that is, there is no discrimination or preferential behavior—then by the end of Year 10 twenty-four of the one hundred tenants will be white, and the number of Black tenants in the universe will have dropped by 24 percent. As it happens, the number of Black tenants in nine gentrifying St. Louis census tracts studied by Mallach and Beck Pooley declined by 22.3 percent from 2000 to 2010. Alan Mallach and Beck Pooley, "What Drives Neighborhood Revival?"

33. Mallach, *Drilling Down in Baltimore's Neighborhoods,* 45.

34. Janine Bologna, Nava Kantor, Yunqing Liu, and Samuel Taylor, "The Right to Stay Put: City Garden Montessori School and Neighborhood Change," Report, George Warren Brown School of Social Work and Sam Fox School of Design and Visual Arts, Washington University in St. Louis, 2015, https://csd.wustl.edu/Publications/Documents/city-garden_final-report.pdf.

35. Rachel Woldoff, *White Flight, Black Flight: The Dynamics of Racial Change in an American Neighborhood* (Ithaca, NY: Cornell University Press, 2011), especially chap. 6, "Black Flight: Consequences of Neighborhood Cultural Conflict."

36. Most prominently perhaps Spike Lee in a famous 2014 rant. For a complete transcript, see "Spike Lee's Gentrification Rant—Transcript: 'Fort Greene Park Is Like the Westminster Dog Show,'" *The Guardian,* February 26, 2014, https://www.theguardian.com/cities/2014/feb/26/spike-lee-gentrification-rant-transcript.

37. Jake Flanagin, "The Brooklynization of Detroit Is Going to Be Terrible for Detroiters," Quartz, July 15, 2015.

38. Mallach, *The Divided City,* 110.

39. Todd Swanstrom, Karl Guenther, and Nathan Theus, "What People Talk about When They Talk about Gentrification: Creating Whole Communities," University of Missouri-St. Louis, 2018, http://www.umsl.edu/wholecommunities/research/Focus-Group-Report.FINAL.1.17.19.pdf.

40. Stephen Danley and Rasheda Weaver, "'They're Not Building It for Us': Displacement Pressure, Unwelcomeness, and Protesting Neighborhood Investment," *Societies* 8, no. 3 (2018): 74.

41. Ta-Nehisi Coates, *We Were Eight Years in Power: An American Tragedy* (New York: One World, 2017), 86. Coates's formulation has been sharply challenged by other African American commentators. See Thomas Chatterton Williams, "How Ta-Nehisi Coates Gives Whiteness Power," *New York Times*, October 7, 2017, https://www.nytimes .com/2017/10/06/opinion/ta-nehisi-coates-whiteness-power.html.

42. D'Juan Hopewell, "Gentrification Will Save White Supremacy," blog post, June 23, 2018, http://hopewellthought.com/2018/06/gentrification-will-save-white-supremacy/ (site discontinued).

43. Rick Jacobus, "It's Not Either/Or: Neighborhood Improvement Can Prevent Gentrification," *Shelterforce*, July 18, 2013.

44. Census tract 142.

45. A comparison could be drawn with the Bohemian neighborhoods of the nineteenth and early twentieth centuries such as Montmartre in Paris and New York's Greenwich Village, but such a comparison would be far-fetched particularly in light of the aggressively counterculture nature of those neighborhoods. The two have little in common except for the youth of their inhabitants.

46. Swanstrom, Webber, and Metzger, "Rebound Neighborhoods in Older Industrial Cities."

47. Dowell Myers, "Peak Millennials: Three Reinforcing Cycles That Amplify the Rise and Fall of Urban Concentration by Millennials," *Housing Policy Debate* 26, no. 6 (2016): 928–47.

48. Joe Cortright, "Not Peak Millennial: The Coming Wave," *City Observatory*, March 28, 2016.

11. THE CRISIS OF THE URBAN MIDDLE NEIGHBORHOOD

1. Henry S. Webber, "Local Public Policy and Middle Neighborhoods," in *On the Edge: America's Middle Neighborhoods*, ed. Paul Brophy (New York: American Assembly, 2016), 156.

2. For historic reasons, the principal house form in nineteenth-century working- and middle-class neighborhoods in a coastal belt that runs north from central New Jersey and includes most of coastal New England was the two- and three-family house with stacked units, known in Boston as "triple-deckers." Such houses make up only a small part of the residential stock in other American cities.

3. Defined here as tracts in which the median household income was between 75 percent and 125 percent of the citywide median.

4. Ray Suarez, *The Old Neighborhood: What We Lost in the Great Suburban Migration, 1966–1999* (New York: Free Press, 1999), 24.

5. Thomas Sugrue, *The Origins of the Urban Crisis: Race and Inequality in Postwar Detroit* (Princeton, NJ: Princeton University Press, 1996), 33.

6. See Gregory D. Squires, Derek S. Hyra, and Robert N. Renner, "Metropolitan Segregation and the Subprime Lending Crisis," *Housing Policy Debate* 23, no. 1 (2013): 117–98; and Jacob W. Faber, "Racial Dynamics of Subprime Mortgage Lending at the Peak," *Housing Policy Debate* 23, no. 2 (2013): 328–49.

7. While much of the research on homeownership effects has controlled for income and other measurable variables, it is arguably impossible to control for the possibility of self-selection bias in terms of differences in values and behavior between those who become homeowners and those who do not. The body of research on homeownership effects is extensive, however, and virtually all the many studies point in the same direction. While in some cases the effects diminish significantly when one controls for length of tenure, this means less than it may seem, since most of the difference in tenure between renters and homeowners appears to be an inherent property of ownership in

the US cultural context. While the extreme extent of the tenure gap is created in part by instability associated with the revolving door of poverty and eviction, even under the most optimal rental conditions less than half of the tenure gap disappears.

8. For a detailed discussion of milking, or predatory landlord behavior, see Alan Mallach, *Meeting the Challenge of Distressed Property Investors in America's Neighborhoods* (New York: Local Initiatives Support Corporation, 2010).

9. Alan Mallach, "Over the Edge: Trajectories of African American Middle Neighborhoods in St. Louis since 2000," *Journal of Urban Affairs* 42, no. 7 (2020): 1063–85.

10. See Todd M. Michney, *Surrogate Suburbs: Black Upward Mobility and Neighborhood Change in Cleveland, 1900–1980* (Chapel Hill: University of North Carolina Press, 2017).

11. Thomas E. Bier, *Housing Dynamics in Northeast Ohio: Setting the Stage for Resurgence*, (Cleveland, OH: MSL Academic Endeavors eBooks, 2017), http://engagedscholarship.csuohio.edu/msl_ae_ebooks/4.

12. In a policy dating from the long-gone days where cities were generally much wealthier than rural townships, the State of Ohio pays for the maintenance of state highways in townships but requires cities to cover those maintenance costs from their budgets.

13. Joseph McNeely and Paul C. Brophy, "The Middle Neighborhood Movement, 1970–2000," in *On the Edge: America's Middle Neighborhoods*, ed. Paul C. Brophy (New York: American Assembly, 2014), 1–8.

14. The Federal historic preservation tax credit has little impact on residential neighborhoods because it applies only to income-producing properties. It has had a major impact on downtown revitalization in many cities.

15. This point is well described in two strong ethnographic studies of Black middle neighborhoods. See Rachael Woldoff, *White Flight/Black Flight* (Ithaca, NY: Cornell University Press, 2012); and Mary Patillo, *Black Picket Fences: Privilege and Peril among the Black Middle Class* (Chicago: University of Chicago Press, 1999).

16. This is a point stressed by Woldoff, who characterizes the goals of those she describes as Black "pioneers." "Their goal," she writes, "was not to achieve a minimal standard of safety from extreme violent crime and brazen disorder; for them the desire for an improved atmosphere for their families included a neighborhood with a greater representation of conventional families and lifestyles." Woldoff, *White Flight/Black Flight*, 147.

17. While that number is only two-thirds of the 2005 figure, the earlier numbers were inflated by subprime lending, which led to many purchase transactions some of which probably should never have been made.

18. Detroit Future City, *Growing Detroit's African American Middle Class: The Opportunity for a Prosperous Detroit* (Detroit: Detroit Future City, 2019), 47.

19. See especially Courtney Bonam, Caitlyn Yantis, and Valerie Jones Taylor, "Invisible Middle-Class Black Space: Asymmetrical Person and Space Stereotyping at the Race-Class Nexus," *Group Processes & Intergroup Relations* 23, no. 1 (2020): 24–47.

20. Henry Grabar, "Black Space, White Blindness," Slate, September 18, 2018, https://slate.com/business/2018/09/black-neighborhoods-white-racism.html.

21. David Rusk, "The 'Segregation Tax': The Cost of Racial Segregation to Black Homeowners," Brookings Institution Center on Urban and Metropolitan Policy, October 2001, https://www.brookings.edu/wp-content/uploads/2016/06/rusk.pdf.

22. Sandy Smith, "Some Philadelphia Neighborhoods Are Walking a Line between Boom and Bust," Next City, May 15, 2017; https://nextcity.org/features/view/philadelphia-middle-class-neighborhoods-mount-airy.

23. Lauren Hood, "Detroit Needs to Preserve the Cultural Integrity of Its Black Neighborhoods," Model D, February 7, 2017, https://www.modeldmedia.com/features /black-space-detroit-020717.aspx.

24. William Lee, "A Crumbling, Dangerous South Side Creates Exodus of Black Chicagoans," *Chicago Tribune*, March 18, 2016, http://www.chicagotribune.com/news/opin ion/commentary/ct-black-exodus-chicago-20160318- story.html.

25. For more information, see Middle Neighborhoods, middleneighborhoods.org.

12. THE PERSISTENCE OF CONCENTRATED POVERTY NEIGHBORHOODS

1. Matthew 26:11.

2. Charles Duff, *The North Atlantic Cities* (Liverpool: Bluecoat, 2019), 40.

3. Anne Sinclair Holbrook, "Map Notes and Comments," in Residents of Hull-House, *Hull-House Maps and Papers* (New York: Thomas Y. Crowell, 1895), 5.

4. These two numbers are not strictly comparable because the United States did not adopt the current standard for measuring poverty until 1965. For Roosevelt's second inaugural address, see "Inaugural Address, January 20, 1937," Franklin D. Roosevelt Library and Museum, https://www.fdrlibrary.org/documents/356632/390886/1937inau guraladdress.pdf/7d61a3fd-9d56-4bb6-989d-0fd269cdb073.

5. As can be seen from figure 12.1, the census began to distinguish characteristics of the Latinx population only after 1970.

6. Paul Jargowsky, *The Architecture of Segregation* (New York: Century Foundation, 2015), 4.

7. The classic work on neighborhood effects is Robert J. Sampson, *Great American City: Chicago and the Enduring Neighborhood Effect* (Chicago: University of Chicago Press, 2012). See also Harriet B. Newburger, Eugenie L. Birch, and Susan M. Wachter, eds., *Neighborhood and Life Chances: How Place Matters in Modern America* (Philadelphia: University of Pennsylvania Press, 2011).

8. George C. Galster, "The Mechanism(s) of Neighborhood Effects: Theory, Evidence, and Policy Implications," presentation at the ESRC Seminar, St. Andrews University, Scotland, February 4–5, 2010. The 20 percent figure is used by some federal agencies to determine whether an area is eligible for certain federal programs, such as the Opportunity Zone program. Other federal programs, however, use different standards, such as the Low-Income Housing Tax Credit, which makes investors eligible for greater benefits in areas with over 25 percent poverty rates.

9. Galster, "The Mechanism(s) of Neighborhood Effects."

10. For a critique of the conventional approach for studying neighborhood effects and a recommendation of an alternative approach similar to ours, see Peter Dreier, John Mollenkopf, and Todd Swanstrom, *Place Matters: Metropolitics for the Twenty-First Century*, 3rd ed. (Lawrence: University Press of Kansas, 2014), 96–102.

11. Joe Cortright and Dillon Mahmoudi, *Lost in Place: Why the Persistence and Spread of Concentrated Poverty—Not Gentrification—Is Our Biggest Urban Challenge* (n.p.: City Observatory, 2014). The study focuses on the inner core of each metropolitan area, defined as the area within ten miles from the center of each area's central business district.

12. Jargowsky, *The Architecture of Segregation*, 2–3.

13. Jargowsky, 5.

14. Lance Freeman, *A Haven and a Hell: The Ghetto in Black America* (New York: Columbia University Press, 2019).

15. This figure appears in a number of documents and apparently originates in Jeremy Williams, *Detroit: The Black Bottom Community* (Charleston SC: Arcadia Publishing, 2009), 10.

16. Eugene Robinson, *Disintegration: The Splintering of Black America* (New York: Doubleday, 2010), 66.

17. Robinson, *Disintegration*, 66.

18. Kendra Bischoff and Sean Reardon, "Residential Segregation by Income, 1970–2009," in *Diversity and Disparities: America Enters a New Century*, ed. John Logan (New York: Russell Sage Foundation, 2013), 215.

19. Cortright and Mahmoudi, *Lost in Place*, 14.

20. Cortright and Mahmoudi, 19.

21. For dashboards with data for each individual metropolitan area included in the Cortright and Mahmoudi study, see Joe Cortright, "Lost in Place," City Observatory, September 12, 2014, https://cityobservatory.org/lost-in-place/.

22. For an overview of vacant property issues in the United States today, see Alan Mallach, *The Empty House Next Door: Understanding and Reducing Vacancy and Hypervacancy in the United States* (Cambridge, MA: Lincoln Institute of Land Policy, 2018).

23. Jason Hackworth, *Manufacturing Decline: How Racism and the Conservative Movement Crush the American Rust Belt* (New York: Columbia University Press, 2019), 173.

24. Mallach, *The Empty House Next Door*, 27–35.

25. The only exception to this rule is where properties are rapidly appreciating and landlords are willing to take a short-term loss in return for a larger long-term gain. This does not apply to the typical concentrated poverty neighborhood.

26. Matthew Desmond, *Evicted: Poverty and Profit in the American City* (New York: Penguin Random House, 2016).

27. For a review of what the authors call "hypermobility" and its negative effects on children and schools, see Molly Metzger, Patrick J. Fowler, and Todd Swanstrom, "Hypermobility and Education: The Case of St. Louis," *Urban Education* 53, no. 6 (2018): 774–805.

28. Eric Klinenberg, *Heat Wave: A Social Autopsy of Disaster in Chicago* (Chicago: University of Chicago Press, 2002), chap. 2.

29. Klinenberg, *Heat Wave*, 92, 97.

30. Klinenberg, 101.

31. Anne Gunderson, "Breaking the Cycle of Inner-City Violence with PTSD Care," Chicago Policy Review, June 2, 2017, https://chicagopolicyreview.org/2017/06/02/breaking-the-cycle-of-inner-city-violence-with-ptsd-care/.

32. See, for example, Charles C. Branas et al., "Citywide Cluster Randomized Trial to Restore Blighted Vacant Land and Its Effects on Violence, Crime, and Fear," *Proceedings of the National Academy of Sciences* 115, no. 12 (2018): 2946–51; and Eugenia C. Garvin, Carolyn C. Cannuscio, and Charles C. Branas, "Greening Vacant Lots to Reduce Violent Crime: A Randomised Controlled Trial," *Injury Prevention* 19, no. 3 (2013): 198–203.

33. William Julius Wilson, *When Work Disappears: The World of the New Urban Poor* (New York: Vintage, 2011).

34. Wilson, *When Work Disappears*, 65.

35. Sharkey, *Stuck in Place*, 46.

36. Raj Chetty et al., "The Opportunity Atlas: Mapping the Childhood Roots of Social Mobility," National Bureau of Economic Research, Working paper 25147, 2018.

37. See, among others, Raj Chetty, Nathaniel Hendren, and Lawrence F. Katz," The Effects of Exposure to Better Neighborhoods on Children: New Evidence from the Moving to Opportunity Experiment," *American Economic Review* 106, no. 4 (2016): 855–902. Chetty and other researchers point out that the effects of participation in the Moving to Opportunity program are highly uneven; for example, children who were under thirteen when they moved saw significant improvements in school outcomes, while those who were thirteen and over did not.

38. It is known as the Mount Laurel doctrine after two New Jersey Supreme Court decisions in 1975 and 1983 that enunciated the fair share principle in a case brought against the zoning practices of the Township of Mount Laurel, a postwar suburb of Philadelphia in Burlington County.

39. Anne C. Kubisch et al., *Voices from the Field III: Lessons and Challenges from Two Decades of Community Change Efforts* (Washington, DC: Aspen Institute, 2010), vii.

40. Michael S. Rosenwald and Michael A. Fletcher, "Why Couldn't $130 Million Transform One of Baltimore's Poorest Places?," *Washington Post*, May 2, 2015, https:// www.washingtonpost.com/local/why-couldnt-130-million-transform-one-of-baltimores -poorest-places/2015/05/02/0467ab06-f034-11e4-a55f-38924fca94f9_story.html.

41. Rosenwald and Fletcher, "Why Couldn't $130 Million Transform One of Baltimore's Poorest Places?"

42. For a further discussion of the Sandtown-Winchester project, see Alan Mallach, *The Divided City: Poverty and Prosperity in Urban America* (Washington, DC: Island Press, 2018), 196–98.

43. Jason M. Barr, *Building the Skyline: The Birth and Growth of Manhattan's Skyscrapers* (New York: Oxford University Press, 2016).

44. For a good overview of the case for providing legal counsel to tenants in eviction proceedings, see Heidi Schultheis and Caitlin Rooney, *A Right to Counsel Is a Right to a Fighting Chance: The Importance of Legal Representation in Eviction Proceedings* (Washington, DC: Center for American Progress, 2019). Established in 2017, New York City's Right to Counsel initiative provides free legal services to all tenants facing eviction in housing court.

45. Estimates vary but tend to find that between one in four and one in five eligible households are able to obtain vouchers. See "Three Out of Four Low-Income At-Risk Renters Do Not Receive Federal Rental Assistance," Center on Budget and Policy Priorities, n.d., http://apps.cbpp.org/shareables_housing_unmet/chart.html.

46. We refer to an entitlement housing allowance in general terms because we do not want to suggest that simply expanding the present HCV program, with its limitations, is necessarily the best way to accomplish this goal. President Joe Biden's campaign platform included a call for universal housing vouchers. If and when a universal entitlement housing allowance is enacted, policymakers should carefully think through the best and most cost-effective form the program should take.

47. For a more extended discussion of this issue along with examples of successful schools, see Mallach, *The Divided City*, esp. at 218–23.

13. NEIGHBORHOOD CHANGE IN THE SUBURBS

1. Quoted in Tal Axelrod, "Trump Makes an Appeal to Suburban Women at Rally: 'Will You Please Like Me?,'" *The Hill*, October 13, 2020. The regulation that Trump is referring to is the Obama administration's Affirmatively Furthering Fair Housing rule, which required municipalities to identify and address policies that promoted racial segregation. In July 2020 the Trump administration rescinded the rule, which was subsequently reinstated in 2021 by the Biden administration.

2. Douglas S. Massey and Jonathan Tannen, "Suburbanization and Segregation in the United States: 1970–2010," *Ethnic and Racial Studies* 41, no. 9 (2018): 1594–611.

3. Audrey Singer, Susan W. Hardwick, and Caroline B. Brettell, eds., *Twenty-First Century Gateways: Immigrant Incorporation in Suburban America* (Washington, DC: Brookings Institution Press, 2008).

4. Elizabeth Kneebone and Alan Berube, *Confronting Suburban Poverty in America* (Washington, DC: Brookings Institution Press), 20.

5. See Ellen Dunham-Jones and June Williamson, *Retrofitting Suburbia: Urban Design Solutions for Redesigning Suburbia*, updated ed. (Hoboken, NJ: Wiley, 2011).

6. Robert A. Beauregard, *When America Became Suburban* (Minneapolis: University of Minnesota Press, 2006), 124–25.

7. Beauregard, *When America Became Suburban*, 127.

8. Beauregard, 130.

9. William H. Whyte Jr., *The Organization Man* (New York: Simon & Schuster, 1956), 317.

10. Thomas E. Bier, *Housing Dynamics in Northeast Ohio: Setting the Stage for Resurgence* (Cleveland, OH: MSL Academic Endeavors Ebooks, 2017), 28. https://engagedscholar ship.csuohio.edu/cgi/viewcontent.cgi?article=1003&context=msl_ae_ebooks.

11. Samuel H. Kye, "The Persistence of White Flight in Middle-Class Suburbia," *Social Science Research* 72 (2018): 38–52.

12. Whitney Airgod-Obrycki, "Are the Suburbs Losing Status?," Joint Center for Housing Studies at Harvard University, February 4, 2019.

13. See Karen Beck Pooley, "Debunking the 'Cookie-Cutter' Myth for Suburban Places and Suburban Poverty: Analyzing Their Variety and Recent Trends," in *The New American Suburb: Poverty, Race, and the Economic Crisis*, ed. Katrin B. Anacker (Burlington, VT: Ashgate, 2015), 171; and Andrea Sarzynski and Thomas J. Vicino, "Shrinking Suburbs: Analyzing the Decline of American Suburban Spaces," *Sustainability* 11, no. 19 (2019): 5230.

14. Homer Hoyt, *The Structure and Growth of Residential Neighborhoods in American Cities* (Washington, DC: Federal Housing Administration, 1939), 119.

15. Beck Pooley, "Debunking the 'Cookie-Cutter' Myth," 40.

16. As reported in "Levittown, NY Real Estate & Homes for Sale," Realtor.com, https://www.realtor.com/realestateandhomes-search/Levittown_NY.

17. Beck Pooley, "Debunking the 'Cookie-Cutter' Myth," 73–74.

18. This is based on an update of data from Todd Swanstrom et al., *Pulling Apart: Economic Segregation among Suburbs and Central Cities in Major Metropolitan Areas*, Living Cities Census Series, Brookings Institution, October 2004. Middle-income suburbs are defined as those with per capita incomes between 75 percent and 125 percent of the per capita income of the metropolitan area; poor suburbs are those below 75 percent, while affluent suburbs are those above 125 percent.

19. Norton E. Long, "Political Science and the City," in *Urban Research and Policy Planning*, ed. Leo F. Schnore and Henry Fagin, (Beverly Hills, CA: Sage Publications, 1967), 243–62.

20. Richard Child Hill, "Separate and Unequal: Governmental Inequality in the Metropolis," *American Political Science Review* 68, no. 4 (1974): 1557–68.

21. In 1974, a federal appeals court ruled that Black Jack's zoning ordinance forbidding the construction of multifamily housing had a discriminatory effect even if it could not be proved that it had a racially discriminatory intent and was therefore in violation of the Fair Housing Act (*United States v. City of Black Jack, Missouri*, 372 F. Supp. 319 [E.D. Mo. 1974]). The decision was effectively reversed a few years later when the US Supreme Court ruled that plaintiffs must prove discriminatory intent to prevail in such cases (*Village of Arlington Heights v. Metropolitan Housing Development Corp*, 429 U.S. 252 [1977]).

22. It is difficult to prove a causal connection because of the many factors involved, but the weight of the evidence suggests that individual success in school is affected by classmates' socioeconomic backgrounds. For a balanced review of recent scholarly research on this question, see Sarah A. Cordes, "A Reality Check on the Benefits of Economic Integration," Future Ed, Georgetown University, 2019, https://www.future-ed .org/a-reality-check-on-the-benefits-of-economic-integration/.

23. John Pacewicz and John N. Robinson III, "Pocketbook Policing: How Race Shapes Reliance on Fines and Fees in the Chicago Suburbs," *Socioeconomic Review* 19, no. 3 (2021): 975–1003.

24. Listed on Zillow at: https://www.zillow.com/homedetails/1641-N-44th-St-East -Saint-Louis-IL-62204/5224963_zpid/, accessed November 21, 2022.

25. See Alan Mallach, *The Divided City: Poverty and Prosperity in Urban America* (Washington, DC: Island Press, 2018), 166–68.

26. See Scott W. Allard, *Places in Need: The Changing Geography of Poverty* (New York: Russell Sage Foundation, 2017), 137.

27. Sarah Reckhow and Margaret Weir, *Building a Stronger Regional Safety Net: Philanthropy's Role* (Washington, DC: Brookings Institution, 2011), 8.

28. Todd Swanstrom, "Equity Planning in a Fragmented Suburban Setting: The Case of St. Louis," in *Advancing Equity Planning Now*, ed. Norman Krumholz and Kathryn Wertheim Hexter (Ithaca, NY: Cornell University Press, 2018), 110.

29. Gregory Weiher, *The Fractured Metropolis: Political Fragmentation and Metropolitan Segregation* (Albany: SUNY Press, 1991); Eric J. Heikil, "Are Municipalities Tieboutian Clubs?," *Regional Science and Urban Economics* 26 (1996): 203–26; Kendra Bischoff, "School District Fragmentation and Racial Residential Segregation: How Do Boundaries Matter?," *Urban Affairs Review* 44, no. 2 (2008): 182–217; Jonathan Rothwell and Douglas Massey, "Density Zoning and Class Segregation in U.S. Metropolitan Areas," *Social Science Quarterly* 91 (2010): 1123–43; Jessica Trounstine, *Segregation by Design: Local Politics and Inequality in American Cities* (New York: Cambridge University Press, 2018), esp. ch. 8.

30. For disparities in health, see Malo André Hutson, George A. Kaplan, Nalini Ranjit, and Mahasin S. Mujahid, "Metropolitan Fragmentation and Health Disparities: Is There a Link?," *Milbank Quarterly* 90, no. 1 (2012): 187–207. For disparities in life expectancy, see Yonsu Kim and Tim A. Bruckner, "Political Fragmentation and Widening Disparities in African-American and White Mortality, 1972–1988," *SSM—Population Health* 2 (2016): 399–406.

31. We calculated the dissimilarity index using 2015–2019 American Community Survey data at the tract level for two groups: Blacks and all others. We believe this is the best approach because race is the most salient issue in neighborhood segregation, while other racial/ethnic groups are not a large part of the population in either county.

32. Our account of the development of Ferguson draws heavily on Madeleine Swanstrom, *Streetcars and Segregation: Ferguson from the Civil War to Michael Brown* (Honors thesis, Departments of History and Economics, Tulane University, 2018).

33. There is in fact a third Ferguson. North and east of Old Ferguson are neighborhoods with larger, often distinctive postwar suburban-style homes.

34. The barrier was finally removed after demonstrations in 1968 following the assassination of Dr. Martin Luther King Jr.

35. Richard Rothstein, "The Making of Ferguson," Economic Policy Institute, October 15, 2014.

36. Our account of Ferguson and its contrast with University City draws from Napoleon Williams, III, *Role of Municipal Governance in Stabilizing Mature Inner Suburbs: A Study of Five St. Louis Municipalities, 1970–2015*, PhD Diss., Department of Political Science, University of Missouri-St. Louis, 2020.

37. Advertisement, *St. Louis Post-Dispatch*, August 25, 1978.

38. There is a second road into the area, but it was closed due to concerns about crime and only opened for school buses. During a January 2021 visit, both roads were open to traffic.

39. Distressed sales represent all foreclosures and sales of foreclosed properties. Based on data collected by William Rogers, as reported in Swanstrom, *Streetcars and Segregation*, 79.

40. "Investigation of the Ferguson Police Department," US Department of Justice, Civil Rights Division, March 4, 2015, https://www.justice.gov/sites/default/files/opa/press-releases/attachments/2015/03/04/ferguson_police_department_report.pdf.

41. A study of 340 American cities where more than 20 percent of the population is Black found that Blacks were overrepresented in 2 and underrepresented in 129. International City/Council Management Association study as reported in Richard Fausset, "Mostly Black Cities, Mostly White City Halls," *New York Times*, September 28, 2014.

42. An analysis by the *New York Times* found more than 730 municipalities that relied on fines and fees for at least 10 percent of their budget. Mike McIntire and Michael H. Keller, "The Demand for Money behind Many Police Traffic Stops," *New York Times*, October 31, 2021.

43. *Baltimore County, Maryland Strategic Plan 2020*, November 15, 2010, 24.

44. Thomas J. Vicino, *Transforming Race and Class in Suburbia: Decline in Metropolitan Baltimore* (New York: Palgrave Macmillan, 2008), 160.

45. Gregory Smithsimon, "Punctuated Equilibrium: Community Responses to Neoliberalism in Three Suburban Communities in Baltimore County, Maryland," in *The New American Suburb: Poverty, Race, and the Economic Crisis*, ed. Katrin B. Anacker (Burlington, VT: Ashgate, 2015), 195.

46. Smithsimon, "Punctuated Equilibrium," 208.

47. As reported in Bernadette Hanlon, John Rennie Short, and Thomas J. Vicino, *Cities and Suburbs: New Metropolitan Realities in the United States* (New York: Routledge, 2010), 191.

48. Hanlon et al., *Cities and Suburbs*, 166.

49. Vicino, *Transforming Race and Class*, 153.

50. See Cherlin, Andrew J. "'GOOD, BETTER, BEST': Upward Mobility and Loss of Community in a Black Steelworker Neighborhood," *Du Bois Review: Social Science Research on Race* 17 (2001): 1–21.

51. Henrietta Lacks, the wife of a steelworker and resident of Lyons Homes, died of cervical cancer in 1951. She achieved posthumous fame when it became known that a cell line from her tumor, which had been harvested without her consent, had become a critically important resource in cancer and other medical research. The story, which raises thorny medical, racial, and ethical issues, is well told in Rebecca Skloot, *The Immortal Life of Henrietta Lacks* (New York: Crown, 2010).

52. This somewhat overstates the change, because much of the decline in Black-identifying residents is the result of an increase from 1 percent to 5 percent in the number identifying as being of two or more races.

53. This is impossible to prove in the absence of a clear and agreed-upon definition of "suburban," but there is compelling evidence to support the assertion. See Jed Kolko, "America Really Is a Nation of Suburbs," Bloomberg CityLab, November 14, 2018.

54. In *Bowling Alone* Robert Putnam concluded that "residents of large metropolitan areas incur a 'sprawl civic penalty' of roughly 20 percent on most measures of community involvement." Robert Putnam, *Bowling Alone: The Collapse and Revival of American Community* (New York: Simon & Schuster, 2000), 215. The research on the relationship between sprawl and social capital, which is bedeviled by the challenge of separating sprawl from other characteristics such as education and income, is extensive and cuts both ways. One early careful study of the issue found that "at least one characteristic of sprawl—automobile hegemony—is inimical to neighborhood social ties." Lance Freeman, "The Effects of Sprawl on Neighborhood Social Ties: An Exploratory Analysis," *Journal of the American Planning*

Association 67, no. 1 (2001): 69–78. Thad Williamson found that sprawl has negative effects on certain kinds of civic and political engagement. Thad Williamson, *Sprawl, Justice, and Citizenship: The Civic Cost of the American Way of Life* (New York: Oxford University Press, 2001). Measuring sprawl at the county level, Doan Nyugen found no relationship between sprawl and social capital. Doan Nyugen, "Evidence of the Impacts of Urban Sprawl on Social Capital," *Environment and Planning B: Planning and Design* 37, no. 4: 610–27.

55. See, for example, the website for the Fox Meadow Neighborhood Association, https://www.foxmeadowna.org/.

56. Whyte, *The Organization Man* and Beauregard, *When American Became Suburban.*

14. THE THEORY AND PRACTICE OF NEIGHBORHOOD CHANGE

1. Louis Wirth, "Urbanism as a Way of Life," *American Journal of Sociology* 44, no. 1 (1938): 12.

2. Mark S. Granovetter, "The Strength of Weak Ties," *Social Networks* 78, no. 6 (1977): 1361.

3. See Maxime Felder, "Strong, Weak, and Invisible Ties: A Relational Perspective on Urban Coexistence," *Sociology* 54, no. 4 (2020): 675–92.

4. Iris Marion Young, *Justice and the Politics of Difference* (Princeton, NJ: Princeton University Press, 1990), 237.

5. Michael Sandel, "What Money Can't Buy: The Skyboxification of American Life," Huffington Post, June 20, 2012.

6. Robert D. Putnam with Shaylyn Romney Garrett, *The Upswing: How America Came Together a Century Ago and How We Can Do It Again* (New York: Simon & Schuster, 2020), 13.

7. See Alan Ehrenhalt, *The Lost City: The Forgotten Virtues of Community in America* (New York: Basic Books, 1996) and Ray Suarez, *The Old Neighborhood: What we Lost in the Great Suburban Migration 1966–1999* (New York: The Free Press, 1999).

8. "St. Louis Tries to Integrate Its Pools, Causing Race Riots and Social Change," *St. Louis Post-Dispatch*, June 21, 1949.

9. Heather McGhee, *The Sum of Us: What Racism Costs Everyone and How We Can Prosper Together* (New York: One World, 2021), 25.

10. According to the National Swimming Pool Foundation as reported in Jeffrey Collins, "Swimming Pools Dry Up after Draining City Budgets," *Telegram & Gazette* (May 30, 2011).

11. Research by Jessica Trounstine supports the negative association between racial integration and public goods provision, but she finds the causal arrow pointing in the opposite direction: cities with the largest public sectors resisted racial integration the most. Jessica Trounstine, *Segregated by Design: Local Politics and Inequality in American Cities* (New York: Cambridge University Press, 2018), chap. 4.

12. With thanks or apologies to the *Ladies Home Journal*, which ran the "Can This Marriage Be Saved?" column from 1953 until the magazine's demise in 2016.

13. A study conducted by the Rand Corporation in the late 1970s meticulously documented the negative impact of federal policies on older urban areas. The findings are summarized in Roger J. Vaughan, Anthony Pascal, and Mary E. Vaiana, *The Urban Impacts of Federal Policies*, Vol. 1, *Overview* (Santa Monica, CA: Rand Foundation, 1980). Most of these antiurban policies are still in place.

14. In recent years there have been a number of proposals to withhold federal community development and housing funds from municipalities that maintain exclusionary practices. While reasonable in intent, these proposals all miss the point that federal assistance is of relatively little importance to the more serious offenders, which value their ability to exclude far more than they do the occasional federal grant they receive.

15. A study of the distribution of federally sponsored or incentivized community development capital to all US counties with more than fifty thousand population found that "the level of distress a county experiences does not directly relate to level of funding." Brett Theodos and Eric Hangen, "Tracking the Unequal Distribution of Community Development Funding in the US," Urban Institute, January 31, 2019.

16. There is a growing body of literature on this subject. For a good statement of the issues and conclusions, see Vicki Been, Ingrid Gould Ellen, and Katherine O'Regan, "Supply Skepticism: Housing Supply and Affordability," *Housing Policy Debate* 29, no.1 (2019): 25–40.

17. Joe Cortright, "A Solution for Displacement: TIF for Affordable Housing," *City Observatory*, November 6, 2019.

18. Andrew Volmert, Moira O'Neill, Nat Kendall-Taylor, and Julie Sweetland, *Mixing It Up: Reframing Neighborhood Socioeconomic Diversity*, Frameworks Institute, October 2016, 8.

19. See Miriam Axel-Lute, "Talking about Revitalization When All Anyone Wants to Talk about Is Gentrification," *Shelterforce*, October 24, 2019.

20. George Galster, *Making Our Neighborhoods, Making Ourselves* (Chicago: University of Chicago Press, 2019), 299.

21. Illustrating neighborhood feedback effects, a recent study in Philadelphia found that the blocks where homes were repaired experienced a 22 percent reduction in crime, although the causal link is unclear. Eugenia C. South, John MacDonald, and Vincent Reina, "Association between Structural Housing Repairs for Low-Income Homeowners and Neighborhood Crime," *JAMA Network Open* 4, no. 7 (July 21, 2021): e2117067, https://jamanetwork.com/journals/jamanetworkopen/fullarticle/2782142.

22. As quoted in James Heckman, "Early Childhood Development ROI," Heckman: The Economics of Human Potential, https://heckmanequation.org/resource/early -childhood-development-roi/.

23. For a discussion of strategies to revive Black middle neighborhoods, see Alan Mallach, *Making the Comeback: Reversing the Downward Trajectory of African American Middle Neighborhoods in Legacy Cities* (Cambridge, MA: Lincoln Institute of Land Policy, 2021).

24. Donald R. Haurin and Stuart S. Rosenthal, *The Sustainability of Homeownership: Factors Affecting the Duration of Homeownership and Rental Spells* (Washington, DC: US Department of Housing & Urban Development, 2004), v.

25. Michael Schubert, "Through a Glass Darkly: Trying to Make Sense of Neighborhood Revitalization," Paper prepared for the Workshop on Neighborhood Change in Legacy Cities sponsored by the Center for Community Progress and the Lincoln Institute of Land Policy, 2016.

Index

Note: Page numbers in italics refer to figures and tables.

of, 38, 40, 75–77, 272; in the rise of urban neighborhoods, 68–69; suburban, 70, 282, 283–86, 297–98; in successful integration, 180–81, 183; in urban neighborhood decline, 75, 83
Hoyt, Homer, 38, 39, 73–74, 178–79
HUD (US Department of Housing and Urban Development), 39–40, 84–85, 88–90, 204–5, 214
Hunts Point-Longwood, South Bronx, 198–200
Husock, Howard, 194–95
Hymowitz, Kay, 61
Hyra, Derek, 185–86

immigrants/immigration: in concentrated poverty neighborhoods, 275–76; in demographic change, 57–58, 145, 154–59; and good neighborhoods, 24, 30–31; immigrant neighborhoods, 51, 53–63, 67–68, 99, 145, 155–57, 202, 263–64; Immigration Act of 1924, 65, 67, 154; integration of, 186, 330n32; in neighborhood change theories, 35, 37, 38; in neighborhood markets, 131–32; in the rise of urban neighborhoods, 51, 53–63, 65–68; significance of race for, 168, 186, 187–88; in suburban change, 280–81
income gap/inequality, 8, 21–22, 25, 91, 160–63, 188, 230–31, 241–42. See also equality/inequality; polarization
income/income level: in concentrated poverty neighborhoods, 260, 263–64, 270, 272–74, 275, 277–78; demographic change and economic restructuring in, 145–46, 156, 160–63; and gentrification, 225, 226–28, 229–231, 232; and good neighborhoods, 8, 13–14, 19–23, 25, 29; in middle-neighborhood crisis, 234–35, 239, 241–42, 243–44, 246–47, 250, 255; in neighborhood change theories, 35–36, 39, 41–43, 45–46, 316–19; and neighborhood markets, 124–26, 127, 129–33, 139–40; and polarization, 30, 102, 104, 106–10, 112–13, 118, 119–20; and race, 175–76, 177, 180–81, 187, 188; in suburban change, 281, 283, 286–87, 289–90, 292, 294–95, 296–97, 298–300, 301, 302–3; and urban neighborhood decline, 84–86, 90–91, 92–94, 95–96, 97–98
Indian American communities, New Jersey, 156, *157*
industrial cities, 29–30, 32–33, 38, 53–63, 100, 159–61, 216, 220. See also under *city name*

industrialization, 9, 51, 55–56, 57, 59. *See also* deindustrialization
infrastructure, 55, 77–78, *126*, 128, 190, 240–41, 245, 270–71, 278, 289, 298, 320
in-migration: Black, 64, 72–73, *84*, 169–70, 172, 175, 184, 262; in decline of neighborhoods, 28–30; in demographic change and urban restructuring, 148–52, 153–54; in gentrification, 215, 217, 218, 232–33, 315–16; in growth of concentrated poverty neighborhoods, 262, 263; in middle-neighborhood crisis, 248–49, 252–53, 256–57; in neighborhood markets, 144; in polarization, 100–102, 104, 106, 107. *See also* out-migration
institutions/institutional frameworks, 47–48, 61–63, 127, 288–90, 291–301, 303–4, 305–6, 309, 312–13
insurance, 39–40, 320. *See also* FHA (Federal Housing Administration)
integration, racial, 178–85, 186–87, 289, 292–93, 330n32. *See also* segregation, racial and ethnic
Interstate Highway and Defense Act, 77–78
invasion-succession model of neighborhood change, 35–37, 168, 237, 305, 310–11, 317
investment/investors: change agents in, 191–95, 205–6, 207–8, 209–11; community development systems in, 92–93, 94–96; in concentrated poverty neighborhoods, 263, 266–67, 273–75, 279; in decline of neighborhoods, 28, 250, 252–53; in downtowns, and urban decline, 90; and gentrification, 216–17, 218–19, 229–30, 231–32; in good neighborhoods, 21, 29–30, 318–19, 321; in middle neighborhoods, 240–41, 243, 245–46, 248–49, 321; in neighborhood change theories, 41–42, 45; in neighborhood markets, 123, 126–27, 134–35, 139, 140–42, 144; in suburban change, 293, 295, 296, 300, 301–2. *See also* speculation/speculators
Ironbound neighborhood, Newark, 240

Jackson, Kenneth, 74
Jacobs, Jane, 15, 40, 78, 80, 136–37, 213
Jacobus, Rick, 230
Jargowsky, Paul, 260, 261
Jewish neighborhoods, 64–65, 67–68, 275
Johns Hopkins University and medical complex, 151–52, 202–3

Kahneman, Daniel, 134–35
Keller, Suzanne, 13–14

Printed in the USA
CPSIA information can be obtained
at www.ICGtesting.com
LVHW051053271023
762238LV00005B/544